ANGELS of DEATH

ALSO BY JULIAN SHER AND WILLIAM MARSDEN
The Road to Hell: How the Biker Gangs Are Conquering Canada

INSIDE THE
BIKER GANGS'
CRIME EMPIRE

JULIAN SHER
AND
WILLIAM MARSDEN

CARROLL & GRAF • NEW YORK

ANGELS OF DEATH
Inside the Biker Gangs' Crime Empire

Carroll & Graf Publishers
An Imprint of Avalon Publishing Group, Inc.
245 West 17th Street
11th Floor
New York, NY 10011

AVALON
publishing group incorporated

Library of Congress Cataloging-in-Publication Data is available.

ISBN-13: 978-0-78671-931-0
ISBN-10: 0-7867-1931-1

9 8 7 6 5 4 3 2 1

Printed in the United States of America
Distributed by Publishers Group West

Authors' Note

——

Several of the criminal cases described in this book were still before the courts at the time of printing, though some may have since been resolved. All the accused are innocent until proven guilty, and the allegations against them remain to be proven in court. The charges and the details of their alleged activity are taken from public court and police documents. In the few instances where biker associates asked to remain anonymous for their protection, we have noted this. In all other cases, the names of the biker informants and the undercover police officers are real and have not been changed. Because this book spans several continents, measurements and currencies are given in the way they appeared in court documents or are commonly used in the respective countries.

CONTENTS

PROLOGUE

"American Legend"

Hells Angels will continue to ride to the ends of the earth.
The sun never sets on a Hells Angel patch.
—HELLS ANGEL SONNY BARGER

They had not planned on beheading her.

But Cynthia Garcia needed to be taught a lesson. The forty-four-year-old single mother of six had committed a fatal error. Nobody disrespects the Hells Angels, especially in their own clubhouse. In their minds, "the stupid bitch" deserved to die.

It was a cool fall Thursday night in Mesa, Arizona, in October 2001. Ten bikers had just returned to the Hells Angels clubhouse after one of their favourite drinking holes shut down at 1:30 A.M. But the boys were still hungry for some action.

The clubhouse was in a rundown part of town just east of Phoenix, on a small street lined with busted-up pickups, faded brown palm trees and broken-down white fences. The Mesa headquarters was prettier than most biker hangouts, which often look more like bunkers than clubhouses. The local Angels had taken care to keep up appearances. The Spanish shingles on the slanted roof were not cracked; the white stucco wall was immaculate, except for a striking logo—two big yellow Death Heads bracketing the name "Mesa" in blood red. A Death Head also adorned the black mailbox on the sidewalk.

The winged Death Head is the Hells Angels' proud emblem: an angry-looking skull with a helmet and feathers streaming behind

1

him. It's frightening—as it's meant to be: don't fuck with the Angels. We'll eat you alive.

Inside the clubhouse, the Angels sent out one of their eager recruits to hunt down some women. He came back with Cynthia Garcia, five foot five and weighing 120 pounds—tiny compared to most of the beefy boozers in biker leather. She started drinking with the boys and having a good time, but then things turned nasty.

According to a gang officer who investigated her murder, "They brought her back for some recreation, and she didn't want to recreate. So they beat her down. She still got mouthy with them. So they threw her in the trunk of a car and finished her off out in the desert." She was barely alive, beaten and bloody, when the three bikers who'd taken it on themselves to deal with her dragged her out of the car and threw her on her back in the sand. They stabbed her repeatedly, according to a later confession from one of the killers.

"I want to cut the bitch's head off," the confessed killer claimed one of his bikers said. But his knife was too dull to finish the decapitation, according to the same testimony.

A bad knife was the least of the bikers' problems. They could not know that for one of the killers, the slaying of an innocent woman had pushed him over the edge: he would turn traitor, rat on his biker brothers and start working undercover for the police. In the end, he would help bring down not only the two bikers he said helped kill Garcia but more than forty Hells Angels from five states on murder and drug charges in the biggest federal sweep against the bikers in American history.

Half a world away, Don Hancock, the retired chief of the Criminal Investigations Branch in Western Australia, drove through a quiet suburban neighbourhood in Perth with his friend Lou Lewis. The two men had passed the day at the racetrack, won a bit of money and were now enjoying the serene pleasure of time well spent. As they pulled into Hancock's driveway, a powerful bomb positioned under his seat blew Hancock out of the car, shredding his body like a rag doll and killing him instantly. His friend died soon afterwards. A cellphone had triggered the bomb, and the outlaw biker who had dialled the number assured his mate that they wouldn't be charged for the call.

A year earlier, outlaw bikers had literally blown to bits a small town in Australia's outback where Hancock had retired. The former police officer had fled but was relentlessly tracked down.

Australians call outlaw bikers "bikies," but there's nothing friendly about the apparent diminutive. The murder of Hancock would launch a massive police investigation and inspire tighter laws designed to bring the bikies under control. But it was too late. Aussie bikies, bold imitators of their American brethren, had already become the country's first nationwide crime syndicate, dominating Australia's underbelly.

Three years later and another continent away, three bodies were discovered in a stream near the town of Eicht, in the southern Netherlands. This time, all three victims were elite bikers, members of the Dutch Hells Angels Nomads chapter, and one was the chapter president. Nomads are often the most powerful among fully patched bikers, not restricted to operations in a specific geographic turf. But not even Nomads are always immune to insider treachery.

It was late in February 2004. All had been shot several times point-blank, execution-style, their assassination sparked by the theft of 293 kilograms of cocaine with an estimated street value of $11 million. But this was much more than your usual burned drug deal. The murders revealed a hitherto undisclosed story in the outlaw biker chronicles: their international ties to Colombian drug dealers and narco-terrorists.

Police later arrested a member of the Hells Angels chapter in Curaçao, an island in the southern part of the Caribbean that is part of the Dutch Antilles. The biker flipped and informed on thirteen Hells Angels Nomads back in Holland, who were then arrested and charged with the murders of their leaders.

The cocaine was reportedly shipped to Amsterdam, via the Angels' new chapter in Curaçao, from the Revolutionary Armed

Forces of Colombia (FARC), an insurgency group labelled narco-terrorists by the U.S. State Department. Police frequently compare the bikers to terrorist organizations because of their explosive violence and cell-like structure, and the killings in the Netherlands revealed direct connections between the two.

For the first time, Dutch authorities, who had been notoriously reluctant to take on the country's Hells Angels, the most powerful bikers in Europe, decided to act. Justice officials investigating the murders eventually charged almost the entire Nomads chapter, not just with murder and cocaine smuggling but also with being part of a criminal conspiracy. Their trial would send shock waves through the European biker underworld.

Three murderous evenings, three different continents, three faces of the Angels of death: the killing of innocents, the killing of cops and the killing of fellow bikers.

Not to mention the hundreds of thousands of lives ruined, brains fried, bodies withered by the methamphetamines, cocaine and other drugs pushed by the bikers.

And yet while the body count kept mounting, Sonny Barger, the legendary patriarch of the biker gang, was being feted by the international media as he promoted his latest bestselling book. Even the usually thoughtful British press fell for the rebel Yankee. *The Times* of London called him "affable, big-hearted, warm." *The Independent* labelled him an "American Legend."

And in many ways he is.

Over five decades, Sonny Barger helped to build an empire patiently crafted in his own self-image. He was the poor kid with a tough upbringing. A cast-off, abandoned by his mother and neglected by his alcoholic father. Yet the Hells Angels became an international corporation that today is as much a part of the modern American ethos as Microsoft and McDonald's.

The Hells Angels brand is as recognizable an American logo as the burger chain's golden arches or the Nike swoosh. And like all good merchandisers, the Angels have learned to adapt: their local boys speak the native language and mix well with the drug and party scene of their home countries. But the Hells Angels also come with the international clout and discipline—and the ability to reach out and strike an enemy anywhere—that would make the American military jealous.

The Hells Angels play a supporting role central to America's image of itself—America the free, America the faithful, America the invincible. Barger's genius was to clothe a criminal enterprise with the trappings of American folklore and myth.

To many, Sonny Barger is a folk hero. The myth of the rebel biker—from Marlon Brando in *The Wild One* to the heroes of *Easy Rider*—is still strong, playing to the heart of the growing biker community. It is all part of a carefully staged PR campaign, right down to the motorcycle rides to raise money for children's charities.

No other biker gang has been so successful in building and controlling its public image. Other biker leaders don't go on book tours or have their own Web sites. Barger, however, sells his own brand of sauce on the Internet—"hotter than a Harley-Davidson's manifold"—and beer "to satisfy your thirst for the flavor of adventure and the passion for freedom."

But Barger has another passion: a plan of uniting outlaw motorcycle gangs under one banner—the Big Red and White, the official colours of the HA. The Hells Angels are now the dominant criminal biker gang on the planet, with an estimated twenty-five hundred members in twenty-three American states and in twenty-five countries on five continents. Their vertically structured "franchises" allow them to control trafficking in cocaine, marijuana and methamphetamines from manufacturer down to the street level. Their infiltration of major ports assures the smooth flow of drugs and guns into North America and Europe. Extortion, loan sharking and murder round out their business interests.

It is globalization on a scale multinationals can only dream of. Indeed, OMGs (the acronym for outlaw motorcycle gangs) are the United States' only homegrown contribution to international organized crime. Italy gave the world the Mafia; Asia spawned the triads; Russia and the collapsing Soviet empire gave birth to the new eastern mob.

But America gave the world the bikers.

Rivalling the Hells Angels for international dominance are two other American players that have also exported their terror: the Bandidos out of Texas and the Outlaws from the Midwest. The bloody rivalry between these gangs has left a trail of bombs, bullets and bodies in the U.S., across Canada, Australia and Europe.

Over the past decade, the expansion of outlaw biker culture has been so successful that almost every country with a biker franchise has sprouted special police task forces and new anti-gang laws to combat their violent criminality. In country after country, the pattern is predictable: brutal territorial wars break out with rival biker gangs using guns, grenades, bombs and rocket launchers to intimidate and murder each other, while police initially stand back and watch the carnage. Then an innocent "civilian" is killed and the public outcry sparks a toughening of the criminal codes, more power to police and mass arrests. The bikers back off and sue for peace. But by then they have become well entrenched, and life returns to a new kind of normalcy, the kind that has bikers running the show.

While you have to demonstrate absolute loyalty to the club in order to become a full patch Hells Angel, this does not always mean you have to be a criminal to join. It is a popular myth that one must carry out a murder or a similarly serious crime to sign up with the outlaw gang. Many members, indeed, can spend years in the club without taking part in any overt criminal activity. But that is hardly the point. It would be hard to miss the illegal acts your brothers were committing around the world. And when was the last time anyone saw a Hells Angel quit in protest over the outrages carried out in the name of the patch?

Biker gangs are unique in the underworld because they are so obvious. They parade their criminality in patches on their leather jackets and use them as a sign of where they stand in the club's hierarchy. An aspiring Angel must spend a lot of time as a club "hangaround"—essentially a gofer. Then with luck he graduates to being a "prospect." Only after a year of prospecting are the lucky few who make the grade allowed to wear the club's insignia on the back of his jacket. He becomes what is known as a full-patch or patched member. It is a long and painstaking process, carefully crafted to weed out not just slackers but also informants and undercover cops. It gives members a very public identity—and at the same time, makes them among the most difficult criminals to infiltrate. In their world, there are no secrets. Gang members are expected to be openly ruthless and savage at the slightest insult. Few cops could last in such a demanding world. But some have, and in this book, you will learn of the handful of men and women who have tried to stop the outlaw bikers.

Angels of Death is the story of how the Hells Angels grew so powerful and how the police—with only a few successes—have tried to stop them. For the first time, police officers who have infiltrated biker gangs tell their secrets—revealing the challenges, fears and horrors they discovered going undercover.

The bikers also tell their stories, in their own words—not in careful PR statements but in never-before-disclosed wiretaps, secret emails, confessions and court evidence.

From the Angels and their pursuers comes the true story of how this once ragtag group of rebels, outcasts and felons succeeded in becoming one of the world's most sophisticated criminal enterprises.

"Hells Angels will continue to ride to the ends of the earth," says Barger. "The sun never sets on a Hells Angel patch."

It is not an empty boast.

PART I

THE INFILTRATORS

ONE

Death in the Desert

———

She's nobody. No one cares. No one probably even reported her missing.
They probably found her . . . probably fucking [put a] Jane Doe on her.
—Arizona Hells Angels Paul Eischeid

A man turns rat and squeals on his friends for many reasons. For a Hells Angel, breaking the code of biker loyalty means taking your life in your hands. You might as well sign your own death warrant. You do it only for money. Or fear.

For Michael Christopher Kramer, it was mixture of all those things. His moment of truth came on a cool night in the middle of the Arizona desert when a dying woman, her blood and breath draining out of her, grasped his pant leg and then let go.

Kramer was in many ways no different from most of his fellow bikers in Arizona.

His drug of choice was methamphetamine, or speed. "There are a lot of meth addicts in the club," he later testified, admitting he "might do a snort here and there." But his real vice was alcohol—lots of it, with a particular fondness for Bud Lite. Drunk or sober, the six-foot biker was prone to violent outbursts: he thought nothing of beating the crap out of somebody just because he could.

Kramer had served four years behind bars on a robbery charge, from 1986 to 1990. When he got out, he eventually landed a decent-paying job as a garbage truck driver. But he got his kicks and his status by becoming a biker. He joined the dominant club in the state of Arizona—the Dirty Dozen, an excessively vicious gang even by biker standards. "[I] thought it was cool to hang around with the bikers," he later told a court. "Liked the image and at times the violence. [I] wasn't in it for the chicks or the money."

If Kramer liked the image and violence of the bikers, he got a boost in 1996 when Sonny Barger, the legendary leader of the Hells Angels, moved to Arizona and absorbed most of the local Dirty Dozen into his worldwide organization, giving them exalted status in the biker world. Kramer became a member of the HA chapter in Mesa, a quiet suburb just east of Phoenix, thus earning the nickname "Mesa Mike." And it didn't take long for Kramer to prove he was worthy of the patch. In 1997, while at a weekend motorcycle festival, he got into an argument with another biker over who had the faster bike. He slammed the guy with his fist, splitting his lip and making his nose bleed. The man took out a handgun from his back pocket, but his friends dragged him away. Kramer was not amused: that showed disrespect, and no one impugns the power of the patch.

"When anybody pulls a gun on me, it belongs to me," he said. He took the gun and ordered the man and his friends to leave the area: "You do not report your gun stolen or lost or make a report on this incident, or you're done. I will kill you with your own gun."

By 2001 Kramer was a five-year veteran of the Angels. He had mellowed somewhat since his wife had given birth to a baby girl. His thick eyebrows and deep-set green eyes seemed to suggest something brooding, almost sad. At times after "church"—that's what the Hells Angels call their regular club business meetings—he would head home to his newborn daughter instead of drinking with the boys.

But on the cold Thursday evening of October 25, 2001, Kramer decided instead to hang out with the boys, a decision that would change his life forever.

And help end the life of Cynthia Garcia.

———

"Funny. She was real loveable."

That's how Angelina, who was eleven years old when the bikers murdered her mother, remembers Cynthia. "Fun" is not something many young girls associate with a parent, but Angelina insists her mom "was a real cool woman." Cynthia would take Angelina and her friends swimming and listened to their music—mostly. Angelina's only beef with her mom was that she also liked country music.

Married as a teenager, then divorced a dozen years later, Cynthia did her best to raise six children alone in the tough, poor neighbourhoods and streets of Mesa. There were four girls and two boys, ranging in age from the baby of the family, Angelina, to her twenty-six-year-old eldest daughter, Bianca. "She always wanted the best for us," says Olivia, the second eldest. "She taught us to be honest. To live a good life."

But life wasn't that good for Cynthia. She had a former boyfriend who had abused her and was now incarcerated. Unemployed, she was forced to live with her parents and Angelina, the only child still at home, in a cramped apartment. The handful of family photos they have show Cynthia clutching her youngest daughter, her long reddish brown hair falling below her shoulders. At forty-four, she retained much of her youthful beauty, though it was an open family secret that Cynthia was often on the streets, finding refuge in the bottle. "Drinking was her downfall," says one family member.

So it was not a complete surprise that Garcia would be out late at night on that Thursday, October 25. Cynthia called her eldest daughter from a pay phone around 8 P.M. and said she'd be back to pick up some money.

A few hours later, a security camera captured a brief image of her outside a local convenience store on the corner of Valencia and Broadway, in Mesa, just three miles west of the Hells Angels clubhouse on South LeBaron. It was the last time she was seen alive by anyone but the bikers.

After a long night of drinking, Mike Kramer and his friends were getting a little restless. Joining Kramer that night were two of his biker buddies. Paul Eischeid was a "prospect"—meaning he was on probation for a year and not yet a "full-patch" member. Eischeid had the fire of a new recruit: he was a walking tattoo parlour, his torso front and back covered with black ink; his name was plastered on his stomach, and eventually a Hells Angels' Death Head and "Hell 666 Bound" would be emblazoned across his lower back. But he was very different than your average biker; he was clean shaven, handsome and intelligent enough to work as a stockbroker for one of the large financial institutions in the area.

Kevin Augustiniak, on the other hand, although already a full-patch member, was basically just a loser with a temper. With green eyes and at five feet nine inches, he weighed only 140 pounds, and he had an arrest record that included trespass, assault, driving under the influence of alcohol and resisting police.

In February of 2001, according to police accounts, he had bumped into a woman and her children at a local bar holding a special "family day" where children were invited. The mother told the biker to watch where he was going; he promptly slugged her, breaking her jaw, according to police.

Less than four months later, Augustiniak came home after working a security detail for Hells Angels to find that his neighbour, busy cleaning out his boots to get ready for his construction job, was making a lot of noise by banging the boots against a wall between the two homes. The two men quickly got into a shouting match through the wall, then stormed outside to confront each other. Packing his weapon, Augustiniak approached the man with typical Angel swagger.

"I don't care what club you're with, that gun don't mean shit to me," the neighbour said, according to police accounts.

So the biker promptly shot the man twice, wounding but not killing him.

Augustiniak calmly walked back into his house and waited for the police to arrive. He placed his gun on a table and emptied out the bullets. He told his girlfriend to wait in the bathroom in case

there was a shootout and took the precaution of calling "the boys
to notify them. The Hells Angels arrived about the same time the
cops from the Phoenix suburb of Tempe did.

"He was emotionless," says Chris Hoffman of the Tempe gang
unit. Adds his partner, Sgt. Chuck Schoville, "Let's face it, when
you shoot a neighbour for making noise, that's not normal. Kevin
was just a loose cannon."

A loose cannon that was set to explode on that last Thursday
night in October 2001. According to Kramer's later sworn testimony in a separate HA trial unrelated to the murder and police
records disclosed to defense lawyers, this is what transpired.

Augustiniak and Kramer, along with four other full-patch
members, headed out with Paul Eischeid and two other prospects
to a local bar in nearby Gilbert. They all wore their colours, led by
Mesa chapter president Robert "Bad Bob" Johnston. When the bar
shut down about 1:30 A.M. on Sunday, most of the boys headed
back to the Mesa clubhouse to continue drinking at their well-
stocked private bar. The late-night revellers included the Mesa
club's sergeant-at-arms, Denis Gillard, who had a long history of
aggravated assaults, weapons and drunk driving charges, and
Gary Dunham, who had flames and skulls tattooed on his arms,
while across his stomach he sported the slogan "Death Is Certain.
Life Is Not."

The Angels sent out Kelby Randolph, one of the club's dimmer
prospects, to find some female companions—what Sonny Barger
had once described as "a scavenger hunt for pussy."

Kramer and the other Mesa boys wanted the prospect to bring
back a woman in a red dress spotted earlier that evening. Randolph
returned shortly afterwards empty-handed, reporting he had
failed to track her down. So this time the bikers dispatched him
"in search of any female that he could find," as Kramer later
recalled.

This time, Randolph somehow met Cynthia Garcia. She
agreed, for whatever reason, to go back with him to the clubhouse.
Though she didn't know the Angels, Garcia would not have been
nervous in that neighbourhood, even in the dark of night. Her

mother used to live not far from the clubhouse; an aunt and other family members still did. On her way in, she could not have missed the large, neatly painted red-and-white sign nailed to the gates in the driveway:

> HAMC Mesa does *not* allow the use or possession of
> illegal substances at our clubhouse.
> Please *do not use* or possess any illegal substances on
> this property.
> Thank you,
> HAMC Mesa

How much trouble could she get into, Garcia must have thought, if they didn't allow drugs? But once inside, Garcia quickly discovered to her horror that the only rule the Hells Angels follow is that they make the rules and everyone has to obey. The Angels plied her with alcohol, and everyone, according to Kramer's account of the evening, was "having a good time." But "after some time had gone by, [she] started to 'talk trash' about the patched members," Kramer would later recall.

He warned her not to talk that way around those guys, but, according to Kramer, Garcia wouldn't back down. He grabbed her by the hair. Don't talk trash about the HA, he repeated.

"She's acting stupid," Augustiniak said, according to Kramer's account to police. Kramer alleged Augustiniak knocked her off the bar stool, and as she lay on the ground, he and Paul Eischeid "proceeded to kick and punch her."

"She was bleeding and semi-conscious," Kramer later remembered. He turned to two other bikers who were watching and told them to get a car and back it into the clubhouse driveway so they could dump her in the trunk.

Kramer stared at the woman lying on the floor: she was bleeding from the face—enough, he feared, to stain the carpet. Eischeid and another prospect dragged Cynthia's limp body out of the clubhouse and threw her into the trunk. "Eischeid got in the driver's seat, Augustiniak got in the front passenger seat and

I got in the backseat. We drove to a remote location in the desert," Kramer said.

Kramer claimed the plan had been simply to dump the woman, injured though still alive. But Augustiniak "wanted the female dealt with in a more severe manner." It was a long and, if Kramer is to be believed, miserable drive out to the desert. Augustiniak drove fast. Kramer, alone in the back, could hear noises coming from the trunk. Cynthia, beaten and dazed, was terrified and trying to fight for her life. "[I] had an idea what was going to happen and could not believe it," Kramer later told police. The report on his debriefing does not explain why he did nothing to stop his buddies.

Eischeid—again according to Kramer—drove past Apache Junction and turned off at an isolated patch in the desert, just off Usury Pass Road near the Salt River. The three men stepped out of the car and were careful to take off their Hells Angels jackets before pulling Garcia out of the trunk. They then dragged her to the other side of a fence near some bushes. Kramer could no longer feel the woman moving.

Garcia lay before them, motionless, on her back. According to Kramer's police statement, Eischeid pulled out a knife and stabbed her over and over in the chest. Then Augustiniak yanked out his knife and joined in. By Kramer's account, they had stabbed the woman at least twenty times. Eischeid then tossed Kramer his knife, expecting the full-patch member to join in. According to Kramer, he made "a slashing motion" on the right side of Garcia's neck: "I . . . intentionally stabbed the victim in the neck area."

Then he handed the bloodstained knife back to Eischeid, who went on stabbing the now nearly dead woman. In the eerie silence of the desert night, Kramer could hear her gurgling and gasping for air. At one point, her blood and her life draining from her, Cynthia grabbed on to his pant leg. Then she let go, and Kramer knew it was over.

Augustiniak, however, was not finished if Kramer's account is to be believed. He decided he wanted to cut off her head, perhaps to make sure she could never be identified or maybe just as a sick trophy. He said he wanted to put her head on a fence post.

Augustiniak took his blade to Garcia's neck but found his knife was too dull to complete the decapitation. They buried her body, partially severed head and all. Drenched in blood, the three bikers climbed into their car and drove back to Mesa.

That, at least, is the story Mike Kramer told police; his account has yet to be challenged, much less proven in court. But Kramer did secretly record his buddy Paul Eischeid, telling him not to worry about the killing: "She's nobody. No one cares. No one probably even reported her missing. They probably found her . . . probably fucking [put a] Jane Doe on her," he said in a conversation recorded by the police.

It would not be the last time that Paul Eischeid would make a mistake about Cynthia Garcia's murder.

Bianca, Cynthia's eldest daughter, thought it was strange that her mother had not shown up to pick up the money they had talked about earlier that evening, but she figured she'd hear from Cynthia sooner or later. The weekend, however, came with no news and then more days slipped by with a worrisome silence. Finally, about a week later, at 2:15 P.M. on Wednesday, Halloween day, two men driving through the desert made a gruesome discovery by the side of the road—the bloated, decomposing body of a woman.

Detectives on the scene spotted tire marks by the side of the road, shoe impressions and drag marks, along with a couple of empty cigarette packs and butts. At the county medical examiner's office, Dr. Laura Fulginiti's autopsy revealed twenty-seven stab wounds "in four groupings." She also discovered that "the throat had been cut at least three times." Through dental records and fingerprints, they were quickly able to establish the victim's identity, but that's all they had—a name. No one knew how she had ended up in the desert or who had killed her. It would take many months before police would connect Garcia's murder to the bikers.

"For a long time we didn't know what happened," remembers Bianca.

And the police didn't know either. "At this time, all leads have been exhausted and this case will remain open," read the police reports. "Suspect/s information is unknown."

The bikers had done their best to keep it that way. After the desert slaying, according to Kramer's story to police, Garcia's three killers had sped back to the Mesa clubhouse, where they took off their clothes and boots and handed them to a prospect named Richard Hyder, who burned them on a grill. Kramer and Eischeid then drove the car to Kramer's home; they tore out the carpeting from the trunk and hosed down the entire vehicle. Eischeid gave Kramer the two knives; he later dumped them at a waste disposal station.

But disposing of the grisly memories of Cynthia Garcia's execution would not be as easy. The killing appeared to have badly shaken Kramer—and he made a fateful decision to rat out his beloved Angels to the cops. "What happened in the desert was screwed up. The murder was screwed up," Kramer would later testify. "[I] didn't become an informant to make money or to retaliate," he said according to court notes. "I got a conscience."

Nonsense, says defence lawyer Ellen Barry, who would later cross swords with Kramer in a Hells Angels drug case. "He characterizes himself as a somewhat passive participant in this whole event. He portrayed himself as having this big crisis of conscience. But the fact of the matter is he knew his ass was going to jail for the rest of his life, and he ratted first. He realized that somebody was going to rat, and so he got out first."

Whatever his motivation, within days of the murder, Kramer made a call to the police that would alter his life—and ruin the lives of numerous Hells Angels in several states. It was not the first time he had snitched; by his own admission, when he was twenty-one, he had "set up a guy" he thought was stealing a motorcycle. So once again, Kramer reached out to the cops: he contacted a friend who put him in touch with the stocky detective in charge of the gang unit in the nearby town of Tempe, Chuck Schoville.

Schoville loves bikes—and hates outlaw bikers. He began riding mini-bikes when he was just six and could afford his first

Harley only after more than a decade of policing. The Mesa club-house borders the city of Tempe, and several Hells Angels live in his town, so Schoville has to keep on top of the biker wars. Just about every week he gets a call, and it's always the same old story: some desperate soul in jail or in trouble with the law claims to be connected to the Hells Angels and he's willing to flip over on the whole world. It's almost always a lie. But Schoville remembered a lesson of patience he learned when he used to go deer hunting with his dad: "He wanted the big one. Look for the big one."

So it was with a cop's healthy dose of skepticism that Schoville agreed to meet Kramer at Stuart Anderson's, a popular steakhouse thirty-five miles west of Phoenix. The anguished Angel was nervous about anyone spotting him in town. Sporting a crew cut and trim leather jacket, Kramer didn't look at all like the biker Schoville was expecting. But when Kramer took off his jacket, Schoville spotted a Hells Angels tattoo on his arm—and realized this was "the big one."

Kramer was cagey. He kept talking in circles, asking what if this, what if that. He liked using the word "hypothetical" a lot. "He was testing the waters to see if we were legit or not," says Schoville.

After two hours of this delicate dance, the Angel and the cop agreed to meet again.

"There's something a little strange here," Schoville said as they prepared to say goodbye in the parking lot. "You keep telling me, 'what if, what if.' But what is it you want?"

Kramer would say only that he needed money, and that he wanted to get out of the biker lifestyle.

The biker and the cop met a couple more times over the next few weeks, and only then did Kramer make indirect mention of the Garcia murder. He referred vaguely to a stabbing. Kramer was a smart snitch: he wasn't going to give up his most valuable com-modity—the details of a biker murder—without a big payback from the cops.

Schoville knew his small gang unit in the city of Tempe could not run a major undercover operation with a full-patch Hells Angel. Besides, Kramer was nervous about leaks within local law enforcement. He knew the bikers had their spies. Schoville mentioned the case to Steve Trethewy, an analyst with the Rocky Mountain Information Service, a regional police intelligence service, who had been a respected and plugged-in Arizona biker cop. They both decided the best person to call was a young case agent for the federal Bureau of Alcohol, Tobacco and Firearms, the ATF, in Los Angeles. John Ciccone was making a name for himself as one of the brightest biker investigators, especially against the HA's feared rivals, the Mongols.

"Are you sitting down?" Trethewy asked Ciccone when he got him on the phone. "Because I'm going to hand you something, buddy."

He told the ATF man he could deliver him a full-patch Hells Angel informant. Trethewy, like many others in Arizona law enforcement, was frustrated with the lack of action against the HA in his state: Man, if we could just do a big case on the Hells Angels in my backyard, he thought.

"I'll be out there tomorrow," Ciccone said.

But when Ciccone first met Hells Angel Mike Kramer, Schoville feared the two men were off to a shaky start. Within the first two minutes, the Californian ATF man was ribbing Kramer about how tough the Mongols were in California, where they had inflicted numerous beatings and shootings on the Angels.

"How come the Mongols are kicking your guys' asses?" Ciccone teased Kramer.

Well, this relationship isn't going to go very far, Schoville thought to himself. If I were this guy, I would just get up and tell Ciccone to eat shit and die.

But Kramer took a liking to, or at least found a grudging respect for, the tough-talking ATF agent. By November 26, 2001, he was sitting in the ATF's Group II office in Los Angeles being debriefed as a confidential informant by Ciccone. He might have been Mike Kramer, Mesa Hells Angel, to the bikers, but now in police intelligence files he was CI-78400-376.

The new CI "revealed a significant amount of intelligence" about unsolved murders, narcotics trafficking and firearms deals, according to the official ATF account of the debriefing, later disclosed in court files. Kramer also promised he would "be able to provide information regarding the current tensions between the Hells Angels and the Mongols"—an avenue of investigation that in just four months' time would prove vital when a major clash between the rival gangs exploded.

What Kramer did not yet reveal were details of the Garcia murder, much less his direct role in it. During his first one-hour meeting with the ATF, only about ten to fifteen minutes were devoted to a "hypothetical murder" when Kramer, according to later court disclosures, indicated only that "something crappy happened."

"We didn't know," insists John Ciccone. "He gave us bits and pieces, but there wasn't enough for us to pursue as far as looking to solve a murder."

On December 1, Kramer got an early Christmas present. He signed a formal "Informant Agreement" with the ATF. The standard nineteen-clause, one-page deal made it clear he could not "take part in any unlawful activities . . . in acts of violence . . . [or] initiate any plans to commit criminal acts."

When Kramer's role as an informant eventually became public in 2004, there would be accusations that the ATF had unwittingly signed up a murderer to do its dirty work. In fact, it was a little more subtle than that. Ciccone was no fool. He knew that a full-patch Hells Angel doesn't come knocking on police doors unless he has something really onerous that he wants to get off his back. But Ciccone was willing to bide his time, gaining Kramer's trust. "The more you do for me as an informant, the better off it'll be in the long run. No promises, no guaranties," he told the biker.

"I knew at some point in time, we'd get the full story."

Mike Kramer didn't realize it yet, but he had just signed on to be the eyes and ears for a rising ATF case agent who, in only a few short years, had become a master at burrowing into and busting up biker gangs. John Ciccone, standing about five feet five inches, is short by the standards of biker cops. Many of his fellow officers—not to mention the bikers—tower over him, but Ciccone takes no guff from anyone and easily dominates a room or a meeting with a take-charge attitude, an easy smile and a sharp investigative mind.

His main interest in college in Michigan was playing baseball, but while pursuing a minor in criminal justice he interned at a local police department and caught the bug. Determined to work for the feds, he applied to all the major agencies; the ATF gave him his first job offer.

The ATF was gaining substantial experience in tackling outlaw biker gangs. There was a new generation of young, well-trained agents and undercover operatives eager to get a crack at the Hells Angels. But within the agency there were also plenty of bureaucrats and senior managers loath to take chances on anything as risky as the bikers.

Ciccone's first case in LA in the mid-1990s was against a gangsta-rap record company suspected of hiring a lot of street gang members and laundering dope money. Just as that case was winding down, he started helping out a good friend and fellow ATF agent named Darrin Kozlowski. "Koz," as everyone calls him, looked intimidating enough as a police officer—tall, heavy and broad-shouldered, but when he went into full disguise, with long, greasy hair to his shoulders, a goatee and bulging biceps, he looked as mean as the meanest biker.

Koz was among the growing army of young agents the ATF was training to penetrate street gangs, firearms traffickers and biker gangs. There was no textbook, no manual on how police could infiltrate outlaw motorcycle gangs. They made plenty of mistakes, but that's how they learned—from experience.

Though they dominate the biker scene worldwide, on their home turf in Southern California the Hells Angels are actually outnumbered by two rival groups, the Vagos and the Mongols. In early 1997 Koz was nurturing a confidential informant (CI) named Junior, who was at that time prospecting for the Vagos. But thirty days into the job, Junior got himself killed in a motorcycle accident. Koz decided he would try to penetrate the gang himself and walked into a tattoo shop in Hollywood known to be the hangout for many of the members of the main Vagos chapter. They invited him to their clubhouse that night.

The ATF now needed someone to cover for Koz, and Ciccone stepped in. From the start, it was what Ciccone calls a "fly by the seat of your pants" operation. "That was the first time we were involved in that kind of thing," he says. "Management wasn't prepared. Koz wasn't prepared."

Outside the Vagos' clubhouse that evening, a lumbering giant of a biker came out to greet Koz: "Hey, we need to ask you some questions," he said as he put his massive arm around him. "We got a situation where we believe Junior was working with the ATF and informing on us."

Behind him, the bikers were padlocking the gate. They ushered him inside, through a steel door and into the cinder-block building without a single window. In the surveillance car, Koz's watchers mistakenly assumed it was all going to plan: "Hey, it's looking good, man—he's going in with them!"

But inside the dark, dingy clubhouse, with graffiti scrawls everywhere on the green walls, the Vagos were grilling the undercover cop: "My heart's beating fast," Koz says.

The ten bikers put their guns on the table and wanted to know why Koz had a gun in his boot. "Hey, I'm not giving up my gun," he retorted. They asked for his address and phone number; he didn't have any undercover information ready, so he just made stuff up. The Vagos were mollified enough to invite him out for beer. As they left their clubhouse, they turned one way and a rattled Koz sped off in the opposite direction.

After that narrow escape, Koz was ready to call it quits. But, as luck would have it, the Vagos recontacted Koz through a real pager number he had supplied. He told them he was furious at being grilled; they respected his tough attitude and invited him back to hang with them. Over the next year, Koz managed to win the confidence of the Vagos, getting in tight with them and eventually earning his full patch. "Every time we had a hurdle, we seemed to be able to talk our way out of it," Koz says. "Once I got patched, I figured the hurdles were over." But then the girlfriend of Junior, the deceased confidential informant, supplied the Vagos with a police business card Koz had given him. Suddenly, the jig was up. The ATF scrambled to take the case down in early 1998, still managing to make more than a dozen arrests and shutting down the Hollywood chapter for a short period.

Ciccone and the ATF took away some useful lessons from that experience. They had been forced to rush in before Koz had been fully "backstopped." That meant he did not have his cover story completely worked out with all the proper IDs, credit history and personal background in place to support it. "It was just moving way too fast, before everything was in place," Ciccone says. "You get too far ahead of yourself, then you are constantly forced to make up stuff. It's too risky. But we didn't know any better."

Next time, Ciccone would be on top of the situation. Big time. His next target was also bigger: the Mongols. The Mongols dominated Los Angeles with three hundred members in the city and another hundred or so scattered through Southern California and a few other states. They started doing something rarely seen in biker circles: recruiting young, mainly Hispanic, street gang members. Police noted a rise in stabbings, assaults and shootings in dance clubs and hip-hop parties where typically bikers don't congregate; now the Mongols were turning these youth hangouts into their territory.

Ciccone wanted to take a hard look at these guys. He developed a CI who had been in prison with the Mongols. He started sending the CI into bars where the Mongols hung out. He met some high-ranking members and got hold of the gang's application form, so this time the ATF had an idea of what they were going to ask. Another informant, a woman close to the Mongols, offered to introduce someone to the gang.

Ciccone now needed an agent—and Billy Queen was the natural choice. The grandfather of ATF undercover operatives, Queen, at forty-eight, had been with the ATF twenty years, eighteen of them undercover. He knew how to ride a bike, and he looked the part. Ciccone had become friends with Queen when they worked on a SWAT team, so he approached him about the Mongols.

"I got this case going. Would you be interested?"

Queen, naturally, jumped at the chance. Fortunately, he had been backstopped for years. He had an established credit history and a fake criminal history. He'd had an apartment under his assumed name for the past few years. The bikers often hired private investigators to check out prospects or people with whom they did business. If the neighbours were questioned, no suspicions would be raised about a new tenant who had suddenly moved in just before applying to be a Mongol. The ATF also had a fictitious business front, so they could provide Queen with six years of W-2 tax forms, as the bikers requested. The Mongols wanted phone numbers for family members, so the ATF put an undercover line in the home of Queen's brother back East and told him what to say if it rang. They even had to plant a fake high school yearbook photo under Queen's undercover name. The Mongols checked for that, too.

Ciccone ran all the backup surveillance on Queen. It was constant stress. Watching Queen walk into bars filled with fifty bikers, Ciccone never knew if this was the night the Mongols would confront his agent. "They would always say shit like 'Hey, Undercover'—stuff like that, just to fuck with him, I guess," Ciccone recalls.

But as later recounted in his book, *Under and Alone*, Queen earned the Mongols' confidence and became a full-patch member, riding undercover for a remarkable stretch of two years and two months.

Queen finally came out of role in March 2000, and the ATF struck hard two months later. Police executed seventy-six search warrants in four states and arrested fifty-one full-patch Mongols. Queen had made recordings of dozens of firearms and drug crimes; he also helped solved a murder. "We made a significant hit on their membership," Ciccone says with a smile.

Though the arrangement had been a success, Ciccone realized they had done some things wrong. For one thing, he was doing all the paperwork, all the money management and all the surveillance while Queen was handling all the undercover. "We were running 24/7," he says. "We didn't have the people we needed." The ATF would have to make sure the next infiltrations had more administrative support.

Ciccone also had to grapple with bureaucratic short-sightedness. "We had constant headaches from management: 'We're spending too much money; where are the results?'" In a way, it was to be expected. Managers are interested in results that can be measured: how many arrests, how many guns, how many kilos of drugs. But sending in a cop to become an outlaw biker takes time: you have to hang around for a few months, then prospect for even longer and then—even if you get the patch—you still have to gain the full trust of the other members before you penetrate the inner circle. From a statistical point of view—arrests and convictions—it would be at least a year of nothing.

"All our management was seeing was tens of thousands of dollars being spent on repairs to the bikes, the undercover apartment, utilities, phones, this and that—and no arrests and no search warrants were happening. They were so hung up on that, they wanted to shut the case down every other month," says Ciccone.

Still, Ciccone felt he had learned a lot from the successful penetrations against the Vagos and the Mongols. Now he was eager to use his latest catch, full-patch snitch Mike Kramer, to go after the Hells Angels.

Back in Arizona, that's just what the ATF's Joe Slatalla was aiming to do as well. Like Ciccone, Slatalla knew only too well how bureaucracy and institutional wrangling could screw up an investigation. The beefy, seventeen-year agency veteran had tried once before to stop the Angels dead in their tracks in Arizona. He had failed—and he wasn't about to let his second chance slip away.

Slatalla had started out in the ATF's Detroit office before moving to the desert state in the 1990s, working everything from narcotics trafficking to organized crime and street gangs—and at least a dozen biker cases. "Slats" is the nickname used by both his friends and enemies, and he has equal numbers of each. In the mid-1990s Slatalla figured that the best time to stop the HA in Arizona was just as they were making their big push to win over the local Dirty Dozen biker gang and before they got a foothold in the state. His plans quickly ran afoul of managers in his own agency and other police forces. "He's got a very strong will, very confident," says one insider. "He was a threat to the other investigators and he was frustrated at the missed opportunity." Slats left Arizona for a supervisor's job back in Miami.

Taking advantage of police infighting and inaction, the Hells Angels flourished in their new-found desert playground. "When the Hells Angels came, for almost four years nobody in law enforcement did any enforcement on them," says Chuck Schoville of the Tempe gang unit. "Everybody said it was organized crime, the Mafia of the new day. Well, my question was, If this is organized crime, what are we doing about it?"

By late 2001 Joe Slatalla had returned to Arizona, determined to shake things up with the Angels: "I felt they were pretty ripe to be exposed and to be beaten," he says. Only this time, he was going to run a tight ship and not let the bureaucrats screw it up.

He began from a straight intelligence standpoint, going through hundreds of police reports dating back twenty years. He identified members and associates and tried to figure out what sources might be out there for recruitment as snitches. He began planning for wiretaps and other traditional investigative techniques; then suddenly—in December of 2001—he caught a lucky break.

That break was named Rudolph "Rudy" Kramer, a repeat offender who had had the misfortune to get nabbed with a dirty gun. Kramer (who shared a surname with Hells Angel Michael Kramer but was no relation) sported a ponytail, at least ten aliases—and a drug problem. He was looking at serious jail time, so in an interview with the ATF he bragged about his association with the Hells Angels and how he could broker an introduction to the secretive club. Kramer was not blowing hot air. According to court-filed affidavits, as far back as 1999 he had requested permission from the Hells Angels chapter presidents in Arizona to start a Nomad chapter of the Solo Angeles in the state. The Solo Angeles were a

Mexican biker gang based in Tijuana with about 125 members. They had a handful of members in the U.S., mainly in Southern California, but no formal chapters, an organizational weakness Slatalla would later exploit.

Some Angels, including Mesa chapter leader Bob Johnston, were in favour of Rudy's idea of setting up a local Solo Angeles Chapter. But the powerful president of the Cave Creek chapter, Daniel "Hoover" Seybert, voted against it. So Rudy joined a small gang known as the Loners, ever careful not "to infringe on the Hells Angels' drug distribution turf . . . which consists of the entire state of Arizona," according to Kramer's reports to the ATF. He remained close to the HA, just the same. As late as December 2001, they asked him to join their puppet group, the Red Devils.

Slatalla saw a rare opportunity here. He knew that no successful operation against a well-structured organized crime group like the Hells Angels had ever taken place without infiltration. Using cops was always more reliable than sometimes dubious snitches—but also a lot more dangerous. In California, the ATF's John Ciccone had run undercover cops inside two Hells Angels rival gangs, the Vagos and the Mongols. In Colorado, the ATF had infiltrated a smaller gang called the Sons of Silence. But no cop had ever gotten close to the illustrious—and super-cautious—Angels.

Slats felt there was a disadvantage in trying to become outright members of the HA. For one thing, they were so well insulated that it might take too long. For another, even once inside, a cop might find that the illegal activities carried out by the club raised serious dilemmas: "You can't play by their rules and beat them," Slatalla says. "You can't go to parties and do dope; you can't go to parties and take advantage of the women offered to you. So it's a very rare law enforcement official who gets in."

But now Rudy Kramer had given Slatalla a novel idea: what if the cops set up their *own* biker gang and used that to cozy up to the Hells Angels? If Slatalla and the ATF engineered the creation of a branch of the loose-knit Solo Angeles, they could spy on the HA but still call the shots by running their own club.

"Nobody to my knowledge has ever actually used a legitimate club, lied their way into that club and then used that club as their credibility cover," Slatalla says. "It was an over-the-top plan that had never been done before. What if we tried this? Could we work it? And we said, 'Yeah, it's so crazy it might work.'"

Slatalla figured the cops could use Rudy Kramer to introduce the undercover cops to the Angels. So about eight weeks after he was arrested on the gun violation, Kramer's charges were tossed out and he was out on the street, hanging around the bikers once again. Now all Slats needed was an equally crazy, over-the-top cop—an experienced but bold undercover police agent who could lead the attack. And he found one in a foul-mouthed, cocky man parading as a Mafia debt collector, a gunrunner to Mexico and cold-blooded hitman in Bullhead City, Arizona. Jay Dobyns had been doing dangerous undercover work for the ATF for more than a decade. And he had the scars to prove it.

Jay Dobyns's first week on the job with the ATF started with a bang, literally. He points to the scar on his chest where the exit wound is still visible. He's wolfing down a hearty plate of bacon and eggs at a noisy diner. Everyone knows him here—the waitresses, the cashier, the patrons—although his garish tattoos and pointed goatee seem slightly out of place amid the middle-class crowd in a conservative suburb of Tucson, Arizona. Many remember him as a university football star; others see him as the friendly dad who coaches Little League; only a handful know what he does as a cop.

Dobyn's six-foot-two stature and lean, powerful build made him a star receiver for the legendary Arizona Wildcats in the early 1980s. He is still ranked among the top ten best receivers in Wildcat history, but he knew early on he wasn't going to make a living playing football. He plotted his career options much like a well-executed pass play: he didn't want to sit in an office; he wanted some kind of service, but no uniform; and he wanted action. That left only one option: police work. And the ATF was the most exciting team in town, "because of their reputation for street work,"

Dobyns says. "The ATF historically had an understanding of street work and what it's like to be a street officer or highway patrolman. And I think that's the beauty of the ATF: the ATF never fully embraced that federal stereotype of showing up with a suit and tie and a notepad and reporting to a crime scene after a fact. It's as close to being a street cop as you can be and be a fed."

Within days of first putting on his ATF badge in 1988, Dobyns, at only twenty-six, got his first taste of blood. A team from the local Phoenix office was hunting for an armed ex-convict. "I'm the new guy, so everybody is trying to protect me," Dobyns says.

The prey was hiding in some deep weeds behind a trailer park. Dobyns was walking behind his supervisor when he caught something out of the corner of his eye. But by the time he turned, the felon had grabbed him from behind and put a gun to his head. He dragged the rookie agent to a nearby car as the other cops scattered and cocked their guns.

"We're getting out of here!" the ex-con yelled. "Drive!"

"This guy is probably going to shoot me one way or the other," Dobyns remembers thinking, "I'd rather have him shoot me with my people around me versus driving me twenty miles out into the desert and killing me there."

So the new recruit grabbed the keys out of the ignition and made a lunge for the door, but not before the ex-con's gun went off. The bullet went right through Dobyn's back, between his shoulder blade and spine, and came out his chest, ricocheting off the car window and nicking his hand. The ATF agents exploded with fifteen rounds of fire, killing the hostage taker. But Dobyns lay on the ground, spitting blood and falling in and out of consciousness.

"I was lying in the desert thinking, I got shot before I even got my first paycheque! You know what, I'm going to fuckin' die. I have been on the job a week, and I'm going to die in this fuckin' trailer park."

The police rushed their fallen comrade to hospital, where he was stabilized and stitched up. But Dobyns found that patching up his wounds was easier than patching up his year-old marriage.

His twenty-one-year-old wife was completely overwhelmed by the shooting: "I don't want you to do this any more," she told him.

"This is what I'm supposed to do," said Dobyns. "This is what I want to do." The childless couple divorced quickly, but it would not be the last time Dobyns's family life would suffer.

The shooting of a former football star turned cop had generated a lot of local heat in the media, not the kind of publicity a budding undercover agent needed. Back at work after a quick recovery, Dobyns got into his first of many dust-ups with management.

"Well, I guess your days of undercover work are done," his boss said.

"Absolutely not," insisted Dobyns. "I didn't freaking come here to sit behind a desk and sit on the phone and make my case by using a fax machine and a computer."

So a compromise was struck: the ATF shipped Dobyns out to Chicago. For an adventure-seeking rookie eager to sell guns and dope and bust some bad guys, the crime- and gang-ridden Windy City was a dream assignment.

And it didn't take long for Dobyns to get shot again.

He fell in with a group of young investigators working street gangs. He befriended an equally gung-ho agent named Chris Bayless. "Jay is probably one of the best undercover guys, bar none," Bayless says. "What makes you good is being able to keep your shit together when everything around you is just spiralling into the ground."

In the tough alleyways and streets of Chicago's South Side, Dobyns learned the tricks of the undercover trade—how to stay cool, how to speak the lingo, how to push the envelope without breaking the law or cracking any skulls.

But not without picking up some more scars. When a machine-gun deal went sour, Dobyns and Bayless found themselves chasing a couple of gangsters in a car. They blocked one street and leaped out of their car, but the bandits sped toward them; one of them rolled down the window, leaned out and fired off two quick rounds. Dobyns managed to shoot the driver in the shoulder, but not before the fleeing gun merchants careened into him, sending him flying over their car. "He flips up in the air, his shoes go flying off," Bayless remembers. "I could see his eyes go back in his head. I thought he was dead."

Dobyns hit the windshield with his head, shattering the glass. The blow spun him over the roof. Bayless could not fire any more because Dobyns was blocking his shot.

"Jay flew into the air, but he had enough sense to catch himself, twist his body around and fire another round at the car before he hit the ground," says an amazed Bayless. He dashed over to check on his friend. Both of Dobyns's kneecaps had been blown out; he was badly bruised but not broken.

"Are you all right?" Bayless asked him.

"Go fuckin' kill them," Dobyns replied.

Bayless sped off after the felons, who were apprehended shortly afterwards. He could only marvel at his partner's courage under fire. "This was a guy who had been taken hostage and shot back in Arizona. Then he comes here and gets run over and almost shot and killed a second time," says Bayless. "He still sucks it up and goes out there every day and works harder than anybody else I know."

Dobyns had remarried just four months earlier. His new wife Gwen was a tall, striking blonde, a graphic artist he had met in Tucson. Dobyns called her from the hospital that night.

"I was in another shooting and I wanted you to hear about it from me before you heard about it on TV," Jay told his new wife.

Gwen took it in stride. She knew what she was getting into when she married the ambitious ATF undercover agent. "I'm not a worrier—it's just not my thing," she says.

She had more to worry about when her husband joined Bayless for a trip to Colorado in the fall of 1999 to help two ATF agents who had spent two years infiltrating a local motorcycle gang, the Sons of Silence. Dobyns and Bayless had a simple task: they wore patches from the Unforgiven, a fictitious gang set up for the operation. They would start showing up in bars, elicit threats from the Sons of Silence and then stand down—but not before gathering evidence that bikers used intimidation and violence to maintain their criminal monopoly.

Dobyns and Bayless arrived late one night at one bar with three other undercover agents, all dressed up as members of the Unforgiven. They had been told the bar was clear of any full-patch members of the Sons of Silence, but they soon ran into a prominent leader named Doug Luckett—all six feet nine inches and three hundred–plus pounds of him.

"Hey, you guys can't wear that shit around here," Luckett ordered, pointing to the Unforgiven patch.

The ATF agents' plan was to simply drop their colours and walk out like a bunch of wimps. Two of them made it out the door, but then the doorman locked it really fast.

Luckett then grabbed Dobyns and started punching him. For the next fifteen minutes, the three remaining undercover ATF agents slugged it out with most of the bar patrons.

"They tried to rip off our colours, but we wouldn't let them," says Bayless.

Bruised and bleeding, they made it to the door. Luckett glared at Dobyns: "You're dead, man. Your colours—that shit is all coming off in about two seconds."

Bayless had thought the fight was over, so he gasped as his partner tackled Luckett, knocking him to the ground. Then it seemed as if the whole bar piled on top of them.

From the bottom of the pile came Dobyns's muffled taunt to the Sons of Silence: "Hey, my shit is still on, motherfucker!"

Somehow the ATF agents eventually managed to get the bar door open and escape without having to fire a shot, though they had several loose teeth, contusions on their heads and were pissing blood for a few days. It all seemed worth it when, a few weeks later, the ATF with more than 250 law enforcement agents dismantled the three chapters of the Sons of the Silence by arresting Luckett and thirty-eight other members, seizing dozens of guns, pipe bombs and handmade grenades; $25,000 in cash; and ten pounds of methamphetamine.

It was Dobyns's first brush with biker gangs, and he learned three things. He learned that if you look the part and talk the talk, it's not that hard to pass yourself off as a member of a fictitious bike gang. Second, he saw how brutal and explosive bikers can be. And, most important, he realized that when you walk into their territory and the door locks behind you, you're all alone. Cop or no cop, badge or no badge, there is no cavalry coming to save you.

It is just you and a bunch of bikers and nobody else.

Jay Dobyns and Michael Kramer didn't know it yet, but soon they would both be working undercover in separate yet parallel infiltrations of the Hells Angels, run by Joe Slatalla and John Ciccone. A cop and a killer, working for the ATF to jail as many bikers as possible.

Neither the police nor the bikers knew that those two investigations would eventually culminate in what every gang fears the most: sweeping arrests not only for guns and drugs, but also charges under the U.S. government's powerful RICO—Racketeer-Influenced and Corrupt Organizations—laws, enacted in 1970 and initially used to break up the Italian mob. A conviction as a "criminal enterprise" under RICO had always been Sonny Barger's nightmare, a devastating blow to his attempts to sanitize the image of his beloved Angels. He would narrowly escape it once in California, but had no idea he was going to be hit by a double storm of racketeering trouble from Jay Dobyns and Mike Kramer.

Ironically, it was a prison term in Arizona for Barger that set everything in motion. Less than four years before Dobyns and Kramer started their operations, the Hells Angels did not even exist in Arizona. Their phenomenal explosion of operations—in the American Southwest and around the world—was largely due to the driving ambition and killer instinct of a scrawny kid who grew up in the slums of Oakland, California.

TWO

Arizona Dreamin'

—

In the '60s we got a lot of publicity. It was all fun and games.
In the '70s, we all became gangsters.
—SONNY BARGER

Sonny Barger came to Arizona and liked what he saw. Granted, the most famous biker in the world, the international face of the Hells Angels, wasn't there as a tourist. He was a guest of the U.S. federal government, with free room and board for five years at the Federal Corrections Institution in Phoenix.

Inmate number 82740–011, after all, was guilty of conspiring to murder several rival bikers.

But aside from the barbed wire and mediocre food, life in the early 1990s was pretty good for the aging biker. He even sent a picture to one of the prosecutors who had put him behind bars: Sonny was lying on the grass, bare-chested, soaking up the desert sun, a big smile on his chubby face.

Barger liked the dry air, the craggy mountains, the long, flat desert highways. Unlike in California, an easy rider could rev up his Harley and race down the roads with no helmet required. "I dig the desert; it's the new California," Barger later wrote. "It's wide open and free."

Ironically, it was Barger more than anyone who made California synonymous with bikers and vice versa. Now the Hells Angels leader was thinking the unthinkable—he would leave his Hells Angels Oakland club, the mecca of motorcycle mayhem, for a sprawling state that did not even have a Hells Angels charter.

And therein lay the rub. The King of the Bikers could hardly settle in a state where the Hells Angels were as rare as Democrats. So if Arizona didn't have any Hells Angels to bring in Barger, Barger would have to bring the Hells Angels to Arizona.

"Barger has got so much power, it's incredible. So what does he do? He turns the whole state," says Steve Trethewy of the Rocky Mountain Information Network. "That's one of the trends for the Hells Angels around the world: growth. They have just exploded over the past ten years. It's just been phenomenal the way they have built up."

By his telling, Ralph "Sonny" Barger, born in 1938, never had it easy: his father was an alcoholic Teamster, and his mother ran off with a bus driver when he was an infant.

"What I really liked to do in schools was fight," the future biker leader boasts in his autobiography, *Hell's Angel.* And he was good at it. He got kicked out of the fifth grade after jumping on the teacher and suspended again when he smashed another student on the leg with a baseball bat. He spent time in local taverns with his dad, learning to steal pretzels and hard-boiled eggs.

At only sixteen, Barger joined the U.S. Army by forging his birth certificate; there he learned how to take weapons apart and became a machine gunner—training, he writes, that "later on . . . would come in handy." He bought his first Harley, a used 1936 model, for $125 after being discharged from the army; he had tried to re-enlist, but the psychiatrist ruled he was "too aggressive."

That aggressive streak came in handy on the rough-and-tumble streets of Oakland. Barger also displayed the charisma and shrewdness that transforms punks into leaders. While still in high school in 1954, he founded his first club, the Earth Angels, just "a small street-corner club," as he remembers it: eight kids trying to look and act cool with jackets and a name stitched on the back. Two years later, he joined his first bike club, the Oakland Panthers, but quickly grew disenchanted with them.

They were just recreational riders; Barger says he was hungry for a tight-knit "second family" that was devoted to "raising hell."

He found that family in the spring of 1957, when he began roaring through the streets of Oakland with what he calls "a new wild bunch." One of them had adapted a patch featuring a small skull inside a set of wings—later to become the famed Death Head. Sonny's new group took inspiration from the patch and called themselves the Hells Angels, not really knowing much about the club until they ran into other bikers who told them there were already official chapters with the same name in Fresno, San Francisco, the San Gabriel Valley and San Bernardino.

Sonny learned that it was in Berdoo, as San Bernardino is popularly known, that the club was first formed back in 1948, taking the name from a B-17 Bomber Group stationed in England during the Second World War. The Angels back then were still a ragtag army of ruffians that revelled in their anarchy. But that would soon change under Barger's stewardship. Sonny's group became the Oakland chapter on October 1, 1957. Within a year, Barger took over as president at age twenty. "With big plans of my own," as he put it.

It didn't take long for power to shift to Sonny and the Oakland club, which became, in effect, the mother chapter. The scrappy kid from Oakland was a natural leader. He didn't impose his leadership through brute force—though he never shied away from beating the crap out of his enemies or shooting someone. "He's not a big guy, not a physically threatening guy," says Jay Dobyns, the ATF undercover cop who would infiltrate the Angels and meet Barger several times. "But he's got this charismatic leadership personality that allowed him to build this club. When you talk to him, when you speak to this guy, he makes you feel that there is nothing going on in his life except that conversation with you. He makes you feel important, like he is personally interested in you."

What Barger was interested in was bringing some purpose and discipline to a rowdy army. For the first time, he laid down basic rules and structures. No fighting or swearing at meetings. Strict limits on how close club charters could be to each other. Barger later spelled out more regulations: "No using dope during a meeting" (though presumably any other time was fine) and "no drug burns"—in other words, if you make a drug deal, go through with it and don't rip anybody off. The HA rule book would eventually set the standard for biker gangs around the world.

The repeated reference to drugs was telling, since arguably next to their bikes and their girls, drugs were what the Hells Angels cared about the most. At first, in the 1950s and early '60s, they were heavy recreational users and only part-time distributors. By Barger's own admission, he was at times "totally crazed on cocaine." He named the bike he built by hand "Sweet Cocaine" (and dubbed the smaller model for his girlfriend "Little Cocaine"). Sonny says he eventually kicked his habit in jail, but his first of many wives became so addicted that she had to check into a detox centre.

Barger was not so crazed that he lost his shrewd sense of business. In 1966 he incorporated the Hells Angels under the laws of the State of California, and shortly afterwards trademarked the rights to the name "Hell's Angels" and the winged Death Head insignia. Over the years, the Hells Angels also developed an elaborate pecking order to preserve their elite status. A club or charter had to have six full-patch members to be operational and had to be sponsored, in turn, by an already existing, legitimate club. A full patch consisted of a bottom "rocker" with the name of the club's city or region and a top rocker with the HA name, with the trademarked Death Head in the middle.

From the start, Barger and his Angels jealously guarded their name and status. Barger admits he nearly killed an Oakland bar patron in 1965 simply for bad-mouthing the Angels. He first jammed an automatic pistol into the man's mouth; then when he slammed the pistol against his head, it accidentally went off, hitting the man's skull. "The first shot had been an accident," Barger wrote in his book. "But since the motherfucker was already shot in the head, I bent him over the pool table and shot him again." Barger was convicted of assault with intent to murder.

When a rival gang stole his treasured motorcycle by mistake, the Angels rounded up the suspects, bullwhipped them, beat them with spiked dog collars and broke their fingers with ballpeen hammers—heavier, steel-headed hammers used for metalwork that became favourite weapons of the HA. Another time, Barger admits, when they found two bikers who dared to pretend they were officially HA, they stuck their hands in vises and beat them senseless with bullwhips and mallets.

The turf the Angels were so eager to protect, in the middle of the 1960s, was still exclusively Californian. But in 1966 they formed their first out-of-state club in Omaha, Nebraska. They would never look back, eventually expanding to almost two dozen states in America and another two dozen countries across five continents.

That expansion paralleled another important change within the Hells Angels: the personal drug abuse that Barger and his boys boasted about turned into professional profit-making in the late 1960s—and it transformed the organization forever. Over the next decades, drugs and crime came to define the Hells Angels around the globe: the drug business—cocaine, marijuana and especially methamphetamines—became a multibillion-dollar enterprise for them. And they would take on anyone who threatened their profits.

It was a crucial transformation that the Hells Angels have desperately tried to gloss over: they have largely succeeded in convincing the media and the public that the image of beer-drinking, bike-riding, drug-toking rebels from the early '60s has not substantially changed: whatever damage they cause, the story goes, is mainly to their own brains and beat-up bodies. But this dated myth simply hides the seismic shift that took place in the late '60s when the Hells Angels began an inexorable transformation from club to crime empire. And like so many other cultural tremors that shook the U.S. and eventually the world, the spark was lit in California.

It was called DOA. Dust of the Angels. As in Hells Angels.

It was 1967. The Summer of Love. It was the height of the hippie movement, and hippie heaven was in Haight-Ashbury, San

Francisco, just across the bay from Hell headquarters at Sonny Barger's Oakland chapter. And for a brief period, one of the hottest drugs on both sides of the bay was the white dust from the Angels.

Its real name was PCP, a water-soluble crystalline powder that can be snorted or mixed with tobacco or marijuana and smoked. It wasn't the only drug the Angels pushed. Barger admits that his pals "used to move most of the LSD" in the area. But Angel Dust gave the bikers status. "They got popularity for the first time," says Tim McKinley, an FBI agent in San Francisco who would become one of Barger's fiercest opponents. "It gave them a taste of what they wanted: money, recognition and status—all three things they desperately craved."

The bad news was that DOA also stands for Dead on Arrival. It was phencyclidine—basically a horse tranquilizer and a deadly recipe for severe hallucinations and delirium. The ultimate bad trip. Eventually the drug lost its popularity. Angel Dust bit the dust, so to speak, though it continues to pop up to this day. But the bikers had caught the bug. Unlike marijuana or cocaine, which started as natural products that could be grown domestically or imported, Angel Dust was basically a chemical product you cooked. It was cheap and easy to make. And easy for the Angels to make a fortune with.

So it was a natural progression from manufacturing phencyclidine to manufacturing methamphetamine. Like PCP, meth is a chemical product, usually in the form of a white powder that easily dissolves in water and can be snorted, smoked or injected. But unlike Angel Dust, meth had staying power: its popularity has lasted for decades. Under its various names—meth, speed, crank—its abuse has skyrocketed, becoming the single most important drug sold by the bikers in the U.S. And it is now considered the fastest-growing drug problem in the United States and Canada, ruining countless lives and leaving tens of thousands of people wasted, washed up—or dead. Thanks to their international network, the Angels would be instrumental in spreading the drug to Australia, Europe and Canada. Eventually, it would rival cocaine for the profit it put in the pockets of the Angels and the plague it unleashed on city streets. In more ways than one, the Angels were to build their empire on speed.

In the late '60s, as Barger boasts, "Backroom chemists tested their shit on us because we'd try anything." One of those back-room boys was a chemist from Shell Oil named Kenny Maxwell. Known as the Old Man, he taught the Angels how to cook meth. "He would get convicted, go to jail, do his time, get out, manufacture, get convicted, go to jail," says McKinley.

But he taught the Angels well. They mastered what became known as the fishbowl synthesis: at the time, a revolutionary way of cooking meth using phenyl-2-propanone (P2P), a controlled but not illegal substance that they got in bulk through their ties to the emerging Australian Hells Angels.

"They really got organized," explains McKinley. "They would teach people who were not Angels the technique. They would then supply the lab site, the equipment, the precursor chemicals and they got virtually all the product. They weren't taking huge risks but they were getting the lion's share of the profit."

Meth quickly supplanted Angel Dust as the bikers' leading chemical product. The bikers said goodbye to Angel Dust. They also said goodbye to that brief Summer of Love. The flower children's fling with the Angels as their drug suppliers turned sour when Barger's Angels came out solidly in favour of the Vietnam War. The 1960s ended decisively twenty-five days early on December 6, 1969, when the myth of flower power—and the myth of peaceful motorcycle gangs—died at the now infamous Rolling Stones concert in Altamont, California.

The rock stars with the outlaw image hired the outlaw bikers for security. When some concertgoers got too close to their bikes, the Hells Angels, as Barger later wrote, "beat fuck out of them." They jabbed a pistol into the side of guitarist Keith Richards to force him to keep playing. It all culminated in death when the Hells Angels later stabbed and killed an armed black man who rushed the stage. "That was a turning point in terms of national attention and recognition that this is more than just a bunch of guys having a great old time, drinking beer and carrying on," says

Ted Baltas, who would eventually help lead the first coordinated attacks against the bikers by the ATF.

By April 1970 a police report described Barger as "probably the most powerful and well-known outlaw motorcyclist in the country." It went on: "The subject is influential with motorcycle clubs all across the nation. Barger has been unemployed for years and yet is seen with large amounts of money. This money may come from the dues he collected from his own chapter and . . . the franchise money he obtains from chapter charters he has sold in various states. It is known that all Hells Angels deal extensively in the narcotic trade."

It wasn't just the cops who were saying that. "In the '60s we got a lot of publicity," Barger told *The Washington Post*. "It was all fun and games. In the '70s, we all became gangsters." Later in his autobiography, the Angels leader was blunter: "The seventies were gangster era for us. I sold drugs and got into a lot of shit."

Barger's quips about "fun and games" and the "gangster era" reflect well the double attraction of outlaw motorcycle gangs and the Hells Angels in particular. What makes someone become not just a criminal but a biker? And not just a recreational biker but a gang member?

Surprisingly, part of the answer is that they love to party, says Montreal criminologist Maurice Cusson, who has written extensively on what motivates criminals. "It's not the fact that they like to party that distinguishes delinquents from common humanity," Cusson says. "What separates them from the rest of us is that they make partying the centre of their existence."

They live purely in the present. Criminals lack the kind of self-discipline and control that enables normal people to plan for the future, educate themselves and build careers. As adolescents, criminals are impulsive, hyperactive and easily bored. They are addicted to the moment. And the supreme moment is the party. Sex, drugs, fast cars and alcohol. No inhibitions. They commit crimes not because they are poor or disadvantaged but because living the life of a criminal allows them to perpetuate their party lifestyle. In fact, studies show that the most accomplished criminals, the ones who make the most money, are the ones that have the least self-control, party the hardest and act the most impulsively.

"Like warriors of the past, the criminal of today has to be able to face danger and concentrate totally on the moment," Cusson says. "He has to act without caution, without self-control and without any concern for the future. He has to shoot first.

"Few people understand the enormous advantage of never hesitating and always daring," he says, citing the fifteenth-century Dutch humanist Desiderius Erasmus.

This is life on the edge. But too often the biker criminal falls off the edge and pays the price in debt, addiction, prison and poverty. By the age of forty, an outlaw biker may find that the party lifestyle takes its toll and begins to wear thin. But for many of them, the party goes on forever. That's because, says Dr. Stephanie Wagner, a clinical psychologist, many of those she sees are psychopaths.

Wagner works inside the heavy granite walls of California's second-oldest penitentiary, Folsom State Prison. In this massive, overcrowded stone cage, she has written psychological profiles of a number of Hells Angels, all of whom are serving long sentences for violent crimes and are eager for parole. "I don't believe that I have ever recommended that a Hells Angel be released," she says. "I consider them psychopaths."

Wagner relies heavily on studies by Canadian psychologist Robert Hare and his psychopathy checklist, which is widely used in prisons around the world to identify psychopaths. Hare has written that about 25 percent of inmates are psychopathic and should never be given parole. This is because their brains are hardwired not to lose the thrill of living on the edge. In other words, they cannot be rehabilitated. "Most inmates after the age of forty kind of lose interest in the criminal lifestyle," Wagner says. "Psychopaths never lose interest. They con. They love to con. That's part of their being. They are real pathological liars. They love to prey on the helpless. And that never goes away for them. And so they are always dangerous when they are released." She says the Hells Angels itself is a psychopathic organization. "They don't have a conscience. The endgame is to perpetuate itself by any means."

Studies show that criminals are at least twice as likely to be violent when they are members of a gang as when they are not. The gang influence turns crime into a blood sport. And the tighter the gang, the more violent its members become.

Membership in any outlaw biker gang depends largely on how far the potential recruit is prepared to go to protect the club. "It's clear that the facilitating effect of a gang is strong," Cusson says. "You are violent when you are part of a gang. You are not violent when you leave the gang."

Gangs are by nature territorial and therefore have more to protect than a freelance criminal. Like wolves, they mark their boundaries, and anyone who dares to cross them is dealt with harshly. Whether to maintain the honour of the club or protect a drug monopoly, it all amounts to the same thing. Kill or be killed. A simple slight can spark gang warfare. Vengeance becomes the dominant factor. But whatever the cause, it all comes down to protecting territory. And for outlaw bikers that means protecting the integrity of their patch.

In the first three years of the '70s, Sonny Barger's self-described "lot of shit" included charges of attempted murder, illegal possession of a weapon, kidnapping, assault and possession of narcotics. Barger, found guilty of heroin, cocaine and marijuana offences, along with false imprisonment, began serving time in Folsom prison in 1973. While he was behind bars, authorities slapped him with tax evasion and three more weapons charges.

Still, he was able to walk out of Folsom in 1977; a few years in the joint were just a minor inconvenience to the biker hero. Nevertheless, there were changes afoot in the police world that would eventually have a profound impact on the easy ride his Hells Angels had enjoyed so far from law enforcement.

Just as Barger was getting ready to leave the prison walls behind, two men—Ted Baltas and Tim McKinley—signed up with two different federal police agencies; the two investigators would eventually meet in San Francisco, join forces and cause Sonny Barger his biggest—and to date his only real—grief with the law.

Ted Baltas signed on with the ATF, which had been set up formally as an enforcement branch of the Treasury Department four years earlier. In one form or another, the department had been going after booze and guns and tax cheats for two hundred years. Its most famous enforcer, as part of what was then called the Bureau of Industrial Alcohol during the Prohibition era of the 1930s, was Eliot Ness, who eventually nailed Chicago's organized-crime king, Al Capone, on tax-evasion charges.

Nearly five decades later, it was inevitable that Eliot Ness's successors at the ATF would clash with the Al Capones of the Hells Angels. "The violence that is associated with these fellows—the amounts of guns and bombs—that's pretty much ATF's background and expertise, so from the onset it was pretty much a natural area for us to get into," says Baltas.

Baltas had his first posting in the Northeast, where the Angels had begun to try to build up a strong presence: Barger himself had travelled to Lowell, Massachusetts, to check on a prospect club and approve them as the Hells Angels' first full charter on the East Coast in 1967. Chapters in Salem, New York and Rochester soon followed in 1969. It didn't take long before local police were spotting more Angels coming in from the West Coast, more inter-chapter contacts . . . and more meth in the bars and on the streets.

"We started seeing network building here, but it was frustrating: the local state and county law enforcement people were not equipped. They have limited resources and their issues are on a day-to-day basis," Baltas says.

Barger's Angels, on the other hand, always seemed to be one step ahead of the law. "There are no boundaries for them—they don't look at state lines or county lines as a restriction. And that's what has helped them survive so much," the ATF man says.

The answer, to Baltas and others at the ATF, was obvious: only a federal agency, with the broader resources, ability and time, could take on a national organized crime group. Baltas recalls the mood at the time: "We're the feds. We get paid to go after the biggest and the baddest. These guys are challenging the state and local authorities, so let's see what we can do."

They ran some early infiltrations and operations against the bikers, but nothing systematic—"there weren't any real national strategies," as Baltas puts it. Intelligence gathering at first was purely reactive. But by the late '70s, the ATF partnered with the Drug Enforcement Agency (DEA) and set up a biker desk in El Paso, Texas. The mandate of the new El Paso Information Center (EPIC) was to identify for the first time the known members of the biker gangs, and to determine where they were located and who was in charge. EPIC published a book every year—sort of a beginner's guide to bikers for the police—and slowly but surely they began the education of American police forces: what the different patches meant, what a prospect was, how the gangs were structured.

"It was a kind of walk-before-you-run thing," Baltas admits.

But Sonny Barger was about to prove he could still run circles around the cops.

In 1979 the U.S. government tried to prosecute the Hells Angels under the RICO anti-gang and racketeering laws. Barger was arrested again, along with dozens of other members—charged not just with drug trafficking, prostitution and the attempted bombing murder of two policemen but also with being members of a criminal group devoted to breaking the law. It was the first time the authorities were going after the Hells Angels *as the Hells Angels.* "It's not only an indictment of individuals, it's an indictment of the organization," explained one DEA director.

Talk was cheap, though. It was one thing to talk about indicting an organized crime group and quite another to convince a jury. It takes a meticulously documented investigation and an extremely well prepared prosecution. The RICO case against Barger had neither, as one young recruit to the FBI was about to find out.

Tim McKinley had been a law student, working at the district attorney's office while waiting for his bar results to come in, when an astonishing case came across his desk. One of his law school classmates was arrested and charged with murder. He had set up a cocaine deal, then had his supplier assassinated. A key witness against him had been a topless dancer, but the FBI had lost track of her. A gritty McKinley resolved to pursue the case. He spent every weekend touring every topless joint in Northern California until he finally found her. The man quickly pleaded guilty—and the FBI suggested that McKinley, the eager lawyer-to-be, should trade in his bar degree for a badge and sign up with the G-Men.

He did, and after a stint at the academy he was posted to San Francisco, where one of his first assignments was protecting one of the judges in the Barger RICO trial. The U.S. marshal's office had intercepted a few telephone threats to the judge; McKinley was able to trace the calls to a biker bar in Richmond.

"The problem was, in the FBI we didn't have any idea who was in the Hells Angels," McKinley remembers. "I thought, This was weird: this may explain why we're not doing very well in the trial."

Indeed, they weren't. The U.S. attorney's office was in over its head. There had been no electronic surveillance of the suspects; no independent corroboration of what informants were alleging. Two hung juries had been unable to come to a decision on thirty-eight of forty-four separate charges. The $15 million federal prosecution resulted in two mistrials. When it was all over, a triumphant Barger threw a big bash for the jurors.

"They've drawn a family tree with a little square at the top that is supposed to be me. But that's not the way it is. There is no top. This is a democracy," Barger later said in a newspaper interview. "People like DEA, ATF, they talk about how bad and rotten the Hells Angels are. Then they break down people's doors, ransack their houses, find out they're in the wrong place and leave without even apologizing. DEA and ATF on their best days would make the Hells Angels look like a bunch of Boy Scouts on a Sunday picnic."

It was classic Barger—over the top but on target. No one could deny that by beating the feds on the RICO rap, Ralph "Sonny" Barger had scored big. "He got a lot of power," admits the FBI's McKinley. "He got a lot of status, and he just kept building on it. It allowed the Hells Angels within the organized crime community to become quite powerful."

McKinley took away one overriding lesson from the RICO disaster: "There was then—and there continues to be to this day—a grotesque underestimation about what the Hells Angels are doing." He was not going to make that mistake when he got his chance to take on Barger.

It would be more than two decades—in 2003—before American law enforcement, much wiser and craftier, would have the confidence and expertise to charge the Hells Angels again under organized crime and racketeering charges. The Angels would have a much harder time throwing off those accusations, coming after lengthy and sophisticated undercover operations.

But back in the late '70s and early '80s, his RICO victory helped cement Barger's image as the ultimate American rebel, the outlaw on a bike thumbing his nose at authority. Far from impairing his ability to expand the Hells Angels empire, his run-ins with the law only heightened his prestige across the United States and around the globe.

From a handful of charters in California in the 1950s, the Angels had slowly spread across the country. By the end of 1970, Sonny had overseen the expansion to fourteen chapters across the States. Over the next two decades, the Death Head patch spread to the Midwest—with Chicago being a particular hotbed of violence—as well as the Northwest, Alaska and many of the Southern states.

From the start, Barger had also set his sights far beyond the shores of America. The first chapter outside the United States was formed in New Zealand in 1961. Much more significant was the initial beachhead in Europe, when the Hells Angels formed a chapter in London, England, in 1969, followed by Zurich, Switzerland, in 1970. To the north, Canada would prove the most fertile land for the HA to take root in; the Angels planted their flag on Canadian soil on December 5, 1977, when a chapter opened up in Sorel, just outside Montreal. Eventually, Canada would grow to be become one of the largest Red-and-White bastions, with over thirty chapters and 560 members and prospects.

"We've been expanding like wildfire," Barger boasted—and he

was right. By the end of the 1970s, the Hells Angels had added twenty-three chapters in the United States, Canada, Europe, and Australia, for a total of thirty-seven. During the '80s the HAMC (Hells Angels Motorcycle Club) expanded even faster, creating another thirty-three new chapters. And by the time '90s were over, on the dawn of a new century, the Hells Angels would spread to South America and Africa with a total of more than two hundred chapters worldwide.

As the Angels expanded their global empire, police forces tried desperately to catch up. But it was an unequal race. Barger had built an organization that was agile and flexible—he could quickly dispatch emissaries to England or South America to solve disputes or help set up a chapter.

"They can shift at a moment's notice; we can't," says Ted Baltas of the ATF. "We're the big ship in the ocean; they're the little rowboat that can move around wherever they want."

It was the beginning of the computer age—and as usual, the bikers were far ahead of the cops. A computer expert in Cleveland helped the Angels set up software to exchange intelligence and information on the cops. "You got to hand it to them—they were able to take advantage of technology better than we were," says Baltas. "We'd see these computers in their offices on raids, and we didn't even know how to work them. They had a better intelligence base than we did in law enforcement."

The authorities were able to score some sporadic successes. In November 1981, police in Cleveland uncovered an Angels weapons cache that included an anti-tank rocket, hand grenades and a supply of dynamite. In December, members of the Hells Angels in Omaha were jailed on several charges, including murder and torture, in their attempt to keep control of the local drug scene. Asked in 1982 by a reporter about police reports that his members were connected to contract killings, Barger offered only a weak denial: "I can't say some members haven't done that. I don't know."

But Barger himself would soon be involved in a murder conspiracy himself—thanks to Baltas and McKinley, the two cops who had kept on eye on him since he had beaten the RICO rap, and an enterprising infiltrator they ran named Anthony Tait.

Tait worked as a bouncer at a couple of topless bars in Anchorage, Alaska. And while he was pals with the bikers, he also was friendly with the cops. He had been passing information to the police about biker activity for some time. Nothing serious, nothing full time. Then one night, on a dare, he'd bet two Alaskan police buddies that it would be a snap for him to infiltrate the Hells Angels. They'd scoffed. Tait had bet them a steak dinner and a bottle of whisky he could do it.

He won.

It didn't take him long to become the sergeant-at-arms for the local chapter of the Hells Angels. Tait could never have imagined that his little wager would for the first time open up the inner workings of the Hells Angels to the FBI and the ATF. It would eventually send Sonny Barger to an Arizona prison and set in motion a violent series of events that would dramatically change the biker scene in the Southwest.

The surprised Alaskan police suddenly had a full-patch spy on their hands; they quickly passed Tait on to the FBI, and Tim McKinley was tasked with figuring out how they could make maximum use of Tait nationally and internationally.

"What he wanted to do was to just give us a bunch of information, and we do wiretaps, and everybody would go to jail." McKinley smiles at the memory. "He was kind of shocked to find out just how complicated it was: 'What do you mean?' Tait had asked. 'You guys are not going to break the law to do it?'"

McKinley's game plan was deceptively simple: use Tait as "a walking electronics platform." Record everything he could to gather intelligence and evidence in ways that conventional wiretaps or surveillance could never do. "What he was tasked to do was to identify the upper-level leadership of the Hells Angels, identify the criminal structure of the organization, track the money, track the dope."

And from the start, McKinley knew he would run up against Sonny Barger. "He was a focus from the beginning because he was always such a shot-caller within the organization." But McKinley also knew Barger would be a formidable opponent: "Balls—the guy certainly has balls."

By that point, McKinley had spent almost a decade with the FBI. He had more than a hundred investigations involving the buying and selling of drugs under his belt; more than fifty operations against the Hells Angels in particular that had resulted in four dozen bikers going to jail. But in the years since Barger had walked away from the bungled RICO charges, McKinley had also seen enough corruption, incompetence and infighting to know how not to run a biker investigation. Don't underestimate the Hells Angels, he concluded. And above all, build a tight team.

Fortunately, the ATF's Ted Baltas had recently transferred from the Northeast to San Francisco. "Kind of like going from the frying pan into the fire," says the agency's top biker expert, who now found himself at the epicentre of the Angels empire. He quickly met up with McKinley. The two men shared a passion for nailing the bikers and a passionate hatred for the petty rivalries that had plagued police agencies in the past.

"In early days, each agency wanted to control its own investigation—the DEA doing drugs, the FBI doing their thing, the ATF guns and bombs," recalls Baltas. "The whole idea of collaborating and sharing wasn't there. We didn't have the resources, the knowledge, the manpower—or we weren't smart enough to do it."

"If anything, the Angels taught us to do it," the ATF man continues. West Coast chapters readily exchanged intelligence on police tactics with their East Coast affiliates. Even on a global scale, minutes of important meetings at Sonny Barger's Oakland chapter show that Canadian Angels came down to report on their legal hassles, and there were regular updates on Europe.

So Baltas and McKinley decided this time they were going to do things differently. They broke down the bureaucratic barriers from the ground up. Simple things, small steps, but they meant a lot: Baltas had a key to the FBI office and came and went as he wanted. "The fact that ATF and the FBI worked together so closely left a lot of people speechless," says Baltas.

McKinley wanted more than just better cooperation: he wanted complete control over who was going to be on his team. Because, simply put, McKinley didn't trust a lot of people when it came to taking on the Angels.

And for good reason. In an earlier operation against the bikers, McKinley recalls how wiretaps on the phones of the Frisco chapter kept blowing up—always on the twelfth or thirteenth day. There'd be about one hundred calls a day, and then suddenly the traffic would drop to zero. A biker would come on the line and bellow, "You rats are on the line. Fuck you, feds!"

McKinley was pretty sure the leak came somewhere within the legal department of Pacific Bell; the police had to notify the phone company about taps, but it took time for all the paperwork to get through. Once, as a test, McKinley delayed the paperwork slightly—and sure enough, this time the wiretap lasted one more day.

There were more serious signs of biker penetration within the federal police agencies themselves. McKinley was all too aware that spying worked both ways. Not only did the police try to infiltrate the bikers, but the bikers tried to infiltrate the police.

McKinley was cooperating with the DEA on a joint operation against Kenny "KO" Owen, who police believed to be a major meth cook for the Angels. They had been doing surveillance non-stop late in 1984—from Thanksgiving through Christmas and into the new year. Then suddenly, the day before the searches were to go down, the DEA pulled the surveillance for two hours, supposedly for an administrative meeting. At just about the same time, Owen got a call.

"You stay here," Owen told his partner. "I got to go meet a guy. It's important."

The meth man returned within a half hour, with the details of all the locations the police were planning to search.

"The feds are coming tomorrow," he said. "We got to get this shit out of here!" McKinley only found out about the phone call later, when he eventually busted Owen. But he was convinced that the fact that Owen cleaned out his labs just before a raid was not a coincidence and that it proved a "high level corruption within DEA."

Then there was an operation McKinley helped run on the East Coast bikers that was compromised "at a high level within the FBI." An FBI agent in the press office happened to be buddies with a journalist who also happened to be friendly with a New York Hells Angels leader—friendly enough to be seen riding on his bike the day before the police searches went down.

"You know it's a clue something has gone wrong when you go to search a place at six in the morning and the Hells Angel is up— and he's freshly bathed," McKinley says. "He's on his second cup of his coffee. He's wearing starched blue jeans. A clean, crisp shirt. His cowboy boots are shined, and there's four inches of paper ash in the fireplace, and it's still warm—and it's a spring day!"

McKinley knew even his own office was not safe. He had two good-looking women who worked as clerical staff. They loved to dance but were also strict Mormons. The bikers put pressure on them to get them to turn. They refused and reported the incident. Still, it indicated the bikers had the wherewithal to find out who was working for the FBI in the first place.

So with Tait, McKinley took extreme caution. He formed his core team with just eight other FBI agents and two other ATF men besides Baltas. "The whole concept behind Tait was to minimize the number of people involved so as to minimize the likelihood of a leak. Because the leaks were just killing us." The FBI man used the same system as the Hells Angels to communicate with his spy Tait—no cellphones, no home phones, no business phones. It was all pager to pay phones. Tait would page McKinley with an agreed-on code, and then McKinley would call back from a pay phone.

McKinley codenamed the operation CACUS after a character in Dante's *Inferno*. "All the best names were taken," he jokes. He had tried for Charon, the mythological boatman who takes the condemned across the river to Hades, but had to settle for Cacus, the centaur creature in Dante's seventh pit of Hell.

And sure enough, Tait did a good job of bedevilling Barger and the Angels. "In my experience, he's better than any undercover [cop] I've seen," says McKinley with uncharacteristic praise. "He's got an ego the size of Montana, but he is perfectly willing to follow instructions and report accurately."

Tait's bravado and flashy style allowed him to climb quickly up the Angel ladder, becoming the West Coast representative. Never suspecting he was an infiltrator, Barger accepted Tait as a successful biker drug pusher: "Judging by the way he threw money around, I figured he dealt drugs or something," Barger later wrote.

Tait almost always wore a recording device—usually two, because McKinley was a stickler for details and always wanted a backup. He often concealed a bug in his pager, transmitting to the FBI on a frequency they were sure the bikers had not already discovered, and then for safety carried a separate, tiny digital recorder. He attended hundreds of biker parties and business meetings in homes, bars and clubhouses across the U.S. and even around the world. His work eventually helped lead to the conviction of more than five hundred persons on federal and state charges and the seizure of more than five hundred kilos of drugs.

Just as Operation Cacus was hitting its stride, the stakes suddenly got a lot higher. On August 12, 1986, two members of the rival Outlaws gang gunned down a Hells Angels member named John Webb in Kentucky. Barger and a few other members immediately flew there to investigate. The Angels wanted revenge—and they picked Anthony Tait to lead the charge against the Outlaws. Tait was a rising star with the Angels who also happened to have been a chapter mate of Webb's when he was in Alaska.

The turmoil and plotting unleashed by the subsequent biker war gave the FBI plenty of fresh investigative leads. But Webb's execution also became "the four-hundred-pound gorilla that just ripped our ass," as McKinley puts it. That's because the case was never designed to deal with spontaneous violence. "As a government agency you can't let anyone actually get killed," he says. It was a dilemma that would haunt future police infiltrations into the Hells Angels organization in the years to come.

Five days after Webb's killing, on August 17, Tait attended the weekly meeting of the Oakland chapter. Barger and other members were discussing addresses for the Outlaws; Barger specifically talked about "identification numbers" and "street names" for their hated rivals. What's more, he had a gold mine of police intelligence—a publication put out by EPIC, the El Paso Information Center, on bikers that Ted Baltas had helped set up. It had the names, addresses, biographies and photographs of the Outlaws. That the leader of the Hells Angels could get his hands on a confidential police intelligence bible just confirmed McKinley's suspicions that the Angels' fingers reached deep into the police infrastructure.

"[The] book would be useful in setting out targets . . . to 'hit' simultaneously," another HA chapter president told Tait.

On September 29, Tait dropped by Sonny Barger's home on Golf Links Road in Oakland. The two-storey house, surrounded by lush greenery, was a comfortable step up from the tough streets where Barger had grown up. Sonny went to the desk in his study and pulled out the EPIC book for Tait. "Barger told [Tait] how to retaliate against the members of the Outlaws motorcycle club by murdering them one at a time," an FBI affidavit states.

Barger and his vengeful Angels apparently had little worry about ever being brought to justice for killing their rivals. At a November 30 meeting in the Oakland clubhouse, the bikers passed around photographs of the two Outlaws suspected of killing Webb. The conversation then turned to the Hells Angels' much-publicized defence fund—tens of thousands of dollars the bikers collected not just from members as part of their obligatory dues but also from an easily conned public encouraged to help the Angels fight so-called government harassment.

Barger told the meeting he tried to stay ignorant of the use of the money. "There was a judge back East that got convicted of accepting some of that," he said, making a gesture under the table as if paying a bribe. Indeed, a judge in Cleveland had been convicted of accepting a bribe from the Hells Angels to issue a directed verdict of acquittal in a capital murder case, allowing an HA member to literally get away with murder.

Early in the new year, on January 17, 1987, Barger once again greeted Anthony Tait at his home in Oakland. This time the talk turned directly to killing. Tait asked the leader for his advice in taking out the Outlaws.

"It doesn't matter which one," Barger said. "You're not going to get the guys that did it. . . . You can snipe one of them. . . . Don't get caught."

(By Barger's own account, he admitted telling Tait, "If two Outlaws were involved, then shoot two of them and call it even.")

The war was heating up. In September of that year, the Outlaws brazenly attacked two Cleveland Hells Angels and a prospect in Joliet, Illinois. They seized their colours—a deliberate insult and one of the surest ways to shame a biker—and shot one of them in the foot.

One month later, on October 18, 1987, Tait was set again to drop by Barger's home. It would be a crucial surreptitious recording, and even a bold infiltrator like Tait was nervous. "There were six or seven separate points that all had to hit, preferably in the right order," Tim McKinley remembers telling his spy. "I still had to pour two or three shots of whisky into him to get him to go and do it because you don't use the 'K' word with Barger."

But Tait did explicitly talk about "killing," and Barger showed no hesitation. Tait showed Sonny several photographs of the three-storey brick building that served as the Outlaws' clubhouse in Chicago. He then calmly told Sonny how he planned to plant charges of plastic explosives to destroy the walls and collapse the roof.

The blast would "kill five or six " people, Tait said.

"Good," replied Barger, "especially after Joliet."

Barger's memory of that fateful discussion is only slightly different and, if anything, even more damaging. As he later recounted it, he okayed the bombing: "If that's what you gotta do, do it."

"There might be innocent people there," Tait warned.

"That's what they get for hanging around with guys like that," Barger said.

Tait also asked Barger to help him create an alibi by messing up his hotel room in downtown Oakland to make it look as if he had spent the night there; a more than willing Barger sent another Oakland club member to do the job.

McKinley and Ted Baltas knew they had him. Sonny Barger, the patriarch of the Angels who kept boasting to the media that his boys were just a bunch of fun-loving, misunderstood rascals, had been caught on tape scheming, plotting, aiding and abetting the cold-blooded murders of his rivals.

The police came for Sonny Barger on November 10, 1987. It was not a pretty sight. McKinley had given strict written instructions to the arresting officers to cuff the fallen Angel behind his back. They didn't, leaving his manacled hands in front. ("Good help is so hard to get," McKinley quips.)

So as he walked into the FBI operations headquarters, Barger still had his balance—and his temper. The ATF's Ted Baltas walked over to take custody of him. In a flash, Barger exploded and took out Baltas's right knee with a side kick. McKinley, who was in an interview room, came running out.

"What did you do that for?" he yelled as he bounced Barger off the wall, then jumped on him with both knees on his belly.

"Fuck you, McKinley, you're an asshole!" Barger barked back.

"You know what—you're right, I am an asshole," replied the FBI agent. "Always was, always going to be. So what else is new?"

Those were the last words the two men ever exchanged.

On trial for conspiracy to murder, Barger was frantic. "When he gets scared and under pressure, he reverts to type. Cornered, trapped, he lashes out. Several other bikers arrested in the sweep were ready to plead guilty, but Barger forbade it: plead, and you're out of the club."

It was clear to the jury who ran the Hells Angels. McKinley was on the stand for two weeks, Tait for six. When Barger wanted a question asked, he would write it down, walk up to podium where his lawyers stood and stand there, jabbing with his finger if necessary, until the lawyer complied.

It didn't help. After a five-month trial, Ralph "Sonny" Barger was convicted of conspiracy to violate federal law to commit murder. The day after his conviction, the floodgates opened, and suddenly the other bikers were allowed to plead. "It was all about Ralph," says McKinley.

Barger ended up doing fifty-nine months in the Federal Corrections Institution near Phoenix, Arizona. Released in 1992, he was fifty-four years old and recovering from throat cancer. The dry, hot air of Arizona no doubt appealed to him, but it might not have been the only attraction in a move. The business climate back in Oakland was drying up. The Tait operation had taken out some of their biggest meth producers. "They had enough money and product stashed away for about five years," says McKinley. "Everybody had run out of money; the shit had hit the fan." As one member told the FBI man, "When the money left, the brotherhood left."

It was good time for Sonny to leave. But while the barren landscape of the Arizona desert beckoned, Barger also knew that the state was barren of Hells Angels—not a single member or chapter in the sixth-largest state of the union.

Nothing that the leader of the Hells Angels couldn't fix.

You can tell a lot about a man and the team he leads when you look at the people they recruit. And to establish their foothold in Arizona, Barger and the HA chose the meanest, baddest, bloodiest bikers in the state—a gang of thugs and killers aptly known as the Dirty Dozen.

"They were absolutely the largest and most violent gang in the state," says Joe Slatalla, the ATF case agent in Phoenix who would later direct an ambitious infiltration project against Barger's bikers. "They had a history of being the real dirty biker types."

The ranks of the Dirty Dozen—despite their name, they numbered well over a hundred—included psychopaths like "Puff" Huey who molested and tortured a thirteen-year-old girl; he had her branded with the tattoo "Puff's Pig" and raped her with a baseball bat. He got 166 years in prison.

Another Dirty Dozen thug was so upset when a rival biker from Tucson bad-mouthed his club that he had two pals hold down the victim while he tried to cut out his tongue; he didn't quite succeed but managed to cut his cheeks ear to ear.

Though based only in Arizona, the Dirty Dozen had a national reputation for violence. Police arrest records for other gangs often listed drug charges as the leading offence, but the number-one reason for Dirty Dozen bikers to end up behind bars was assault, followed closely by weapons violations. In one bust in 1992 police seized thirteen hundred guns, including several "street sweepers," automatic shotguns that can fire off twelve rounds in three seconds. The weapons haul was so huge that the cops had to rent a Ryder truck to lug away the armaments. The Dirty Dozen's reach extended well into the drug and sex trade; as one member who later became a Hells Angel boasted to the police, the Dozen "ran the dope, the whores, the bars."

Barger obviously liked what he saw in the Dirty Dozen. "They were friends and allies, having ridden in Arizona for over twenty-five years," he wrote in his history of the Angels. Once Sonny got out of prison, he worked hard to broker a patch-over with the Dirty Dozen, putting them on the fast track for membership in the world's most elite biker gang and bypassing his own club's strict rules. Barger extended the Dirty Dozen the courtesy of allowing them to wear a small red-and-white "prospect" badge on their vests under their own logo, and he cut their prospecting year in half. After only six months, they rode down to Laughlin, Nevada, for an annual biker run and came back with their Arizona bottom rockers in the spring of 1999. The Angels had made it into Arizona.

Then the Hells Angels machine kicked in. They sent several ex-Dozen men over to California to learn the ropes and brought over some of their stronger members who were close to Barger to ease the transition.

"They went in and they cleaned house," says Steve Trethewy of the Rocky Mountain Information Network. "There were guys wearing T-shirts saying 'Come in peace or leave in pieces.'" Of the 120 original Dirty Dozen members, the Angels chopped out half and then whittled away again until they were left with only forty-two members.

Not that the Hells Angels were weeding out criminals. On the contrary, Barger and his crew were looking for the most talented, aggressive but controllable badasses they could find. A police analysis in 1999 of the Dirty Dozen members who had successfully patched over showed that 85 percent had felony arrest records. Part of the reason the Phoenix chapter to this day has the reputation of being among the most vicious is that they have a majority of ex–Dirty Dozen members: "typical, nasty road war bikers" is how Joe Slatalla of the ATF puts it.

It was a classic Hells Angels success story. The Dirty Dozen had beaten off the rival gangs like the Vagos, the Devil's Disciples and the Mongols to keep control of the drug trade in Arizona. But they could not resist the lure of the status and clout of the biggest outlaw motorcycle gang in the world.

Back in Oakland, California—the mother chapter of the venerable Hells Angels organization—Sonny Barger stood up at an August 1997 meeting and uttered the words few had ever expected to hear: he requested a transfer. Joining him would be hardcore bikers like Johnny Angel, the appropriately named veteran of the gang.

Ten days after his sixtieth birthday, on October 18, 1998, Sonny Barger officially became an Arizona Hells Angel. He bought a comfortable ranch house in an isolated desert suburb north of Phoenix. On paper he was just a simple member of the Cave Creek chapter, but no one doubted he was still the powerhouse. He published his autobiography in 2000, and it became an international best-seller. There was talk of a movie deal. New Hells Angels chapters were being formed across the globe.

In a few short years in Arizona, Barger had taken the Angels from zero to four dozen members. With its booming population and flourishing drug and illegal gun trade, the entire region was the Angels' for the taking. "The Southwest is a growing area for the Hells Angels," Barger said. "We're shaking it up good."

What Barger didn't know was that the ATF was finally getting ready to shake back.

After four decades of leading the Angels, Barger had grown crafty and cautious. But the ATF was also smartening up. From Ted

Baltas's early work with Tait in the 1980s through to John Ciccone's direction of undercover cops inside the Vagos and the Mongols, the ATF was learning how to penetrate the bikers in more sophisticated ways. The FBI had pretty much abandoned the field. After McKinley's successful work with Tait, the FBI bureaucrats decided to transfer the Hells Angels from the Organized Crime unit to the Violent Gang section, which tended to handle quick investigations. "It was a stupid move," McKinley complained. "You can't do a Hells Angels case in three weeks."

That left the ATF as pretty much the only team on the field to go after the bikers in any systematic way, with Ted Baltas coordinating operations from headquarters in Washington, D.C. As a new century dawned, the stage was set for a showdown in the Southwest. ATF case agent Joe Slatalla was nurturing a bold plan to infiltrate deep into the criminal activity of the Arizona Hells Angels by setting up a fake bike gang manned by undercover cops and informants.

And the man Slatalla had picked to lead the charge—Jay Dobyns, the driven ATF agent who got shot his first week on the job and went on to more and more dangerous assignments in Chicago and Colorado—was in position to strike.

By 2001 Dobyns had moved back with his wife and two young children to Arizona. In September of that year, the ATF dispatched him to Bullhead to target several local bounty hunters who were running wild, selling guns illegally. Bullhead is the kind of dusty, dirty desert town once so popular in cowboy movies. Just across the river on the Arizona border overlooking the casinos of Nevada, it's a backyard dump heap to the glitzy Vegas strip. Gun shops, seedy motels and even seedier bars play host to boozers, bikers and bandits—just the kind of place where a cop like Jay Dobyns would fit in. "Operation Riverside," as it was called, was off and running.

Dobyns wrapped up the bounty hunter aspect of the case quickly, but soon discovered Bullhead was a hotbed for firearms crimes. "It was nasty," Dobyns says. "I did not cross paths with anybody in that town who wasn't involved in something they shouldn't be doing." Dobyns's cover story was just deliciously devilish enough to work. As "Jaybird," or simply "Bird"—a nickname he had used since he was child—he was a baseball-bat-wielding debt collector for the casinos. But secretly he was also supposedly a gunrunner to Mexico.

"Underneath the table, we were firearms traffickers," Dobyns explains. "We buy guns, we buy bombs, we have connections in Mexico, we take them across the border. There are strict gun laws there so there is a huge markup value: a gun you buy in the United States for two hundred bucks, you can sell in Mexico for two to five times that price."

As Bird's reputation grew, more and more low-lifes from Bullhead were not only selling him guns but also soliciting him to commit murders. Dobyns and the ATF set up five independent murder-for-hire investigations—getting the offender to make a down payment or provide a weapon and then making the arrests before they had to fake a murder. It also didn't take long for word of the brash, loud-mouthed debt collector/hitman/gunrunner to move to the top of the criminal food chain in Bullhead City: the Hells Angels.

"I was already credible in their eyes—I didn't need an introduction," says Dobyns. "They knew more about me initially than I did about them." The Hells Angels started dropping by Dobyn's home to crash or knock back a few beers.

The ATF now had an undercover cop with a solid reputation as a gunrunner cozying up to Angels in Bullhead. Meanwhile, in Phoenix, case agent Joe Slatalla was setting the stage for a fake biker club to penetrate the Hells Angels in the state. Out of Los Angeles, John Ciccone was just beginning to run Mike Kramer as a high-level full-patch informant—to catch the killers of Cynthia Garcia and anybody else he could nab. Finally, in San Diego, the DEA and the ATF had a major drug investigation code-named Operation Five Star well under way against the Angels chapter there.

That meant that by the start of 2002, there were four separate operations circling around the Hells Angels power base in the

Southwest. Though no one expected or planned it, within a few months these investigations would come together in a multi-pronged assault. Slatalla, Dobyns, and Ciccone would find themselves thrown into a two-year battle that would pit the ATF against the Hells Angels in Arizona, California and Nevada.

What kicked all these investigations into high gear and brought them together was a bloody biker shootout in the spring of 2002 in a small Nevada casino town.

THREE

Hell at Harrah's

———

A lot of things changed after the shooting at Harrah's.
It basically forced law enforcement to take another look at the bikers.
—BILLY GUINN, SAN DIEGO SHERIFF'S DEPARTMENT

"Officer needs help, shots fired!"

Las Vegas police Sgt. Gary Hood was the first cop on the scene at Harrah's casino in the desert town of Laughlin, Nevada. Hundreds of bikers were going at each other with hammers, wrenches, knives and guns—anything they could grab. It was carnage and confusion. Blood was splattered on the windows and floor. "Every door out of the place has blood trails," said one witness.

Hood quickly radioed the dispatcher for reinforcements. Two armed bikers suddenly jumped out from behind a row of slot machines; Hood quickly returned fire.

Officers from the Las Vegas gang crimes unit and other reinforcements start rushing in. Officer Michael Ford caught sight of Hells Angel James Hannigan running away from the battle zone, a knife dripping blood clutched in his left hand

The Angel hesitated as if he was weighing his chances of stabbing the cops or trying to get away, Ford later recalled in court testimony. He didn't seem to want to surrender.

"Either do it or you're going to be killed. I'm going to kill you," Ford barked. Hannigan chose to drop his knife.

It lasted only a few minutes, but the battle between the Hells Angels and their hated rivals, the Mongols, would leave more than a dozen injured and three dead. Police picked up no fewer than fourteen guns and 107 knives, two hammers, two wrenches and nine flashlights.

But the shots that were fired at Laughlin were heard across the country, in police headquarters everywhere. Finally, the top brass began getting the message that the bikers meant business. And their business meant blood.

Laughlin is one of those desert gambling towns where the only sure bet is the booming tourist trade. Just eighty miles south of Vegas, it boasts nine casinos, eight thousand inhabitants and five million visitors every year trying their luck. One of the town's biggest draws is the annual River Run, the largest gathering of motorcycle enthusiasts in the western United States. Every April, as many as 100,000 recreational bikers, vendors and spectators stream into the bars, casinos and hotels.

Several thousand outlaw bikers are also on hand, and the Hells Angels are always the stars. They pack into the Flamingo Hilton, throw around lots of cash and put on a show of wheelies and bike tricks for the whooping and hollering crowds of tourists. Great PR: the classic image of good ol' rowdy boys having fun.

In recent years, though, the Mongols had shown up to spoil the party. As the Angels' bikes rolled in, the Mongols walked right through the entourage and into the casino. "They just stood there and eye-fucked everybody," recalls the ATF's John Ciccone. "The HAs didn't do anything. And every time the HAs didn't respond, that made the Mongols in everybody's eyes look like they were the 'badder' group. And the Hells Angels were just biting their lips because they were trying to keep up this clean image."

Around the world, the Hells Angels were the largest and dominant outlaw motorcycle gang. But in the American Southwest, they are facing serious challenges to their hegemony by larger and faster growing gangs like the Mongols. Hatred between the two groups had been brewing for years, ever since the Mongols had had their first major skirmish with Angels in the late 1970s and early '80s—and won. The dispute was over the bottom rocker, the half circle lower patch on the back of a biker's vest that identifies the location of his club. Traditionally, the HAs forbade any other club to use the name "California" spelled out in full. But the Mongols challenged the ban. There were car bombings and several stabbings; two Mongols were shot and killed as they rode their bikes on the freeway. But in the end, the Hells Angels finally conceded and the Mongols won the right to wear the "California" rocker.

The truce was short-lived. In the mid- and late nineties, the Mongols became an increasing threat to the Angels: they were growing faster, recruiting younger and setting up chapters like wildfire. They started swallowing up street gang members, especially in East LA, so much so that what was once a 60 percent white club had become a 90 percent Hispanic organization. They sped up their integration process: while Hells Angels protocol meant prospect members still had to wait at least a year before becoming full patch, the Mongols started to let their recruits wear their full colours right away, with just a small "P" on the side to indicate they were still on probation. The Mongols went for smaller, more numerous chapters while the Angels favoured fewer, larger local clubs. So while there were only five HA chapters in all of Southern California, there were thirty-nine Mongols chapters in LA alone.

Mongol chapters started popping up all along the California coast, which had always been Red and White. In Reno, they set up four chapters and shot up the Angels' clubhouse; in San Jose, four new Mongol chapters surrounded the HA chapter. There were shootings and stabbings; pipe bombs were left underneath cars.

The Mongols tended to be younger and more aggressive than the more established Hells Angels. A lot of their members didn't even own bikes. They had been street gangsters since they were teens; now they were just street gangsters with leather vests and colours. "You had Mongols, young kids, doing drive-by shootings and no HAs are responding," says Ciccone. "You have a lot of older HAs that have already been to prison. Now they are living a comfortable lifestyle, they are wealthy. Are they going to want to go kick the shit out of some young Mongols, which would put them back in prison for another ten years?"

That really burned the younger Angels, who were itching to strike back and frustrated by their elders' caution. "The younger guys were saying, 'We have to fucking stand up for ourselves. They're letting the Mongols run amok, and it's making the HAs look bad,'" says Ciccone.

The cops knew the volcano was going to erupt—they just didn't know when and where. "It was bound to happen," says Ciccone. "It just happened at Laughlin."

In the days leading up to the Laughlin explosion, Sonny Barger as always was busy promoting his latest book—and his image.

While Barger's first book, his internationally bestselling autobiography, gloried in self-congratulatory tales of rapes and murders, his new opus, *Ridin' High, Livin' Free,* reflected his attempt to reposition himself as a mainstream rebel, as it were: it was a tribute to the motorcycle culture, with paeans to everyone from Steve McQueen to rock legend David Crosby. Barger was trying to promote himself as a quiet, semi-retired easygoing rider—and the media were buying it. On Sunday, April 21, 2002, a *Los Angeles Times* reviewer gushed that it was "fun to listen to romantic tales of hell-and-heck-raising" in Barger's latest book. He reported that the Hells Angels leader had "settled down in a ranchette near Phoenix . . . with a pretty young wife" and a preteen stepdaughter. Every morning, he claimed, Barger raises the American flag on his flagpole "and takes it down at sunset, folding it reverently against his bosom."

On Tuesday, April 23, the biker leader spent three hours signing books for the three hundred fans who turned out at a San Diego Harley-Davidson dealership. The next day, the crowds were just as big outside a local bookstore, where two dozen bikes lined the street as a radio boomed out ""In-A-Gadda-Da-Vida." Said one anxious autograph-chaser: "He's a living legend."

By Thursday, Barger was leaving his adoring fans in California to head to Laughlin, only to see his carefully nurtured image as a peaceful rascal explode in a hail of bullets the next day.

Tensions had been mounting all week in the Nevada town. By Friday, April 26, the Mongols had massed in great numbers to party at Harrah's casino in Laughlin, while the Hells Angels, as usual, made their headquarters at the Flamingo Hilton. As luck would have it, the Vegas police brass had chosen this year to cut back on biker intelligence. Det. Tom Allen had been keeping an eye on the bike gangs in the area since 1993 with the Las Vegas police department's Criminal Intelligence department. He knew his local Hells Angels had strong ties to the Mafia and local Teamsters. At previous runs, the police had had a full squad of five to seven intelligence officers on the ground, sometimes even two squads. In 2002, there were only four officers. "It was basically useless; we caught a lot of stuff but we missed a lot of stuff."

The ATF, on the other hand, had blanketed the town with as many controllers and undercover operatives as possible. John Ciccone, for one, was busy at Laughlin, keeping on eye on both the Mongols and the Angels. He had several reliable informants inside the Mongols. And his new star recruit, full-patch Hells Angel Mike Kramer, was expected to show up Saturday morning to start spying on his HA pals. Too late, as it would turn out, for the big show.

Then there was Jay Dobyns, the ATF undercover cop who was hanging out with gunrunners and bikers in nearby Bullhead City as part of Operation Riverside. The ATF had also sent out Darrin Kozlowski, the agent who had infiltrated the Vagos with Ciccone, to help Dobyns mingle and mix with the bikers in Laughlin. Koz would ride shotgun for Dobyns, pretend to be his Californian connection and build up his reputation as a mover and shaker. Late Friday night, the two of them strolled into the Flamingo, Dobyns with his tattoos up and down his arms, Koz sporting a thick headband and sunglasses.

"The casino came to a stop when we walked in," Dobyns recalls. He turned to his partner and whispered, "Dude, every eye on this place is on us: they are all eye-fucking us." Dobyns at first flattered himself, proud he had made such a startling impression at his first big biker event. Only later, in light of the terrible events about to unfold, did he realize the Angels had been staring because they suspected the strangers might be Mongol spies.

Dobyns started drinking, hanging out with the Angels, making new contacts. He met Donald "Smitty" Smith for the first time, an influential member of the Arizona Nomad chapter who happened to live in Bullhead City. Dobyns chatted with Maurice "Pete" Eunice, a Californian Angel who was about to play a bloody role in the battle that would explode shortly.

There were also more undercover ATF agents on the scene: the San Diego bureau had sent two operatives to Laughlin, hoping they could ingratiate themselves with the Hells Angels. It was part of the major investigation code-named Operation Five Star. The ATF was helping the DEA probe two drug trafficking rings through which the Hells Angels were moving marijuana, cocaine and methamphetamine throughout the United States from Mexico. To provide surveillance, the ATF had also sent out the cover team from San Diego.

One member of that team was a pretty, twenty-nine-year-old female agent with long hair and a quick smile on her first ATF assignment. Jenna MaGuire was fresh out of the ATF academy; her training officer in San Diego happened to be the ATF's point man on Five Star. MaGuire caught sight of Dobyns and Koz in their biker getups; she had never met them before, but she knew from her briefings that they were cops. They began to talk at the bar. Three cops chatting, but to the other bikers, it would have looked as if Bird was hitting on some chick. MaGuire was impressed with how authentic Dobyns and Koz acted: "Those guys looked so scary, they looked so intimidating," she says. The young ATF recruit could scarcely imagine that within a few months, she would be joining Dobyns as his biker girlfriend in a perilous two-year undercover operation.

While the cops were mingling with each other and the bikers in the Flamingo, tensions were ratcheting up outside. At 9:30 P.M., a few dozen Mongols left Harrah's in taxis and made their way to another casino, called the Golden Nugget. They marched up to a booth where a Hells Angels motorcycle was on display; when police tried to block them, the bikers encircled the cops. The nervous police radioed for their SWAT team, along with police horses and dogs. They also called in more officers from Las Vegas.

It was going to be a long night.

Two hours later, the Mongols left, defiantly walking in a single file back to their encampment at Harrah's. About the same time, a Las Vegas police captain and a lieutenant were meeting with a Mongol leader to try to calm things down.

We know you're here to have an "in your face" with the Hells Angels and we don't want that to take place, they told the biker, according to later grand jury testimony.

We don't want to have trouble, the Mongol insisted.

The two officers then went over to the Flamingo to meet with three Hells Angels leaders.

"We asked that they allow the police department to maintain order," the police later testified, urging the Angels to "remain on the property."

"We have chosen a life of outlaws; we plan to live the life of outlaws," the Hells Angels responded. "We don't need the police department. . . . We don't care what the fuck you do, we're going to do what we have to do to protect ourselves."

Back at Harrah's casino, the worried staff could all but hear the ticking of the bomb that was about to explode. Packed mainly with Mongols, Rosa's Cantina at the west end of the sprawling gaming palace also hosted a fair number of Angels. Near the craps table, a Mongol intentionally bumped into an Angel. "You could just see daggers coming out of this guy's eyes," one casino employee later testified. "They were restless, they were uneasy, they were on edge," said another.

Just after 2 A.M., at his blackjack table, dealer Jay Buhr saw a Hells Angel and a Mongol face off against each other.

"We don't want to start this in here. Let's take it outside," the Hells Angel said.

Buhr rushed over to his supervisor: "We don't have enough security for what's going to happen here real soon," he warned.

Within less than a minute, all hell broke loose.

What happened in the next few minutes inside the casino led to more than one hundred criminal charges that have yet to be adjudicated in a court of law. What follows is a version of events as pieced together from state grand jury testimony and federal indictments. The events described are based on witness accounts, but the allegations of involvement by individuals have not been proven.

Outnumbered and probably spooked by the more aggressive Mongols, the Hells Angels inside Harrah's put out a distress call to their comrades at the Flamingo, where a lot of the younger, more hot-tempered Angels were staying. They had had enough of giving in to the Mongols; now was the time to kick some ass. The Angels had massed from across the country—and they knew they were not going to Harrah's for drinks.

"Do you know what's going to happen if we go up there?" a Nomad member from Washington named Smilin' Rick asked.

"Yeah, I do," said David "Monty" Elliot, the president of the Anchorage, Alaska, chapter. "What choice do we have?

"You're right, goddammit!"

"Let's mount up!" cried a third biker, according to a later ATF affidavit.

Like avenging cowboys, they sped through the city. Outside Harrah's, Sgt. Gary Hood had already pulled into the valet area in time to spot about thirty Hells Angels arriving. "They jumped off their bikes in this area and ran into the entrance," he said. They didn't intend to stay long: several of them had left their keys in the ignition.

At the front desk, guest Jeff King was registering when the bikers stormed by. "Better get the fuck out of here because trouble is about to start," a biker warned. King saw one Angel with a clawhammer, and six or seven with knives.

Leading the pack was Raymond Foakes, the sergeant-at-arms in the Sonoma County chapter in California, according to grand jury testimony. The Angels and the Mongols came face to face at Rosa's Cantina. The Angels acted with military precision, a small group acting as sentries around the bar. The casino's surveillance tapes show Mongols leader Roger Pinney and Hells Angel Pete Eunice talking briefly. It was just after 2:16 A.M.

Suddenly, according to court filings, "Foakes kicked a Mongol in the face and started the fighting." Within seconds, more than a hundred bikers were brawling on the casino floor with guns, knives, wrenches and hammers.

"Boom! Boom! Pop! Pop!" is how tourist Kerry Richard later remembered the sound of gunfire exploding all around him as he dropped to his hands and knees.

"Help me, help me! I'm hit, I'm hit!" he heard a man cry. "I saw blood all over the floor, all over his hands."

"Lie down. You've been hit real hard—just stay right here," Richard told the man. But then he noticed the victim was furiously kicking something in between a row of slot machines and realized it was his biker vest. "Then it dawned on me that he wasn't a regular patron like myself, he was a Mongol and he was trying to hide his colours," Richard later told a court. He crawled away, fearing the Angels would come back to finish off the Mongol.

Another tourist, John Davidson, testified that he ducked underneath one of the blackjack tables. He grabbed his $1,200 in chips, then reached up to pull down the dealer as well. "She was screaming out of control," he said.

A bartender's cellphone rang. It was his wife. She was working the roulette wheel in another part of the casino—only now she was under it. Bullets were flying everywhere. She called back later to report she was safe, but there was a corpse next to her.

With little regard for innocent bystanders, the bikers went at each other like Vikings on a battlefield—and it was all captured on more than four hundred surveillance tapes. The Mongols were pulling out guns "like a peanut vendor at a fuckin' ball park," recalled one Hells Angel. The Angels responded in kind. According to police affidavits, "as soon as the fighting starts, [Hells Angel Pete] Eunice pulls out a handgun and fires several times at Mongols."

One Angel tackled a Mongol and held him while his buddy stabbed him. The casino videotapes, according to state grand jury testimony, show an Angel from Arizona named Cal Schaefer swinging a ballpeen hammer at two Mongols and then pulling out a handgun and firing several rounds. At 2:16 P.M. the security camera captured him aiming in the direction of a Mongol named Richard Nolan, who was later hospitalized with a gunshot wound.

Over at one of the blackjack tables, another Hells Angel was busy reloading his gun after firing off half-a-dozen rounds.

"Hey, buddy, get out of the pit, because if somebody starts to shoot at you, all the rest of us are in danger. You're using us as a shield basically!" shouted Jay Buhr, the rather brave blackjack dealer. "If he hadn't had a gun, it went through my mind to go over there and knock the piss out of him."

At another blackjack table, there was more pandemonium. The Hells Angels dragged one of their fallen comrades who had been shot and propped him up against the table, then surrounded him to protect him.

"This is my area. I'm protecting my friend here—get away!" yelled Hells Angel Rodney Cox, wielding a crescent wrench if the grand jury account is accurate. When a Mongol came around the corner, Cox sprang into action with his heavy weapon.

"[He] literally jumped up, ran after him, buried it in his head, and then turned around and ran back to watch his friend again," blackjack dealer William Southern later testified.

The Angels seemed to be enjoying themselves. "The shit was happenin' and we were rockin' and rollin,'" a biker named Michael Hurn later boasted. At one point, two Hells Angels ganged up on Mongols leader Roger Pinney. Angel Henry Leedom "has Pinney on his knees while he is punching him in the face," according to a court-filed police account. Fellow Angel James Hannigan grabbed the Mongol by the hair with his right hand and stabbed him twice with the knife in his left hand.

Hannigan wasn't done yet. Right next to him, a Mongol named Benjamin Leyva was fighting with an Angel. Hannigan grabbed the Mongol's left shoulder and plunged his knife into his torso, according to a police affidavit. Leyva's grief wasn't over. Arizona Angel Cal Schaefer pointed a gun right at Leyva and fired three shots, police allege. The Mongol tried to flee. Schaefer fired a few more shots, police claim. Leyva—with bullet wounds in his elbow, back and stomach and a knife wound in his belly—somehow managed to survive.

Several other Mongols, bleeding and staggering, also survived their wounds from the gun, wrench and knife attacks in the casino. Enrique Muñoz got a bullet in the chest, Davey Carmargo got one in the leg and Raymond Santos was stabbed. But luck run out that night for their fellow Mongol Anthony Salvador Barrera. He was stabbed to death in the chest.

Two Hells Angels also paid for their pride with their lives. Police found the crumpled body of Jeramie Dean Bell in the casino pit area with a serious gunshot wound in his right upper chest. They rushed him to hospital, but he did not recover.

The security videotape also showed fellow Angel Robert Emmet Tumelty tossing chairs during the battle, until he was felled and killed by a bullet to his abdomen.

The bedlam and the bloodshed was all over in a matter of minutes.

Las Vegas police Sgt. Gary Hood, the first cop on the scene, managed to make his way to the centre of the casino floor, amid the bodies, the moaning of the injured and the shouts of still-frenzied bikers.

"Everything just kind of stopped," Hood told the grand jury. "We're standing there looking at them and they're looking at us, and we're waiting for them to do something and they're waiting for us to do something, I guess."

"Everybody get on the floor!" the police ordered, finally taking control of the situation. In all, police arrested seventy Angels and forty-two Mongols and associates. They seized fourteen firearms and 107 knives—ten of them with apparent visible blood.

Homicide detectives made the rounds of various hospitals in the area. They found a dozen severely wounded bikers, not one willing to talk or cooperate. Many of the bikers not nabbed by the police at the casino sped away, back to California or Arizona for safety.

Not all of them made it.

Less than an hour after the Laughlin shootout, Christian Tate, a twenty-eight-year-old Hells Angel from San Diego, was found dead on the Interstate 40 in California, about 115 miles west of Laughlin. His wrecked bike lay strewn on the road, bullet casings not far away. He had been shot off his bike. The Laughlin River Run had claimed its fourth, and for the moment its final, victim.

Many of the Hells Angels and the Mongols dispute the accounts given by either police or rival bikers. But regardless of how the pending legal cases turn out, the Laughlin shootout dramatically changed the biker landscape.

Miraculously, not a single tourist, employee or cop was injured or killed. More than any other recent explosion of biker violence in the United States, the Laughlin shootout exposed just how brazen the Hells Angels and their rivals were. It wasn't the toll of the dying and injured that shocked people; there had been deadlier biker confrontations in recent years. It was the audacity of the Angels—and the Mongols—the outright contempt for the law, the flaunting of biker bravado. In a packed public arena, in full view of hundreds of security cameras, they waged a pitched battle to see who would be king of the outlaw jungle. And while the Mongols fled, stuffing their vests in garbage cans and air vents to avoid being identified by the police after the battle, not a single Hells Angel took off his colours.

The bloodshed led the TV newscasts and made headlines across the country, even earning the Hells Angels a spot on *The New York Times* front page. "Publicity is good, no matter what," Sonny Barger said shortly afterwards. "Publicity has always been good for the Angels." But Barger told reporters the Laughlin shootings were spontaneous, isolated and overblown: "I'm not going to talk about that. There are people like that in any group— doctors, lawyers and everybody. You know as well as I do that was a drop in the bucket compared with what is going on anywhere else in the world."

The initial reaction to the Laughlin shootout inside the ATF— the main federal agency tasked with taking on the bikers—was panic. Management in Los Angeles ordered the immediate with-drawal of the two undercover agents working with Operation Five Star. "Our management freaked out and pulled them," says one disappointed ATF officer on the scene.

With dead biker bodies around, the ATF figured it was either too dangerous—or too compromising—to have undercover agents trying to infiltrate the Hells Angels. The hasty retreat forced Operation Five Star to scrap its original plans. The two agents had only begun to cozy up to the Angels and had not made much progress so far; now their sudden disappearance from the scene smashed all hope of establishing any street credibility.

Curiously, the agents had been staying at the Bullhead City house of another undercover ATF cop at Laughlin, Jay Dobyns. Dobyns recalls the panicky scene: the ATF made tactical evalua-tions of the two California agents, swooping down in cars with other agents riding shotgun, hurrying the undercovers into the vehicle and then dashing away.

"These guys are being taken away under armed guard, and I'm back at the house by myself watching TV," Dobyns chuckles. "And it's my house and the Angels know that's where I am. But I was fine with that: I'm not burned in this." Indeed, in the days and weeks following the Laughlin shootout, Dobyn's reputation as a local gangster was such that several local Hells Angels dropped by to discuss the Harrah battle. Dobyns's bosses in Arizona reasoned he was not in danger, because up to that point, his undercover work in Bullhead had not been directly targeting the Hells Angels.

After the initial panic, however, the Laughlin shooting spurred police forces into action. "A lot of things changed after the shoot-ing at Harrah's," says Billy Guinn, a veteran investigator with the San Diego sheriff's department. "It basically forced law enforce-ment to take another look at the bikers." Once the Nevada dust settled, Laughlin changed the political map for biker cops.

Dobyns could feel it almost right away. Some of the supervisors within his chain of command had been pooh-poohing his biker work: "They would look at bikers as nothing more than burned-out Vietnam vets who liked to ride and smoke dope," Dobyns says, remembering their attitude: "They are not hurting anybody; we're wasting our time with these guys; why are we spending money on them?" Now, management's tune was changing: "Well, you know, maybe you guys are on to something. Maybe we ought to go after them." Within a couple of months after the Laughlin shooting, Joe Slatalla was able to pull Dobyns out of Bullhead, recruit a large team from several police agencies and begin a long-term assault on Barger's Angels in Arizona.

John Ciccone could see it, too. Suddenly, his informant inside the Hells Angels, Mike Kramer, became much more valuable: "I was able to sit here and see what was happening on the inside," he says. Kramer now had a new, major assignment: find out the dirt about who did what at Harrah's. Ciccone, like most people, assumed that the hundreds of hours of casino surveillance tapes would make the case against the bikers an easy roll of the dice. But nothing goes as planned when it comes to taking on the bikers. The police and prosecutors in Nevada would get bogged down in jurisdictional disputes. In the end, it would be two years before any significant progress was made—and it wouldn't happen until John Ciccone took charge.

In country after country where the Hells Angels and other biker gangs fought their bloody wars, it was the same, tragic story as at the Laughlin shootout. It would take a particularly gruesome display of biker bravado—all too often at the cost of innocent lives—to alert a disbelieving public and politicians to the threat posed by the biker gangs. In Canada, it was an eleven-year-old boy killed by a piece of flying shrapnel from a biker bomb. In England, it was the Hells Angels bold hacking to death of two rivals in broad daylight at a music festival.

And in Australia, eight thousand miles away from the casinos of Nevada, it would take a nighttime assassination in the isolated outback and the car bombing of a retired policeman to wake up a nation to the perils of the bikers and the failure of its justice system to cope with them.

PART II

AUSTRALIAN ASSAULT

FOUR

Murder in the Goldfields

——

Fuck you and your ways. I'm going to take care of it my way.
—Gypsy Joker Graeme "Slim" Slater

Det. Jack Peter Lee was certain nothing good would ever come of this. He had one dead outlaw biker. A bikie, as the Aussies called them. And his chief murder suspect was his former boss and commander of the Criminal Investigations Branch (CIB), Don Hancock. What a mess, he thought, his hand sweeping over his bald head. And it was getting worse by the minute.

He grimaced and turned to gaze out the window of the police sedan. An endless line of all-too-familiar gum trees flew by as he travelled along the Great Eastern Highway, deeper and deeper into the Australian outback. The murder had happened Sunday night, October 1, 2000, in an isolated mining town called Ora Banda. Lee had been briefed Monday. That's when the worry set in. It hit as soon as he heard the word "bikie" and the name Hancock in the same breath. "Extreme apprehension," as he later described it. "Because I knew that this was one of those career-changing moments." Not scared of Don Hancock and what he could do. But aware that the bikies were involved, and a former head of CIB involved. This would attract repercussions down the track. "I knew someone was going to suffer."

Tuesday morning, and Lee was on the highway heading from Perth, the thriving government and financial centre on Australia's west coast, toward Kalgoorlie in the Goldfields district, a seven-hour drive. Lee knew the area. He had worked in the Goldfields as a teenager before joining the navy. After nine years at sea, he left with a tattoo on his right arm—"Blood Group A positive"—and an acceptance letter from the Western Australia Police Service. It was a natural progression. Lots of servicemen joined the police when he did. Now, after twenty-two years of slogging up the ranks, he had no real desire to go back to a place that was well beyond the reach of McDonald's, Red Rooster and Hungry Jacks. A place where men outnumbered women four to one and too many bored miners feasted on booze and amphetamines. It held nothing but salt-scarred red dirt, struggling vegetation, scorpions and a whole lot of trouble that could easily destroy his career. "Desert, really," he said. "There's nothing else out there." If this had been just about a bikie killing, he would have been comfortably back at his office in sun city Perth. But this wasn't about a bikie killing. Jack Lee had been called in because this murder was about a legend.

To friends and colleagues, Don Hancock was the Don or the Silver Fox. Few police officers commanded more respect. He was considered one of the top cops in all of Australia, one of the most esteemed detectives the job had ever produced. And now this was the guy Lee was gunning for.

It was hard to believe. Lee sat in the back of the car, juggling his thoughts. He recalled that Hancock had signed his appointment when he became a detective. The certificate hung on a wall in his Perth bungalow. The Don had the appearance of a courtly gentleman, with his trim white hair, smooth pink skin and easy smile. He wore finely tailored sports jackets and slacks. He liked to quote poetry, especially the "Bush Ballads" and "Galloping Rhymes" of Australia's nineteenth-century poet-balladeer Adam Lindsay Gordon, a mounted policeman and fellow horse lover.

Of course Hancock had his darker side. Who doesn't? But Lee had sensed that it was a little harsher than most. "Hancock was an absolute gentleman of the old school. And I think that he was not the sort of guy who would back down in front of what he saw as scum." That's what made Lee nervous. He was aware that Hancock was a tough, competitive cop who could get surly over the loss of a friendly game of billiards. He was part of what younger cops referred to as the old school. It meant a penchant for frontier justice, and the vast empty Goldfields were still very much frontier.

Hancock's biggest case had been the 1982 Perth mint swindle. He put three men—the Mickelberg brothers—in jail for stealing sixty-five kilos of gold. It was Australia's biggest gold theft and quickly assumed the aura of folklore, alongside the feats of one of the country's greatest heroes, Ned Kelly, the nineteenth-century bushranger and police killer. The brothers, however, had always claimed that Hancock and a junior detective had fabricated evidence and beaten one of them in a police interrogation room after stripping him naked. Initially, few people believed them and the Mickelbergs lost all their appeals. Yet even after twenty years, the scandal wouldn't dissipate. Hancock quietly took his retirement, left Perth and moved with his wife, Elizabeth, to Ora Banda. The Perth mint swindle case made Lee wonder about Hancock. He wondered what this icon was capable of.

Ora Banda was a place few people other than miners had ever heard of. A tiny outpost with a revolving-door residency of forty to fifty people, all engaged one way or another in the local mining industry. Gold is what made the entire region viable, and gold is what still makes it viable today. Or at least the hunger for gold.

For Hancock the place was home. His family had deep roots there. His father and grandfather had prospected and mined gold in the area for almost a century. According to the briefing Lee had received the day before, the Hancocks basically owned the town. The Ora Banda Historic Inn, the pub, the beer garden and restaurant, the trailer park, the general store, seven motel units and three houses and a number of single men's quarters, plus the old diesel gold crusher that still worked like a charm. All of it belonged to the Don, held under a company called Wentworth Holdings WA Pty Ltd. He had spent two years restoring Ora Banda and was trying to resurrect it as a small mining centre and tourist destination. Outside the pub was a racetrack. It was sculpted out of the dirt, and every year Hancock held several race days as part of the Kalgoorlie racing round. Hancock re-established the old Ora Banda Cup day, and thousands of people drove up from Kalgoorlie and other local communities, even Perth. It was as good a reason as any for friends and tourists to spend the day gambling, boozing and firing up their barbecues. Inside the track was a cricket oval. Each year Hancock organized a match between police and local miners. The only rules were that the game ended in a tie, everybody got drunk and Hancock ran the show. Strictly speaking, the oval and racetrack were public ground. But as far as the Don was concerned, he owned them. Five miles east of Ora Banda, Hancock also owned a gold lease called Grant's Patch. Three generations of Hancocks had mined there. Now Don and his son, Stephen, ran a small open-pit mine in the area. It was little more than a huge hole blown and hacked out of the ground. A tin-roofed shack contained tools, explosives, a plastic bag with fifty-one rounds of .303 ammunition and a rifle. Something to shoot kangaroos with for a bit of fun. Roo shooting, as the Aussies call it. Roos have lean meat that cooks up red and gamey and is quite tasty on a barbecue. Still, it seemed a pretty powerful gun just to knock down an oversized rabbit.

But it wasn't dead kangaroos that Jack Lee had in mind on that Tuesday morning. It was the dead bikie. Monday's briefing revealed only the standard info. His name was William Joseph "Billy" Grierson, thirty-nine. No criminal record. Originally from the east coast. One of fourteen kids. Mechanic for a local mining company. Divorced, father of two. Recently made full-patch member of the Gypsy Jokers chapter in Kalgoorlie.

Bikies were new terrain for Lee. Even though he was a veteran murder investigator, he had never had a bikie case. He knew them by reputation, though, and the Gypsy Jokers were said to be the most violent biker gang in Australia. They were also one of the oldest, started in 1969 by a Hells Angel from Melbourne. The gang adopted the original Hells Angels' "1%er" patch and used the Angels' blood red as a dominant colour on their Death Head patch, but they always refused to patch over to the HA, reflecting the independent streak in the Western Australia gold digger mentality.

The Jokers were created just as the American outlaw biker culture began to gain a permanent foothold in the Aussie underbelly. The Gladiators, started in 1963 in Sydney, were the first and for a long time the only recognized outlaw bikie club. It took Aussie soldiers returning from Vietnam to get a wider bikie movement going. By the 1970s there were outlaw biker clubs in every major Australian city. Many were homegrown, such as the Jokers, Rebels, Finks, Coffin Cheaters and Black Uhlans. They essentially imitated the rules, dress and firecracker temperament of their American cousins, the Hells Angels and Bandidos.

The first national biker run that captured the attention of Australia was in 1972, and it quickly dissolved into a fight over colours. The Angels—who had two chapters and would eventually expand to nine—demanded that the Rebels change their red-and-white banner. The fight turned into an ongoing feud that ended when members of the Rebels invaded the Hells Angels' president's home and beat him to death with a baby's pram. Patches, emblems and colours were fought over across the country as Mad Max Aussies formed new clubs and staked out their territory. In 1976 the Coffin Cheaters in Melbourne challenged the Resurrected, demanding that they change their name. They visited the club president, known only as Pig, raped his nineteen-year-old girlfriend and beat him almost to death. They then visited a second member, beating him unconscious before turning their attention to his three girlfriends, who had taken refuge in a closet. When the Cheaters pried open the locked door, they got a big surprise. One of the girls, age eighteen, had a gun. She didn't hesitate. She shot one Cheater dead and wounded another. The rest fled as she fired off even more rounds. Six Coffin Cheaters were convicted of assault, burglary, wounding, theft and rape.

Police took little notice of the mounting death toll until the Father's Day Massacre in the Sydney suburb of Milperra in 1984. The Comancheros had declared war on a former chapter that had patched over to become the first Bandidos OMC outside the United

States. It was to be a deadly welcome for the American-based club. The two sides shot it out in a tavern parking lot. Five bikies were killed, plus a fifteen-year-old girl. Many others were wounded.

The massacre dominated the front pages for weeks, and police immediately clamped down. Task forces proliferated. Cops regularly stopped bikies on the highway for no other reason than to check their licences and registrations. In Western Australia, when a hundred bikies went on a run, 150 cops went with them, racing ahead simply to obstruct their activity and to make sure they were policed to the limit even on the lowest-level crime. As one police officer said, "If it's stealing a hamburger or a cool drink from the local country store, then we will police them to the nth degree." Mom, Dad and the kids would be protected from bikie invasions, the police promised.

But despite all the attention—or maybe because of it—bikie gangs only grew stronger. Over the next twenty years, the Bandidos spread to almost every major urban centre in the country. The Comancheros doubled in size and opened a chapter in Brisbane. They also established a handful of feeder clubs.

Financed by the growing trade in methamphetamine, motorcycle gangs had their largest growth spurt after the massacre. This was followed by a violent consolidation beginning in 1994, as the major clubs either absorbed or destroyed the weaker gangs. Thirty-five people died in the gang wars, and the number of clubs was reduced from 178 to about 32.

The battle for Australia was not an isolated event. It was part of a worldwide outlaw biker gang conflagration sparked by the Hells Angels' dream to paint the universe red and white. In Europe, Canada, and the United States, hundreds of bikers and many innocent citizens lost their lives in biker killings. Hundreds more were seriously maimed in beatings, bombings and shootings. When the smoke cleared, the Hells Angels ruled Canada. Europe was divided between the HA and the Bandidos. The United States had become primarily Hells Angels, Bandidos and Outlaw country.

Australia, however, was a different story. While the Bandidos' national president, Michael Kulakowski, flew to the U.S. in July

1996 to participate in peace negotiations between the HA and Bandidos in Europe, at home he was powerless against clubs such as the Gypsy Jokers. Unlike in Europe or North America, neither the Hells Angels nor the Bandidos succeeded in entirely vanquishing the fiercely independent Australian bikie gangs. Nor have they ever succeeded in penetrating Western Australia, home to the Jokers and the Coffin Cheaters. Instead, they made peace.

The Gypsy Jokers emerged as the most violent. Whether their targets were enemy bikies or police didn't seem to matter. They fought all comers. They didn't hesitate to bash or threaten a cop who got in their way. Jack Lee had seen the video clips. Shots of bloodied police officers and handcuffed gang members.

Many bikies became rich in the process, as bikie business became big business. Drug trafficking financed legitimate businesses in construction, security sevices, entertainment and automobile mechanics. A steel company owned by two Gypsy Jokers even constructed a suburban Perth police station.

So by the time Lee headed toward Ora Banda, bikie gangs were firmly entrenched in the Aussie subculture, dominated by the big five: the Hells Angels, Bandidos, Rebels, Coffin Cheaters and Gypsy Jokers. And those members who had survived the culling process—estimated by police at more than three thousand (more per capita than any other country)—were hard-core, dedicated bikies.

This was the world Jack Lee was entering when he headed east to Ora Banda.

"Yeah, I was bloody apprehensive," he said. "It was the biggest job that I have ever taken on in my career, and I have investigated quite a few homicides. That was an extremely long drive."

Sunday, October 1, 2000, had been a gorgeous spring day. The air was warm and comfortable, the sky a cloudless, shimmering blue. Perfect for a long holiday weekend and a barbecue with family and friends. Don and Elizabeth Hancock were expecting a big crowd at the Ora Banda Historical Inn. "It was a really lovely sunny day and we had lots of people out," Elizabeth Hancock recalled. "The bar and the beer garden were full, and everybody was really happy." Among the guests in the beer garden were two police officers, Det. Senior Sgt. Kim Gage and Det. Senior Const. Sean Gartlan, with their wives and children. Gage and Gartlan had just transferred the week before from Perth to take command of the local CIB in Kalgoorlie. They had driven to Ora Banda that day to have lunch and visit Hancock. Gage's father had been at police college with the Don, and anyway Gage felt he couldn't very well start their new jobs without first paying their respects to the Silver Fox.

Hancock had spent the morning on his favourite hobby—prospecting. He was still dressed in his dusty old boots, bottle-green shorts and cotton shirt. He needed a shower, but he was too busy working in the office, helping Elizabeth with the accounts. After Gage and Gartlan arrived, he and Elizabeth went out and shared a drink under the hot sun.

It was about then that they heard the deafening rumble and roar of Harley-Davidson motorcycles. There were only seven bikes, plus two run trucks to bring the camping gear, beer, extra gas and spare parts. They immediately smashed the desert calm. Elizabeth Hancock cast nervous glances at her husband, worried about his reaction but not wanting to say anything. The bikies were Gypsy Jokers. They wore their colours as they roared around the racetrack several times before parking under two shaggy gum trees at the far side of the cricket oval, where they began setting up camp. They attached a large Gypsy Joker banner between the trees, cut down one of the larger trees in the area with a chainsaw, stripped it of its branches and dragged it onto the track for a bonfire. A tall, thin, bearded bikie named Sid "Snot" Reid attached a rusting car hood to his bike and began tearing around the track, with a couple of his fellow bikies riding on the hood screaming and hollering like teenage boys out to wake up the neighbourhood.

Hancock watched the performance and then withdrew to the pub. He became unusually busy clearing tables and collecting cans and just generally checking in and out of the bar to make sure his forty-odd patrons were being served, clearly trying to ignore the fact that his town had been invaded and his sacred cricket pitch desecrated by people he considered, using one of his favourite phrases, "criminal scumbags." Seeing them raise their flag over his territory like a conquering army was even more galling.

Gartlan suggested that this was simply an advance party, a scouting expedition for an invasion of five hundred bikers from the Rebel motorcycle gang due to descend on the area the following week for a national bike run. Hancock was thinking, Not in my town.

Rebecca Price, the Ora Banda Inn's head cook, was busy preparing barbecues. She realized Don was drunk when he came in to use the toilet; Elizabeth was already in the washroom.

"Who's in there?" he yelled.

"I am."

"Well, I'll just have to piss in the sink."

Rebecca was used to Don's occasional belligerence. "When Don has been drinking, he's generally a lot worse. He's got that typical policeman's attitude that he's higher up than anyone else and can do what he wants. . . . When he really does drink, he doesn't drink in moderation, he drinks like a fish."

Hancock's daughter, Alison, was serving drinks when four of the Gypsy Jokers entered the pub at about 4 P.M. and took a table at the far end of the bar. They purchased bread rolls from Elizabeth Hancock and started drinking, talking and laughing. Don sat near the cash register toward the other end of the bar. Alison kept clear of the bikies, who were drinking shooters and beer, and for a time everything seemed fairly normal. Some patrons played pool while others watched the closing of the Sydney Olympics on TV.

Rebecca noticed that Elizabeth was unusually fidgety. As she prepared herself a salad in the kitchen, she talked nervously about the bikies, repeating stuff like "I wish these damn bikies would go" and "I'm just worried about Don."

Patricia McQueen, the inn's breakfast cook, came in for a chat with Rebecca. She told Elizabeth, "Well, if you leave them alone, they'll leave you alone." Elizabeth ignored her and took her salad into the bar.

The trouble started at about 6 P.M. Gage and Gartlan and their families had by then left Ora Banda for Kalgoorlie. About fourteen people were still in the bar and the beer garden when one of the bikies, James "Spud" Manson, walked over to Robbie Mitchell, a local prospector sitting at the bar, and said, "You're a fucking wanker." Just like that. No hello. Nothing.

"What are you talking about?" Mitchell said.

"You know what I'm talking about. You're a fucking wanker."

Hancock sat sipping a drink, listening to the exchange. Elizabeth was nearby, nervously eating her salad.

The bikie walked back to his mates; Mitchell had one more drink and left. The confrontation had frightened him. Later it was claimed that the bikie thought Mitchell had screwed him a few years back on a mining lease, but at the time the exchange seemed to come out of nowhere.

The atmosphere calmed somewhat, and Alison served the bikies a fresh round. They invited her to their camp, but she politely told them she had to work all evening. As she walked away she heard one of the bikies joke about "creaming my pants." Alison was thirty-six years old and had heard enough "dirty talk," as she called it, not to let it bother her. But it bothered her father. He stood up, walked over to their table and said rather stiffly, "This is my daughter behind the bar. I'd appreciate it if you would refrain from talking like that. If there's any sign of trouble, I'm going to close the pub."

Bikie Billy Grierson stared up at the silver-haired bar owner and said, "No worries," and then went back to his drink. The bikies lowered their voices, and the foul language stopped.

But the atmosphere was tense, and Alison was worried. She wanted to keep the peace. So she walked to their table and nervously apologized for her father's warning.

"I hope you understand. He's being a protective dad."

"Hey, it's better that he cares than that he doesn't," Grierson said.

But that wasn't the end of it. Five minutes later Grierson stood up to go to the toilet. On the way he stopped by Hancock, put his arm around his shoulder and said in a low voice loud enough for Alison to hear, "Don't you threaten us. We'll go and drink our own [beer]."

Hancock was startled. "What are you on about?" he asked.

Grierson said, "If that's your fucking attitude, we'll just go down and drink piss out of our own esky [cooler]."

"That's it. I don't need this. I'm closing the pub." Hancock got off his stool and angrily bolted the double doors.

"Alison, the bar is closed," he told his daughter. "No more drinks."

The confrontation seemed petty, but Hancock was clearly furious. Rebecca saw him walk into the passageway to the kitchen and say something to Elizabeth. Don then left the inn by the kitchen door and drove off in his white Ford 100 utility truck— what the Aussies refer to as a ute—kicking up gravel, fishtailing down the road toward Grant's Patch. "I mean, he obviously dropped the clutch and cracked a shit," Rebecca said. "That's the way I felt. He cracked a shit." Meaning he was furious. "Minutes later Elizabeth came up to me in the kitchen and said, 'He's gone to Grant's Patch. He's gone to get his gun.'"

As patrons finished their drinks and retired to the beer garden where the giant barbecue was sizzling, Elizabeth grabbed the till, covered the money with a tea towel and carried it into the kitchen. "At least they won't get the money," she told Rebecca.

Kirsten Forster, twenty-three, a mining technician, had arrived in time to see Don stomping out of the pub; she asked Alison, "What's going on, Ali?"

"Dad's closing the bar and he's going to get his gun."

Elizabeth told her that Don was worried that the bikies were scouting the place as a possible venue for an upcoming biker rally, and he wanted it stopped.

Grierson and the other Jokers finished their drinks and returned to their camp across the oval. It was about 6:50 P.M. The sun was setting and the air was cooler. The bikies had set up a generator to charge a floodlight that lit up their camp and the Gypsy Joker banner. Grierson and Manson joined Snot Reid, Graeme

"Slim" Slater and the other bikies sitting around the bonfire. Slater and Grierson sat together with Manson on a wooden park bench, while Reid lay on the ground. Grierson recounted the incident in the pub with the white-haired publican, and the bikies had a laugh and continued drinking. Nobody thought anything more about it.

At about 7:15 P.M. Rebecca heard Don's car come down the Kalgoorlie road, apparently returning from Grant's Patch. She noticed the car circle around the pub and head in the general direction of his home.

Meanwhile, Elizabeth hurried out to her car with the evening's take, plus money from the safe. As she left the inn, she told Patricia McQueen, "I'd better go and find Don before he does something stupid."

"If you're that worried, call the police," Patricia said.

"Don wouldn't like that," Elizabeth said.

The Gypsy Jokers had actually come to Ora Banda by chance. They had originally planned a weekend run from Kalgoorlie to Laverton, another mining town in the area. But when they arrived, they discovered the town was holding an aboriginal festival, so after a few drinks in the pub, they drove on to Leonora, where they spent the night. The next morning they held a meeting to discuss whether to go back to the Kalgoorlie clubhouse. Sid Reid thought that was boring. They could do that any time. He was a truck driver and knew the area. He suggested Ora Banda, with its camp ground, beer garden and bar. Spend the night there and return to Kalgoorlie in the morning. The others agreed, so they packed up the camp and rode off to Don Hancock's fiefdom . . . and right into trouble.

The first shot cracked the still night air at about 7:45 P.M. Snot Reid felt the bullet pass by his left ear. It hit the fire, kicking up a small explosion of embers. The bikies immediately dived for cover. The shot seemed to come from across the oval in the general direction of the battery. But nobody was sure. Two of the bikies jumped in the run truck and drove off to investigate. One of the bikies suggested it was a stray shot from a roo shooter.

Another suggested that it might be that prospector Robbie Mitchell firing a warning shot, trying to scare them because they had called him a wanker.

Billy Grierson disagreed—he figured it had to be Don Hancock: "If it was a gunshot, it would just be the old prick trying to scare us," he said. Reid took a walk over to the inn where he asked Ray Pinner, one of the other prospectors hanging out at the bar, if there happened to be any roo shooters in the area.

"Not to my knowledge," Ray said. And Reid returned to the camp, where he found Grierson and Slater back on the bench drinking and joking, the gunshot seemingly forgotten.

The shot was also heard in the beer garden, where people immediately assumed it was the bikies raising hell around their campfire. Some patrons left the garden and rounded the corner of the inn to check on the bikies. All they could see was the distant bonfire and floodlight and a few shadowy figures. Soon everybody went back to drinking and barbecuing.

Elizabeth had been at home in the Hancock bungalow across from the battery when she heard the shot. She ran to her car and drove back to the inn to check on Alison.

The second shot rang out about ten minutes later. Slim Slater heard the recoil at about the same time as he saw Billy Grierson fall off the bench. Billy was a huge man, six feet four inches and well over 220 pounds. But he was probably dead before his head hit the ground. The bullet passed just over the top wooden rail of the bench he was sitting on. It made a clean entry hole just under his left shoulder blade, severed his spine and exited the right chest cavity under his arm, bruising the inside of his arm before dropping to the ground. Grierson collapsed over the spent slug.

The stunned bikies quickly loaded Billy onto the run truck and drove off to the Cawse nickel mine nine miles away. It had the nearest first-aid post. Two ambulance attendants immediately went to work trying to revive him, but it was no use. With their comrade dead, the bikies stripped off Billy's bloodied denim vest with its Gypsy Joker patch, its iron cross and Nazi swastika badges and removed his Gypsy Joker belt buckle and his boots. They then left his body on the dirt road with the attendants—there was nothing more they could do for him—and drove back to Ora Banda.

By then, the police had arrived at the scene of the shooting.

"Where's the white-haired guy, the one we'd been having trouble with this afternoon?" the bikers demanded.

Uniformed cops had already taken various statements and cordoned off the murder scene. The town was full of whispers and suspicion, with angry bikers demanding answers and, police feared, bent on revenge.

There were about forty people still in town when Billy Grierson was murdered. They were almost all miners—the holidaymakers had left by then—who had been in the beer garden behind the inn. They all had alibis. None of them could have shot Billy, so they were quickly eliminated as suspects. The problem with most of the beer garden witnesses, however, was that they were drunk. When they were interviewed they didn't have a clear recollection of what had actually occurred.

This was not the case with Rebecca and Patricia. They had been together in Rebecca's caravan. Both cooks described the tense atmosphere in the pub that day and mentioned that Elizabeth and Alison had told them Don was going to get his gun. Elizabeth had also questioned Rebecca and Alison about what they told the police.

Rebecca was shocked when Elizabeth walked into her caravan without knocking.

"What did you say to the police?" Elizabeth asked without so much as a hello.

Patricia was sitting behind Elizabeth and motioning to Rebecca not to say anything, and Rebecca muttered something inaudibly.

"What do you mean? Did you say there was an altercation?" Elizabeth asked.

"Oh, yeah. I just told them that we closed the bar early and generally what happened."

Elizabeth said, "I left the pub at 7.20 P.M. I went home and Don was having a shower. He was home all the time. I sniffed Don's guns and they didn't smell as if they'd been fired."

With that, Elizabeth left.

Rebecca thought, Why would she say that?

One of the first coppers to arrive on the scene, at about nine o'clock, was Senior Const. Dave Roper. As soon as he saw him, Gypsy Joker Spud Manson approached and pointed out a man in the beer garden as the person the Jokers believed had probably pulled the trigger.

"That's him," he said.

Roper thought, Christ, that's Don Hancock. He noted that Hancock was wearing dirty green shorts and shirt.

"My wife just told me somebody has been shot," Hancock told Roper. He appeared calm and composed.

Roper said, "Apparently so."

Hancock said, "Well, my wife said so. What do you mean 'apparently'?"

"Well, I wasn't here at the time, so I can only say apparently."

"What do you mean?"

"Mr. Hancock, I'm aware of who you are and what you used to be, so you know what I mean when I say 'apparently.'"

"It sounds as though I'm a suspect."

"At this stage everybody here is a suspect."

Hancock took a step backwards, held up his hands in surrender and said, "I'm saying nothing. You'll have to speak with my solicitor."

"You're not prepared to say anything further?" Roper asked, surprised that the former policeman was not being more cooperative.

"Nothing," Hancock said.

Roper said, "Fair enough. I will have to ask you to remain here. Do you understand?"

Hancock said, "Yes, I know the score." He walked over to the beer garden and spoke to some of the patrons.

But he didn't remain in the beer garden. Within minutes he

had quietly slipped away in his ute—a pickup truck— and driven back to his house. The police didn't notice his absence until a bikie pointed it out.

"Where's the fucking publican?" Gypsy Joker Sid Reid asked, referring to Hancock.

"He's in the pub," a cop said.

"Like fucking hell he is. He's just left."

Slater said, "Good job, mate. You've let him go."

The Jokers were furious. Many were certain that Hancock was the killer, even though it was hard to imagine that a person would kill somebody over such a minor altercation as the one between Grierson and Hancock. Still, as Reid said, "Hancock had done it and that was fucking it. . . . I watched [Hancock] going from blind rotten fucking drunk [to] flat-out standing up in the space of an hour." The bikies couldn't see him doing that without a "big adrenalin rush" and that must have come from the murder of their mate Billy Grierson. They were angry that the police had not searched Hancock's home and seized his guns. And now it appeared that the police had let him go.

Roper sensed the situation could get dangerous. He sent two constables, Justin Dwyer and Max Janse, to find Hancock. When they arrived at his house, two dogs were barking out front. So they waited a bit in their patrol car. The dogs stopped barking when Hancock and Elizabeth finally came out a few minutes later. The police noticed that Hancock had freshly showered and changed his clothes. He was wearing beige slacks, a clean shirt and shoes. His silvery hair was still wet. They also noticed that he was eating an orange. The juice was all over his fingers. Janse thought it was odd to be eating an orange at this time of night, especially after he'd been boozing all day.

Janse was angry. "You were told to wait at the inn."

"I'm home now. They can come and speak to me here."

Janse couldn't believe what he was hearing. A former senior police officer appeared to be impeding his investigation.

"We are conducting an investigation and you are hindering us."

"I don't have anything to say. You can speak to my solicitor."

"You were asked to wait at the inn while we were conducting our investigation. The demons [detectives] are coming to speak to you."

"I don't have to come with you."

Janse began reaching for his cuffs. "I will have to arrest you for hindering police."

Hancock retreated a step and tried to be chummy. "Don't be ridiculous."

But Janse was not about to back down. "You'll come back to the inn under your own steam, or I'll place you under arrest and take you back."

"This is stupid. Oh, all right. I'll just finish my orange."

Hancock walked back inside the house and returned a short time later with a flashlight. He and Elizabeth got into his ute and drove back to the hotel with Janse following in his police car. When Hancock got to the inn, one of the bikies walked over to him.

"I know you done it, you bastard," he said. He was calm but direct.

"You have to prove that," Hancock said just as calmly.

Hancock went to his office to call his lawyer in Perth. By this time Det. Senior Sgt. Kim Gage, one of the officers who had been drinking with Hancock earlier on, arrived on the scene, accompanied by Det. Noreen O'Rourke.

When he had received a call from O'Rouke that a bikie had been shot at Ora Banda, Gage had cast his mind back to that afternoon and hoped against hope that Hancock wasn't involved. But O'Rourke quickly dashed any such thought when she informed him that Hancock had had an argument earlier in the evening with the dead bikie. On the road to Ora Banda, Gage called Perth headquarters on his cell to ask for a computer check on any firearms registered to the Hancocks. He discovered they owned three .22-calibre rifles and a single-shot shotgun. So by the time he arrived back in Ora Banda and had been briefed by the other cops on the scene, he knew that Hancock was a suspect.

Gage ordered the entire town cordoned off as a crime scene. He entered Hancock's office and found him on the phone. Hancock quickly hung up. Gage started on a friendly note.

"How are you doing?"

"Good," Hancock said.

Then Gage got more to the point. "The person shot here tonight is deceased."

Hancock went grey and became fidgety and agitated. The sudden change startled Gage. He also noticed that Elizabeth Hancock, who was in the room, began to shake and her hands trembled. He decided he would try to talk to her later, when Hancock wasn't around to influence her answers. From the way they were eyeing each other, Gage got the impression that they had already discussed their stories. He had been told about Hancock showering and changing his clothes and about the orange. As far as he was concerned, Hancock was in a lot of trouble

"What happened here tonight?" he asked.

"I'm not saying anything until I speak to my solicitor," Hancock replied.

Gage tried to question him further, but Hancock just waved him off. He then asked Hancock if police could take his firearms. Hancock readily agreed, so Gage sent Janse and Roper back to the house to seize the firearms. Hancock led them to his house. Janse used the opportunity to see if he could find Hancock's discarded work clothes—the dirty green shorts and shirt and the brown boots. He had a quick look through. "I didn't have a really good look," Janse said. "The reason I didn't was because we didn't have a warrant, so I thought if it's a chance discovery, then it's good and if it's not a chance discovery, then the evidence would be useless."

With Hancock out of the picture, Gage tried to question Elizabeth. He didn't get far with her, either.

Ignoring his questions, she asked, "Do they think it was Don?"

Who "they" were was not clear.

"Yes, I believe so," Gage said.

"It couldn't be him. He was at home."

"What time was this?"

"I went home about 7.30 P.M., and he was watching the closing of the Olympics. About ten minutes later he got up and had a shower."

It was a crude lie. Elizabeth knew it; so did Gage. As Gage questioned her further, she became incoherent, and he frequently had to repeat himself because he couldn't understand her answers. He told her he wanted a detailed statement, but she said that she would have to discuss it with Don. When Hancock returned, having handed over his .22s and his shotgun, he immediately told his wife she didn't have to give a statement, so she declined.

Gage decided he didn't have enough evidence to obtain a warrant to search Hancock's house for the clothes or any other guns. It would prove to be a fatal error. And not the last one. None of the detectives ever pressured Hancock to hand over his clothes. Nor did they ask him what he had done with them. The clothes were crucial to the investigation, because if Hancock had pulled the trigger, his clothes would likely have gunshot residue from the blowback of the gunpowder used to fire the bullet. Hancock agreed to have swabs taken of his hands, but that was after he had showered. Any residue would likely have been washed off by then.

What's more, word got around that he had been eating an orange. Rumour had it that the citric acid in the orange would help destroy or disguise gunshot residue. It wasn't true, but the bikies believed it. And they believed it was further evidence of his guilt. And further evidence that the police were not doing their jobs. Why didn't the police just search his house as they had done so often to the bikies? Police thought nothing of stopping and searching bikies on the highway whenever they pleased. They didn't seem to need a warrant for that. Clearly Hancock was getting special treatment because he was an ex-cop. No one seemed to be seriously looking for the missing clothes. No one had even asked Hancock what he had done with them, or if he would retrieve them for the police. And it didn't help that both Gage and Gartlan had been seen drinking with Hancock that afternoon.

Gage decided there was nothing more he could do. It was too dark to search for the weapon or conduct basic forensic examinations of the crime scene, so he ordered his team back to

Kalgoorlie, leaving behind a couple of constables to guard the town. What the police were now calling Operation Sandalwood, after the aromatic trees common to the area, was put to bed for the night.

Even though Gage regarded Hancock as his chief suspect and had declared the entire town a crime scene, he allowed Hancock to return home and retain the keys to all his buildings. Police consider the first forty-eight hours of a murder investigation as crucial to its success. They had eaten up four hours, and the situation had already turned into a debacle. The consequences would be tragic.

Gage returned to Ora Banda the next morning at eight. Even though the bikies had remained fairly calm and showed no signs of aggression, Gage feared the situation was too dangerous for the Hancocks. Gage suggested that Hancock immediately return to his suburban home in Perth, and by 11 A.M. the chief murder suspect and his family had disappeared down the Great Eastern Highway, protected by two constables in a police patrol car.

Gage had given Det. Noreen O'Rourke the difficult task of communicating with the bikies. She had had to persuade them to hand over the jacket and colours they had stripped off Grierson's dead body. She promised to return them after a forensic examination, which was slightly unusual since police would want to keep them for a trial, if there ever was one. She also succeeded in getting statements out of Slim Slater and Spud Manson, the two most senior members of the Jokers' Kalgoorlie chapter. This was in and of itself a coup. The Gypsy Jokers' number-one rule is never to talk to the police. The two bikies refused to sign the statements, but at least police had something to go on.

Now she wanted further statements, but Slater said she would have to wait until he got permission from his Joker leaders. Next morning O'Rourke got an earful of the bikies' volatile temperament. Slater called her and asked to meet in front of the police station. Ten minutes later he drove up to the station with Manson. Both men got out of the car. Manson sat on the hood as Slater marched over to O'Rourke. She immediately realized that Slater's formerly polite demeanour had changed for the worse. "He was very angry, very agitated, aggressive toward me," she said.

The Gypsy Joker launched at the cop, swearing and yelling, demanding to know why Hancock hadn't been arrested.

The investigation was still continuing, O'Rourke tried to say.

"Fuck you and your ways!" retorted the furious biker. "I'm going to take care of it my way."

He got back in his car and they drove off. The Jokers never spoke to the police again. War had been declared.

It was into this hostile setting that Det. Jack Lee from the Criminal Investigations Branch arrived.

Lee didn't mess around. He quickly told Det. Kim Gage that he was off the case. "It was a conflict of interest. He was there during the afternoon. He was a material witness. There was no way in the world he could be seen to be bringing an objective viewpoint."

In fact, after the initial briefing at the police station in Kalgoorlie, poring over police notes and witness statements, Lee was convinced that Hancock was his man. It wasn't so much the altercation in the pub—that seemed piddling to him. Nor was it the missing clothing, the shower, the talk of guns, the drinking and lack of cooperation. Certainly they all played a part, but it was more something Elizabeth had said that convinced Lee of Hancock's guilt.

Elizabeth had told the police that she had heard the shots while watching the closing ceremony of the Olympics with her husband. Worried about her daughter, she went to see her, at Alison's bungalow near the inn.

Lee knew that last part was true—Alison confirmed that her mother had come to check on her. But it made no sense that Don Hancock would let his wife wander about a town filled with bikies to check on a shooting.

"It's wrong," Lee says. "It doesn't happen. It's not police behaviour. A copper doesn't send his wife to see if his daughter's been shot."

That could only mean Don Hancock was not at home when

the shots rang out. "Don Hancock killed Billy Grierson," Lee concluded. "That's what I believe."

But he soon realized that unless he could get Hancock to confess, he would probably never prove it. The investigation was now riddled with missed opportunities.

Police did find two high-calibre slugs near the bonfire. Forensics showed from the weight of the lead that they were probably from a .303. But some of the lead had been fragmented, so it could have been a .308 or a .310. Lee believed the gun was probably an unregistered First or Second World War .303. The old army stock issue, bolt action, holds a clip of five rounds. Not easily available but not uncommon in this bush setting.

An examination of the path of the bullet through Grierson's body indicated that the shot came from the top of a small incline about a thousand feet away and not far from Don Hancock's house and the battery. But where was the gun?

For the next ten days, Lee's team combed the desert for miles around but found nothing. Nothing except prospectors' drill holes. Drill holes riddle the desert around Ora Banda, spaced about every 350 feet, often more than 1300 feet deep and filled with groundwater. Few people knew the location of those holes better than Don Hancock; his family probably sank many of them. Lee figured that the missing firearm lay at the bottom of a drill hole. He tried plumbing a few but quickly realized it was an impossible task. Between the time of the murder and the time the police arrived, the killer had had ample opportunity to drive far into the desert and slip the gun into oblivion.

Lee began to paint a picture in his mind of what had happened: Hancock was fearful of a bikie invasion of his town, furious at their arrogant behaviour on his holy sports grounds and in his own pub. He wandered around the bush in an alcoholic rage and shot his .303 rifle into the bikie camp to scare them off. Whether he meant to kill Billy Grierson or not didn't really matter. Lee preferred to believe he didn't mean to kill anybody. He reasoned that from about a thousand feet shooting from pitch-dark into the distant light of a bonfire and floodlight, Hancock would have had to be a hell of a good shot. And he was pretty smashed, which would have made the shot even harder to nail. Whether it was aimed or an accident didn't really matter. It was still murder. What worried Lee now was his strong belief that unless he was able to bring Hancock to justice, the violence would not end with Billy Grierson.

But by Friday, October 13, Lee figured he had done all he could do. The bikies had buried their murdered colleague under a simple wooden cross in Kalgoorlie cemetery. A hundred and eighty bikies came from all over Australia to ride in the procession through the mining town in what looked more like a show of force than a funeral march. Police received numerous threats of retribution and tightened security at their stations. Nothing happened. The bikies dispersed as quickly as they had arrived. Everything seemed to return to small-town normality.

Lee left that afternoon, driving down the gravel road with a fistful of alibis for the thirty-eight people who were in Ora Banda that evening. All except Don and Elizabeth Hancock, who refused to give statements. Overnight, Ora Banda had become a ghost town. A few residents stayed on to look after the buildings for Hancock, but most had fled or simply moved on, fearful of repercussions. Afraid of the bikies.

And they were wise to be afraid. That night, the desert silence was again shattered. Don Hancock's Ora Banda Historical Inn was bombed. It was the first act of what would be a long, creeping vengeance.

The Gypsy Jokers were embarking on a well-trodden road to hell that other bikies in the country had already taken. Because almost two decades before the Gypsy Jokers began plotting revenge against Don Hancock, the Hells Angels had already paved the way for a violent bikie culture in Australia.

And killing cops was considered fair game.

FIVE

The Original Speed King

———

Yea, though I walk through the valley of death I fear no evil because
I am the evilest mother fucker who ever walked through the Valley.
—TATTOO ON THE ARM OF THE AUSTRALIAN HELLS ANGEL
PETER JOHN HILL

Obsession.

That was always a danger. The bikies had a tendency to get under a cop's skin. They could be so up front and in your face about their criminality, just challenging you to do something about it. Fight them. Arrest them. They didn't give a fuck.

That's what worried Sgt. Bob Armstrong. Letting the bastards get to you. This time he was convinced that Peter John Hill and his Melbourne Hells Angels wanted to kill him. Worse thing was he knew there was not much he could do about it. He just had to let the game play out. Hope it went his way. It was August 1982.

If Armstrong had learned anything from tracking the Melbourne Angels, it was that Hill was a special guy. Different from the rest. A little less predictable.

That was because he had a business side to him. A marked efficiency and management capacity. Not all that common in a bikie. But then Hill didn't have the usual bikie pedigree. He wasn't a high-school dropout from a low-income background. He was a rich private-school kid from upper-class Melbourne whose father, Roger, was a senior bank executive with one of Australia's largest financial institutions— the ANZ (Australia New Zealand Bank)— and whose mother, Audrey, was a housewife and socialite. What got Hill interested was a passion for motorcycles. What kept him interested was the beginning of a business that would be embraced by almost every bikie gang in Australia and New Zealand, flooding Oceania with the white powder of speed (or "crank," as they called it) to the same degree that North America and Europe were flooded with cocaine.

Hill emerged at a time when Australia's underworld was dominated by a host of unruly crooks of Italian or Irish descent, who wore shiny suits and bad ties and hung around nightclubs and cafés. Leather, motorcycles and sweat were not part of their criminal scene. Hill helped change all that. He embraced the American outlaw subculture and made it the dominant business force in Australia's underbelly. Through him and his mates, the Hells Angels set the trends and established the rules of this new-look underworld.

Hill crowned himself the country's original speed king, the real Thunderdome road warrior.

"It was party time," Hill recalls in an interview. "Parties, women, bikes, fast cars, all the good things in life when you are young. Live for the moment. I did that for fourteen years. It was a big slice of my life. It was a lot of fun. I thought so at the time, anyway."

Hill became one of the original members of the Melbourne Hells Angels in 1972 when he was nineteen, patching over from a small homegrown gang called the Phantoms. A Hells Angels club photo taken several years later shows him standing tall and lean in the back row with long, black curly hair, a narrow face, determined eyes, a straight but slightly off-centre nose and a small mouth with a hint of a smile. He's aged since then, lost some hair, but otherwise hasn't changed much. Still is a bit of the party animal.

In heavy black ink he'd had tattooed on his arm his personal version of Psalm 23: "Yea, though I walk through the valley of the shadow of death I fear no evil because I am the evilest mother fucker who ever walked through the Valley."

That was Hill trying to be tough. More of a joke than anything. Hill was like that; he took everything in stride, or at least tried to. When a cop raided his house one Christmas day, seizing $10,000 and a packet of speed, he didn't bark or sneer at him like other bikers. He invited him for tea.

But there was a deadly serious side to Hill. It was his vision that brought speed to Australia and initiated its meteoric ride up the drug charts to number one in the country there and in New Zealand.

"The Hells Angels wanted to become the dominant club in Australia, which created a lot of animosity and resentment," he recalls as he takes a break from his fruit farm. "We had a strategy for expansion. It was a desire to control the drug business. We set up a structure to sell all over Australia, and get other clubs to distribute it on the street."

Bob Armstrong was getting in the way of Hill's big plans. The Melbourne sergeant had been investigating the Hells Angels since 1977 and had grown accustomed to their threats. "There had been numerous threats. They range from 'We're going to land a plane on your station; we're going to drop a bomb,' to 'We're gonna kill Bob Armstrong and his team of bloody detectives. . . .' If you let them get to you it'll drive you mad. So you just got to learn to deal with it. You carry a gun and you learn to handle it."

There's nothing particularly imposing about Bob Armstrong. He's medium height and reasonably muscular but nothing over the top. He has a round, ruddy face and a slightly mischievous, boyish smile. People claim he looks like the comedian Benny Hill. There's a bit of Benny in him, no doubt, but not much. His eyes are too direct and too tough. He was born on a dairy farm in the green, rolling country near Gippsland, up on the Victoria–New South Wales border. After he graduated from high school, he kicked around the lumber business, performing menial jobs. Not interested in farming. "Then in 1967 I was putting down a couple of beers with a mate and said, 'Let's join the cops.' People always ask you 'Why did you join the cops?' No real reason."

Almost from the moment he obtained his detective shield in 1975, Armstrong's life seemed inextricably linked to Hill's in a sort of perilous dance. In the early 1970s, the Hells were just getting started. The police didn't know much about them, and Armstrong knew almost nothing. Until, that is, he raided the home of Roger "Rebel" Pexa, treasurer of the Melbourne chapter.

He found a long list of firearms—.38s, .45s, .357s—and next to each gun was a nickname: Ball Bearing, Pug, Rye and others.

"They're into drugs, they're into guns—who are this mob?" Armstrong asked.

He made a few inquiries, took out a few warrants, kicked in a few doors and found some guns, phony licences, stolen jewellery and some marijuana plants. Nothing unusual in terms of seizure. But he also found a recipe: *Speed Made Easy: How to manufacture amphetamines.* He took it to his drug experts and they said, "Oh geez, we haven't found this before." More raids revealed some primitive speed labs in the back laundries of Hells Angels' homes: an old washing machine, a few pipes and hoses and a few glass jars, nothing sophisticated. Then Armstrong went on TV and talked about how the Hells Angels were into gunrunning and a new drug called speed.

The Hells Angels sued him for defamation. Even though they later dropped the suit—their lawyers told them they had no character or reputation to defame—it pissed off Armstrong: "That got up my nose. That's where it started."

What Armstrong didn't know at the time was that Peter Hill was determined to turn the amphetamine business into a sophisticated money-maker. He'd made several visits during the late 1970s to the Hells Angels mother chapter in California, right at the time when the boys in Oakland were becoming expert meth manufacturers. The former Shell Oil chemist Kenny "Old Man" Maxwell had passed on his skills to three Oakland Angels in particular: James Patton "Jim-Jim" Brandes, chapter president Sergei "Sir Gay" Walton and Kenny "KO" Owen, all of them close to Sonny Barger. Owen, the Angel whom FBI agent Tim McKinley had under surveillance for such a long time and would eventually bust, was by far the most prodigious cook. Owen had developed an expertise in manufacturing amphetamines using methylamine mixed with phenyl-2-propanone (P2P) and methanol in a reactor vessel. He added tinfoil, cooked it to 134 degrees Fahrenheit, cooled it and then refined the resultant grey sludge using caustic soda, hydrochloric acid and acetone to extract and crystallize the meth. (The result is not to be confused with pure crystal meth or "ice," the highly addictive modern form of speed that's smoked to give an immediate and lasting rush.) It was a fairly sophisticated process that required careful handling. Carelessness could cause the reaction vessel to overheat and explode.

Peter Hill's visit was well timed. The California Angels needed money for the defence fund, and Hill's Melbourne chapter could help. These were wild times for Barger's Angels. They were under assault from the federal government. Barger, Brandes, Owen, Walton and the Hells Angels as an organization were awaiting trial on racketeering RICO charges—a case that would eventually collapse in disaster.

Hill became good friends with Jim-Jim Brandes, who organized a visit between Hill and Walton, who was in prison on weapons charges. Walton described the equipment and chemical ingredients, how to set up the laboratory, amounts and combinations of chemicals, cooking, heating and refining. It was all very detailed and a lot to remember. Prison rules forbade pens or pencils. When Hill left, he quickly scribbled it down in his own personal shorthand onto three pieces of paper and flew back to Melbourne. Walton escaped days before he was to be transferred to a federal prison in Texarkana, Texas. He was recaptured two months later, but not before he had mailed a more complete recipe to Hill.

In return for the recipe, Hill agreed to ship P2P, which was illegal in the U.S. but not in Australia, to the Oakland chapter. "It's an example of one of things that makes the Hells Angels so powerful: their international capabilities," says Tim McKinley.

The Aussie bikers shipped the chemical in three-litre Golden Circle pineapple cans, piercing the side of each tin with two small holes, draining the juice and refilling the can with P2P. They then soldered shut the holes and glued the labels back on. From 1980 to 1982, they shipped three hundred litres to the U.S. by surface mail (two cans a shipment)—enough to manufacture about US$50 million worth of speed. Melbourne received no payment for the P2P. The shipments were simply the chapter's contribution to the defence fund for the California RICO cases against the Angels.

"The recipe from the United States was the actual starting point, and it was a matter of teaching ourselves how to use the various chemicals involved," Hill says, paying tribute to the California HA biker, Sergei Walton. "He was the only one who knew how to do it."

When Hill got back to Melbourne, he sat down with three other Hells Angels—Ray Hamment, John Madden and Roger "Root Rat" Biddlestone—to set up a business plan. They were nothing if not precise, calculating the exact size of the glass vessels they needed to cook the meth, whether they had to be at angles or straight up and down. "We'd draw up a design of the glassware we needed and then we'd have a glass blower make them," Hill says.

With startup capital of $15,000 from the proceeds of stolen motorcycles, in late 1980 they began a trial-and-error process of making speed. Most of the effort was in increasing the yield. The P2P and other chemicals were imported from the Calaire Chemical Company in Calais, France, with the help of an uncle of Hells Angels Terry "Pop" Faulkner, who had an import licence. Hamment was put in charge of distribution through the Hells chapters and associate chapters, and Hill, Madden and Biddlestone would oversee the manufacturing.

These four bikies essentially represented the Hells Angels front-line troops in Australia. Profits from the drugs were divided equally, while Faulkner was paid a commission—usually in speed—for procuring the chemicals. (From the beginning, Faulkner overcharged his partners, but they did not find out until it was too late.) They also gave money to the Hells Angels Melbourne chapter, financing its expansion and allowing the club to buy property and put on some of the city's largest rock concerts. "Without the cover of the club, we wouldn't have been able to do it and distribute it," Hill says. "Without the club, it would have been a lot more difficult."

The Angels initially rented a house in Belgrave, a semi-urban suburb east of Melbourne, but quickly ran into the lingering problem with speed labs: the long-lasting and distinctive sweet, sometimes rosy, smell of cooked methamphetamine. It attracts too much attention. So they rented a property called Greenslopes, thirty miles outside Melbourne in Wattle Glen, an area of bush, hills and cows. They paid the landlord twice what he asked, and he asked no questions. The property had a large house plus a small bungalow concealed from the road, ideal for their lab. They covered the windows with black plastic, sealed the doors and installed air conditioners and fans. The fumes from the manufacturing process were so toxic that they ate the chrome off the fans. The Angel cooks had to wear gas masks.

But it wasn't long before they could cook up five pounds of speed in twenty-four hours. They initially sold it for AD$10,000 a pound on the wholesale market. But demand quickly grew and they jacked up their prices to $12,000. They also increased the size of their reactor vessel from five to twenty litres, allowing them to make four times as much speed. Eventually, they cut the purity with white sugar from 66 to 50 percent—"out of greed," says Hill—substantially boosting their profits.

The bikies shipped their speed in powder form to HA chapters in Sydney, Adelaide and Brisbane, and to allied clubs in Western Australia, including the Gypsy Jokers. As the Angels worked to expand their markets, the cash rolled in. "There wasn't anybody else in the market," Hill says. "Fucking hell! Customers were our last worry. We had more customers than we could supply. Of course we tried to stop anybody else doing it."

By 1982 they had perfected the process to produce 100 percent yield. This meant that their twenty-litre reactor vessel produced 4.5 to 5.5 kilos of pure speed in twenty-four hours. After expenses, which included a cut to the HA club, those 4.5 to 5.5 kilos would yield profits of $70,000 to $100,000 for the four main partners. Not bad for a day's work.

"We sort of spent it as fast as we got it on our lifestyle," Hill said. They bought property, cars and motorcycles. Unfortunately,

Hill and the other Angels were also snorting large quantities of their own product and giving away speed to other Hells Angels. Soon the entire club was on speed. As they tried to turn a nation on to methamphetamines, they were already riding the knife's edge. And they began making plans for an even bigger operation. They ordered a 100-litre reactor vessel and started looking for a new location. What they didn't realize was that their high times were about to end. Bob Armstrong was patiently watching and listening.

Sergeant Armstrong and his detectives discovered the Hells Angels Greenslopes lab in late 1981 more or less by accident. An alert area resident reported a suspicious car to the local police. Armstrong was working bikie intelligence and had tagged all the Hells Angels as an "alert" on his computer. This meant that every time a policeman ran a search on an Angel or on his vehicle, it rang bells on Armstrong's computer. Armstrong phoned the cop who had filed the report, and then decided to check it out himself. So he drove up to Wattle Glen. When he spotted Hill and his crew, he knew he was on to something. He waited for the bikies to leave, sneaked into the bungalow and was astonished to find such a complex operation.

Hill had installed a voice-activated tape recorder to detect an unauthorized entry, but he had forgotten to turn it on. Armstrong turned the tables on the Angel leader, bugging Hill's cottage for six weeks, listening from a vacant house nearby and often observing from an even closer white van. When he finally raided Greenslopes at 6 P.M. on March 10, 1982, he found a machine gun that could shoot seven hundred rounds a minute, $18,000 in cash, three kilos of newly refined speed and two pistols smuggled from the American Angels. To their horror, police also stumbled across sixteen sticks of gelignite and more than thirty electric detonators hidden in the cottage; it brought home the dangerous game they were playing. The radio frequency of the transmitters, which were concealed in the cottage roof, could have set off the detonators and blown the entire lab to hell.

Armstrong finally had enough to bust Peter Hill and his partners. The arrests at first appeared to be a major setback for the
Australian Angels. Hill's factory was the only major speed lab in
the country, and the Hells Angels had big expansion plans. His
partners also knew the secrets of cooking speed, but Hill was the
chief chef. He was the speed king. He was the man who brought
speed to Australia from America, and within two years made it the
drug of choice.

No other Australian Angel knew how to cook it as well as Hill
did. Indeed, outside his Greenslopes parternship of four bikies, no
Hells Angels in the country knew how to manufacture speed at all.
Hill and his partners had a monopoly and were damned if they
were going to share their secret with anybody. They possessed the
technical know-how and were the guardians of the three-page
recipe from the Americans.

With the Greenslopes speed lab out of commission, the HA's
money source was in danger of drying up. But as things turned out,
the problem was quickly solved. Within a day of their arrests, all
four members of Hill's speed team made the $20,000 bail. Two days
later, they returned to Greenslopes where, unknown to the police,
they dug up one kilo of speed buried on the property. They then
opened another, smaller, lab about seventy miles west of Melbourne
outside the gold mining city of Ballarat. The Angels had manufac-
tured about $1.8 million worth of speed in Greenslopes; they hoped
Ballarat would become their new Eldorado.

When the trial started, Hill and his crew were working in the
Ballarat lab at night and driving to Melbourne in the morning. It
was no picnic, and they often fell asleep in the courtroom, despite a
heavy intake of their own speed. But the game was on and they were
soon making more money from Ballarat than ever before.

Yet, to keep the cash flowing, they had to beat the charges. If
desperate times call for desperate measures, the Hells Angels went
all out.

One day, Armstrong got a call from Hill's mother, Audrey.

"Look, I think you should be careful," she said.

"Why?"

"You better be careful. I think Peter is going to try and kill you."

"What makes you say that?"

"What I've heard is there's some bloke coming from America. He's called the Assassin and Peter has hired him to come in and kill you."

"Thanks for that," Armstrong said and hung up.

Australian federal police had started Project Wing Clipping to gather intelligence on bikie gangs, primarily the Hells Angels. So Armstrong called them up and asked if they could check out a bikie nicknamed "the Assassin." They quickly called back.

"'Guess what. We've found one whose nickname is the Assassin."

"Who is he?"

"His name is James Patton Brandes. Named after General Patton."

Brandes. The same Oakland Angel who was Hill's closest American friend. The same biker to whom he used to send the pineapple cans of P2P. Armstrong didn't know about Brandes's ties to Hill at the time, but what he did find out spelled trouble: "And by the way," the cop told Armstrong before hanging up, "he's applied for a visa to come to Australia."

Armstrong couldn't ignore this. Further checks showed that Brandes had recently been acquitted on charges that he had murdered a biker and—more worrisome from Armstrong's point of view—had attempted to kill two police officers. San Jose Police sergeant John Kracht had once arrested Brandes and soon afterwards was himself injured by a bomb. The second cop was California Bureau of Narcotics enforcement inspector William Zerby. Zerby had also "locked horns" with Brandes, as Sonny Barger put it in his autobiography. Aware of threats against his life, Zerby was in the habit of checking his car each morning for explosives. On the day he was supposed to testify against Brandes in county court, Zerby stepped back to look under the car and trod on a pressure pad, triggering a bomb that severely crippled him.

The news unnerved Armstrong. He approached his senior

commanders about clamping twenty-four-hour surveillance on Brandes when he arrived in Australia. Maybe catch him in the act. The bosses weren't keen on that idea. It would consume too many resources. And what if they lost Brandes? They were still contemplating that possibility when the phone rang.

"Bob, he's got his visa," an agent from Project Wing Clipping said. "He's landed in Australia, and he's sitting here in Melbourne Airport."

Armstrong decided it was time to meet his assassin.

It was August 26, 1982, and customs had Brandes locked in a holding cell. In his luggage, police found news clippings of his murder cases, transcripts of his trials, a pair of thumb screws, a bug detector and a copy of the U.S. Treasury Department's forensic handbook, with passages highlighted about how to take fingerprints off metal. Plus a description of Bob Armstrong. What was most surprising for Australian and later U.S. police was what they found in Brandes's notebook. He had scribbled onto one page high-level computer access codes that allowed the Hells Angels to tap into secret U.S. Justice Department files on outlaw biker investigations. "That scared the hell out of them," Armstrong says.

The customs officers were still wondering whether they could legally bar him from entering the country when Armstrong and his detectives walked in. "We didn't tell him who we were," Armstrong recalls. "We didn't have to. He knew. He just looked at me and said, 'Shit, you look like Benny Hill.'"

"I shouldn't really be here," Brandes said to no one in particular. Armstrong didn't reply. Didn't say anything to his would-be assassin. Just stared at him like an animal in a cage. "I should have stayed in California," Brandes continued. "I should have flown my plane down to Texas and Arizona. I should have been doing that this weekend."

Armstrong figured there was no point in interviewing him. "You could tell he was a hard nut. He wasn't going to give you the time of day. You just were not going to get anywhere at all with him."

Further checks revealed that Brandes had failed to mention his prior convictions for gunrunning and drug dealing when he applied for his visa. So authorities cancelled his visa and the next day they put the Assassin on a flight back to America.

"I used to go and see Audrey every once in a while and thank her very much," Armstrong said of Hill's mother. "I have a bottle of wine with her at Christmastime. Thanks for the advice you gave me."

To this day Hill denies he hired Brandes to kill Armstrong. So who was the guy caught trying to enter the country with thumb-screws and a description of Armstrong? "Oh, he was just a friend of mine." A possible explanation is that Hill told his mother about Brandes. At the time, the two were estranged, but Audrey tried to keep in touch because she was worried about her two grandchildren. So she probably overheard Hill mention the name, the Assassin. Perhaps he did it on purpose, hoping she would warn Armstrong. All Hill will say about his parents is that they were "far from impressed" with his career path.

Back in the courthouse, Hill and his Angels had other tricks up their sleeves if outright assassination wasn't going to work. They concocted elaborate stories to justify their lab. Their defence lawyers dug up an eccentric chemist from England named Colin Fleet, who tried to convince the court the Angels were simply manufacturing racing fuel additives and polymers for plastics in their lab.

The eager English chemist proved to be more expert than the Angels could have imagined. Hill was so pleased with Fleet that he invited him to help with the Ballarat lab. Fleet perfected Hill's work by reducing the odour produced in the manufacturing process, thus allowing smaller labs to produce large quantities without fear of detection from the smell. But Fleet himself became a problem. He grew addicted to speed and began suffer-ing paranoid delusions. He eventually committed suicide.

The Hells Angels were far from crazy when it came to trial tac-tics. They showed up at the trial of Hill and his mates in full colours. They always sat at the front of the courtroom staring at the jury, in an obvious attempt to intimidate. Hill's trial took four months and ended in a hung jury. As Hill later revealed, they bribed one of the jurors with a suitcase full of money.

In 1983 a judge aborted a second trial when a book was published containing evidence that had not been presented to the jury. John Peter Hill and his Angels appeared to be riding high, operating their Ballarat production facility and churning out meth and profits. But the Angels were facing renewed threats to their empire—and they came from within.

Armstrong and his detectives had been playing a heavy psychological game that convinced the Hells Angels that there was a mole in their ranks. Whenever Armstrong found drugs or guns during a search of a Hells Angel's home or clubhouse he'd make sure they heard him mumble to a colleague, "That was good information that bloke gave us."

That prompted Hill and his speed team to go on a witch hunt. Certain that somebody in the club had squealed, they forced all the members to fill out a psychological questionnaire and read their answers into a tape recorder. The tape was sent to the Angels in Oakland, who hired a voice stress analysis expert. They never found the informer, because there wasn't one.

But they cleaned house anyway. Five members were kicked out of the club. One member was thrown out because he couldn't read or write. A member from the Nomad chapter was severely beaten because he had warned a fellow Angel that he was suspected of talking to the police.

At the same time, they were trying to clean up their public image. They started a Christmas Toy Run for children, another tactic they learned from Oakland.

The Angels also had to contend with outside enemies. Other clubs were hankering to get into the meth business, including an American club that would prove to be the Hells Angels' greatest and most vicious adversary—the Bandidos.

William "Jock" Ross was a transplanted Scotsman from Glasgow who had served for six years in the Royal Engineers and had disturbing visions of running his own private army out of Sydney, Australia. Like Hill, he was crazy about motorcycles and thought of starting his own gang. One day in 1973 he was watching an old

John Wayne western on TV called *The Comancheros*. He thought it was a great name and took it for his club.

The Comancheros were not like most other bikie clubs. Ross appointed himself the "Supreme Commander" and demanded that members swear allegiance to both him and the club. He hung a Nazi flag in the clubhouse. That in itself wasn't unusual for bikie gangs; swastikas decorate the clubhouses and jackets of bike gangs the world over, including the Gypsy Jokers. What was unusual was that Ross drilled his troops like a parade ground sergeant, marching his men around the clubhouse yard and practicing mock attacks on rival clubs. His Comancheros were constantly at war with other Sydney bikie gangs, and he plotted his attacks with military precision. He even formed an elite attack unit, which he called his Strike Force.

By 1983 he had forty full-patch members in two chapters in Sydney. Still, some members had grown tired of Jock's imperious ways. As one of the Comancheros said, "If I wanted to march around the fuckin' backyard, I would have joined the fuckin' army." In 1984, Anthony Mark "Snodgrass/Snoddy" Spencer and another dissident Comanchero flew to the United States on a mission to buy Harley-Davidson parts, still relatively scarce in Australia. It was no accident that they travelled to Albuquerque, New Mexico, where they met up with Ronnie Hodge, president of the Bandidos Motorcycle Club.

The Texas-based gang had been started in 1966 by an ex-Marine who named the club after the fat Mexican cartoon rascal Frito Bandito, used to sell corn chips. But there was nothing comic about the Bandidos. The FBI was investigating them for the murders of a federal judge and an assistant U.S. attorney in San Antonio, Texas, as well as a police officer in Louisiana. There was also an investigation into the Bandidos' connections with a Montreal gang of drug traffickers, gunrunning into wartorn Lebanon and a plot to murder a Lebanese politician. The Bandidos had twenty-eight chapters in the U.S., more than living up to their motto, "Fuck the World—We are the people our parents warned us about."

Snoddy couldn't care less about these investigations. What interested him was that the Bandidos specialized in exporting stolen and used bike parts and were eager to open a supply line to Australia. They had also started secret laboratories for manufacturing speed. Hodge suggested that the Comancheros patch over to the Bandidos and supply the U.S. club with the base chemicals, primarily methylamine and P2P, just as the Angels were doing. In return, the Bandidos would teach their Aussie brethren how to cook crank.

Snoddy jumped at the chance and quickly convinced his mates back in Sydney of the wisdom of joining the Bandidos and ridding themselves of Jock Ross's military obsessions. It wasn't a hard sell. The Aussie Angels were making millions of dollars trafficking in speed. Snoddy saw an opportunity to break into their market with the full force of the American Bandidos as backup.

The Comancheros' Supreme Commander, however, didn't let this treachery go unpunished and picked a crowded bike rally on Australia's Father's Day in early September to strike back.

The British Motor Cycle Club, one of the country's many popular clubs of weekend riders, had organized a Father's Day swap meet for Sunday afternoon, September 2, 1984, in the parking lot of the Viking Tavern, a barn-like building in Milperra, a Sydney suburb. Here bikers and the outlaw bikies came together to exchange and buy motorcycle parts, trinkets and memorabilia amid barbecue picnics and ample amounts of booze.

Ross knew the Bandidos would be there. He armed his troops with shotguns, rifles, knives and baseball bats and set up one of his vintage ambushes. As members of the public innocently roasted a lamb on a spit, the Bandidos arrived and all hell broke loose. Ross hadn't expected the Bandidos to be so heavily armed. The tavern parking lot was soon a war zone.

When the guns finally fell silent, six bikies were dead. And so was a fifteen-year-old girl, a misguided bikie groupie who had been caught in the crossfire. Many more were wounded. Thirty-one bikies were convicted of murder or manslaughter. A despairing Snodgrass, his dream of leading the Bandidos' invasion of

Australia destroyed, hanged himself in Parklea Maximum Security Prison near Sydney while awaiting his murder trial. Another desperate bikie named "Flash" spent three days building a guillotine at his home and chopped off his own head. Jock Ross was shot in the head during the shootout but survived. He was given a life sentence.

The killings were front-page news, and editorials blamed police and called for tougher laws to stop the bikie violence. Yet the outcry had little effect; nor did Snoddy's and Flash's deaths or Ross's imprisonment. None of it spelled the end of the Comancheros or the Bandidos or bikie subculture in general. Despite a massive police crackdown, the Bandidos gradually expanded into every major urban centre in the country. It was as if the bad publicity from the massacre had given them new life.

The Comancheros endured the absence of their leader. Despite his life sentence and an ugly head wound, Jock Ross was not about to let his creation die. He served out his sentence and, after his release in the early 1990s, reclaimed his old position as supreme commander, although in a much more tranquil setting. He lives with his family in the countryside outside Sydney.

The Father's Day Massacre did give the Hells Angels some breathing room. Their policy had been to take immediate and violent action against local clubs that started their own speed labs, burning down rival clubhouses and bashing their members. With support from America, the Bandidos would have proved a far more difficult adversary. But the massacre delayed the Bandidos' invasion of Australia. Peter Hill's biggest problems, however, weren't coming from outside clubs. They were coming from within the Hells Angels themselves. Success had bred distrust and jealousy in the membership.

Old resentments were beginning to surface within the Melbourne chapter. Angels outside Hill's immediate circle grew envious of the large sums of money Hill and his crew were making and the power it gave them. They wanted a bigger share for the club. They wanted a bigger share for themselves. And they were bitter over increased police surveillance, raids and arrests, even though they weren't directly involved in Hill's business. What's more, Hill's and Roger Biddlestone's lax attendance record at club meetings angered some members, who talked of expelling them. Members also discovered that Hill and Biddlestone were using a rival club called the Black Uhlans to distribute their speed.

Distribution networks had grown massively. Speed was now often sold at major truck stops. Long-haul truckers discovered that a bit of crank kept them awake. The truckers blew the market wide open by helping to spread Hill's product throughout the country. "It was jealousy that was the big problem," Hill says of the malcontents within his club.

But an even bigger problem for Hill came from one of his own partners. Ray Hamment had been stealing profits. Money was missing from the sale of methylamphetamine that Ray couldn't explain. "Roger and meself weren't happy with his explanation," Hill says. "Things were just getting a little bit greedy." Then after the raid on Greenslopes, Hamment made off with about 100 litres of P2P the police had not seized, intending to start a rival speed lab. That amount could make him almost 100 kilos of speed, valued at the top end at $2.4 million wholesale. Hill and Biddlestone wanted it back.

Hamment and his brother, however, who had recently joined the Melbourne chapter, skilfully managed to turn other Angels against them, triggering a palace coup aimed at the king of speed. The timing was perfect. The king's power had been slipping. Until then, Hill had relied on his friend John Madden, the Melbourne chapter's sergeant-at-arms, to keep the dissidents in check, but in 1985 Madden was killed in a motorcycle accident. His death isolated Hill and Biddlestone.

The last straw was the discovery of the Ballarat operation. Hill had tried to keep it secret, not just from the police but from some younger members of the club as well. Since the Greenslopes arrests, Hill had increased the security measures. That's one reason Armstrong hadn't found their new lab, until one day in 1985 when two police detectives were in Ballarat checking into a motel and saw Hill's and Biddlestone's names on the registry. Surveillance led police to the Ballarat lab, and Hill was again busted. Police then came down hard on other members of the club. Hamment saw his chance to rid himself of Hill and Biddlestone.

Hill felt cornered. He surrendered his colours and resigned from the club. "I just had had enough. Enough of everything. I was getting it from all sides. It was a little bit too much."

But nobody simply resigns from the Angels. His former mates ransacked his house, claiming he had not turned in all his HA paraphernalia. A few weeks later, a posse of Hells Angels tried to abduct his wife while she was shopping. Hill drove them off with a shotgun. He and his wife went into hiding.

His partner, Biddlestone, stubbornly resisted all demands to leave the club. The old guard still supported him, but in the end that didn't help. He was beaten when he refused to take part in the raid on Hill's house. Two Oakland Hells Angels flew to Melbourne to mediate the dispute, but the trip was in vain. A year later the bikies took Biddlestone to a home outside Melbourne, handcuffed and beat him unconscious with iron bars. They moved him to another house, where he was revived and beaten again. He endured fifteen hours of torture. Finally, the HA dumped his broken body outside a hospital and drove away. Almost every major bone in his body had multiple fractures. He was alive, but barely. The Hells Angels had sent him a personal message. His membership card had been cancelled.

The unrelenting pressure from the Hells Angels drove Hill and Biddlestone into the welcoming arms of Bob Armstrong. Hill gave a taped confession that lasted almost five hours and eventually testified against his fellow bikies. Biddlestone also confessed on tape but refused, out of fear, to testify in court against Hamment and the rest of the Angels who were arrested and charged with his beating; consequently, charges were dropped. "Piece of cake," one accused reportedly said as he left the courtroom.

Five years after the original charges were laid for the Greenslopes lab, Hill was sentenced to five years in prison with eligibility for parole after two. Biddlestone and Hamment got six years and Faulkner got four.

The reign of the Australian Hells Angels' first speed king was over. When he got out of jail, Hill took his family far from Melbourne to the edge of the outback in rural Australia and now makes his living driving transport trucks and growing oranges.

Colleagues of Sgt. Bob Armstrong cautioned him about the danger of becoming obsessed with the bikies. "They'll destroy your career," they warned him. Armstrong agreed. By the mid-1980s, he was sick of Hill and his Angels and wanted a new challenge. But somehow he seemed powerless to shake them. If Sergeant Armstrong thought his biker worries were over, his old nemesis Peter Hill had reserved one final surprise. Before Hill and Biddlestone disappeared from the speed scene, they took one last swing at the Hells Angels and the cops. They sold their amphetamine recipe to the Black Uhlans. The rumour was they sold it for a measly $1,000.

For the next fifteen years, the Black Uhlans and their founder John Higgs became one of the major suppliers of speed in the country. Born in 1946, Higgs was a career criminal long before he supplanted Hill as the new speed king. He already had an impressive list of convictions, including manslaughter, assaulting police, drugs, theft and trading in illegal firearms.

The Uhlans were a distant offshoot of the Hells Angels. After the Hells Angels helped spawn the Gypsy Jokers in Western Australia, the Jokers came east in the early 1970s and formed the Fourth Reich in Wollongong, a seaside town just south of Sydney that calls itself the gateway to the south coast. Soon afterwards, ten of its members moved to Brisbane, just ahead of a police investigation into allegations of rape. There Higgs and his mates established the Black Uhlans, taking their name from German cavalry lancers. Like the Jokers, they adopted the Hells Angels rules and colours but remained a fiercely independent gang.

No bikie club in Australia is considered more secretive and more difficult to penetrate than the Black Uhlans. This was why Hill turned to them to help distribute his speed, and it was also why members such as Higgs ultimately became so successful in the business of drugs. When he was finally arrested in 1994, Higgs was considered the biggest speed trafficker on the east coast. Police found seven tonnes of chemicals on his property, enough to make amphetamines with a street value of AD$400 million. Through his bikie connections, Higgs had built a vertical network, controlling production and distribution all the way down to the street level. He had built up a financial empire that included real-estate holdings, a fishing trawler, clubs, restaurants, tattoo parlours and interests in manufacturing companies. His speed empire stretched from New Zealand to the west coast of Australia.

Five times the police investigated Higgs; five times they came up empty. Police hoped they'd be luckier the sixth time, after a businessman approached them and described how Higgs had asked him to secure precursor chemicals for his numerous amphetamine labs. Now police had a man who was already close to Higgs and ready to go undercover. Codenamed E292, he spent the next two years building a case against Higgs. His evidence first led to Higg's arrest in 1994.

It looked as if Higgs would slip away once more when the case almost fell apart after someone broke into the police evidence room and stole files revealing the identity of the source. An investigation revealed that a policeman had been paid $250,000 for the burglary. Higgs, of course, was the chief suspect. E292 had to go into the witness protection program with his wife and children but in the end was able to testify. Higgs was sentenced to six years in prison.

With him out of the picture, it wasn't long before territorial outlaw biker wars broke out. Over the next five years, thirty-two bikies would die and many more would be beaten as the Hells Angels, Bandidos and other clubs fought over the amphetamine trade. Desperate to expand their memberships, gangs grew sloppy. Melbourne officer Bob Armstrong—now with almost two decades of bikie investigations under his belt—used the opportunity to infiltrate the Ballarat chapter of the Bandidos. On May 31, 1996, he sent in two cops accompanied by two female agents. For the next eighteen months the men infiltrated the gang, eventually becoming full-patch Bandidos.

But Armstrong shut down the operation just as one of his agents was about to be named club secretary with access to all the books. "Three of the leaders of the Bandidos were murdered during this time," Armstrong says. His agents were showing signs of exhaustion. They were unarmed and very much exposed in the drug wars. "It was getting too dangerous," he concluded.

Still, Armstrong regretted pulling the plug at such a critical stage. "I've often thought about what would have happened if we just kept it going. One of them could have gone on to be national secretary, communicating with all the other chapters across the world, keeping the network going."

In the end, police managed to arrest most of the twenty club members, plus numerous associates in four different states, but the busts were minor and the investigation took longer than any of the prison sentences.

That only made the bikies more confident. Over the next few years, the various Australian-based gangs would unite into national alliances and even expand abroad, stretching into Europe and Southeast Asia. As Armstrong and other beleaguered officers would discover, the bikie wars in Australia were far from over.

And while Armstrong had escaped an assassination plot, former police commander Don Hancock would not be so lucky.

SIX

The Bikies' Revenge

———

Hey buddy, what to say? You were taken from us by a cowardly dog
but remember, buddy, every dog has its day.
—BILLY GRIERSON'S DEATH NOTICE

The Gypsy Jokers had a long memory. If they'd ever doubted their
creed of violence, Billy Grierson's murder had re-ignited their religion. The murder, they were convinced, had been carried out by
retired police officer Don Hancock.

Ora Banda—Hancock's town —had to be destroyed "because
it's Billy's resting place," Gypsy Joker Snot Reid said. Although
Billy's body was not buried in Ora Banda, Reid dreamed of retribution in the desert town. An attack on one bikie was an attack on
all of them. It demanded immediate and furious reprisals.
Without it there was no power and without power, no drug business. Reid was a Gypsy Joker drug dealer and understood the
power of bikie intimidation.

The first attack occurred on Saturday Oct. 13, 2000—two
weeks after Billy Grierson's murder. The bikies secured a load of
Power gel explosives, a sausage-shaped gelignite used by the mining industry. They hid the explosives in a concrete coffin belonging to a teenage boy—sliding back the lid and stuffing them in
among his bones—whose Kalgoorlie grave was not far from Billy
Grierson's. They made two bombs: Powergel packed around
boosters, inserted in PVC pipes with a lighting fuse. Nothing complicated. They just had to light the fuses and toss the bombs.

125

The day before the bombing, Graeme Slater—the Gypsy Joker leader who had warned a police detective three days after Grierson's murder he intended to "do it my way"—took his wife and children, along with Reid and his girlfriend, to the Southern Ocean resort of Esperance for the weekend. Meanwhile, Reid said, three Gypsy Jokers drove to Kalgoorlie from Perth. When they arrived, they hopped in an old Toyota utility truck Reid had bought for $500—a "throwaway vehicle," Reid called it—and that evening drove to Ora Banda. When they arrived at the inn, they quickly tossed the bombs on the front veranda and left. The blast blew out the front of the inn and just missed killing or injuring Hancock's son, Paul, who had left the inn minutes earlier. The Jokers figured the police wouldn't suspect bikies from Perth, and both Reid and Slater had alibis.

The second attack came two weeks later, on November 1. Slater and Reid drove up to Ora Banda. They parked their ute near the caravan park. They noticed two lights coming from a caravan and heard voices, but ignored them. They took two jerry cans of gasoline—one green, one red—and two Molotov cocktails out of the ute and walked up past the inn with its splintered debris, broken veranda and boarded-up windows. They kept on walking until they got to Don Hancock's house. It was about 9 P.M. The stars lit the way. "We threw the green jerry can of petrol around on the veranda," Reid said. "Then we smashed a window next to the back door and poured some petrol out of the red jerry can into the house.

Without waiting to see the results of their handiwork, they drove back toward Kalgoorlie, stopping along the way to torch the ute. The two bikies then headed to town in Slater's Land Rover, which he had stashed in the bush.

The next day they expected to read about their exploits in the newspaper but were disappointed to find no mention of the attack. They checked the next day. Still nothing. Finally, they sent up a prospector friend to take a look. He reported back that the house was still standing. "It obviously hadn't gone to plan," Reid said. They had made the mistake of using plastic bottles. When they tossed them through the window, they didn't break, the cloth wicks flared out and the gasoline failed to catch fire. The house was still standing. They had been foiled by their own stupidity. Undaunted, they began planning a third and, they hoped, final attack.

Mike Bezemer, Don Hancock's part-time yardman, had been in Tasmania on October 13 when the first bomb went off. He returned five days later to find that the bar and front veranda had been damaged, but it was nothing that couldn't be repaired.

Bezemer took care of Hancock's properties and tended his grounds. He was thirty-seven years old and was dating Hancock's daughter, Alison. The bombing scared him, but not enough to leave. As it stood, he was one of only five people still in town.

On Saturday, October 21, Bezemer was sitting in the beer garden, drinking with Ray Pinner. Two men in a white Toyota ute pulled up. Mike knew one of the men as Gyspy Joker Spud Manson but didn't recognize the other man sitting in the passenger seat with a black hat pulled over his face. He was Sid Reid.

Spud called out to Ray Pinner to come to the car. Ray walked over and leaned through the window.

Spud asked Pinner who was around town.

"Basically nobody," Pinner replied. Then Spud and Sid drove off.

Mike soon forgot about the visit, and for the next two weeks he went about his daily routines.

Until Sunday, November 5, when the bikers launched their third and final attack. It was brutal.

That evening Bezemer had been watching TV. At around ten o'clock, he went outside to get some air and pat his dog, Ollie; then he heard a vehicle coming from the direction of Hancock's house and decided to investigate. There were no headlights, and that scared him. "I raced into my van and grabbed a kitchen knife and a broomstick handle just for something . . . for protection."

Sid Reid parked a stolen BMW between the house and the battery mill. He and three other bikies got out of the car. They had three bombs. They placed one bomb in Hancock's house and the second in the mill. Each bomb had a fuse long enough to give the bikies time to get out of town. They also doused the interior of Hancock's house with gasoline. But when they lit the fuse, they accidentally ignited the gas and a flash fire blew the front door shut. They frantically pulled the door open and ran out. They were still laughing about it as they drove toward the hotel.

This time Reid cut the fuse to the third bomb half as short as the others.

"Just chuck it out the door. It'll go off before the others," he ordered.

As Mike Bezemer ran toward the hotel, he saw the shape of the BMW as it drove under the town's only street light, close to the pub. He heard the car pull up in front of the inn. Then he heard voices. He first thought they were girls' voices, but then he wasn't sure. They just seemed high-pitched. Someone yelled, "Get in, go!" He heard the car skid and take off down the road and out of town. He reached the back of the hotel when the first bomb went off. A huge explosion ripped through the hotel facade.

"My ears were ringing a bit, I tell you, and I ran. I had corrugated iron and rocks and stuff flying all around me. I took cover and ran behind the back of the hotel," he recalled. He nervously peeked around the bushes, but all he could see was the BMW racing down the dirt road. Then the second bomb went off and Hancock's house blew up. "It went up in flames, probably a hundred feet in the air. Flames, pieces of timber in the air."

Bezemer dashed to the front of the hotel, where there was a pay phone that miraculously still worked, and called the police. He then called Alison in Perth and was describing the destruction when the third bomb went off, shattering the mill and destroying the ore crusher and the old Crosley diesel motor her father had restored. About 430 miles away, at the other end of the phone line, Alison could hear the sound of her father's world exploding.

By the time the firemen arrived, Hancock's house had burned to the ground, the mill was destroyed and so was a good part of the hotel. Ora Banda was rubble. It no longer existed. The Jokers had blown it away.

———

Jack Lee couldn't believe it. He was the lead investigator in the Grierson murder case and his chief suspect was Hancock, the powerful former director of Western Australia's Criminal Investigations Branch. Now his crime scene had gone up in flames. Blown to hell by bikies he'd thought would allow him to complete his investigation. He was proven wrong. All he could think was, What's next?

"There were a number of threats by the bikies in relation to police officers," he said. "We were told that a police officer was going to be shot dead. Chasing after the former head of the CIB was one thing, trying to protect myself as the senior investigator, well, that was another."

What filled him with fear was the bikies' impenetrable clannishness and their sense of being above the law. And the fact that there seemed to be nothing he could do about either.

With Ora Banda destroyed, Reid and his mates turned their attention to Hancock. Kalgoorlie police had arrested Reid and Slater on December 5, 2000, for assault, deprivation of liberty and threatening to kill a Kalgoorlie man in a dispute over money. Their bail terms stipulated that they could no longer live in the same town as the victim of the assault, so in January 2001 they moved to Perth and became members of the Perth chapter of the Gypsy Jokers. As it turned out, their banishment worked in their favour. Hancock was now close at hand.

Reid shacked up with his girlfriend, Natasha Moutinho, a barmaid, and worked to expand his business in drug trafficking—amphetamines and cannabis—and in stolen cars. He had been addicted to speed since he was a teenager, when he changed his name from Glue to Melville before settling on Reid. "I don't like me fucking family," he said. "There was a fucking incident where there was child molesting going on in me family and I disowned me family."

By the time he moved to Perth, Reid was a speed freak who had long forgotten what life was like without drugs.

Slater, on the other hand, was a family man. His father spent his life in the army, and his mother was a nurse and midwife. One of his two sisters was married to a cop. He married his childhood sweetheart and had three children, two boys and a girl. He dressed his boys in bikie T-shirts and had their hair cut into mullets just like their dad's. Slater didn't take drugs. He boozed. After he moved his family to Perth, he spent a lot of time at the Joker clubhouse drinking under the Nazi flags that hung over the bar. Fridays he'd binge all night before returning home to his wife. "I usually start off drinking the Hahn Premium Lights, and once I've knocked down a dozen or so of them, I'll change later on to rum and Coke," he said. "I can knock'em down too." Or so he claimed.

When the Gypsy Jokers went looking for Hancock, they used government contacts. A female employee of the department of transport was friends with Gary White, the Gypsy Joker who helped bomb Ora Banda to the ground. White owned a trucking business and frequently visited the licensing office to pay for vehicle registrations. The woman later admitted she would personally take his payments and handle them herself—"to make it quicker or easier," she said.

But that wasn't the only favour she did for her bikie friend. On August 10, 2001, White asked her to check the licence number and make of a car that Reid had under surveillance. He wanted the address of the owner. (The Hells Angels in Canada had acted similarly to locate their murder victims. But they went a step further. They bribed government workers in the licence bureau.) When White's friend first entered the information into the computer, the numbers didn't match the make of car, so White told her to reverse the last three numbers—700 to 007. The address that flashed up on the screen belonged to a man named Lou Lewis who lived around the corner from Hancock.

It didn't take the bikies long to find out that Lewis was Hancock's best friend, and the two of them went to the Belmont Park Raceway every Saturday. Don Hancock and his wife lived in a modern two-storey red-brick house on Enfield Street in the suburb of Lathlain in east Perth. Surrounded by a high brick wall, the property had a large swimming pool and an extensive patio shaded by palm trees. Their tidy residential neighbourhood had the sleepy ambience common to middle-class suburbs the world over: tree-lined streets, manicured lawns, wide driveways and large garages. It all spoke of a life of comfort and tranquility.

Hancock knew his life was in danger. He could have imprisoned himself in his own private fortress, but he wasn't that kind of man. "If they're going to get me, they're going to get me. There's nothing I can do. You can't run, you can't hide," is how Insp. Stephen Brown characterized Hancock's attitude. Brown was one of the detectives in charge of protecting the ex-police officer. The police installed two video cameras outside Hancock's house to help identify any perpetrators, but left it to him and his family to check and change the tapes on a daily basis—a critical error. "Hancock made it clear throughout that he wasn't going to alter his lifestyle, so basically his safety couldn't be assured from that point on," Brown said.

Still, police couldn't very well stand by and do nothing. They sent in regular patrols to cruise Hancock's neighbourhood, check on prowlers and any suspicious vehicles. On June 22, 2001, two patrolmen discovered Lenny Kirby, president of the Perth Gypsy Jokers chapter, and club treasurer Stevie Adams at 11:04 P.M. sitting in a silver Ford ute parked in an empty lot with a clear view of Hancock's house. The bikies claimed they had stopped to urinate. Police would later find out how well the Jokers had cased the neighbourhood. If they had been more watchful—or if Hancock had bothered to check the tapes—they would have seen Sid Reid and others lurking in the vicinity both in their cars and on foot.

The incident with Kirby unnerved police. They urged Hancock to move away. "Don Hancock could have run away from this," Lee said. "The measure of the man was that he knew that if he had run away—and we could have hidden him; we could have put him in New Zealand—these people would have killed another police officer in retribution, and they might have killed two, and he knew that. There was no way he was going to hide from them. That's the sort of man he was."

Police then requested that Hancock at least stop or curtail his weekly visits to the racetrack. But Hancock's outing with his best friend, Lewis, a retired bookmaker, was a ritual he refused to change. It often included a stopover at the same Lathlain pub before taking the same road to the same members' parking lot and then sitting at the same racetrack bar where they spent the day drinking and watching the horses charge across a video screen. What Hancock didn't know was that sharing the bar with him most Saturdays was Mark "Moonie" Barrie, a full-patch member of the Gypsy Jokers.

Meanwhile, Lee's investigation into Billy Grierson's murder was going nowhere. Hancock, his wife and daughter would talk only through their lawyer. They demanded that Lee present them with written questions, and they would write out statements in reply.

The statements eventually received from each family member often matched word for word. Lee found them unbelievable, but the Hancocks declined to answer any further questions about any matter contained within their statements. It was clear to Lee that Hancock was working the system as best he could. It was also clear to him that there was nothing he could do about it. He couldn't very well start pushing Don Hancock around. Not if he wanted to keep his job.

His only hope was a coroner's hearing, which, in Australia, police can request. The coroner could compel the Hancocks to testify under oath and even lay charges. Lee set the date for October 1, 2001.

Saturday, September 1, 2001, was just another beautiful sunny warm day in Perth. Don Hancock got a call from Lou Lewis asking what time he should pick him up to go to the races at Belmont Park. It was the end of season. Lou didn't want to miss the action. Hancock was less enthusiastic. He owned a stake in a horse called Don's Record running that day in the last race in Kalgoorlie—a race that would be broadcast on the TV at Belmont. He thought he would drive over later in the afternoon to watch his horse run. He had too many errands to do and didn't want to spend the whole day at the track. Lou knew his friend and easily persuaded him that whatever he had to do could wait. It was race day.

Lou picked him up at about twelve-thirty in his 1981 Holden

Commodore station wagon with a flatbed trailer hooked to the back. He had been towing some material to build a cubby house for his grandsons and hadn't bothered to detach it. His wife Irene had suggested he take a taxi because she didn't like the look of him riding off to the races in an old car and trailer, parking in the members' lot next to the Mercedeses and BMWs. But he didn't care. The two friends drove out to the freeway, along the winding banks of the Swan River and into the members' lot. They parked the Holden across two spaces and headed directly for the Parade Ring Bar, where they took their usual seats at the far end, where smoking was permitted.

Across the street from the Hancocks' house, Lorenzo Bordoni was preparing for his daughter's thirteenth birthday party. He was expecting ten schoolgirls over that day and tied party balloons to his mailbox to give the place a festive atmosphere and to make it easier for parents to find his house.

Sid Reid had been up all night dealing drugs and partying. He spent time with one of his best customers. Sold her drugs and collected money. They didn't talk much. "The closest thing we come to having a nice conversation was a root [a fuck]," he said. So he didn't confide much in her about anything he was up to.

Reid didn't wear a watch. Rarely knew what time it was. Didn't care. When he got back to his house later the next morning, all he knew was that it was Saturday morning, September 1.

This is how Reid later claimed in court the rest of his day unfolded: fellow Gypsy Joker Graeme Slater dropped by in the early afternoon with a white van and told him to get in. They drove to Belmont Park, where they spotted Lewis's Holden. Slater slid the van into the empty space next to it.

"That's a bit of good luck," he said. "Got a park right beside it."

Reid opened the sliding door and climbed out to check the doors on the station wagon. The front and back were locked, but the tailgate door was open. Reid slipped in and opened the rear passenger door nearest the van. Slater handed him a shoebox-sized gelignite bomb. It was wrapped in thin white packaging foam held together with tape. Two wires—one green, one red—

stuck out the top. Reid tried to slip the bomb under the passenger seat, but it wouldn't go all the way. Only about a third. He didn't care. He left it like that and climbed back into the van. Slater then armed the bomb by plugging the two wires into a cellphone. Then the two men drove to a nearby parking lot to wait for Hancock.

Hancock and Lewis watched Don's horse come in third in the last race at Kalgoorlie. Hancock won a fistful of $50 bills, which he stuck in his pocket. Then the two friends walked to the Holden and drove away.

Reid was sleeping when Slater nudged him. "Come on, it's time to go." Reid drove the van onto the Graham Farmer Freeway, following behind Lewis's station wagon. Lewis soon turned off the freeway but Reid didn't follow. He could see the station wagon drive down the off-ramp and then head toward what he thought was probably Enfield Street. Lewis was still in traffic when Slater pulled a cellphone out of his pocket, turned it on, punched up a number.

Then he pressed Send.

"Rest in peace, Billy," Slater said, thinking of his murdered bikie pal Grierson.

It was that easy. He could have done it from anywhere. Paris or London. Slater then slipped the phone into a cloth bag, smashed it to pieces with a hammer and later sprinkled the pieces into a ditch along the side of the road as Reid drove the van.

That afternoon, Irene Lewis made soup for the evening meal. She watched television and at about five forty-five took the dog for a walk up Enfield Street. She passed in front of the Hancocks' house and noticed there was a party across the street at the Bordonis. She smiled when she saw the balloons. It reminded her of her own daughter's birthdays. She walked to the top of the street, then returned home, where she started getting the dinner ready.

For most of the day, Elizabeth Hancock had been entertaining her daughter, Alison, and her three grandchildren. They left at 5:30 P.M. Half an hour later, Elizabeth and her son, Paul, drove to the video store to return a movie. They picked up Chicken Treat for dinner before heading home.

Slater's call to the cellphone under Hancock's seat should have ignited the bomb immediately, but it was delayed. A bomb scare that evening at a nearby casino had forced the evacuation of about twenty thousand gamblers. Many immediately dialled their cellphones, overloading the nearest transmission tower. That meant Slater's call had to be re-channelled. By the time it sent the deadly signal to the bomb, Reid and Slater were several miles away, and Lewis was just pulling into Hancock's driveway. It was 6:30 P.M.

The blast was heard for miles around. It tore the roof off the station wagon, releasing a massive fireball high over the community. Thousands of deadly bits of shrapnel pierced the air. Glass, metal debris and body parts rained over a broad area of the neighbourhood. Hancock, sixty-four, was killed instantly, his torso ripped from his lower body and catapulted over the garden wall and onto his patio, face up next to the pool. His organs and lower body parts were found on front porches, yards, in trees and on roofs. Lewis's body remained intact in the car, but the pressure from the explosion destroyed most of his internal organs. He was sixty-three. Hancock's video surveillance cameras captured the awful scene.

As Hancock's $50 bills fluttered through the air, neighbours emerged from their houses and evening meals.

Lorenzo Bordoni had been watching the news on Channel 7. His daughter's party was still in full swing. She and her ten friends were playing on the back veranda when the explosion rocked the house.

It shattered his front door, smashed the glass panes and rained debris down on his roof. "It was frighteningly loud," Bordoni said. "I don't think I've ever experienced anything as loud." Through the broken glass he saw a fireball rise off the street. Horrified, he dashed to the back veranda to make sure the girls were okay. He told them to stay put and called the police and fire departments. He had his camera on hand for the birthday, so he grabbed it and started taking pictures of the carnage.

Farther down the street another neighbour, Cornwall Hoete, had sat down with his fiancée to watch the Rugby Union game between New Zealand and Australia. The national anthem was being played when the blast shook his windows. He went outside, saw Lewis's car on fire, and ran up Enfield Street. Lewis lay slumped across what had been the car's front seats. Hoete pulled him out of the burning car and, with the help of two other neighbours, carried his body across the road.

Brenda Austin, a nurse, was at home with her family. A friend's mom had just dropped her daughter off when she heard the explosion. She ran over to see if she could help. A crowd stood around Lewis's body, with many people crying. She pushed through, bent down and felt for a carotid pulse. There was a faint beat, but then it was gone. She began CPR, chest compression. A second nurse came and performed mouth-to-mouth. The ambulance arrived soon after and paramedic Michelle Murdoch put her defibrillator pads on Lewis. Her monitor showed an agonal rhythm. Murdoch knew his heart was about to seize. She could do nothing to save him.

Irene Lewis came running out of the house when she heard the explosion—and immediately recognized her husband's car ablaze. "I could see the station wagon with the trailer out in the street and then all the flames come up."

By the time Elizabeth Hancock and her son turned up the street with their Chicken Treat, police had already arrived.

"I knew something terrible had happened," she said. "The police moved me over and I asked them what was happening and they wouldn't tell me."

Glancing up the street, she caught sight of Lou's body and the fire engine: "I knew it was at my house." She tried to move closer, but the police blocked her. Her son got out of the car, but they stopped him, too. Irene Lewis finally came up and told her about the explosion. Elizabeth stared down the side of the road and saw Lou's body. "I didn't know where Don was. Nobody would tell me what had happened. Nobody would tell me where he was."

On the side of the road, a cop picked up Don's loaded .38 revolver and slipped it into a plastic evidence bag.

Back in their car, far away from all the carnage, the bikies had no idea if the bomb had actually gone off. Slater reassured Reid that an identical bomb had been successfully tested. He added, "You don't actually get charged for the call."

Only after dropping off Slater and doubling back did Reid get his confirmation. He stopped at a gas station for some food and overheard a conversation about a bomb in the area. To be really sure, he then drove by Hancock's neighbourhood, where he saw the cops and emergency vehicles and the smouldering car. Satisfied with his reconnaissance, he drove home, made up a couple of "eight balls"—three and a half grams of speed—and went back to work.

The attack stunned the community and enraged police and government officials. Western Australia had never seen anything so cruel and brazen. Separated by desert, sea and an entire continent, Perth was once a safe distance from the violent criminality that scarred so much of the world. The Perth underworld had once been populated by Italian Mafiosi and Irish gangs that respected the rules. Now the bikies had destroyed the playing field and moved the game onto the streets. Over the previous eleven months they had levelled the town of Ora Banda and triggered a murderous bomb in the middle of the city, killing two citizens and endangering many others. The bikies had signalled their intentions and defiantly executed their revenge. Their actions seemed calculated to mock law enforcement authorities. The murder of Hancock was a message to police that they had failed. That they couldn't solve the Grierson case; that they couldn't even protect one of their own; and that, when all was said and done, their laws meant nothing to bikies. The fact that one of the victims was a former senior police officer deepened the loathing against the bikies. It was clear to the police and politicians that laws had to be strengthened and the bikies taught a lesson.

That lesson was Operation Zircon.

Warrants were quickly issued for raids on bikie homes, businesses and the Gypsy Jokers' fortress clubhouse. Police found a loaded unlicensed .357 Magnum pistol in Reid's home. They also found shrines dedicated to the memory of fallen bikies. Slater kept his concealed behind cupboard doors in his bedroom, the photos of Grierson and others tacked on the walls like icons. Reid had a framed photograph of Grierson prominently placed on a wall in his living room, along with a newspaper clipping of Grierson's death notice, which Reid had written and signed "Snot": "Grierson, Bill: Hey buddy, what to say? You were taken from us by a cowardly dog but remember, buddy, every dog has its day."

Police targeted every Gypsy Joker in the state and offered a reward of $500,000 for information leading to the arrest of the killers. Three covert surveillance teams tracked senior members of the Jokers, hoping to undermine the leadership. They laid 130 charges for drug trafficking and firearms violations and seized millions of dollars in assets. "It was a no-tolerance approach," Stephen Brown said. Police acted with a speed and determination that had seemed absent in the Grierson murder investigation. For the Jokers, it all smacked of double standards—a contrast that would return to haunt the police when the case finally went to trial. For now, the key was to destabilize the Gypsy Jokers and scare them into giving up the killers.

Police thought they got a break when they managed to put out of commission Jokers chapter president Lenny Kirby, who had long been a stabilizing force in the group. He wasn't a drinker and never took drugs. For him, the club was a business, and he was the man who kept it together. Three days after the murders, he had summoned the Jokers for a special meeting. "Police had seen a couple of people. . . . Everyone was just to keep their mouth shut and not talk to the coppers" is how Reid recalled Kirby's stern warning. A month later, Kirby again called a meeting. This time it was held in an empty construction lot so they couldn't be bugged. Again he harangued and threatened the members about keeping their mouths shut.

Police were thrilled when they nailed Kirby on a drug charge. Already in prison on another charge, awaiting bail, he had instructed a visitor to go immediately to his home and destroy a stash of drugs he had buried in his yard. Police bugged the conversation and got to the property first. After six hours of digging, they found a huge quantity—three and a half kilos—of amphetamines, plus $363,000 in cash. Kirby got ten years behind bars. Now with the Gypsy Joker president out of action, the investigators hoped the club's cohesion would crumble.

It was not to be. Police wiretapped twenty cellphones and land lines and concealed another twelve bugs in homes and vehicles, obtaining 120,000 hours of conversations. Despite the extraordinary efforts, no real evidence surfaced. No bikie would talk. When Kirby went down, an equally strong leader in Graeme Slater filled the void. Hammered almost daily with arrests and police surveillance, the bikies would not surrender their own. Police simply couldn't breach the Gypsy Joker wall of silence.

One Operation Zircon detective, however, was making progress. It was slow and ponderous, but he felt that with patience his work would pay off.

Det. Sgt. John "Jock" Robertson had been a police officer in Glasgow, Scotland, before he got a job with the Western Australia Police Service in 1983 and moved his family to the other end of the world. A slim man of medium height, Robertson had a soft Scottish brogue, which helped him gain the attention of his targets. He was a counterterrorist negotiator. He knew how to get friendly with outlaws and persuade them to confess. Other Zircon investigators from the major crimes branch were trained in the American FBI method of intelligence gathering, building a profile of the killer, surrounding the target without actually getting close. It was a process of wait and see. Robertson was all face-to-face, hands on. Go right to the target, make him think you know more than you really do. Get him to confess. By the time police discovered which approach worked best, it was too late.

The Jokers' Kalgoorlie chapter members were at the top of the police watch list. Particularly Sid Reid and Graeme Slater. Both had been close friends of Billy Grierson and both had moved to Perth. And police knew only too well the account of Slater's warning that he intended to "do it my way." Police also had a "one-time" informant who had simply told them that Reid and Slater were involved in the Hancock/Lewis bombing. The informant refused to testify, so police could not use the evidence, but it helped reassure them that they were on the right track.

Four days after the murder of Hancock and Lewis, investigators got a call from the police station in Freemantle, the port town just south of Perth. They had picked Reid up on drug charges and were about to release him on bail. Did the investigators want to talk to him? Robertson left immediately to check it out. A search of Reid's car uncovered media clippings of the bombings.

"Fuck off! I'm not talking to you!" were Reid's first words to the cop.

That's when Robertson believed he could get this guy to speak to him. After all, Reid *is* talking, Robertson thought. Most bikers would simply have turned away. Reid didn't seem so hard core. His rap sheet showed little more than petty crimes, getting more serious only after he joined the Jokers. He was a drug addict and had been for a long time. He also had been a bikie for just two years. He wasn't yet wedded to the club. All the evidence indicated to Robertson that Reid was the weak link. "I never did doubt that Reid was either involved or knew who was," he said. Zircon detectives decided that Robertson would concentrate 100 percent on the man the bikies called Snot.

"My role was to befriend Sid Reid, get Reid's trust and show him another life besides the bikies," Robertson said. "I wanted to isolate him from the bikies and build up a distrust by the bikies for Sid Reid—get into their heads."

Reid was let out of jail on the drug charges, but police bugged his house and car and tapped his telephones. Each morning Robertson read the transcripts of Reid's conversations and those of his live-in girlfriend, Natasha. He knew the two were constantly arguing and were worried about money and how they were going to live and eat. Reid was also increasingly anxious about his life, concerned that someone would kill him.

Robertson went to Reid's shabby bungalow at 50 Weston Avenue almost every day. He was the unwanted visitor rapping on his door, talking to him on his veranda or through the screen door, often nattering on about anything.

"Sid, are you behaving yourself? That looks good. What're you eating?"

Though Reid ignored him, Natasha said, "A bacon-and-egg McMuffin. You going to confiscate it?"

"Natasha has attitude," Sid said, laughing.

He sometimes tempted Reid with the lure of the $500,000 reward that police had announced for information leading to the arrest and conviction of the murderers.

"A half a million," Natasha said. "You could blow that in a day."

"What about you, Sid?" Robertson asked.

"I'd blow it in a week."

Robertson was always there to remind Reid that the other bikies were not there for him. While they were making money, he was always short. Guys like Slater and Kirby were rich; they sat back and did nothing while reaping the rewards. But not Reid. Robertson told Reid the police would protect him, give him a new identity, a new life.

Robertson's prodding of Reid was all very public. He made it obvious to everybody that Snot was his target. While other bikers looked on, Robertson would be standing by his car in front of Reid's house or walking up to Reid's front door, rapping on it, calling out to him. Every day, seven days a week. It was psychological warfare, and it began to infuriate the bikies.

"Irish cunt" was how they addressed him, mistaking his Scots accent.

One bikie at Reid's house told him, "If you come up this driveway again, you won't be able to walk back. You'll need an ambulance to take you out of there."

Finally, the bikies erected a security cordon around Reid's house, barring Jock's entry. So Jock would talk to him through the gate, quietly reminding Reid of everything that was going wrong in his life.

"I knew exactly Sid's state of mind. As time went on, he began to accept me attending wherever he might have been, out driving, visiting friends or at home. It was during these times that I noticed a change in his state of mind from confrontational to acceptance and then to some sort of friendship and trust."

Jock tried not to push too hard. He rarely talked to the bikie's girlfriend or wife. "Bikies don't like you to touch their family." But he and other cops talked to Reid's friends. Everybody Reid hung around with inside and outside the bikie community became targets, including two of his best friends, Tony Sarros and Big Al Wishaw. Robertson always made sure he told Reid who he was talking to and what they were saying.

The Jokers decided to counter the police surveillance with their own. Across from Curtin House, the faceless glass-and-concrete downtown headquarters of the major crimes unit and Operation Zircon, they rented a room at the Blackcap Backpackers Hotel in January 2002. For the next six months, they videotaped everyone who entered and exited the high-rise building. They recorded names, faces and car registration numbers. (Police found out about the bikies' operation only the following July, when they arrested a bikie associate with two of the videotapes in his car.)

Meanshile, Jock Robertson was working hard to sow distrust among the bikies. Jock questioned Lenny Kirby's brother Thomas about a cannabis shipment that had arrived the previous day. Police wiretaps showed the bikies suspected Sid had squealed. As the days, weeks and months passed, Jock watched as the bikies grew increasingly distrustful of and anxious about Snot. But there was little they could do. Kicking Reid out of the club could simply drive him into the arms of the cops. Killing him was not an option, what with the "Irish cunt" always hanging about and the police surveillance that, they suspected, blanketed the entire club. At one point, Jock watched as Slater and several other bikies met Reid in Gosnell Park. They warned him not to talk to the police or anybody outside the club, including his friend Tony Sarros. Bikies had seen Sarros talk to the police on several occasions.

Six months of pressure finally paid off on February 13, 2002, when Slater and Reid had a furious confrontation outside Reid's house. "If you fucking talk to Sarros again, you're fucking dead,"

Slater told him. Slater was a tall, beefy man with a round boyish face and beady eyes. He glared at the thin speed freak, shoving him, trying his best to intimidate him, but clearly frustrated at his sense of impotence in the face of all the police surveillance. Jock watched the entire confrontation from across the road and smiled. He thought it was time to bring Reid in.

The next evening, Robertson and six other detectives stopped Reid and his girlfriend on the Berkshire Road near the Roe Highway. They took him in for questioning without formally arresting him.

It was a gamble.

Police brought Reid into a small interrogation room on the fifth floor of Curtin House. He sat behind a round white Formica table, facing a one-way glass that concealed a video camera. He smelled of stale sweat and filth, as if he hadn't washed for weeks. Later prison officials would have to implore him to shower.

At 9:07 P.M., detectives Stephen Brown and Peter De La Motte began the interrogation. After three minutes, Reid asked that the video camera and audio recording be shut off. He didn't want to be interviewed on tape. The interrogation went on for four hours. Police took notes only afterwards, so there is no actual written record of the interview, other than what the detectives noted from memory.

Brown and De La Motte had been preparing for the interview for weeks. They broke it down into four parts. First, they talked about the Gypsy Jokers, asking Reid about club rules and initiation rites. He refused to talk about them because, he said, they were too embarrassing. Then they moved on to his involvement in the surveillance of Hancock at the raceway and the placement of the bomb. They showed him items police had collected at the crime scene, hoping to impress Reid with the thoroughness of their investigation. Make him see that the walls were closing in. They even lied to him, claiming they had found his DNA at the crime scene.

When that didn't work, they pretended that Reid's good friend Tony Sarros had told them that Reid had described how to make bombs triggered by cellphones. Finally, they told him what his friends had revealed about his movements the day of the bombing, and they reminded him about the threats made against him by bikies such as Slater, claiming that Slater had said he wanted to kill him. They talked for an hour and twenty-five minutes. Throughout it all, Reid said nothing. Finally, Brown and De La Motte took a break.

They started up again at 10:52 P.M. with more questions about Reid's movements. They talked about a white Toyota van belonging to a former Joker president that they knew was used in the surveillance and bombing. Brown talked to Reid about the forensic reconstruction of the cellphone that had been attached to the bomb. For impact, he pinned a photo of the reconstructed phone on the wall facing Reid. Still, Reid said nothing.

After almost three hours, it was beginning to look like their gamble had not paid off. At midnight, they took a second break.

They had one final card to play. They started again at 12:23. In a raid on Slater's home in December they had discovered a Nokia phone manual with the licence number of Hancock's Holden station wagon scribbled on the cover. They asked about it, but Reid said nothing.

They began to explore more personal issues. How did Reid feel about murdering a completely innocent man like Lewis? They could see how Reid might be angry at Hancock, but why Lewis? Reid remained stone cold.

How did it feel always to be ordered around by Slater and then having to take the heat for it while Slater sat back and got rich? They kept pushing emotional buttons, hoping he had some. They talked about his relationship with Natasha and his possibly putting her in danger. They talked about his life, his drug addiction and threats from the club and Slater. Still, Reid did not bite. He just sat there stroking his beard, hunched over, looking tired and bored.

Brown and De La Motte were running out of topics. Four hours of a one-way conversation. At 1:29 A.M., the frustrated detectives left the room and told Det. Sgt. Jock Robertson—the experienced counterterrorist negotiator—to try his hand.

All Reid wanted was a cigarette. So Robertson took him up to the ninth floor, which was being renovated. Amid the debris, Reid dragged on his cigarette as Robertson quietly warned him that he couldn't ignore the fact that his life was in danger.

"Do you remember the walk in the park in Gosnells?" Roberston asked.

"Yeah," replied Reid, remembering the heated discussion he, Slater and several other bikies had had in the city park.

"We believe there was going to be an attempt on your life," Robertson said. "Do you realize that?"

"Sid, I've been dealing with you for the last five or six months and I believe that there may be further attempts on your life."

"You can't protect me if I go to jail."

"I can guarantee your safety."

"What about Tash?" he said, calling his girlfriend by her nickname. It was the first sign of a breakthrough—Reid was testing the cop to see what they could offer.

Robertson grabbed the opening.

"I can guarantee Tash's safety."

Robertson assured Reid that the police could supply him with a new identity, a new life. He told him he was "only living an existence. It wasn't a life." To Robertson's surprise, Reid casually said that he was willing to help the police, but he wanted assurances that both he and his girlfriend would be protected.

The investigators were ecstatic. That night, Reid confessed and was charged with the wilful murder of Hancock and the murder of Lewis (though Reid claimed he hadn't known Lewis was in the car). Police had finally broken through the wall of silence. The murders of Hancock and Lewis, the biggest crime in the history of Western Australia, were solved. Zircon had paid off. With a stoolie like Reid, police believed they were about to deal the Gypsy Jokers, the most violent bikie gang in Australia, a crippling blow. While a gratified Robertson went home to his wife, his colleagues shared a celebratory glass of champagne.

The triumph, however, wouldn't last.

———

Over the next few months, Reid gave up Graeme Slater as his principal accomplice in the murders, plus three other Jokers who he claimed had helped with the bombings in Ora Banda. He also told police about a third murder. In August 2001, Gary White killed a drug dealer who owed him $1,000 as an example to other dealers who didn't pay their debts. He shot the dealer near Perth and drove his body to Northam, where he burned it in a bonfire large enough to be seen by several residents of the small rural town. Reid himself had witnessed the killing. On the basis of Reid's testimony and human bone fragments found at the site, White was convicted of murder and sentenced to life in prison. It was the first test of Reid's credibility as a witness, and he passed with flying colours. Then the troubles began.

Mistakes in the handling of Reid proved costly. While he confessed to his part in the murder, he lied about the actions of Slater and others. Over the next seven months, Reid gave three signed statements plus a videotaped interview to the police about the bombing, and each one would be different. Slater played a lead role in all of them but the details of Reid's involvement kept changing. It didn't bode well for his credibility in front of a jury.

Even more costly, however, were the mistakes in the handling of Slater. Perhaps they were the inevitable result of Australia's classic struggle between its British roots and its American longings. Or maybe it was just that police were so overconfident about Reid's confession that they took their eye off the ball.

The investigation into Reid had been along the more traditional British style of actively stalking the target with face-to-face interviews on the street, in his home, at the police station; interviewing everybody around him, his family, his friends, his neighbours, his business associates. Make him think you have far more than you actually have. Break him down.

The approach to Slater was strictly FBI. It was covert and heavily reliant on technology such as bugs and telephone intercepts. Investigators created a blackboard profile of their target, red-flagging evidence from wiretaps and phone records that pointed to his guilt. They neglected, however, to conduct extensive and repeated interviews with his friends and relatives about Slater's activities on the day of the Hancock's and Lewis's murders, so they had no real historical record against which they could check Slater's alibis. Nor did they ever try to get close to Slater himself, as Robertson had done with Reid. Instead, they took a wait-and-see approach, hoping to accumulate enough incriminating evidence to charge him with murder. Hoping, basically, that Slater would make crucial mistakes that would reveal his guilt. Now with Sid Reid's confession, they thought they had made their case. They thought Slater had made the fatal error of driving Reid into their arms. The final red flag was in place. What they didn't realize was that they had underestimated Graeme Slater.

Police arrested Slater the morning after Reid's confession. They still had not obtained a full written statement from Reid. But they thought they would bring Slater in to feel him out. Slater didn't mind. He was keen to find out what Reid had said, so he spent the whole time listening, refusing to answer questions but posing the occasional one of his own. Finally, at three in the afternoon, they let him go—for a month.

They obtained more statements from Reid. And then—when they thought they had enough—they picked up Slater and charged him with wilful murder of Hancock and Lewis and also with the bombings in Ora Banda. Robertson thought the arrest was premature. The only case they had against him was Reid's story. And, as police would discover, Reid couldn't get that straight.

Slater's lawyer, Colin Lovitt, clearly relished the approaching trial. Lovitt was a Melbourne barrister with a well-deserved reputation as a fearless, highly theatrical pleader. He clearly liked his work. His performance in court was straight out of the Rumpole of the Bailey novels. He admonished judges and prosecutors alike, much to the fury of some jurists. He was once cited for contempt and almost kicked out of the bar. Lovitt didn't seem to care. He welcomed all comers. He pounded them with his obstinate but deft debating talents and his mastery of both the proof and the English language. For him, the Slater murder trial was an obvious case of double standards and outright lawless behaviour by a police department bent on avenging the death of one of their own. He thought police had become "obsessed" with bikies and were ready to sacrifice the most fundamental democratic principles to throw them in jail.

The trial in the fall of 2003 lasted eight weeks and was surrounded by heavy police security. Fearful that the bikies might intimidate the jury, officials refused to allow the public in the courtroom. Spectators had to watch on a video screen in another room. Reid himself testified via video camera. The danger, however, was that by erecting an electronic cordon around Reid, the police were blunting the jury's ability to make human contact and assess Reid's credibility. The police simply turned him into a talking head on a TV screen. Slouching in his chair with the long beard and crazy eyes, he became almost cartoonish. It was make-believe.

And Lovitt cherished the moment. During his cross-examination, he tore into Reid for his conflicting stories. He raised doubts about the Nokia phone manual found in Slater's home with Lewis's licence number scribbled on the cover. Tests showed that Reid's DNA was on the manual and not Slater's. Police hadn't found that out until well after they charged Slater. Lovitt implied that the police had planted the manual and craftily noted that it was discovered by an officer who later committed suicide.

What really made the difference was that Slater had an alibi. His mother and sister, as well as his mother's elderly friend, all testified that Slater was a hundred kilometres away at his mother's house in Northam celebrating Father's Day—even though Slater's father was dead—when Hancock and Lewis were murdered. Slater testified that he had spent that Saturday sleeping off a hangover from an all-night binge and then driven with his wife and son to his mother's early that evening.

The Crown produced phone records purporting to show that Slater had been in Perth using his wife's cellphone to call another bikie when he claimed he was a hundred kilometres away at his mother's house in Northam. The Crown claimed this proved

Slater's alibi was nothing short of a carefully constructed fraud. Still, the prosecution was unable to refute the testimony of Slater's relatives.

Then suddenly in mid-trial, at a time when the Crown felt their case was slipping away, what seemed like a gold nugget fell into their lap. While in prison, Slater had written a bikie friend asking him to lie under oath. During the trial, police found the letter in the glove compartment of the recipient's car:

> Hey ya buddy, I want to know if ya can do me a favour, mate. . . . I need you to take the stand at my trial and say that you saw Sid [Reid] a day or two before he got arrested and he asked you to buy all of his tools and car parts for instant cash and you asked him why. His reply was that he had just been thrown out of the club. . . . (It's not a big request, mate, but it is a very important one.) It's also important that you don't visit me 'cause that eliminates me and you from consorting about this. . . .
> Always your mate, S.
> P.S. Can you read this a few times over and memorise it (then destroy this letter). Don't discuss this with anyone.

The Crown waved the letter as solid proof that Slater's entire defence was a well-crafted illusion. Lovitt claimed it was simply a desperate attempt by a wrongly accused man to buttress his defence. As it turned out, the letter was too little too late. Reid's testimony didn't hold up against Slater's story. The jury acquitted after deliberating only a day and a half.

Slater and the bikies were jubilant. Billy Grierson's murder, which they laid at the feet of Don Hancock, had been avenged, and in the process they had beaten back the largest police investigation ever launched in Western Australia. They had utterly routed their adversary.

As for Reid, his lawyers bargained a sentence of life in prison with a minimum of only fifteen years. He was sent out of state to a maximum security prison, where police supplied him with money for cigarettes and candy. Natasha Moutinho soon left him. No family or friends ever visit him.

Slater did plead guilty to the firebombing of Hancock's house but was freed, having already spent two years in jail awaiting trial. Other Gypsy Jokers also went free when a second jury hearing the Ora Banda bombing cases refused to believe Reid. The Hancock murder case was closed.

That left the Billy Grierson murder. It was still officially unsolved. But Det. Jack Lee didn't want his investigation to die with his chief suspect, Don Hancock. That wasn't justice. It had always been his intention to hold a coroner's inquest. He had hoped it would break open his case by forcing Hancock and his wife to testify under oath, but the bikies had destroyed whatever chance he'd had of putting Hancock on the stand. Now Lee was left with an unsolved murder case and a dead suspect. Yet he still wanted his inquest. He thought he could at least ferret out the truth about what happened that night from Elizabeth Hancock and her daughter.

"Don Hancock killed Billy Grierson," Lee says. "That's what I believe. Can I establish that in front of a coroner's court, where the requirement is within the realm of probability? Yes, I believe I can. Can I establish it in a court of law, where the requirement is beyond a reasonable doubt? No, the evidence simply isn't there."

Aside from Lee, however, no one else seemed to have any taste for dragging the family of a former respected police officer—a legend in Western Australia—back over the painful history of that hot Sunday in Ora Banda when Billy Grierson was shot in the dark by a sniper's bullet.

Lee is still waiting for his date with the coroner.

PART III

UNDERCOVER ANGELS

THE YOUNGEST VICTIM

Five-year-old Dallas Grondalski is hugged by the man she called "Uncle Chuck," Hells Angels member Charles Diaz. Later he would slit her throat after the rest of her family was murdered. The Hells Angels ruled that her father had left the club in "bad standing." Diaz is currently serving a sentence of twenty-nine years to life. (Grondalski family photo)

THE MURDER OF

Cynthia Garcia, a forty-four-year-old
Arizona mother of six, was murdered
because, according to one Hells
Angel, she talked back to them
at their Mesa clubhouse (below). The
case is still before the courts. (Garcia
family photo/Clubhouse photo
Julian Sher)

CYNTHIA GARCIA

Informant Mike Kramer, shown in a police photo (above left), told the Bureau of Alcohol, Tobacco and Firearms (ATF) that he and two other bikers, Kevin Augustiniak (above right) and Paul Eischeid (left), killed Cynthia Garcia. Kramer then worked for the police to spy on his fellow Angels. Paul Eischeid, whose torso is completely covered in tattoos, skipped bail and is now a fugitive, listed as "armed and dangerous." Augustiniak awaits trial.

Chuck Schoville of the Tempe Police gang unit and his partner, Chris Hoffman, examine the isolated site in the desert outside Phoenix where Cynthia Garcia's body was found. She was stabbed multiple times. (Julian Sher)

UNDERCOVER ANGELS

ATF agent Jay Dobyns in his role as "Bird" at a biker event (right) and pulling guard duty outside an HA clubhouse (below). His face is blurred because he continues to do undercover work.

Undercover ATF agent Jenna MaGuire, whose face has been blurred to protect her identity, parties with members of the Mesa chapter of the Hells Angels. On her left are Cal Shaeffer, charged with murder in the Laughlin casino shootout, and Paul Eischeid, charged with the murder of Cynthia Garcia.

Skull Valley Hells Angels
June 2003

Pops Rudy Teddy Joby Timmy Bird
'the Graveyard Crew'

Only half of the Skull Valley Hells Angels pictured above are real bikers: "Timmy" and "Bird" are police officers and "Pops" is one of their informants. The photo on the left shows Sonny Barger (middle, white shirt) at a Hells Angels party in Phoenix. All but one of his companions are undercover cops. ATF agent Dobyns is to Barger's immediate right.

SONNY BARGER:

Sonny Barger, at the Hollister run in 2005, is 60 but still looks fit. He signs books as his tattooed bodyguard, Louie Valdez (right), keeps back the crowd. (William Marsden)

AMERICAN LEGEND

A younger Sonny Barger during a visit to Arizona in the 1990s.

The clubhouse of Sonny Barger's Cave Creek chapter in Arizona. The president of the chapter, Dan Hoover (inset), a protégé of Barger's, was murdered in March 2002. (Clubhouse photo Julian Sher)

THE "AL CAPONE" OF VENTURA

George Christie of the Hells Angels chapter in Ventura, California, is the longest-serving chapter president. Police call him the Al Capone of his town. "I take it as a compliment," he says. (Julian Sher)

George Christie (centre, second row, hands across waist, in sunglasses) invited hundreds of bikers from around the U.S. and the world to celebrate the fiftieth anniversary of the Hells Angels in Ventura in 1998.

SEVEN

Black Biscuit

———

No one knew we were going to get into these guys as fast as we did. . . .
No law enforcement officer in the history of this country has ever worn
the patch of the Hells Angels. A month into it, we said, "Hey,
you know what? We're going to kick these guys' asses."
—ATF AGENT CARLOS CANINO

Back in America, where the legend of the outlaw biker was born, Sonny Barger was doing his best to keep alive the image of the Hells Angels as rowdy but basically good-hearted outlaws.

Since moving to Arizona in late 1998, Barger had enjoyed the good life and had helped build the state into a new Hells Angels stronghold. Aside from Sonny's Cave Creek chapter, there were five other flourishing clubs in Phoenix, Skull Valley, Tucson, Mesa and Flagstaff, for a total of about eighty full-patch members. And they were not all stereotypical greasy bikers. One was a clean-cut pilot for America West; another was a stockbroker; a third was a manager at a car dealership. Several bikers also owned nightclubs, a bail bond company and, of course, motorcycle shops.

For years after Barger's arrival in Arizona, the Angels were largely unimpeded by local, state or federal police. A drug bust here, an arrest there for a beating or a shooting. Nothing major. Nothing the Hells Angels couldn't handle.

To be sure, the bloody shootout at the casino in Laughlin, Nevada, in April 2002 that left three dead and a dozen wounded put a temporary dent in Barger's campaign to soften his gang's image. It didn't help when the violent hatred between the Angels and the Mongols struck closer to home in Arizona. On June 11,

Josh Harber, a twenty-five-year-old Angel from Ventura, California, was shot dead on a visit to Phoenix when he stepped outside a bar where the HA had been partying. He'd been gunned down execution-style by a single assassin, believed to be a Mongol.

Six days later came more bad news for Barger. Greg "Snake" Surdukan, fifty-one, the vice-president of the Arizona Nomads chapter, was sentenced to fifteen years in prison, along with fellow Nomad Chris "Porker" Baucum, for running a sophisticated meth ring that spread from South Africa to both coasts of the United States. The huge trafficking network was a tribute to the Angels' global empire. Thanks to members of the Nomads chapter of Hells Angels in South Africa, Surdukan imported "South African Brown" methamphetamines, then distributed the drug through affiliates in New Mexico and Massachusetts. In all, seven Hells Angels were convicted.

But despite the murders and drug busts, Barger never lost his celebrity draw—thanks in no small degree to his undeniable status as an American icon. Hundreds of fans greeted him at his many book-signing appearances, not just throughout the U.S. but in Europe as well. The London *Daily Telegraph* echoed England's enchantment with the Angels, repeating the oft-worn accolades of Barger as "a legend" in a favourable review of his tales of "the biker cowboys."

He had an uncanny ability to ride out what to most organizations would be a series of public relations disasters, but he had no inkling that ATF agents had devised a series of bold undercover manoeuvres that targeted the seemingly untouchable Hells Angels.

Barger himself was not directly singled out in the operations. To a large degree Barger had become a figurehead, relinquishing day-to-day decisions to many of his underlings. Yet to the extent that Barger had worked so hard over the years to make sure that he was so closely associated with the brand name of the Hells Angels—and vice versa—any stain on the HA would inevitably tarnish his own reputation. And the ATF would try to tar the Angels with what they most dreaded: charges under American racketeering laws that they were a criminal organization.

The Angels were facing a two-pronged assault from two different ATF case agents—John Ciccone and Joe Slatalla—running an undercover snitch and undercover cops. Slatalla's focus was exclusively on Arizona; Ciccone's started in Arizona, moved to California and eventually expanded to several states. At first the operations were separate, but they inevitably became intertwined and ended up targeting some of the same bikers.

Ciccone's operation had started earlier, from the time Mesa full-patch member Mike Kramer signed up as an ATF informant in December 2001. Ciccone eventually named his case "Operation Dequaillo"—he chose the title because the Hells Angels were beginning to sport small patches with the slang Spanish word to signify the wearer had violently resisted arrest or had confronted a police officer. Ciccone figured it was an appropriate label for payback.

There was a lot of give and take as the cop and Kramer worked out their relationship: a delicate dance of disclosure, detective work and deal making. Each man was trying to size up the other, deciding how much he could trust the other. Mike Kramer was being deliberately cagey, obviously wanting the best possible deal from the cops for his snitching. The ATF case agent, for his part, wanted to use his full-patch spy to get convictions of as many guilty bikers as possible on drugs, guns or whatever crimes they could document.

And from the start, Kramer expressed an eagerness to betray his fellow bikers. At his first formal debriefing with Ciccone, Kramer promised he "could immediately start purchasing firearms and narcotics" from his buddies—and not just in the Mesa club. He vowed he "would be willing to visit not only Hells Angels chapters in California and Arizona but chapters located nationwide as well."

"We had him going everywhere," says Ciccone. "It's a once-in-a-lifetime shot. We got as much mileage as we could out of it."

Ciccone, based in Los Angeles, could not run Kramer in Arizona, so they came up with the fiction that he was tired of

Mesa and wanted to transfer to California—specifically the San Fernando Valley (SFV) chapter in Ciccone's own backyard. Kramer's family initially stayed in Arizona and he made frequent trips back and forth. Such transfers between HA charters were common, and it did not take long for Kramer to make new friends, particularly with an SFV associate named Daniel Fabricant, a notorious meth dealer with a long record of drug busts.

Ciccone began schooling his new recruit in the tradecraft of spying on the bikers. He gave Kramer a recording device disguised as a battery pack for a Nokia cellphone. Kramer kept it in his vest or shirt pocket where he could have easy access to its On/Off switch.

According to court documents, Kramer's first undercover drug buy for the ATF took place on Valentine's Day in 2002. Kramer was so excited about it that he called Ciccone to tell him because it had not been a planned purchase. He dutifully gave Ciccone all the meth in a small Ziploc bag—an honesty he unfortunately would not always maintain. Ciccone, naturally, did not have blind faith in his spy, so after drug buys he would routinely "pat him down to be sure he didn't take any off the top." Kramer soon boasted—not without reason— that he "got pretty good at playing the game." He would remember important tricks of the trade, like counting out loud the amount of drugs and money exchanged so it could be captured on tape.

On the one event that had prompted Kramer to reach out to the cops in the first place—the murder of Cynthia Garcia—he was still largely silent. He had not given many specifics about where and how the murder went down, much less about his role. He had no deal for immunity from prosecution. He had told the cops it was a stabbing in the desert, not a shooting.

It was an odd situation where almost everyone was half-blind. The medical examiner's office had a body found in the desert that had been identified as Cynthia Garcia, but it was an unsolved homicide with no leads. Her family knew she was dead, not how or why. Kramer knew the bikers had killed a woman, but he didn't know her name or if her body had been found. And the biker cops were stuck with an informant who was hinting about a murder, but they had no body or name to go with it.

"We knew it was in the desert, but that's like telling someone up in Alaska it's in the snow," says Chuck Schoville of the Tempe police. He started digging through file after file—unsolved murders, missing persons. He phoned every police agency in the Phoenix valley, talking to nearly every homicide detective. Nothing matched.

On a whim—more out of desperation than design—he picked up the phone in early February 2002 to call Dr. Laura Fulginiti, a Maricopa County forensic anthropologist he had met during a particularly gruesome search for a body at a landfill.

"Hey, Doc, here's the deal," Schoville said, his voice betraying how thin he knew the clues to be. "I'm looking for a homicide—a female, stabbed multiple times sometime in the last six months, and she was dumped in the desert."

Without a moment's hesitation, Fulginiti said, "Cynthia Garcia." It was Fulginiti who had done the autopsy on Garcia back in October 2001. She told Schoville how many times she had been stabbed and that her killers had tried to cut her head off.

Fulginiti—the doctor who'd performed the autopsy on Cynthia Garcia—had a body and a name but no clue about the killers; Schoville had hints about the suspected killers but no body. Now the pieces began to fall into place. Mike Kramer still was not ready to completely fess up to his role in Garcia's murder, but he was willing to try to get his fellow bikers, Paul Eischeid and Kevin Augustiniak, to talk about the events of that fateful October night in the desert.

So the ATF came up with the idea of secretly recording some conversations between Kramer and his former Mesa pals. Ciccone knew Kramer could not keep raising the sensitive topic without setting off alarm bells: "We're only going to get one shot," he said. Even raising it once was fraught with danger. They tossed around different scenarios and eventually came up with the idea of a giving Augustiniak and Eischeid each a gift. Some little memento by which they could remember what a great guy Kramer was after his announced departure to join the California Angels—a going-away present, so to speak.

Ciccone prepped Kramer on how to approach the targets, how to get them to talk about the murder without being too obvious or pushy. The ATF installed microphones and a camera in the house Kramer still kept in Phoenix and gave him portable recording devices as well. Then on March 15 and March 16, 2002, Kramer set out to meet his two buddies.

The clandestine recordings have yet to be examined or challenged in court, but they have been disclosed to defense lawyers in pending trials. What follows are excerpts from the police transcripts.

Eischeid, the financial worker whose business suits hid the gaudy tattoos that covered almost every inch of his torso, was the first target. At 8:45 P.M., he showed up at Kramer's fully wired place in a small green car and stayed until 10:10 P.M. The biker buddies began knocking back some cold beers, chatting about trucks and bikes. Then Kramer pulled out his gifts: a large knife he had bought for Eischeid and an even more impressive blade he was going to give Augustiniak. Perfect for hunting—or killing.

"Between me, you and Kevin, he's now 'The Decapitator' for me, you know," Kramer said.

"Decapitator Kevin, there ya go," Eischeid agreed. "Oh yeah, that's what he needs."

"I got each of them for a particular reason," Kramer went on.

Eischeid laughed. "Yeah, you could finish the job better."

"You, me and Kevin are fucking forever together, I guess," Kramer declared.

Later on in the conversation, Eischeid said, "I'm more concerned about, fuck, about everybody that's involved. There's six of us that know."

Kramer suggested there was nothing that tied the victim back to the club: "See, I've thought of everything else. There's no . . . sex, she didn't give anybody a fucking blowjob."

"Yep," Eischeid agreed.

"She wasn't a regular. You know what I'm saying?"

"Yeah, I mean, unless somebody connects the two. There's no

way anyone would connect it back to us," Eischeid said. "And you know what? She's probably a fucking crack whore, a fucking bitch; no one's gonna miss her. I think she's a Mesa whore. . . . And that's why there's no connection, there's no DNA."

Eischeid was not completely cocky, though. He remembered the carpet in the clubhouse, apparently stained during Garcia's beating: "I was worried about the carpet and all. . . . Hey, they took it away in that car; they'll never be looking there."

"That was all shampooed," Kramer assured him. "I don't think there's anything left. I really don't."

"I hope not. Unless someone puts two and two together," said Eischeid. "So they can speculate all they want, but the full story will never be known."

Eischeid bragged that he had only few weeks left before he graduated from prospect to full patch. "No one can say shit about me fucking skating through, that's for sure."

"No, you didn't skate," Kramer agreed.

Eischeid seemed almost proud: "That was just the icing on the cake, but I did a lot of other shit that most people don't do, you know."

One down, one to go. Now Kramer had to work on Augustiniak. The next day, Ciccone met Kramer at 11 A.M. to prepare him. Never one to take chances, the ATF agent gave his informant two separate recording devices to conceal, in case one failed. Kramer drove his truck to Augustiniak's apartment on North Emelita, in Mesa. From there, the two bikers went on to a popular restaurant called Long Wongs in Tempe, where they chatted from noon until three.

"Here's your present," Kramer began, handing Augustiniak the special knife.

"This is the King Shit, bro. This is special," the biker said.

"Well, see . . . I'm moving to California, you know. I wanted to make sure you're comfortable with our deal. You know what I'm saying?"

"Right."

"I figure me, you and Paul [are] kind of, like, bonded for life."

Augustiniak said there had been some talk about going out to the desert to "check that place out . . . but [the] Mesa [chapter] doesn't feel" that it was necessary—a statement that to Kramer and his ATF handlers indicated that several members of the Hells Angels seemed to know about the murder and its cover-up. Before they parted, Kramer carefully manoeuvred the conversation back to the new knife he had handed Augustiniak.

"That's got the good edge on it, you know."

"That edge—I won't have a problem like I did last time," Augustiniak said.

"Yeah, fucking take it all off," Kramer said. "That's actually why I got you that particular one. It looked like you enjoyed yourself, but it was just too hard for ya, so—"

"I still couldn't accomplish what I was trying to do, so it sucked," Augustiniak admitted. "I was yelling at her and everything."

"Yeah, yeah . . . that's kinda why I bought that."

"Yep . . . gotta have the bone chopper," said Augustiniak.

"That's a good blade, brother."

"Oh fuck, yeah."

On that note, the two bikers said goodbye, and within an hour, Kramer had handed over the recordings to Ciccone. Kramer must have felt he had done a good job, soliciting what the cops considered very damaging boasts from his knife-wielding buddies. Now his "hypothetical" was a lot less hypothetical. It was clear to the cops that a fatal stabbing had indeed taken place. And it was also becoming painfully clear that their own informant had been involved. Still, Kramer held back from divulging much. "He apparently wasn't going to incriminate himself until he had some kind of deal in writing."

Ciccone, for his part, was in no rush. He had Eischeid and Augustiniak on tape. Kramer, in any case, was way too busy buying drugs from California bikers. Then, just a month after Kramer's secret recordings in Arizona, all hell broke loose in the Laughlin casino shootings. Suddenly Ciccone's full-patch spy had a much more urgent assignment: he was going to help the ATF take down not just a couple of alleged murderers in Mesa and some drug dealers in California, but he was going to go after dozens of Hells Angels all over the United States who had taken part in the Laughlin brawl.

"When the Laughlin shootout went down, we figured out who we were going to indict, and Kramer went all over," Ciccone says. In his home state of Arizona, in Nevada, in his new base of California, even as far as Fairbanks, Alaska, Kramer rode with his biker pals and secretly recorded hours and hours of compromising conversations. The Laughlin run had attracted bikers from across the country, and Ciccone was determined to have his informer catch as many as possible. For his part, Kramer had a vested interest in staying in the spy game against his patched brothers for as long as he could: the better he performed—and the more Angels he ensnared—the better his chances of getting his deal.

The Laughlin shooting also gave new urgency to another infiltration plot against the Arizona Hells Angels that was being hatched by case agent Joe Slatalla in the ATF's Phoenix office. For some months now, Slatalla had been squeezing his snitch, Rudy Kramer, eager for every scrap of information he had on the Arizona Hells Angels. Kramer was a pill-popping, gun-dealing biker affiliated with the Mexican-based Solo Angeles. Facing serious jail time, he had agreed late in 2001 to become an ATF agent, earning an official designation as "Confidential Informant 785000–790."

Slatalla had been laying the groundwork for his scheme of setting up a fake branch of the Solo Angeles made up of undercover cops and informants. His idea was brilliantly simple: using the fake Solo Angeles to befriend the Arizona Hells Angels. The beauty of the plan was that because the undercover cops would have their own club, they could keep their distance even as they penetrated deeper into the subculture of the toughest outlaw biker gang of them all. The only thing Slatalla didn't count on was that the scheme would work so well that the Angels would want to bring the cops right into their club.

Kramer was already busy buying guns and drugs from the Hells

Angels and their associates, namely the Red Devils. He was cozying up to Mesa chapter president Bob Johnston and dropping hints about setting up a Solo Angeles chapter in Arizona.

Slatalla, known as a meticulous organizer, was leaving nothing to chance. He coordinated the installation of ten court-authorized telephonic pen registers on various lines belonging to assorted Hells Angels members and their network, enabling police to trace the outgoing and incoming phone calls of the targeted bikers. Eventually the electronic surveillance would extend to dozens more bikers and thousands of hours of secret recordings.

With Kramer buttering up the Angels, Slatalla had to assemble his team of undercover cops who would become the Solo Angeles in Phoenix. He wanted the leader to be Jay Dobyns, the cocky agent who had been shot a couple of times in the line of duty. Dobyns was already earning a reputation among bikers as a nasty gunrunner in nearby Bullhead City, as part of the ATF's smaller investigation, Operation Riverside. "[Jay] was able to develop quite a bit of credibility with criminal elements that were actually associated with the HA," says Slatalla. Slats first had to convince the case manager running the Bullhead investigation to give Dobyns up. Dobyns's controllers initially balked—not the first or, sadly, the last time internal ATF bickering would obstruct taking on the Arizona Angels. Eventually, Slats got his way—and his key man.

By this time, Dobyns had close to fifteen years of undercover work—everything from the Aryan Brotherhood prison gang to the Calabrese organized crime family. Still, even a veteran operative like Dobyns had good reason to be nervous about penetrating the bikers. "I know I can work undercover. I know I can get over on people," he said. "But can I really get over on these guys?"

The ATF would have had to look long and hard to find a better candidate than Jay Dobyns to penetrate the Hells Angels. Everything about him was pure outlaw biker. His tall, lean, muscular body and his fiery, challenging eyes seem to warn you to keep back, this guy could explode. He didn't have to fake the bullet scars or the tattoos, which covered his arms. The tattoos were not there as an undercover disguise. They were real, and Dobyns had had them inked long before he knew he was going to infiltrate the bikers—though he would add more later as he warmed up to the Hells Angels. On one shoulder was an image of St. Michael, the patron saint of police officers. (Dobyns later would have to come up with a fanciful story to steer the bikers away from figuring that one out.) The other arm had a rifle with a snake wrapped around it. There were plenty of skulls and four strips of barbed wire (for the ATF agents killed in a bloody and controversial shootout at Waco, Texas, in 1993). He also, perhaps fortuitously, had angels painted on both forearms. "I had the skulls and flames, and I wanted some good in there with the evil," Dobyns says.

Across his back was emblazoned his childhood nickname: "Jay Bird." When he went undercover, Dobyns kept his real first name—it's always a good idea to pick a name that you'll naturally respond to—and took his grandmother's maiden name, Davis, as his surname. "She was a very tough, hard-working woman, and I chose this name to honour her with my work," he says.

Right above the bullet hole still visible on his chest from the shooting on his first week on the job, Dobyns had inked in "DOA." Dead On Arrival. He had rings on every finger and chains around his neck. Like many bikers, he had an earring in each ear. His son's friends teased him: "I know that your dad is undercover—is he pretending to be a pirate?"

But the ATF agent knew that even for the bikers, tattoos and jewellery were only skin deep. "The appearance, how you look, is not a big value to these guys," Dobyns says. "Long hair, goatee, tattoos—they're not important to getting you in. What comes out of your mouth and what you can make them believe—that's what counts."

For the second team member, the ATF persuaded the Phoenix department to free up one of its young officers, Billy Long. Long, who went by the undercover name Timmy, had no undercover experience, but he brought several vital attributes to the fake Solo Angeles: he knew bikes; he knew the city; and at over six feet tall he was an impressive martial arts instructor. "The bikers loved the fact that this guy was what they perceived to be a street fighter," Dobyns says. "It was another example of giving them a little and letting them run with it. He never beat anybody up. But they became convinced he was my enforcer, that he was the guy going around with me and putting people down."

To give the ATF's Solo Angeles a much-needed Spanish flavour—after all, they were supposed to be affiliated with drug-dealing Mexicans—Joe Slatalla recruited a talented Puerto Rican agent named Carlos Canino.

Canino jumped at the chance. Not just for the excitement. Since joining the ATF in 1990, he had gone undercover to bust Mexican drug pushers operating in the Pacific Northwest, street gangsters in Los Angeles and Cuban mobsters in Miami. But he also had a big personal stake in joining when he heard Jay Dobyns was leading the undercover team.

Back in 1992, at age twenty-six, with just a couple of years of policing under his belt, Canino had been involved in a violent gang shootout in L.A. He and his partner were cornered by three gang members in a sting that went wrong. Bullets started flying, bodies falling. In the end, one gangster was killed. Canino survived, but his brush with death traumatized him. He was shaken, jarred, on edge. When he looked in the mirror, he thought he saw a coward who didn't belong in the ATF. "In my mind, I thought that I was a lot tougher than I was," he says. "I was ashamed of myself. Why do I have nightmares?" When he thought of committing suicide, he knew he had reached rock bottom.

The ATF has a policy of sending out experienced undercover operatives to talk with other agents after a dangerous incident. It was Jay Dobyns who came out to chat with Canino; he pulled him back from the precipice. "We take care of each other because we know how quickly the tables can turn and the counsellor could be on the wrong end of a bullet and be the victim," Dobyns says. "Carlos is a brave, brave man."

A decade later, Canino saw a chance to pay back Dobyns by working alongside him. "At this point in my career, I had already made my name in the agency," Canino explains, "but I wanted to prove it to Jay. I was going for broke. I was going to do whatever I could to make a good impression—not for my bosses, but for my friend."

Canino had the look, accent and experience to fit his cover story: a dope dealer for the Colombians who had been ripped off in Los Angeles and turned to Rudy Kramer as a broker to help get back most of his shipment.

The fourth and final member of the undercover team was not a cop at all—and that was his strength. He was a wizened, gruff former criminal nicknamed "Pops," a long-time police informant whom Dobyns had known for more than eight years. "We brought him in to do some of the dirty work that we couldn't do," Dobyns explained. Like riding down to Mexico for Solo Angeles meetings, where the ATF agents were not allowed to operate undercover.

"He worked on the same level as the police operatives," said Dobyns. "We consulted him on plans. We exposed ourselves, we let our guard down, but I trusted him."

With Pops, Kramer and the three undercover cops, the "members" of the Solo Angeles were ready to roll. The fact that they were all men didn't strike anybody as a problem at first, but they were quickly going to discover they needed a female agent on board. Backing up the undercover operatives were over a dozen other people—cover teams, support staff and managers. Keeping it all safe from shipwreck against the shoals of the ATF's bureaucracy was Slatalla's job.

It was an unusually large and at the same time secretive task force. Few people outside the team knew of its existence. Even the name of the operation was deceptive. Usually cases get titles that are in some way connected with the targets, but Slats wanted a name that would be so meaningless to outsiders that they would never suspect it had anything to do with bikers. A couple of the investigators happened to be avid hockey fans, so they dubbed the operation Black Biscuit—a slang term for a hockey puck.

Choosing a code name guaranteed to be obscure in the hot desert state of Arizona was the easy part; penetrating the Hells Angels would be a lot harder.

———

It was at a picnic table under a large tree at the back of a church parking lot that the undercovers—Jay Dobyns, Billy Long and Carlos Canino—had their first meeting with the snitch who was going to broker their introduction to the Hells Angels, Rudy Kramer.

"I'll get you next to these guys. I'll vouch for you, but you have to win them over yourself," Kramer told them bluntly.

Canino was struck by how wiry—and wired—Kramer seemed to be: a short man, not more than five five, tattooed from head to foot; he looked like a Mexican gangster. Dobyns liked him from the start, but was wary. "Rudy is smart and stupid. Rudy could tell you a complex formula to solve a math equation, but you'd have to hold his hand to get him across the street without getting hit by a car," he says. "He was street smart but lacked common sense"— a failing that would soon imperil the operation.

"If you guys are coming into this world, here's what it entails," Kramer began, as he slowly laid out the intricacies of the Angels: the rankings, the deference paid to the patch, the strict club rules.

The briefing lasted a couple of hours. Then Kramer exclaimed, "Hey, let's go for a ride!" He wanted to see how well the cops could handle the bikes. They took off for a breakneck jaunt through the jammed, bustling streets of Phoenix out to Apache Junction, weaving through traffic at eighty, ninety miles per hour.

"I'm just hanging on to that motorcycle for dear life." Canino laughs now at the memory. It didn't help that he was riding an old 1984 bike that the ATF had already used—and crashed—in the Sons of Silence investigation in Colorado. As he raced through Phoenix, he says he kept thinking, "If the Hells Angels don't kill me, I'm surely going to get killed on a motorcycle. I'm a dead man. I'm going to die in a motorcycle crash. As soon as I came to grips with that, I was fine."

Learning to harness the Harleys was just one of the simple goals Slatalla had set for his rookie team in those early days of summer: "All I want you guys to do is to get to know Rudy, get to know Phoenix, get out there, be seen. Put the word out that Rudy has a crew. Don't wear your colours yet, but make sure you guys are seen."

The first chance to make their official debut as Solo Angeles came at the end of July. There was an annual bike rally at a campground outside Phoenix known as "Too Broke for Sturgis"—for those bikers who couldn't make it to the popular bike run in Sturgis, South Dakota. Hundreds of bikers from various small gangs roared into the campground to show off their bikes and their girlfriends, all paying homage to the acknowledged top dogs, the Hells Angels.

On this particular hot weekend, the last crew in were four strangers—Dobyns, Canino, Billy Long and Pops—sporting Solo Angeles vests. (They had their flaming orange Nomads patches embroidered at a Tucson shop run by the wife of a retired ATF agent.) They walked behind Rudy Kramer, well known in biker circles but feared because he was unstable and explosive. All eyes turned to the outsiders: "Who the fuck are these guys?" Members of the other clubs started coming around, asking questions. The Solo Angeles were deliberately standoffish. They wanted to save their respects for the exalted Angels.

Kramer spotted the tent where the Angels were holding court. The designated leader was Dennis Denbesten, a meth cook from the Nomad chapter who had been convicted for narcotics and arrested on weapons violations. Looking menacing with his face covered by his long hair and a thick, hermit-like beard, Denbesten was accompanied by a towering biker named "Turtle." As Kramer led his entourage over, the Angels steeled themselves for a fight. "We thought you guys were coming over to shoot us," they later confided.

Kramer moved immediately to defuse the situation: "Hi, how are you doin'? We're guests of Mesa Bob," he said, referring to Robert Johnston, the Mesa chapter president he'd been befriending for months. "We're not here to steal any of your thunder," the Solo Angeles assured the HA. "We got our own business out of Mexico, moving guns out of Arizona to Mexico. We're not here to take any of your dope business."

"I think they liked the fact that we respected the protocol," says Jay Dobyns. "It was one of the things that Rudy brought to us that we really took to heart. We didn't talk out of school; we took our business to the proper chain of command."

Chatting in an open campground was one thing; penetrating the inner sanctum of the Hells Angels' heavily fortified club-houses was quite another. Soon after their successful debut, the new boys in town took their next step as Solo Angeles: an official meeting with Mesa club boss Johnston himself.

Johnston was one of the most influential Arizona Angels, a long-standing tough guy from the Dirty Dozen who had a history of aggravated assault and extortion, along with an arrest for domestic violence and a 1995 drug conviction. Standing six five, he sported a well-cropped black beard, dark glasses and fashionable clothes: he earned a good living as a manager at an Earnhardt's car dealership. Winning over Johnston would be central to the ATF game plan.

On August 1, the undercover cops met with Kramer at a parking lot not far from the Mesa clubhouse, nervously mulling over the different scenarios: what if this happens, what if that goes wrong. "We're procrastinating because the moment of truth has arrived," Canino admits. "I'm scared to go, Jay is scared to go, Billy is scared to go."

Rudy Kramer, the snitch turned teacher, stared at his cop protégés in bewilderment: "Hey, what the hell are you guys doing here? This is what you came to do, isn't it? Either we go or we all just go home and I go to jail. But let's not sit in the parking lot. Let's do it!"

The cops laughed. Dobyns recalled an expression his old partner from Chicago, Chris Bayless, had coined to describe the feeling an undercover agent gets when he senses that danger is all around but there are no obvious red flags preventing him from going forward: "Jesus Hates a Pussy."

It became the Solo Angeles unofficial motto—JHAP for short.

The newly emboldened undercover bikers sped off to the clubhouse on South LeBaron Road—the same clubhouse where

Cynthia Garcia made her fateful visit nine months earlier. It was 9 P.M. as Kramer walked up to the guards on duty in front of the large white metal gates. "I'm president of the Solo Angeles Nomads, and I'm here to see Mesa Bob," he declared.

"It was like going into a medieval castle: this is who I am and these are my knights and I want to meet your leader," Canino recalls.

In a few moments, Mesa Bob strolled out from behind the gates. Rudy made the introductions.

"You guys are more than welcome to my clubhouse. Come on in," said the Hells Angels leader, according to police.

And they did, partying and shooting the shit with the Angels. The Solo Angeles had begun their penetration of the most secretive bike gang in the world.

By 11 P.M., the bikers left for the Spirits Lounge, a favourite biker hangout where, according to an ATF affidavit later filed in court, Mesa Bob told Kramer that the Solo Angeles "were welcome to traffic narcotics in Arizona with [the] Hells Angels support." Equally important, he gave them permission to fly their "cut"— the Solo Angeles patch—in Arizona. It was a key breakthrough: nobody who valued life or limb would dare wear a patch of another gang in Arizona without the Hells Angels' approval.

"My guys have business in Bullhead. We'll be up there next week," Rudy later told the bikers, referring to Dobyns's old gunrunning stomping grounds in Bullhead City. The Solo Angeles were told to make arrangements there with a biker leader named "Smitty."

"Make the arrangements when you get up there," the Mesa chapter president said approvingly. "You need to go see Smitty."

Donald "Smitty" Smith was a porky senior member of the Arizona Nomad chapter who lived in Bullhead; at the Laughlin run, playing the role of "Bird," the local gunrunner, Dobyns had already bumped into Smitty. Now, as a Solo Angele, on August 9, he and Canino strolled into the Inferno, a seedy bar that served as Smitty's sanctum. Sitting next to him was Den Denbesten, the meth cook the agents had first met at the July bike run.

"We know you're the point guy here for the HA," the undercover cops began. "And we're here to back you up." Smitty laid out

the rules, according to police: "The Hells Angels own this territory. Anything you guys are going to do here, you need to run it
through me."

"Fine, we got no problem with that," the undercover cops
quickly agreed.

Remarkably, within a few weeks of operating, the Solo Angeles
felt that they had obtained the blessing of two Hells Angels leaders to operate openly in the state. Then suddenly the pretend bikers discovered to their shock that they did not have the blessing of
their own, very real Solo Angeles leaders down in Mexico. Rudy
Kramer had assured the ATF he had cleared the creation of the
Nomads with the Tijuana boys. But one morning over his usual
breakfast briefing with Carlos Canino at the Waffle House, he let
it slip that he did not have permission from the mother chapter to
fly the Nomad insignia in Arizona.

"I almost choked on my French toast," Canino recalls.

That night, he, Rudy and Jay Dobyns were on a plane to Los
Angeles. They went to see "Teacher," a venerable member of the
Solo Angeles. Kramer introduced his new friends; they wooed
him, promised to send dues back to the club. "We played him very
carefully," says Dobyns. "Respect with just a mix of danger and
fear, enough of each for him to like us and fear us at the same
time." Teacher promised he would vouch for the new gang
members in Mexico.

The ATF figured they were covered: Mesa Bob knew Teacher,
and if he ever bothered to check on the Solo Angeles Nomads,
Teacher would stand up for them. What the ATF didn't count on
were other Angels, less friendly than Bob Johnston, doing some
checking with their own sources in California. In a few months,
that miscalculation would nearly be their undoing.

The ATF opted for a subtle sales pitch, using the power of sug-
gestion, the idea that less is more: letting the bikers' imagination
do the work. The Hells Angels would convince themselves of how
nasty and fearless the Solo Angeles were if the undercover cops
dropped enough hints. As Bird, Dobyns had already earned a reputation as a mean-looking gunrunner and hitman from Bullhead

City without ever actually killing anyone. Bird always carried around his baseball bat, never hitting anyone or even boasting he had used it—but the word spread that this was one crazy dude who would slug people if he felt like it.

He did the same with his house. One of the first homes Dobyns used for the operation had every door, every window barricaded and security cameras in evidence everywhere. "We never said anything about why we did it," Dobyns says with a chuckle. "We just let them see it and they decided, 'Ordinary people don't live like that. I don't know what the fuck these guys are up to, but in that house everything is locked down: you can't get in or out of it. Wow! There is something going on here.'"

The first impressions were so effective that within weeks, the Hells Angels were readily telling the agents their secrets about guns and drugs. On August 20, Smitty told the agents he'd been at the Laughlin shootout and assumed he would be charged with murder, according to a sworn ATF affidavit. The next day, the affidavit continues, Smitty and his wife, Lydia, told the cops their pal Dennis Denbesten was known as "Chef Boy-Ar-Dee" because he was such a "renowned narcotics cook"; once you tried his stuff, they said, you wouldn't want anybody else's.

Guns interested the Angels as much as meth, if the ATF affidavit is accurate. When Dobyns and his crew dropped by Smith's home on Swan Drive in Bullhead City in September, Dobyns showed him several machine guns and firearm silencers. Smitty reportedly said he was interested in a firearm silencer for himself.

In the political geography of the Hells Angels fiefdom of Arizona, though, while Smitty was a potentate in Bullhead and had been Dobyns's first close contact with the bikers, he was not a major leader in the rest of the state. The ATF knew that Sonny Barger, though formally not even an officer in the Cave Creek chapter, still commanded respect; that was also why his disciple, Daniel "Hoover" Seybert, the president of Sonny's chapter, carried such weight in the club's affairs in the state. Initially Hoover had been cool to Rudy Kramer's proposal to set up a Solo Angeles club in Arizona, so Dobyns and his team had decided to concentrate on wooing the equally influential—and already friendlier—leader of the Mesa chapter, Robert "Mesa Bob" Johnston.

Smitty started talking up the Solo Angeles to Mesa Bob, piquing his interest. It didn't hurt that Dobyns gave Johnston a $500 gift for the Hells Angels defence fund. On November 13, at the 5 and Diner restaurant in Chandler, Johnston told Dobyns that he would make it clear to the wary Hoover that the Solo Angeles were his guests in Arizona.

"Hoover is just like me. We have our fingers in everything," Johnston is quoted in the ATF affidavit as boasting. He called Hoover at Sonny Barger's Motorcycle Shop in Cave Creek but was told Hoover was out. He reached the Cave Creek president on his cellphone to tell him he was lunching with Bird of the Solo Angeles. The ATF felt that Hoover was clearly mellowing: he replied that everyone knew the new gang was in town and they were more than welcome at the Cave Creek clubhouse.

The Solo Angeles' endearments to Mesa Bob and his chapter worked so well that it didn't take long for other chapters to start falling over themselves in their rush to recruit the Solo Angeles. It seemed that everyone was eager to get the tough and brash newcomers working with them. In Bullhead City, Smitty told undercover cop Billy Long that he wanted the Solo Angeles to become prospect members under his Nomads. From the small Skull Valley chapter in Prescott, George "Joby" Walters told Bird over drinks one night at the Spirits Lounge how much he appreciated the Solo Angeles' support. Joby's endorsement was significant, considering that he himself had been brought into the club as a prospect by Sonny Barger. Lean and leathery, he often acted as Barger's bodyguard. He was once arrested in Albuquerque for packing a gun during one of Barger's book signings. A rough-and-tumble old-school cowboy, Walters ran a mechanical bull for a living—and introduced Sonny Barger to the Arizona passion for horses. Barger's good friend could never have imagined that his friendliness would eventually help the ATF cops get official status inside the Hells Angels through his Skull Valley chapter.

Like all good stings, Black Biscuit would work best if the targets themselves begged to be stung. Any criminal—especially the Hells Angels—would be suspicious if you came on too strong, too eager. So instead of knocking on the Angels' doors, asking to join, the ATF had gambled that it would be much more alluring—and safer—to set up the Solo Angeles as a friendly club, supportive of the Hells Angels, and let Barger's boys draw them in.

The ATF agents soon began to try and buy guns and drugs from the Arizona bikers. According to a detailed account in an ATF affidavit, on September 19, 2002, Dobyns and Canino met with Tucson member Douglas Dam and chapter president Craig Kelly at Kelly's home on South Winmore. The allegations set out below have not been tested in a court of law, but this is what police claim happened.

Neither man could legally handle guns—Kelly had spent sixteen years in jail for murdering his wife's lover; Dam confided that he had done time in Massachusetts prisons. The cops assured the bikers that they need not touch the guns, just broker the deal; the Tucson men "offered to obtain percussion grenades and smoke grenades along with handguns and AK-type assault rifles."

The next day, police say, Dam escorted the two Solo Angeles into a storage trailer in his backyard. Out of a red nylon bag, he produced a blue steel Taurus .38 calibre five-shot revolver with wooden grips; Carlos said he handed the biker $800 for that gun and another pistol he promised to deliver.

The ATF affidavit also said that Dam showed the cops a 9mm calibre semi-automatic pistol—not for sale, he said, because "the gun was used in a serious crime and it needs to go in the river." The ATF claimed he said that the Tucson chapter of Hells Angels had to okay his dealing with the Solo Angeles gunrunners. Tucson, he joked, would be an easy target for racketeering gang charges if they were not careful.

Those at least are the allegations in the ATF affidavit. Dobyns and Canino were riding high. They felt they had pulled off their first major gun deal with the Angels. "We felt we had scored a touchdown," Canino says, laughing.

But when they pulled up later to meet their controller, Joe Slatalla, he threw a beer bottle at Jay Dobyns's head.

"Hey, what's the matter?" Dobyns exclaimed.

"We've been trying to find you guys all day," Slats said.

Canino and Dobyns felt sheepish. They had deliberately shaken their cover team, with the attitude that, screw it, there's two of us and we can take care of ourselves. It would be the first of an escalating series of confrontations between the frontline troops and the case managers, all too typical of tense, long-term undercover operations.

Still, everyone was thrilled by the speed and ease with which the ATF agents were able to win over the Hells Angels' trust. "I'm thinking to myself, No law enforcement officer in history of this country has ever worn the patch of the Hells Angels," Canino says. "A month into it, we said, 'Hey, you know what? We're going to kick these guys' asses. The only people who are going to stop us are the ATF. The only thing that's going to stop us is us.'"

Canino had no idea how true those words would be. In the end, in-fighting between the ATF and prosecutors would imperil the results of the entire investigation.

In the fall of 2002, barely twelve weeks into the Black Biscuit operation, the undercover team was shaken up with the loss of two key players but strengthened by the arrival of a new, female, operative.

The first to go was Rudy Kramer, whose drug-dealing criminal past gave the cops their ticket into the Hells Angels but also turned out to be his ticket to disaster. He became a handling nightmare. "Rudy was like a wayward kid. He had a good heart, but he was always messing up," Canino says. The team suspected he was "tweaking," back on drugs. On September 6, 2002, police stopped his car near a meth factory and discovered drug paraphernalia inside.

Clearly Rudy was becoming a liability. What's more, they did not need him any more: he had already got them into the circle of the Hells Angels. So the ATF came up with an old but effective way to get rid of him: they re-arrested him on the gun charge that had first led him into the arms of Joe Slatalla back in 2001. They figured his arrest would have the bonus effect of solidifying their credibility with the Solo Angeles, what with one of their own boys being hauled off to prison. With Rudy out of the way, Jay Dobyns took over as the de facto leader of the Solo Angeles Nomads.

Dobyns was pushing himself, playing the tough guy biker while always trying to cook up new schemes to ingratiate the Solo Angeles to the HA. "My job was to run interference for Jay," Canino says, worrying that the ATF was running Jay into the ground. "There's no way he can keep up that pace." Dobyns admits Canino kept him sane: "Carlos was the glue."

That glue was about to come unstuck because of ATF bureaucratic wrangling.

Joe Slatalla had borrowed Canino temporarily from the Miami office, but he now realized he needed the crack undercover operative for much longer. He had a good working relationship with Canino's boss in Miami. Unfortunately, another ATF manager in Phoenix did not—and instead of politely asking for Miami's understanding, he wrote an abrupt email request. That so angered the Miami supervisors that they shot back with distressing news: not only would they not extend Canino's assignment, they were going to cut it short and ordered him back home by October 1.

"I was pissed," Canino admits. "Jay was a friend I'd looked up to for ten years. Now I'm leaving the frontlines, leaving the fight."

The team tried to object to the decision but with no luck, so they had to come up with an exit strategy: how were they going to explain to the Angels the sudden departure of the Solo Angeles' key Spanish-speaking player without raising suspicions? By chance, Canino caught sight of a newspaper article about the arrest of a Chicago drug dealer with the same last name that Canino was using for his undercover identity. He hatched a story and played it out one night when the boys were out drinking with Smitty, the Nomad leader in Bullhead.

"Hey, what's the matter? You look kind of down," Smitty said to a glum Canino, according to police recollections of that evening.

"Oh, something's bothering me," Canino admitted.

"Tell me. I can help you out," Smitty offered, and the ATF agent showed him the newspaper clipping.

"You involved in this?

"No, but this guy's my cousin," Canino explained. "I gotta get away from here because I don't want to bring the heat down on you guys till I find out what the feds have on him. As good as you treated the Solo Angeles, I cannot bring you guys down."

The Hells Angels bought the tale, and Canino was able to disappear gracefully. If anything, his apparent self-sacrifice impressed the Hells Angels. The ATF team had deftly turned debilitating departure into a gain in their stature with the bikers. But with Carlos Canino out of the picture, the ATF undercover team was now down a cop. They also began to realize that perhaps what they needed was not just any replacement but a female one.

In the Hells Angels world, a "chick" is seen as just one more biker accessory. And for Jay Dobyns, that meant problems as he began hanging out more and more with the Arizona Angels. The wife of one biker began coming over to his house and flirting. At one party, Hells Angels tried to foist an eighteen-year-old daughter of another member onto Dobyns. "For me in my undercover role to say no to this young attractive woman, it was weird. 'What are you talking about, you're not interested in her? What the fuck's up with this dude—he doesn't like chicks? What's the deal?'"

Dobyns pleaded with management to find a female operative. During his earlier undercover work in Bullhead City, Dobyns had partnered with one female agent, but she did not work out; another agent sent in to replace her was soon promoted. The ATF hunted for other candidates from their offices all over the country. Either the managers didn't want to free up their agents for that long a period or the women didn't relish playing the role of a subservient biker chick. "It takes a unique and special person with extraordinary self-confidence to operate comfortably in the HA environment, especially for women," Dobyns says. "Tension, violence, and sexuality are in the air at all times around these guys."

By chance, Dobyns thought he had spotted a potential partner in August while attending an ATF training program for undercover agents in San Diego. During a rare break from work, Dobyns grabbed his surfboard and was walking down to the beach hoping to get a much-needed respite from being both a real cop and a pretend biker. He quickly found out an undercover cop is always on duty.

"Hey, baldy!" he heard someone shout, a reference to his clean-shaven biker look. He ignored the call, figuring it was some jerk at a bar.

"You fuckin' heard me," came the taunt again.

This time Dobyns turned to see Smitty, the Nomad from Bullhead City, and Pete Eunice, the California biker Dobyns had last met at the Laughlin shooting. The would-be surfer automatically switched into his biker undercover role.

"Hey, what's going on, man? What are you doing here?" he asked his biker pals.

"Oh, it's my birthday, so we're staying in La Jolla," Smitty said, smiling.

A few moments earlier, Dobyns had been a surfer; now he was playing a biker. But he had to think quickly as a cop. He knew he had twenty-five undercover colleagues at a nearby conference: why not grab this opening and make another play against a major target like Smitty?

"Well, shit, you know what?" he told Smitty. "You can't spend your birthday alone. Let's get together and have some beers."

Dobyns then walked away to catch some waves. But once back at the conference, he grabbed some fellow undercover agents, explained the situation and told them this would be a great opportunity to mingle with their targets. Most of the agents on hand were veterans, but one was a fresh, twenty-nine-year-old recruit named Jenna MaGuire. Dobyns had run into her briefly at the Laughlin Run; now he saw a chance to test her out with Smitty.

"I was six months out of the academy. I had no undercover experience," MaGuire recalls. But she jumped at the chance. Born in Baltimore, she had dreamed of being a secret service agent in high school but ended up with a criminal justice degree at university and a more tranquil job as an immigration officer. In her training, she met people from the ATF and was impressed by their passion and their goal: "Working violent crime and stuff that I thought made a difference." She joined in 2001 and was posted to San Diego.

At the bar that night, Dobyns introduced MaGuire as a some-time girlfriend he had known a couple of years ago. They bought Smitty drinks and a birthday cake. MaGuire hit it off with Smitty's wife, Lydia.

"It was really just to see if I could fit in," MaGuire says. "I felt good; it wasn't stressful, really, because there were so many agents there who knew what they were doing."

MaGuire's debut had been an off-the-cuff and off-the-books operation. Getting approval from management for her long-term deployment would be another matter. The Black Biscuit team put in an official request for her to join, but her management initially refused because technically MaGuire was not even finished her probation.

"You're putting a goldfish in a tank of piranhas" was one of the put-downs MaGuire heard—and she was angry. "There were some people in my management who didn't feel that I was ready for it. They weren't even giving me a shot."

Eventually, management relented and MaGuire was on board. At first blush, she was arm candy, coming out to Phoenix for a couple of weekends a month, playing Jay's girlfriend from San Diego.

MaGuire and Dobyns agreed that she would not play the stu-pid bimbo, which would have been uncomfortable for her and probably still have left Dobyns vulnerable to more aggressive biker women. Instead, her cover story would be that she ran errands for Dobyns and served as a courier for his gun and drug deals. That would explain to the Angels why she always carried a gun, which would be an added security bonus.

Her presence had several advantages, not the least being that it protected Dobyns from unwanted sexual advances. MaGuire could also gather intelligence that the men could not: "People automati-cally were more comfortable with me because they never figured a girl would be a cop." And she hoped the bikers' girlfriends would open up and confide some of their men's secrets to her.

MaGuire's first real test in the field came in early November, when she went out to Bullhead City two weekends in a row as Dobyns's "old lady" with the name of Genevieve—though Dobyns always called her by a nickname, "JJ." The immediate goal was to further win over Smitty and his wife. Dobyns was far from assured they could pull it off. "She's not sure of herself. She's got people at her office saying, 'You're never going to make it. You're going to get hurt. You're going to get eaten up by these guys.'"

MaGuire strolled into the Inferno Bar, where Smitty held court with Dobyns. "They all treated him like a king there," she says. Smitty checked out MaGuire's body for some time and then blurted out, "You know what? You and I could make a lot of money together in wet T-shirt contests. I'll broker you in, you do your thing and we'll split the money."

Dobyns, knowing how tough and spunky his new partner was, shuddered inside. "I'm thinking, Shit—here we go!"

Without missing a beat, MaGuire shot back at the biker leader, "Hey, listen, you know what? I know how these other women who hang around you guys act and how they conduct themselves. I don't act like that. I'm not showing my tits in some wet T-shirt contest so you can put money in your pocket."

Dobyns was mortified. "I felt, Oh, the shit's on now!"

MaGuire had reacted on gut instinct. As Jenna, it took a lot to offend her, but when she was offended, she fired back. As Genevieve, she did the same thing. And it hit home. Smitty stared at the ground around him as he considered her direct challenge and then said, "Okay."

"And that right there set the stage that would carry her for the rest of the case," Dobyns recalls, looking back at that pivotal point. "She wasn't going to be some barstool whore. She conducted herself with dignity."

JJ was quickly accepted into the Hells Angels' circle of friends, and over the next few weeks and months, she would grow close to many of the wives and girlfriends.

Early in the new year she flew out to Phoenix to set up a home with Dobyns and his fellow Solo Angeles. On her first official day on the job full time, she got off the plane and showed up at the designated undercover house, only to find two Hells Angels sitting there—Mark Kruppa and Cal Schaefer, one of the alleged shooters at Laughlin—talking with Billy Long. "Hey, get used to it," Dobyns told her later. "These guys are going to be around all the time."

She did get used to it—and excelled. At a wild biker party her first weekend in town, a photo captures Jenna MaGuire smiling broadly as she nestles in between three Angels from the Mesa chapter: a hard-ass biker named Nick Nuzzo, Cal Schaefer and Paul Eischeid, one of the Mesa bikers whom the police targeted as one of Cynthia Garcia's suspected killers.

It was just a few months into the undercover operation, but Jay and his gang had already established a reputation in the biker world as debt collectors and dangerous outlaw gun dealers. They were known in all the right places. Every bartender, every barmaid and every stripper in town had their numbers. Bullhead City was their town. Then an unscheduled police traffic stop boosted their reputations and credibility beyond their wildest dreams

After one late-night party with the Hells Angels, Dobyns, MaGuire and a troop of bikers were roaring through the back streets to get back to Bird's house. Suddenly, they were pulled over by local police. Except for the ATF task force, which included a few select members of the Phoenix Police Department and other agencies, the police in cities across Arizona had no idea the Solo Angeles were not a real outlaw motorcycle gang. In fact, at joint intelligence meetings, police officers were passing out pictures of the new bikers on the scene. They would tell each other, "We have to figure out who these guys are."

When fifteen local Bullhead cops pulled over Dobyns, MaGuire and a bunch of Hells Angels with their women in tow, the cops had no idea there were undercover agents among the bikers. Riding up front with Bird was Douglas Dam, the two-hundred-pound sergeant-at-arms of the Tucson chapter with a mean reputation as an enforcer. "He just liked to fight; he liked to beat the shit out of people," Dobyns says.

The Hells Angels, accustomed to regular police stops, turned off their engines and put their hands on their bike handlebars, knowing the cops liked to make sure no one was going for a weapon.

"Take your hands off the handlebars and back up toward us," the cops instructed through a bullhorn. "We know you've got guns."

Dobyns did as he was told but was surprised when the cops went after him first—apparently most interested in the tough-looking, heavily tattooed new leader of the Solo Angeles they had heard so much about. The cops frisked Bird and took away his guns. Only then did they move on to the Hells Angels.

According to the ATF, Douglas Dam was dumbfounded and would later spread the word of Bird's prominence throughout the club. "You wouldn't believe it. They were more worried about Bird than they were about me. Who is this guy, what's his story and why are they so afraid of him?"

But the unscheduled traffic stop had briefly rattled MaGuire. As the cops ran her fake undercover ID through the system, all kinds of doubts raced through her mind: "Is my stuff going to fly? Are they going to run my name and is there something goofy in the system that maybe says I'm ATF?"

MaGuire's badge and real identification were locked away in an ATF offsite location. She realized she was in deep. "You can't call time out. You don't get that luxury."

MaGuire had also just made a small drug buy—a "teener bag" of meth—from one of the biker women, placing the dope in her coat pocket. Usually the ATF agents waited until the next morning to drop off and record their drug deals at the ATF office. As luck would have it, MaGuire had decided to drop her dope off right after the party and before the unscheduled traffic stop.

"If I hadn't, I'd be going to jail. They searched my coat pocket several times." MaGuire laughs at the memory. "After that, if I bought dope, I put it in my boots. The cops never checked your boots."

Jenna MaGuire, the fresh recruit from Baltimore, was now thinking as—and being treated as—a full-time Arizona biker chick.

For security reasons, the ATF kept its two undercover operations—Dequaillo with biker Mike Kramer and Black Biscuit with the ATF agents—separate. Kramer knew Jay Dobyns was a cop, but he knew nothing about the other Solo Angeles. Early on, Kramer had helped introduce Dobyns to some of the Arizona bikers, using his own credibility as a full-patch member to ease the way. But that was it. "We did not cross over," says Kramer's handler John Ciccone, "so if someone took a burn it would not expose both cases."

By early 2003—just over half a year after the Black Biscuit undercover operation had officially kicked into high gear—it was clear that the Hells Angels in Arizona had come to accept the Solo Angeles as a friendly club. The bikers were eagerly selling drugs and guns to Dobyns as Bird, MaGuire as JJ, Phoenix cop Billy Long, known as "Timmy," and Pops the informant and they were all partying with the Angels late into the night.

At a drinking party at the Desert Flame Lounge in Apache Junction on January 21, according to an ATF affidavit, Mesa boss Bob Johnston told them he had "hung his ass out" to support the Solo Angeles. The cops believed that Johnston was one of the bikers who had opposed new clubs being allowed in the state. But he assured Bird that he had "vouched" for him to all the Angels he knew.

"The HAs warmed to me because I did not overtly try to impress them," says Dobyns. "I let them see what I knew they would like—confidence, character, intelligence, money, loyalty, courage, pride—and then I stood back and let them come to me."

Eight days later, the cops were partying with the boys at the Mesa clubhouse—the same place where Cynthia Garcia had been beaten. One of her suspected killers, Paul Eischeid, was on hand, and the Hells Angels agreed to take plenty of pictures of their new friends.

"You don't go into an HA clubhouse and start taking pictures," Dobyns notes. "But these guys loved us so much they were asking us to take pictures." Dobyns even pushed protocol by insisting on always carrying his guns—even into Hells Angels clubhouses, a practice normally forbidden to non-members. "I would always say, I'm a debt collector; people don't like me; people are pissed off at me, so I keep my guns with me."

"You come on in—you guys are cool," the bikers agreed.

Bikers whom the ATF agents had won over from the start, like Nomad Donald "Smitty" Smith, were becoming friendlier. At one evening get-together at a Denny's restaurant, Smitty proudly showed off his new "vice-president" patch on his vest.

Bird was widening the circle of Hells Angels who trusted him. He befriended a member of the Tuscon chapter named Robert "Mac" McKay, a gruff, towering member whose bald head and thick beard made him look all the more like the menacing biker he was. McKay ran the Black Rose Tattoo Parlor on Sixth Avenue in downtown Tucson. Though Dobyns was already immaculately tattooed, he had long wanted to get "sleeved down"—his arms completely covered in tattoos. Not because it would enhance his undercover image, just because he felt like it. "I always wanted to do it. Mac was a damn good tattoo artist and ATF was helping to fund it so it was all good for me," he jokes.

MaGuire, as JJ, was also getting closer not just to the women but also to the bikers themselves, making her own drug buys.

By February the Angels thought highly enough of the Solo Angeles to invite them to join their annual prison run, an eighty-mile trek from Arizona to the federal penitentiary in Florence, Arizona. "Ride a Harley, Go to prison" the Hells Angels' poster read. The guards let the inmates line up in the prison yard as the bikers paraded by the fence. Dobyns was appalled at the sight: "You have convicts being honoured by a criminal organization. I don't know how it exists, don't know why it exists. I don't know why it continues to exist."

That wasn't the only policy of neglect that irked Dobyns. As a

biker, he would often ride on the highway shirtless, his edgy tattoos bared for all to see—along with two pistols stuck in the
back of his pants. Carrying a registered weapon is not illegal in
Arizona, but still Dobyns wondered, "How can someone ride
around on a motorcycle with their shirt off with a couple of
guns in the back and not get pulled over at least to figure out
who this guy is. Not one cop ever stopped and challenged me.
Not one cop ever said, 'I'm just going to at least find out who this
dude is. I'm going to run him and see what his story is and see if
there is something to lock him up for because he is acting like
a dick.'"

Dobyns and his team were trying their best to keep up appearances as supposed Solo Angeles. They sent dues to Tijuana regularly when Pops, the informant riding with the ATF, rode down.
The Nomads T-shirts and stickers the ATF had printed up were
also a big hit with the Mexican gang leaders. Bird and Pops went
to California to participate in a Solo Angeles Toy Run. At one
point, a Solo Angeles leader asked them to stand behind him looking tough while he was being interviewed by a local television station. Bird put on his best biker glare and played the part perfectly—never imagining that the incident would soon help save
his skin and salvage the entire undercover operation.

To date, the only Solo Angeles that the Hells Angels had actually seen were Dobyns, his girlfriend and four other members.
Dobyns realized he had to up the ante, so to impress the Hells
Angels the ATF brought in about a dozen undercover agents from
across the United States to play the role of the Solo Angeles. All-
Stars, as they were nicknamed. The beefy, scruffy-looking cops
sure looked the part. One agent—nicknamed "Solo Sonny"—was
a big Southern farm boy, pushing 285 pounds on a massive six-
foot-four-inch frame. He used bungee cords to keep his size sixty-
four vest from blowing around in the wind when he rode.

When they first arrived, the other ATF cops were dubious of
how tight Jay Dobyns could be with the Hells Angels. "I told them
that I was going to walk them into the HAs, based on my word,"
Dobyns says with a smile. "They arrived skeptical. After the first

night [when] I walked them into the Mesa clubhouse, they were believers."

For ten days the cops in biker costumes hung out, rode and partied with the Arizona Angels. They were a huge success, affording Jay Dobyns his first of several encounters with the legendary Sonny Barger at a barbecue party that the Hells Angels held for their friends. Barger's Cave Creek clubhouse was a large white-brick building that stood out in the dilapidated Hispanic neighbourhood of Phoenix called Sunny Slope. Neat red trim made a line along the roof and around all the windows. A small bench below the front window was also appropriately red and white, as was the mailbox. Two large screaming Death Heads dominated the slanted white-metal gates.

Though nominally not even an officer in his own Cave Creek chapter, Barger carried himself with the aura and poise of the international star he was. "He's the shot caller, the deal broker. His reputation precedes him, so when people talk to him they know who they're talking to. Without a doubt you know that he's the Guy," Dobyns says. "He's very personable; he's charming. You can see how he developed this club. He's a politician; he's a salesman."

Bird walked up to the legendary biker to introduce himself as the Solo Angeles leader. "Don't know if you know who I am?" Dobyns asked tentatively.

"Oh yeah, I know who you are," Barger's scratchy voice came back through his tracheotomy. "Glad to have you here. You're a great friend to us. We need to see you around more. Come around more. We want to see more of you at Cave Creek."

Dobyns was relieved that word had got back to Barger about the new boys in town. "I think he knew that we were good for the Hells Angels." So Dobyns decided to push his luck. "Hey, man, you know, I'd love it if you'd come over and take a picture with all of us," he asked. Barger complied.

It was a moment of supreme irony. The photograph shows a proud, smiling Barger in the centre, next to two other senior Angels—Johnny Angel, one of Barger's oldest pals from California, and Dan "Hoover" Seybert, Barger's protegé in the

Cave Creek chapter. Closely packed around them, arms clasped over their shoulders, are ATF agents Jay Dobyns, Billy Long and Pops. And around them are about ten other long-haired, bearded mean-looking bikers—every single one of them a cop.

Sonny Barger could not have been more surrounded by cops if he'd attended a police convention.

EIGHT

Conning the Bikers

___

We reminded ourselves every day when we went out that we're the good guys, they're the bad guys. We're pretending, they're believing.
ATF UNDERCOVER AGENT JAY DOBYNS

March 2003 was going to be a terrible month for Sonny Barger. He would lose his wife, a biker leader he'd nurtured as a surrogate son and much of his reputation.

Just weeks after cavorting with Jay Dobyns and his Solo Angeles, Barger found himself embroiled in a messy domestic spat, charged with assaulting his wife and facing serious gun charges that could have sent him back to prison. To top it off, the aging biker leader had to face the indignity of finding out that the FBI was paying his wife as an informant.

It all began on March 6, 2003, when Maricopa County sheriff's deputies rushed to Barger's ranch on East Galvin Street in Cave Creek, just north of Phoenix, to answer a domestic call. His wife, Beth Noel Barger, and her thirteen-year-old daughter Sarrah accused the biker leader of punching and kicking them. It was not the first time the deputies had shown up at Barger's door. When Beth Noel became the biker legend's third wife in 1999 she was half his age, barely in her thirties. Like Sonny, she came from a rough working-class background. By her own admission, she had "mental problems" for which she took drugs. She once formally listed her education record as attending "Osbourne High School via Juvenile Detention Center." She had two children from a previous marriage; her daughter Sarrah moved in with her and Sonny. A pretty, thin woman with long brown hair, Noel loved horses—a passion she shared with the aging Angel, who was now spending more time on horses than Harleys. Their home on a bumpy dirt road had large corrals in the back to accommodate the animals. Along with Sonny's 2000 Harley Road King, a Camaro and a Chevy pickup, a horse trailer was frequently parked out front. Noel also helped Sonny run his ever-burgeoning business, styling herself vice-president of Sonny Barger Productions.

Their marriage was always rocky, as Sonny's philandering sparked rages from Noel. According to an eighteen-page sheriff's report, Barger himself called the police at 2:26 A.M. on July 14, 2002, to tell them he'd kicked her hard enough that "his wife is paralyzed and cannot move." When police arrived they found Noel slumped in the front seat of her car, moaning in pain. She and Sonny both agreed they were fighting over a "slut," as Noel called the latest woman her husband was seeing.

The tape recording of the 911 call, later played in court, has him at first saying, "She tried to pull a gun on me and I kicked her and she says she can't move." When the police arrived, he told them not that she had tried pulling a gun but that he thought she was going for one in her car, so he struck her. Noel, for her part, insisted the biker chieftain kicked her while she was sitting in a patio chair. Then, as she tried to get up from the ground, "Sonny grabbed her by the hair and threw her" back into the chair. She then made her way to her car, but "she had no feeling in her legs." Subsequent court testimony revealed that she had suffered a broken rib, a broken back and a lacerated spleen. Noel also told the police, "Sonny has beaten her before but she never reported it." Police charged Barger with aggravated assault.

Violence exploded again in the Barger household just over a year later in March 2003.

"Sonny became very angry, grabbed [Noel's] throat with his left hand and . . . struck her on the right side of the face with a closed fist," according to a police report read in court.

"Quit hurting my mom!" Sarrah claimed she said as she burst into the room.

"Get the fuck out of here!" Barger barked as he rushed toward Sarrah, according to police testimony. Sarrah told the police she began to run away screaming, but he grabbed her by her neck and by her right arm. "He bent Sarrah over backwards and punched her two times to temple area and then threw her to the floor."

"He hits my mom all the time. He's going to kill her," Sarrah told police. "I hope he goes to prison forever. I hate him."

According to a handwritten report by one of the arresting officers, Sonny Barger "admitted to me that he did physically grab his wife by the arms and possibly by the throat. He also admitted to pushing his 13-year-old daughter from the top of the head while he and his wife were arguing." Noel Barger, the officer noted, "is in fear for her life."

But the case took an unexpected turn at John Lincoln Hospital that night. FBI agent Stephen Smith visited Noel, who, according to an FBI affidavit, told them not only that Barger "had assaulted both her and Sarrah" but also that "he had a handgun at their residence." For Barger, a convicted felon, to be caught with a weapon would mean a return trip to prison for a long, long time.

Noel described the handgun as a STAR 9 mm semi-automatic handgun, inside a light brown gun case. That same night, FBI agents followed her back to the East Galvin home, where they searched the residence and the detached garage, in which they found the gun in the case so carefully described by Noel. "Beth Barger confirmed . . . that the gun found was Ralph Barger's gun," the FBI affidavit concluded. She claimed Sonny at times kept it on a nightstand on his side of the bed.

The story then took an even more bizarre twist. Noel later told *Phoenix Magazine* that she accepted $1,000 payment twice from the FBI and signed papers as a "confidential informant." If true, the FBI got a bad deal because Noel, seemingly torn between her fear and love of Barger, was hardly reliable. At first she told the FBI at the hospital that "Sonny most likely would try to hide the gun because he knew police were on the way to the house." The next day, after she was informed that her husband was facing charges, she casually said to police, "Well, I guess I'll just have to claim the gun was mine." As the court date approached, she told the FBI, "I'm already getting threatening phone calls out the ass."

By the time a three-day hearing began March 11 at the U.S. District Court in Phoenix to determine if there was enough evidence to detain Sonny Barger and proceed to trial, the defence was asserting that Noel had told several people the gun was hers. It did not take long for the FBI's case to unravel. There was scant evidence—except for the word of a distraught mother and daughter—that the gun was Sonny's or that he had handled it. Under stiff cross-examination from Barger's lawyer, Brian Russo, the hapless feds had to admit they had not even tested the gun for fingerprints. When asked by the incredulous judge if he had an explanation for such an oversight, the prosecutor's lame reply was "I do not. Anything sounds like an excuse."

Ruling there was no "reliable and credible evidence" that Sonny himself possessed the gun, the judge dismissed the case. Sonny Barger walked out of the federal courthouse a free man. He had done it again, escaped the long and often clumsy arm of the law. But this time he came away with scars—with his marriage to Beth Noel and to no small degree his reputation among his fellow Arizona Angels in tatters. Beating up on your wife is tolerated, if not encouraged, by the bikers, but to have your "old lady" in the pay of the feds—especially when you're the world-renowned Sonny Barger—was downright mortifying.

His biker legions were divided over their leader's plight. ATF agent Jay Dobyns, who was riding with the Angels, recalls that many were willing to cut the old man some slack. "But he was also despised for 'turning pussy,'" Dobyns says. "All he's concerned with is promoting himself, promoting his books, his movies, his products."

Nine days after walking out of court, Sonny Barger suffered an even more devastating blow. Dan "Hoover" Seybert was the forty-six-year-old president of Sonny's own Cave Creek chapter. Sonny had made Hoover the powerful person that he was. "Hoover was Barger's puppet," says Dobyns. He was the co-owner of Sonny

Barger's Cave Creek Cycles. Everyone knew that when Hoover spoke, he was speaking for Old Man Barger, who, in fact, treated him like a surrogate son.

In the early morning hours of Saturday, March 22, after a long evening of partying at Brigett's Last Laugh, a bar in north Phoenix, Hoover walked out, surrounded by fellow bikers. His girlfriend was putting on her bandana; Hoover was standing over his bike, adjusting his glasses, and the engines of the other bikes roared as they fired up. Suddenly Hoover keeled over, a bullet in his brain.

Within three days, Sonny Barger's Cave Creek Cycles was closed and never reopened. "I'm just going to miss him," Barger told the local media. "He put the club before anything in his life."

At first the bikers put out the word that Hoover had been yet another victim of the Mongols. Several months later, after Black Biscuit had wrapped up and the ATF's infiltration into the Angels became public knowledge, the Angels tried a different tack, pinning the shooting on the cops. Barger later told the authors that he believed Hoover had been killed by a police sniper positioned on a nearby building. He claimed police wanted Hoover dead because he had never trusted the Solo Angeles and suspected they were undercover cops. "He was shot by the feds because he wanted to run these guys who tried to infiltrate us out of town," Barger said.

But his claim was a convenient fiction, an attempt to deflect suspicion from a much darker conspiracy.

While it was true that Hoover had initially been cool to the Solo Angeles, by the time of his death he had warmed to them. "We brought Hoover around. We had made him an ally," says Jay Dobyns. "The guys in his chapter liked us. When he died, it hurt us because a guy supporting us was gone." Not only was it at Hoover's clubhouse that the Solo Angeles partied and met Sonny Barger, but Dobyns's team was trusted and embraced enough to be asked to Hoover's funeral.

What's more, the police had tested the sniper theory and the physics just didn't work. Hoover had taken a shot dead centre in his forehead, right between his eyes, from extremely close range. Somebody had walked right up to Sonny's man and assassinated him.

That gave the murder the appearances of either a well-orchestrated gang hit or a random bar slaying, but there were problems with both scenarios. If Hoover's death was indeed just a random killing, the unfortunate brawler stupid enough to tangle with an HA leader would have been punished mercilessly. Nothing happened. Homicide investigators were willing to entertain the possibility that a disgruntled bar patron who perhaps had gotten into a tussle with Hoover had managed to walk out and shoot the Hells Angel unnoticed over the deafening din of the roaring motorbikes, but that version of events is unlikely.

Even more implausible was that Hoover had been killed by a rival gang such as the Mongols. "How do you walk up to the chapter president, shoot him in the forehead point-blank, with his girlfriend on the back on the bike, with eight or ten other bikers all standing there and no one fires a shot back at you?" says one police officer familiar with the case. "No one chases you? How does that happen?"

If it had been the Mongols, the Hells Angels would have exacted an extensive, bloody revenge, as they always do. But there was no deadly rampage after Hoover's murder. None. Not a peep from the Mongols or against them.

That left only one option: Hoover's killing had all the markings of an inside job.

Police heard that there was plenty of resentment against Sonny's boy, Hoover. "There is a lot of concern that he was skimming money out of the club," says one investigator. "Doing all kinds of things, travelling around the country, spending money that he's not supposed to be spending. He'd gotten far too big for his own good."

An even darker scenario police were considering was that Hoover's killing was directed at Barger himself, part of a nascent power struggle. "It sends a message because he's Sonny's guy," says one officer close to the case. It was no secret that there was growing resentment among younger members of the club to Barger's self-absorbed approach: all the glory—and the money—from the Hells Angels brand seemed to go to Barger, who was making a personal fortune hawking his books and Hells Angels paraphernalia on his Web site.

Indeed, his fellow bikers had no real idea how much money their leader was making. Court papers later filed in his divorce proceedings give a revealing peek at Sonny's true fortune. Royalties from his autobiography totalled $330,238 in 2001, $340,843 in 2002 and $213,541 the following year, though Barger insisted much of that went to agents and his attorney. Twentieth Century–Fox was also paying him $150,000 over a period of a few years to option the movie rights to his autobiography.

According to his tax returns, he earned $171,332 gross in 2001, $221,686 the next year and $95,579 in 2003. Not bad for a motorcycle rebel.

Police say there was also bitterness among several of the other senior leaders of the Hells Angels who had expected Sonny to step aside gracefully once he moved to Arizona. "You can't be the heir apparent if Sonny continues to keep calling the shots and running things," says one officer. "Sonny didn't leave, and people are still in battle with that."

To this day, Hoover's murder remains unsolved.

On April 4, less than a month after her fight with Sonny, Noel Barger filed papers for divorce. On June 11, 2003, Sonny pleaded guilty to one misdemeanour count of assaulting his wife for the beating back in July 2002. The other counts were dismissed. He got a sentence of eight days but received a credit for time served.

Barger could take some solace from his escape from a badly bungled FBI trap on a gun charge. But he'd lost his surrogate son and an embarrassing wife—and he was only halfway through 2003. The rest of the year would have even more bad news in store for him. The ATF would not be as foolish as the FBI. When they went after Barger's fellow Angels in Arizona, the damage would be devastating.

———

The Hells Angels were also facing pressure in the rest of the country, although it was nothing the HA didn't seem to be able to handle. From their California birthplace, the HA had succeeded in putting down strong roots in half of the states, from Alaska to the Deep South, California to New York.

Through the 1990s they had spread into Illinois and Minnesota, fighting a pitched battle with the Outlaws, who regarded Chicago and the entire Midwest as their turf. By 2000 the HA was well established, having survived the firebombing of their Chicago clubhouse and the murders of several executive members. In Illinois, thanks in part to the work of Jay Dobyns's ATF colleague Chris Bayless, the president of Chicago's Hells Angels chapter, Melvin Chancey and two other former chapter leaders pleaded guilty to a decade-long conspiracy of violence to protect their cocaine and methamphetamine sales; Chancey got more than nine years behind bars. In Minnesota the HA vice president was charged with drug trafficking. The case abruptly ended in a hung jury in 2004 when an Internal Revenue Service special agent investigating money laundering admitted he was having an affair with the wife of the Angels' chief drug supplier. Several months later, though, the HA leader pleaded guilty.

Despite the court cases, HA chapters continued to spring up across America like Wal-Marts. Maryland was the latest. This was Pagan territory, and it wasn't long before the two sides began shooting at each other. The arrival of the Angels immediately sparked a police investigation. In July 2003 John Beal, president of the North Beach chapter of the Hells Angels, was arrested and eventually pleaded guilty to distribution of cocaine and firearm offences. Beal tried to call on some influential friends: a local minister, a mayor and the majority whip of the Maryland House of Delegates penned letters in his support, but to no avail. He got almost four years in prison. Then police charged two Maryland Hells Angels prospects with attempted murder after a barroom shooting that wounded two members of the Pagans.

Deal's ordeal resulted from another successful penetration of the bikers by the ATF. Darrin Kozlowski—who had first worked with John Ciccone on the largely improvised infiltration of the Vagos in the 1990s—this time spent two well-planned years under-cover, eventually becoming a full-patch member of the Warlocks, a large unruly gang close to the Hells Angels. Kozlowski's work—which led to more than thirty arrests and close to fifty search warrants against the bikers—showed how the ATF was maturing in creating false identities and protection for their agents. "I had a lot more confidence in my head," he said. "My backstops were a lot more detailed. Our stories were rock solid. There was no way there was going to be a hole."

Throughout the Northeast, the police continued to give the HA more grief. In Massachusetts two members of the Hell's Angels were indicted on assault and battery charges after they allegedly attacked an off-duty police lieutenant at a bar. In New York and Connecticut more than a dozen people associated with the Hells Angels were arrested in a series of federal drug raids.

It was clear that police had decided that as soon as the Hells Angels came to town they were going to take action. "Because once they get in, you almost can't get them out," Maryland State Police investigator Terry Katz said. "They have influence way beyond just one drug deal. It's kind of like: you don't have a major coke problem, now you do. You have people joining the gang that didn't have a gang to join till they got there. It's like a cancer."

Back in Arizona, ATF undercover agent Jay Dobyns could barely keep himself from laughing out loud.

Arizona Nomad leader Donald "Smitty" Smith was chatting with Dobyns at the biker's home. For months, Dobyns and his team had been burrowing deep inside the HA's circle, but here was Smitty, caustically remarking how the Hells Angels would not be as foolish as the Colorado-based Sons of Silence gang, which had been recently penetrated by two ATF agents.

"The Hells Angels would never allow themselves to be humili-ated," he boasted, according to Dobyns's recollection.

Dobyns could only chuckle to himself, knowing that his bike—the same motorcycle used by the ATF agents in Colorado—was parked in Smitty's driveway.

The Hells Angels prided themselves on being impenetrable. Their long recruitment process, from hangaround to prospect to full-patch member, coupled with extensive background checks, was designed to weed out cops and informers. And even while warmly welcoming the Solo Angeles, the HA never completely let down their guard. The undercover agents got a taste of the bikers' paranoia early in the operation, when Dobyns started doing gun deals with the Hells Angels in Tucson. The president of an HA support club called the Red Devils pulled him aside in the washroom of Peppers Bar, a well-known biker hangout.

"It's not personal, but I have to make sure you don't have a wire," he said as he calmly put a gun to Dobyns head. The ATF agent was forced to his knees, his shirt off, his pants dropped. It was a frightening moment, but Dobyns pulled through. Then he decided to turn the tables. As the biker began to walk away, Dobyns barked, "Hey, motherfucker, you think this is a one-way fucking street here? I have just as much fucking risk in this as you do." He promptly proceeded to force the biker to prove he too wasn't wearing a wire.

What the suspicious biker didn't know was that Dobyns and the other undercover cops did indeed record thousands of hours of their encounters with the bikers—but not with something as primitive as old-fashioned wires and microphones taped to their skin. "We didn't wear wires very often," Dobyns explains, in part because the bikers were constantly hugging each other and slapping each other on the back. "And if you're not comfortable with the equipment you're wearing, it's just the same as if you're not comfortable with the story you're carrying. If you're not comfortable, you're not confident. And if you don't carry yourself with confidence around these guys, you're not going to be believed."

Instead, the undercover agents recorded their conversations in tiny devices hidden in common items everybody carries, such as pagers and cellphones. "We had state-of-the-art electronics," says

Dobyns, though he is careful not to reveal operational secrets. There were glitches, of course: batteries that would die, tapes that would fill up. Generally, though, the technology worked.

On rare occasions, the agents carried tiny cameras. And all their undercover homes were completely wired. Over the course of the operation, Dobyns and his team went through four houses—from a dump in Bullhead City to a decent home in Phoenix with a backyard and pool to a cramped trailer outside of Prescott—that were always filled with visiting Hells Angels. "There is very little that took place that we did not record," Dobyns says.

The agents were also exceedingly well backstopped. The ATF had progressed greatly from the fly-by-the-seat-of-your-pants early days when John Ciccone was directing infiltrations into the Vagos in California. Back then, Darrin Kozlowski had to scramble to get fake ID ready. Now, Jenna MaGuire walked around confidently with her undercover driver's licence, social security card and credit cards. She often left her wallet out in plain view at the clubhouse and on several occasions spotted bikers going through it. "Everything in there I could explain," she says. At her home, she would casually leave her chequebook with her fake name lying around. "We often had visitors," she says. "They could rifle through anything—everything was backstopped."

From the start, Rudy Kramer had cautioned the cops that infiltrating the Hells Angels would be risky. According to an ATF debriefing note, he warned that the biker organization "conducts full background investigations on individuals seeking membership. These investigations include criminal history checks and credit checks. These investigations are conducted via the Internet with special software or by wives, girlfriends or associates employed by government agencies having access to this information."

Armed with that knowledge, the ATF hoped to use the HAs' sophisticated intelligence against them. "They did check us out on at least three occasions that we were aware of, and the private investigators came back and told the Hells Angels everything that we had been telling them," says Dobyns. "So their own people, their own investigators, were substantiating who we were, because we were so well backstopped."

Even in their personal lives agents had to be constantly on guard. Coming out of a Tucson restaurant with some friends one night, Dobyns ran into JoJo Valenti, vice-president of the Tucson chapter. Jay quickly told him his friends were clients in his protection racket.

Even Dobyns's children knew how to react quickly under pressure. As Bird, Dobyns put out the cover story that, though divorced, he tried to visit his two children from time to time in Tucson—just in case any bikers spotted him walking with his son or daughter. One Saturday afternoon, Dobyns was leaving a guitar shop in downtown Tucson with his then twelve-year-old daughter, Dale, when they bumped into Robert McKay, the burly, full-patch member who ran a tattoo shop.

"Go along with what I say," Dobyns whispered to his daughter.

"Hey, what's going on?" asked the biker.

"Trying to spend time with my daughter," Dobyns answered.

McKay said hello and shook Dale's hand. Dobyns could switch into his biker role automatically, but did he have confidence that his daughter could too?

"Absolutely," he says. "I was constantly reminding them, 'If we run into somebody, I'm a bad guy.' My kids know that."

Sure enough, Dale carried it off like a pro, behaving as if it was perfectly natural for her dad to be chatting with a Hells Angel. As they walked away, though, a relieved Dobyns leaned over to his girl: "Do not tell your mother. Do not tell your mother that you met this guy because she's going to be pissed off."

Jenna MaGuire also had her own brushes with blowing cover. While shooting pool one night with George "Joby" Walters, she casually made reference to having Irish roots.

"Oh, so do I," the Cave Creek member said. "What's your last name?"

MaGuire momentarily froze, suddenly realizing her undercover surname, Edwards, was hardly as Irish-sounding as MaGuire.

"Well, my mother's name is McCarthy," she said after a moment's hesitation. To herself she said, That was the longest pause in my life. But he probably didn't notice.

These were the expected accidents and improvisations in the undercover game. The real danger was being discovered by a paranoid biker.

"Get out! Get the guys out of the house!"

A frantic call came one evening early in March, as Dobyns and his team were relaxing in the house they shared as part of their role as Solo Angeles. Dobyns first got an emergency pager code and then he called their controller. It was Joe Slatalla.

"What's going on?" Dobyns asked.

"Don't ask questions—just get out!" Slatalla commanded.

The agents quickly scrambled out and regrouped at the ATF's offsite debriefing location, a nondescript office with a garage in the rear where the agents could meet securely, store their personal effects and work on their bikes.

What they heard there was bone-chilling: the Drug Enforcement Agency had an informant in the Phoenix HA chapter. Not knowing that the Solo Angeles were cops, he had simply passed on a report that some members of the Hells Angels had put together a hit squad. "Hey, look, they want to go kill these Solo Angeles."

The informant's DEA handler, who happened to be on the Black Biscuit task force, immediately passed on the tip. Shit! I'm glad we didn't waste a whole lot of time getting out of there, Dobyns remembers thinking when he heard the news.

The news got even worse when the ATF agents found out that the Hells Angel leading the charge was a six-foot-three, three-hundred-pound behemoth with long black hair and a black goatee nicknamed "Chico." His real name was Robert Mora, the ex-president of the Tucson Dirty Dozen, who had been instrumental in brokering the Hells Angels' takeover in Arizona.

Chico had spent five years behind bars for a manslaughter conviction for the killing of two men. He came out as the Arizona state prison boxing champion. An expert with knives, swords and a whip, he was known for keeping his favourite weapons stuck in special pockets on his biker vest.

"He's definitely the most feared biker in Arizona and one of the most feared bikers in the west," Jay Dobyns says. "He's just a big bad dude. Of the ten Hells Angels I had to stay clear of, he was probably number one on my list. I didn't want him to take my head off in some bar."

Chico had heard rumblings out of California that Jay's Solo Angeles were frauds. They never came to Tijuana, he heard—which was true, since as American cops, Dobyns and his team had no authority to operate in Mexico. Many of the real Solo Angeles had never heard of the new Arizona members. Joe Slatalla's ruse of setting up a fake Solo Angeles group had always been a brilliant but shaky gamble—and now it looked as if Chico was calling their bluff.

What's more, Chico was angry that the Solo Angeles' clubhouse was in his territory but they paid homage to Bob Johnston's Mesa chapter. "'You guys want to kiss Mesa's ass?'" Dobyns says to summarize Chico's beef. "'Then move out to Mesa and get the fuck out of my town.'"

With news that Chico and some Angels might be gunning for them, the ATF agents could take no chances. They lay low for a few days, watching the house. It appeared that Chico's men didn't know exactly where Dobyns and his Solo Angeles lived and never made it to the house. Back at the ATF offsite debriefing centre, nerves were frayed. The Solo Angeles have run out of gas, Dobyns thought, and we're done; the case is over. Let's see who we can arrest right now. This is as far as we can take it.

But like a quarterback in the dying minutes of a losing game, Dobyns tried one final desperate play. He figured that if he could get to Bob Johnston, the powerful Mesa president who had always stuck up for the Solo Angeles, he could perhaps salvage the operation. The task force banged around a strategy, everyone throwing out suggestions for what Dobyns should say and how, but Dobyns knew in the end it would still all come down to his ability to sell it to a skeptical biker.

He set up a meeting with the biker leader, but he was scared: "I thought I was going to get hit that night. That I was being set up to be taken out by the HAs and Chico."

Dobyns smoked a pack of cigarettes before he left. The task force had deployed police officers in full riot gear ready for a rescue, with additional uniformed cops in the area on standby.

According to Dobyns, this is what happened. He sat down with Johnston at a restaurant on Friday, February 28, and immediately confronted him over Chico's allegations. "It's bullshit and you know that," Dobyns told him. "I want you to think back to everything I've ever said to you. Everything I've ever done for you. Everything you know about me. You know that I sell guns. You know that I have been buying and selling dope. We've shown nothing but utmost loyalty to the Hells Angels and to the Mesa chapter."

Dobyns pulled out the photographs of him and Pops mixing with the Solo Angeles at their Toy Run in California. He gave Johnston a videotape of the TV newscast that showed Bird standing guard behind one of the Solo Angeles leaders. Evidence of that incidental trip had now become a lifesaver.

"If I'm not a Solo Angeles, if everything you know about me is not true, how could I show up at this run with this cut on," he asked, pointing to his vest, "and still be wearing it? Would any club allow it? Absolutely not. I'm a Solo Angeles, Bob. He's got it wrong. Chico is wrong."

Bird pointed pictures of him and Pops smoking and joking with the boys, even standing next to a Solo Angeles sergeant-at-arms, always wearing their Solo Angeles patch.

"Why wouldn't someone tell us to turn this shit in and get the fuck out of there?" Bird kept pushing. "It doesn't make any sense, Bob."

Finally Bird pulled out a photograph of the Solo Angeles Nomads that was hanging in the Tijuana clubhouse. "Last but not least," he said, "if I'm not a Solo Angeles, why is my fucking picture up on the clubhouse down there? Look at this physical evidence. I don't know where Chico's getting this, but he's wrong. That's all I can tell you—he's wrong."

Johnston bought it. He got on the phone to Chico, with Dobyns still standing there.

"Hey, you know what? You're wrong on this," Dobyns said Johnston told his fellow Angel. "I got physical evidence that these guys are legit, so I don't know where your sources are, but you stand down."

Dobyns had scored the touchdown. He had saved the operation.

Johnston had to impose some compromises: he told Bird that the Solo Angeles should stop wearing their colours until everything was cleared up. They also had to move out of Chico's turf in Phoenix. By the next Thursday, Bird called Johnston to tell him they had already done so, and Johnston gave him the okay to wear their patches again. That evening, Bird and his gang met with Hells Angels Nomad Smitty Smith and his bikers at his favourite hangout in Bullhead, the Inferno Lounge. Smitty suggested the Solo Angeles consider becoming Hells Angels Nomads operating in Bullhead. The undercover cops were back in the Hells Angels' good graces.

Chico still brooded. A few days later, Bird and the Solo Angeles found themselves at Sonny Barger's Cave Creek clubhouse, drinking at the bar with the bikers. "He eye-fucked us the whole time," Dobyns says, making his hatred clear: "'You know what, man. I don't like these dudes.'"

"Chico was the one guy that really had it figured out," Dobyns says, smiling. "But if everyone in the insane asylum says you're the crazy one, then you're the crazy one. And that's what happened to Chico. He was the one who understood it, but the whole club said, 'You're wrong.'"

For Dobyns, it was the pivotal moment in the case. "I went from the lowest of lows to the highest of highs. I went from feeling like Chico had blown up our operation and feeling like we would possibly be assassinated to the satisfaction of knowing that Bob, an old-school and respected HA, had just vouched for me to his 'brother' of over twenty years. He picked me over Chico. At that point I knew I could take this in any direction I wanted to."

Operation Black Biscuit kicked into high gear. Dobyns and the team devised a series of increasingly complicated ruses and scams. They involved elaborate planning, a good dose of improv theatre and, more often than not, a healthy dash of luck.

One of their first targets was Robert "Mac" McKay, the skilled tattoo artist from Tucson who had befriended Bird. McKay, who had previous arrests for aggravated assault, trespass and disorderly conduct, had already expressed an interest in Dobyns's job as a debt collector for the mob out of Vegas. "Ask your boss if he would like to put a Hells Angel on the payroll," McKay said. What follows is a version of events based on an ATF affidavit and police accounts. McKay was never charged with anything related to these events.

In early March, Bird and Jenna MaGuire as JJ decided the time was ripe to pull an elaborate hoax on Mac McKay. While Dobyns was in McKay's tattoo shop getting some fine artwork done on his arms, his cellphone rang. "Okay, JJ, go!" was Bird's clipped remark.

"What the fuck is going on?" McKay asked.

Dobyns explained that his casino bosses wanted him to collect a debt from a "playboy" who was in town, but the man was always surrounded by bodyguards: "My scam is that JJ will make him think that he's going to get in her pants. She's going to drag him out to a restaurant, and then I swoop in and take my money back."

A couple of hours later, as arranged, Dobyns's phone rang again.

"Mac, she's got him," Dobyns said, telling the biker that JJ had set up a breakfast meeting with the target the following day. "I got no one to back me up. You mind riding with me?"

"This will be a good chance for me," the biker agreed.

The next morning, March 12, Dobyns met McKay outside his shop at eleven o'clock, and they rode their bikes to a nearby Waffle House. MaGuire was sitting at a booth with a clean-cut, college-boy-type ATF agent named Eric Rutland, playing the role of the hapless debtor.

Bird slid into the booth next to the target; McKay sat down opposite him and did his best version of the biker stare-down.

"What's up?" gulped the nervous man.

"You know who I am?" Bird asked.

"No."

"I'm the guy telling you how the fuck it is. You think that money you took out of Vegas wasn't going to come back? You think that you were just going to walk away and no one was ever going to tighten you up for that?"

The ATF agent lowered his head. "Shit, I knew this was coming," he mumbled.

"They could have sent any number of assholes to beat your ass and get that money. I'm not going to do that, man. I just want to help you get that right: give me something so I can go back and tell my people you're trying."

The man immediately offered to write a cheque for $17,000.

Dobyns later gave McKay a couple of hundred dollars. "That's how easy it is: you watch my back and make $200 for five minutes' work."

McKay quickly spread the word to the other bikers, according to Dobyns. Other Hells Angels started calling up Dobyns, pleading for a cut of the action. "Hey, man, when you have a collection to do, don't call Mac, call me."

McKay jealously guarded his new association with Bird. At a meeting at Guillermo's restaurant on Fourth Avenue in Tucson, he suggested that Dobyns should consider using an electric cattle prod during his debt collections; according to an ATF affidavit, he also bragged that he had recently "Tazed" a victim behind his own tattoo parlour using an electric stun gun.

More significantly, McKay not only wanted to join Dobyns's extortions, he also wanted Dobyns to join the Hells Angels. He told Dobyns he was "wearing the wrong patch," suggesting the Solo Angeles should consider prospecting for his Tucson chapter. That made McKay the third Angel—after Smitty of the Nomads and Bob Johnston of Mesa—eager to sign up the undercover cops. McKay pointed out that prospects had to be approved for full membership by a unanimous vote of all the chapter members. That would be a lot easier in Tucson, with only about ten members, than in Bob Johnston's more powerful Mesa chapter, which boasted about twenty.

The ATF took heed of McKay's advice but opted to target an even smaller Hells Angels club in Arizona than McKay's Tucson chapter. The Skull Valley chapter, based in the town of Prescott, was scraping by with five members.

One of them, Joby Walters, had been openly friendly to the Solo Angeles almost from the start, and when the Skull Valley chapter decided they needed a Web site to sell their T-shirts, Bird told them he knew someone who loved the bikers so much that he'd probably do it free. The Angels agreed; Dobyns got a member of the Black Biscuit team to do the Web work, finding it mildly entertaining that the ATF actually built a Hells Angels Web site.

The next target Bird and JJ went after was Bobby Reinstra, the Skull Valley sergeant-at-arms. In court-filed affidavits, they say the following events unfolded. Reinstra, who would eventually be charged with other offences, denies any wrongdoing and the truth remains to be settled in court.

Reinstra was almost stereotypical in his biker look: shaved head; thin, straight eyebrows; piercing eyes; and a pointed goatee. He appeared keen on helping Bird with his baseball-bat-wielding debt collections. "I already know that business," he told Dobyns. "We just call it extortion."

Dobyns chose Las Vegas for the scam, where the Hells Angels were planning a party on the April 18 weekend. "Hey, Vegas— that's where I'm from." Playing up his Mafia debt collector story, Bird told them, "You go to Vegas, man, the town is yours, because it's mine."

He called up his police contacts to broker some rooms in the packed gambling capital. Vegas was all booked, but when the Hells Angels arrived, they were impressed that Bird could swing some rooms at the four-star Hard Rock Café and Casino. Then, having pulled up in their loud Harleys in the parking lot, the bikers were told by security guards that they could not wear their patches inside. It was one year after the bloody Laughlin shootout, and with the next Laughlin River Run just a few days away, everyone in Vegas was on edge.

"Fuck you, I'll sleep in the fuckin' ditch in the rain before I take my cuts off to come into this piece of shithole hotel," one biker retorted. "I don't take this off for anybody."

Bird stepped in to calm things down: "Hang on, hang on, fellows. Easy, we've been riding in the rain for four hours to get here. We're cold, and we do not want to be sleeping outside."

He walked away and called his local police contact. "Look, dude, security is jacking us in the parking lot. You need to make some calls and get this done." He hung up and turned to his Angel buddies. "Give it a few minutes. I'm calling my guys, see what happens."

Sure enough, within minutes the security men came back out. "Say, gentlemen, welcome to the Hard Rock."

The Angels were stunned. "Shit! Bird picks up the phone, makes a call and we're in!"

The bikers knew Bird did collections for a mob boss nicknamed "Mr. Big" in Vegas. They wanted to meet him, but Reinstra insisted he be the only one to accompany Bird: he wanted all the action for himself.

Now Dobyns had to come up with the action—and a Mr. Big. "Look, we need a guy who fits the stereotypical organized crime figure, some guy to play the role so that I can introduce him to the HA," Dobyns said to his Vegas police contacts.

"There's a guy in the Vegas office that fits that role so damn good he could play a mobster on TV," they told him.

But at the last minute the cop was busy. Dobyns got a disturbing call. "He can't be there. Don't worry—I got a guy who's going to play the role. Trust me."

The change unsettled Dobyns, who liked to stage-manage every last detail of his ruses. "Shit! I'm taking these guys to meet my boss who now I don't know. I'm thinking, This is not going to be good. I'm not sure we can pull this one off."

Dobyns and MaGuire met the replacement who was supposed to play the Mafia boss and had less than five minutes to get their story down straight.

"You know, that guy's not going to work," Dobyns muttered to MaGuire as they left. "He doesn't look right."

That night, Bird, JJ and Reinstra headed toward a dimly lit bar on the west side of Vegas called PT's Pub. Mr. Big ushered Bird in and then JJ before Reinstra, treating her as an equal and further humbling the Angel. The biker stood there as if it was his turn to go see the principal.

"You guys want to work for me, huh?" said the mobster in his best Italian accent, having introduced himself as Lou. "Let me get something straight with you guys," he barked back. "I don't give a fuck about you. I don't give a fuck about the Hells Angels. But I give a fuck about Bird. 'Cause Bird's my guy. Anything happens to him in his attempt to become one of you guys, you guys are going to pay for it. And I guarantee you my guys will fuck your guys up. Are we straight?"

Dobyns had to stifle his laughter, watching the Mafia boss treat the Angels the way they all too often bullied their underlings. Dobyns and Mr. Big discussed a shipment of firearms to be delivered the next day, and the meeting broke up by 10:30 P.M.

Dobyns claims Reinstra was so impressed, he said, "Lou is just like the Sopranos—he's like Gotti and all that Godfather shit."

"Yeah, he's the real deal," Bird agreed. In fact, Dobyns had been so impressed by the last-minute replacement he assumed was another cop that he called his Vegas police partners to thank them. "You know your guy played it beautiful. He completely sold it. They're bragging on it."

"Well, he should have sold it," the Vegas cop said with a chuckle. "He's a real mobster from New Jersey that we caught here, and we put him in that deal for you."

The following day, Reinstra asked Dobyns six times, according to the ATF affidavit, about the pending firearms deal with Lou. "This is a chance for me to prove myself [to Lou]," the biker said, according to an ATF affidavit. By 6 P.M., Bird told Reinstra the firearms had arrived and headed out to Palomino Bar to take delivery, asking Reinstra to assist him in checking the firearms—an Uzi pistol, two Mac-10 pistols, a firearm silencer and two AK-47 rifles—and stand in as a bodyguard.

That night over supper at the New York, New York hotel, Reinstra talked about how much he understood the gangster life because he was into "extortion, loan sharking and prostitution— you know, racketeering."

He put out his index finger and thumb in the form of a mock gun and said he didn't know how to tell Lou that he had "done some of this before." He said that it was eagerness to take care of business for the club that propelled him up the ranks to sergeant-at-arms for the Skull Valley chapter. "Some call it stupidity, but it takes balls to walk up and shoot someone between the eyes," he said. "There are few people that can live with that."

He could be called a "rat hunter," the biker explained, again mimicking a firearm with his hand, implying that he had killed an informer. "Three can keep a secret if two are dead," he said, echoing a famous biker slogan. He was a good killer, Reinstra told Dobyns, and a patient one, sometimes waiting four or five years to get even. "I am the guy that will be standing next to your pillow at 3 A.M."

All this, at least, was the ATF's version of events. Reinstra was eventually arrested on other charges and is still awaiting trial. The purpose of the Las Vegas ruse was not necessarily to gather criminal evidence but to win Reinstra's confidence.

Dobyns's reward came when, the police claim, Reinstra assured him that the Solo Angeles were well on their way to gaining the complete trust of the HA. "Everyone already knows you guys and likes you guys," the ATF affidavit quotes him as saying. So much so that the other chapters were jealous of the Skull Valley chapter for "stealing all the Solo Angeles."

If Dobyn's infiltration was rushing along at a breakneck pace, the same could not be said for the investigation and prosecution of the bloody incident that had helped give impetus to Black Biscuit in the first place: the violent shootout at Harrah's casino in

Laughlin back in April 2002 that left three bikers dead and more than a dozen wounded.

"Blow by blow, stab by stab, and shot by shot, we know exactly what happened in that casino," a Las Vegas police investigator had told reporters after viewing the casino's extensive surveillance tapes, but one year later, police still did not have a single biker behind bars or even charged.

True, just a week after the shootings, they had arrested Arizona Angel Cal Schaefer on suspicion of murder. At his bail hearing, prosecutors played a videotape they said showed Schaefer firing his gun eleven times. He was simply protecting himself against the Mongols, his attorney insisted. Schaefer made his $250,000 bail and was released. Barely a month later, state prosecutors dismissed all the charges, saying they needed more time to analyze the massive amount of video evidence. They left the door open to refile charges at a later date.

By the first anniversary of the deadly melee, in April 2003, there was still no progress. Police and prosecutors assured the public that charges were "imminent." But behind the scenes, bitter infighting plagued the investigations. The district attorney's office in the state of Nevada wanted to tackle it as a straight murder case, charging individual Mongols and Hells Angels who had directly or indirectly contributed to the deaths of the three bikers. The United States federal attorney wanted to go after the Hells Angels as an organization under the Violent Crime in Aid of Racketeering Activity (VICAR) law—an organized crime statute that requires proof that the individuals committed violent acts to further the aims of a criminal enterprise.

Under American law, both prosecutions could proceed at the same time—providing there was co-operation and coordination. But authorities on both sides were reluctant to share information. "The U.S. district attorney was having problems with the state DA," says one police insider. "Plus, the homicide detectives with Las Vegas police were protecting what they had, and you had an ATF office where no one had worked big cases and knew what direction to take it in."

It was particularly frustrating for Tom Allen, the detective at the Las Vegas police's biker criminal intelligence unit who had helped stake out the Laughlin run. "I have been living that case since it happened," he grumbled. When he got word that the U.S. attorney's office was considering handing the file over to the FBI, he knew that would be a disaster and quickly got on the phone to his friend John Ciccone, the ATF's top biker expert in Los Angeles.

"Look, you guys are going to lose this case," he told Ciccone. "They're going to give this to the FBI, and that's just not right. They won't prosecute this one the way it needs to be done."

So, much like the way he had taken over the Kramer file in Arizona, Ciccone stepped in to be the point man in Vegas. It was not hard to convince the U.S. attorney that Ciccone should take control of the investigation. After all, he was the expert on the Mongols and had good sources inside the gang. He also had Mike Kramer working as an informant deep inside the Angels. Ciccone flew to Vegas and with his customary zeal was able to butt some heads. "Everybody started working with everybody, and then it all came together," he says.

Kramer was now being an increasingly busy—and important—undercover agent, playing a pivotal role in Ciccone's work to bust Angels across the U.S. for their role in the Laughlin murders. As early as May 18, 2002, less than a month after the Laughlin shootout, Kramer was secretly recording the Hells Angels West Coast Officers' Meeting at the San Bernardino clubhouse. According to an indictment later filed before the courts, they bragged about their heroics on the night of the shooting. Bob Johnston, the leader of Kramer's own Mesa chapter, suggested that if they leaked a copy of the videotapes to the media, the public would "understand the honour and integrity of the Hells Angels" because they had stood their ground and fought. By early 2003, Kramer was recording meetings as far away as Anchorage, Alaska, to get the Angels on tape boasting about "the shit" they did in Laughlin.

In February 2003—more than a year after he had become an

official ATF informant—Kramer also finally came clean on his entire role in the slaying of Cynthia Garcia. In a dry, five-page document named simply "Report 091," the ATF's star informant matter-of-factly detailed how he and his fellow bikers "stabbed the female approximately twenty to forty times." He scrawled a map showing where they had dumped the body.

Still, even with Kramer's signed confessions and the secret recordings of his blunt conversations with his fellow bikers Paul Eischeid and Kevin Augustiniak, which Kramer and the ATF believed could be tied to Garcia's killing, the police faced a double dilemma: Kramer was still central to an ongoing (and dangerous) undercover operation to unravel the Laughlin shootings. So the authorities could not tell the Garcia family much. And they could hardly arrest her suspected killers without tipping their hand and blowing the Laughlin investigation.

Still, they decided it would be wise to bring the family on board in some way before any arrests were made and word got out that the cops were using one of their mother's confessed killers to nail the alleged accomplices. "Quite frankly, we needed their support and their understanding," says Chuck Schoville, the Tempe cop who had first met with Kramer. Schoville was beginning to feel a personal bond with Cynthia Garcia. When he was a rookie cop at age twenty-four, his own mother, a Mexican American, had been murdered by a boyfriend who had kidnapped her and beaten her to death. Her killer was eventually jailed. Schoville, along with a couple of prosecutors, conferred with the family three times to win them over.

"My mother was killed, my mother was Mexican. I know what you're going through," Schoville told Garcia's family when he talked with them. "It will work out in the end."

The family was not so sure. "All of us were upset," says Olivia, the second-eldest daughter. "It was a hard decision. But this was the only way." They finally agreed. They still didn't know the names of the suspects or even that they were Hells Angels, only that the police operation was gang-related and one of suspects was snitching on the others.

That still left Chuck Schoville with a feeling of dread: to protect Operation Dequaillo and Kramer's undercover work on Laughlin, the police also had to hold off arresting Eischeid and Augustiniak as suspects for an indeterminate time. What if the bikers the cops suspected of her slaying killed again while the police left them on the streets to protect an undercover operation?

The police got lucky with the hot-tempered Augustiniak. In the spring of 2003, he was indicted for an assault he had committed before the Garcia murder. So the cops got together with the prosecutors and came up with a scheme: they offered the biker a generous plea of just one year jail time, much less than they normally would have demanded, if he pleaded guilty. Augustiniak couldn't believe his luck and went for it. "It was beautiful deal for him, but he didn't know we just wanted to keep him in jail," Schoville says with a smile. "I knew we had something bigger and better coming against him."

That still left Paul Eischeid wandering around free. All Chuck Schoville could do was wonder how much longer it would be before he could tell Garcia's family that the cops had arrested the men they believed had murdered their mother.

All the family could do was wait.

The undercover cops on the frontlines of Black Biscuit were also beginning to count the days. The long months of intense undercover work were beginning to take a personal toll on the entire ATF team.

Violence was of course the overriding concern—not just the daily dread that comes from knowing that being unmasked as cops could be fatal, but also the challenge of spending so much time with criminals who lived and breathed violence. How do we get close enough to document it and be able to use it in our case and not be involved in it? Dobyns kept asking himself.

It was not only their bodies that were at risk, but their minds and, in a very real sense, their souls. The nightmare for every undercover agent is he that gets in so deep that he forgets to come up for air. Or doesn't want to. "We've all heard the horror stories of these guys who go in and then come out and in their social life they're still acting like bikers," says Jay Dobyns, knowing full well that with his permanent tattoos, shaved head and pointed goatee he could be seen that way.

It was Dobyns's task to make sure his team was separating, as the undercover cops call it—not confusing their undercover lives with their real ones. "We reminded ourselves every day when we went out that we're the good guys, they're the bad guys. We're pretending, they're believing," Dobyns says. "Don't for a fucking second think that they won't put a knife to your throat if they figure out who the fuck you are."

But who would make sure Dobyns—the craziest, wildest member of the Solo Angeles, who was also the tightest with the Angels—stayed on course? His lifeline was Chris Bayless, his former partner from Chicago, and another old friend from the ATF. "These guys contacted me almost on a daily basis just to make sure that my head was right. They called about the case, but it always ended up becoming a personal conversation," Dobyns says. "I didn't figure it out until almost at the end of the case: they didn't care about the case, they didn't give a shit how it was going. They were checking on me."

Bayless knew all too well the risks his friend was running: "You can't do something like that for that long a period of time and not have it affect you. And anybody who says that it doesn't affect you is a frickin' liar because it does," he says. "There are things you don't want to hear, and that's when you know somebody is really going off their track. Like 'Hey, I like these guys a lot. I think these guys are cool.' Or 'I'd much rather be hanging around with these guys than half the agents in my office.'"

When Bayless asked Dobyns about his feelings about the bikers he was spending so much time with, it was always the same answer: "Hey, these guys are degenerate shitheads; they disgust me and they need to be in jail."

"When you hear things like that, then you know the guy's got it screwed on pretty well," Bayless says.

Nevertheless, keeping his head straight while orchestrating

complicated scams and schemes—and all the while making sure his team was safe—was draining Dobyns's health and sanity. "Trying to keep your brain spinning, two or three conversations ahead of time, for eight hours a time, you are physically, mentally, emotionally ripped," he says. "To do that day after day and month after month is nearly impossible."

Nor was it easy for the ATF agents to face the almost daily exposure to drugs and constant pressure to consume them. "The narcotics use is always there, especially meth. They act the way meth users act—they're violent, paranoid," Dobyns explains.

When the bikers kept pressing Bird to try some himself, he pointed to the tattoo just below his shoulder. Dobyns didn't tell the bikers it was St. Michael, the patron saint of law enforcement. "Hey, look, you know what this is?" he began, pointing to the inked design of the angel stabbing a dragon, triumphing over evil. "I got me that because I was a fuckin' junkie. I was a drug user, I fuckin' had nothing. It broke me down, I had no money, I had no home, no family, no car, no place to live. It ruined my life.

"Now you want me to hit this joint or suck that line up to prove to you after everything you know about me that I'm not a cop, that you can trust me? Let me do something else to prove myself to you. You want to go smoke somebody? You want to carjack a car? Let's do something else—don't make me do that 'cause that's going to put me back in that hole."

His tirade worked and the bikers backed off.

Jenna MaGuire, meanwhile, was facing her own burdens. "Being an undercover female in a biker case, you're not going to get to do the glamour stuff. It's not fun being the one who goes to pick up the deli sandwiches or the sodas, but you've got to make it look real."

If any bikers got too fresh with her, Bird would come over and make it perfectly clear she was not up for grabs. But there was little Dobyns or MaGuire could do to protect the other "old ladies" from abuse by their less-than-angelic husbands. "These women have many emotional problems, low self-esteem, narcotic abuse, you name it, they have it," MaGuire notes.

Once, JJ was out with a biker's wife while the men were having an all-day pow-wow. Their orders were to return with food by 5 P.M. The women went shopping, then the biker's wife stopped off at a bar, where she got so drunk that the bartender asked her to leave.

"When do we have to get back and get the food?" JJ asked.

"Oh, we don't have to do that any more," came the slurred reply.

Suddenly, JJ got an angry call from Bird. "Where the fuck are you guys? You were supposed to be here an hour ago with the food."

As they drove home, the drunk woman kept screaming and yelling, grabbing the steering wheel and throwing money out the window. This is not what I went to cop school for, MaGuire thought.

When the women finally made it home, Bird whispered to her, "Get the hell out of here—I'm supposed to beat you up."

The wife was not as lucky. Her husband yanked her out of the car and dragged her into the house. She told MaGuire the next morning that she had been forced to sleep in the closet all night.

"That's the crap you had to go through," MaGuire says with disgust. "For months we dealt with these assholes and that kind of shit.

"I was worried about her. I had already known that I was going to see things that I couldn't do anything about. I had to separate myself. She was a pill popper, she had a terrible childhood, she was just a mess. It's sad and depressing."

There was even less the undercover cops could do to help the children of the bikers when they saw them being bullied or mistreated. "You'd see their kids with a mother who was obviously a crackhead," MaGuire says with a shudder. "They're going to grow up and turn out to be Hells Angels themselves. I just saw the future for these kids and it wasn't pretty."

Dobyns—who had two children of his own—was particularly irritated by the abuse that one Skull Valley biker meted out to his son. The boy was a rolypoly kid, who just had the misfortune of having a father who was a Hells Angel. Dobyns was over at their house one day when the boy came running in, half crying because he had just been squirted in the face with the garden hose.

"You're just a big, fat piece of shit," barked the biker dad. He swatted the child several times. "I'm going to fuckin' kick your ass, embarrassing me in front of these guys. You're a big fuckin' fat pussy."

Dobyns was appalled. "That kid stands no chance, but there's only so much you can do. You can't save the world."

Even more painful for the ATF agents was the unintended impact they were having on the children in the south central Phoenix neighbourhood where they set up their first undercover home. In the poor, mainly Hispanic streets, the image of tough outlaws rolling in on their shiny motorcycles was not exactly the message cops want to send out to youth.

"I don't think we did any service to those kids," Dobyns says regretfully.

MaGuire made it a point to have their freezer stocked with ice cream. Dobyns—this time as a cop and a father, not a feared Solo Angeles leader—tried to talk to the children without blowing his cover: "You know what, you're better than me—do something with your life. Don't be a biker—get an education; don't do this— this is nowhere."

"But they always came back," he says sadly. "They always wanted to hang with us. For the wrong reason, they worshipped us."

All this mental strain, not to mention the exhausting hours, inevitably sapped the agents' physical strength and health. Dobyns, never a heavy drinker, found he was consuming more alcohol than he used to—and, worse, he started smoking heavily. On a rare day off at his home in Tucson, he once slept until five in the afternoon. A neighbour who dropped by was shocked by the changes in his friend: "You looked like a junkie. You looked terrible. You'd lost weight, and you had big bags under the eyes. You looked like you were going through shit."

Dobyns at least could arrange some downtime with his wife and children by inventing a cover story about a business trip to L.A. or San Francisco for a debt collection. Billy Long, the under-cover cop borrowed from the Phoenix police department, lived in the city, so it was even easier for him to grab some time with his family. But for Jenna MaGuire, the rookie agent from San Diego eager to make her mark, there was no easy escape. "I needed to prove myself more than anybody else. I'm new, I'm a girl. They're spending a whole lot of money to keep me out here from San Diego, so I'm not going to give them a reason to send me home."

She worked endlessly. When the men went home to their families, she stayed at the undercover house. "I got a chance to turn my brain off and go be who I was," Dobyns says. "Jenna was always on, she was taking calls, she had people coming by the house non-stop."

When the men would go home for a few days, MaGuire went to the office and wrote reports or typed up transcripts. "I wasn't getting any sleep, any exercise. I started smoking again," she says. "I really wore myself out."

Dobyns, meanwhile, was discovering that even his regular visits back home were far from idyllic. With luck, he'd get home one day a week; sometimes he would be away for a month at a time. "When you come home, your life doesn't stop. Somebody still has to pay the electric bills, somebody still has to mow the grass," he says.

The ATF man was worried about what was happening to him. "There was very little family interaction, very little time when I was able to repair any bonds. I could see my family slipping away from me. My kids don't give a shit that I was trying to be an HA," Dobyns says. "They don't give a shit that I was trying to impact crime in the community. All they want is their dad to come home. All they want is for Dad to read them a book at night or to go off in the backyard and play catch or go to their Little League game. All they want is for their dad to be there and love them.

"And I wasn't there."

The undercover team also had to deal with increasing conflicts with their own management. Dobyns had the deepest respect for Joe Slatalla, the case manager who, after all, was the brains behind the entire Black Biscuit operation. But there is always a natural tension between the undercover operatives who live and breathe the daily grind of infiltration and their supervisors or handlers who try to keep an eye on the longer view.

"You only understand 10 percent of what's going on in this case. You're only dealing with 10 percent of the big picture, I'm dealing with 100 percent," Slatalla once said to Dobyns.

"That may be the case," Dobyns shot back, "but if you make a mistake, you can go back and rewrite a report and fix something. If I make a mistake, I'm going to get hit on the back of the head with a pipe. I'm trying to focus my energy on the 10 percent that's going to keep me and my partners alive. That 10 percent takes 1000 percent of my energy."

All these tensions—the physical, personal and professional strains—would crank up to almost intolerable levels when the Hells Angels put the screws on even tighter: it was time, the Arizona boys told the undercover cops, that they put away their Solo Angeles patches and become Hells Angels.

That would push Black Biscuit and Jay Dobyns's team to the edge.

PART IV

GLOBAL REACH

NINE

The Butcher of Amsterdam

———

*Paul de Vries is the worst human being I have ever known, a filthy rat. [He]
wouldn't do the shooting himself. But Paul can cut. He was a butcher.*
—Dutch Hells Angels Nomad Jan "Old Man" Laughs

Steven John Chocolaad's final resting place was inside a weekend
travel bag dumped into Holland's Juliana Canal.

The canal is a busy waterway that travels along a fairly straight
line down the spine of Holland's most southerly province—
Limburg—linking up with the Maas River and its tributaries in
Belgium, France and Germany. No doubt the wake of the many
ships and barges that regularly ply its waters had something to do
with tearing open the bag containing Chocolaad's body and scat-
tering his butchered body parts along a three-mile stretch of the
canal. When it finally surfaced, the bag contained only pieces of
Chocolaad's discoloured upper body. There were also a few bricks
tossed in to weigh it down, but the gases released by his decaying
corpse were powerful enough to bring it to the surface. At twenty-
nine, Chocolaad was already one of the ageless dead.

May 25, 2003. A glittering spring day in Holland as an elderly
man walks along the canal, observing his dog sniff the grassy
embankment. "The dog was not on a leash, so I watched him
closely. You never know what rubbish washes ashore," the man
later told police. When the dog suddenly darted into the water and
clamped his jaws around a severed human leg, his anxious master
rushed forward. That's when he saw the second appendage—an

221

arm—a few yards away. When police combed the canal banks, their search turned up the bag and torso. The head was never found. They took fingerprints and checked them against their computer records. That's how they knew it was Steven Chocolaad: he had a criminal record for drug trafficking.

An ocean away from the American southwest, six thousand miles from the birthplace of the Hells Angels, Holland seemed at times as if it was in another universe. In Amsterdam—the drug mecca of Europe—police gave the impression that they were unaware, or at least unconcerned, by the activities of the Hells Angels in their own backyard. Even when bodies began piling up—starting with Chocolaad's.

Dutch police at first had no idea why anybody would kill Chocolaad, never mind chop up his body. There didn't seem to be any need to hide his identity. He wasn't a well-known criminal whose fate could easily be linked to the killers. And the last people the Dutch police would've suspected were members of a biker gang. For decades they had totally ignored the growth of the out-law biker culture in Holland. German, American, Swedish and particularly Danish police had all warned their colleagues in Amsterdam about the emerging power and ruthlessness of the Hells Angels and Bandidos.

The Dutch thought they knew better: to them, outlaw bikers were simply a quirky American subculture. If other countries fol-lowed Holland's policy of tolerance and acceptance, the world would be a better place.

Holland was exclusively Hells Angels territory, in no small measure because of politicians who for years had tried to humour what was now a powerful force within the Dutch underworld. Politicians, celebrities, businessmen and even cops mingled with Hells Angels at gala events and occasionally shared their VIP lounges at football matches of Amsterdam's famed club Ajax. HA leader "Big Willem"—a natural born thug whose real name was Willem van Boxtel—became an honored guest at the farewell party of liberal Amsterdam alderman Edgar Peer, who chaired the city's finance committee. As Amsterdam mayor Schelto Patijn looked on, Peer and Willem hugged each other for the cameras.

So it was no surprise that as far as the Dutch police were concerned, the way to solve Chocolaad's murder was to issue notice of a 20,000-euro reward and then sit back and wait for the golden tip. Several anonymous callers did in fact telephone about a ripped drug deal. But nobody paid any attention. The trail went cold and the case slipped into the unsolved file.

Police would wait a whole year before they even began to understand the international intrigue behind young Chocolaad's butchered body, which on a warm spring day had suddenly surfaced in the Juliana Canal. It was a hideous warning of deep trouble to come.

Chocolaad was born in 1975 in Eindhoven, a small high-tech industrial city in southern Holland and home to the Philips Electrical Company. He became a keen billiard player, with talent enough to win the national under-eighteen title. His best friend was the Dutch major league footballer and National team member Orlando Trustfull, who admired Steve for his clear-eyed mastery of the physics of billiards. Hanging around pool halls, however, wasn't just for the love of the game. Chocolaad dealt drugs and mingled smoothly with Holland's outlaw subculture.

In the milieu, he was known as "Vague Steven." He often seemed like a guy who wasn't really all there. Kind of hard to figure out and maybe easy to take advantage of. Yet he was lean and nimble and kept himself in shape. He made his money as an errand boy for drug traffickers—a dangerous occupation that frequently landed him in dicey situations. He was once stabbed in the leg when a drug deal turned ugly inside an Amsterdam apartment. (He jumped out a window and escaped before he could be murdered.) In 1997 he was arrested when police found him in possession of an engine block packed with 7.9 kilos of cocaine. He was convicted of trafficking and thrown in prison, but he won on appeal when prosecutors couldn't prove he knew the drugs were stashed in the engine. While in prison, he met an Amsterdam restaurateur jailed for smuggling a container of marijuana. The smuggler was well connected with the Hells Angels Nomads, and when Chocolaad got out of prison he stayed in the man's Amsterdam apartment. Chocolaad's new-found friend became his link to the bikers.

Steve had been a delinquent since he was young, and his waywardness was one reason his father, a successful dentist, moved the family to Curaçao, an arid, volcanic island at the base of the Caribbean in the Dutch Antilles. It's only thirty-eight miles long and no more than eight miles wide, and for many Dutchmen, it's a favourite holiday retreat with a reliable blue sky. For Steve, however, it was a sun-splashed jail cell. All he wanted was a way out. His key to freedom was the drug trade. Curaçao is situated just off the coast of Venezuela. Like neighbouring Aruba, Curaçao did a flourishing business in smuggling both into and out of South America. Cigarettes, electronics, appliances—anything with high duties flowed into Venezuela and Colombia. Flowing out was cocaine. Curaçao had developed a narco-economy and its bank books bulged with the proceeds. In the port city of Willemstad, Chocolaad met an easygoing islander named Angelo Diaz.

Born on the island of Colombian parents, Angelo Diaz became known in Curaçao society as a charming family man whose wife was a schoolteacher. They had two children. He was a fisherman and caterer admired for the best smoked fish on the island. When he wasn't fishing for tuna, swordfish and shark in his deep-sea sport boat *Make My Day,* he was shipping thousands of kilos of cocaine to Amsterdam. In the greater scheme of the island's underground economy, this wasn't so unusual. What was unique was that Diaz was a major supplier to the Hells Angels in Europe.

His connections with customs officials in Curaçao smoothed his operations. At one point, Dutch Marines smuggled his drugs in their duffel bags on-board air force Orion planes ferrying soldiers back to Holland. Nobody checked the bags until one marine turned informant. Diaz was never arrested. Civilian airlines proved to be an even easier smuggling route for him. Amsterdam's Schiphol Airport had become a massive gateway for cocaine from

Colombia via Curaçao because nobody checked the passengers. As many as thirty to fifty couriers a flight lugged suitcases stuffed with cocaine. KLM's flight path from Curaçao became a conveyor belt for Colombian coke into Europe. When customs began to get suspicious and spot-checked luggage, some Dutch vacationers began returning to Holland with condoms full of cocaine in their stomachs. When the Dutch began checking 100 percent of the passengers in 2003—including obligatory stomach X-rays—they arrested so many people that the prisons couldn't hold them. So the Dutch initiated a policy of simply confiscating the drugs and sending back any courier caught with fewer than 3 kilos of cocaine. These blanket checks quickly reduced the numbers of couriers to between one and five a flight.

Of all the Colombian traffickers in Curaçao moving those drugs, Diaz was perhaps the best placed—with solid criminal connections in Holland, Curacao and Colombia. He moved seamlessly through both Dutch and Latin American communities. His father had moved to Curaçao to work in the phosphorus mines. Diaz himself had married a Dutch girl and lived for a time in Holland. He was also an outlaw biker and a leading member of a Hells Angels support gang in Curaçao called the Caribbean Brotherhood. With his Colombian partners in Curaçao, Diaz organized cocaine shipments that originated from the FARC (a Spanish acronym for the Revolutionary Armed Forces of Colombia). The FARC's guerrilla armies had been fighting a civil war in the Colombian interior and on the streets of Bogotá since they were formed by the Colombian Communist Party in 1964.

The steady cash flow from Diaz and the Hells Angels of Europe were of course part of the reason the FARC could afford to buy a constant supply of weapons. It was a clear demonstration of the criminal and terrorist connections the Hells Angels could forge through their elaborate web of international biker clubs. The Angels in Canada and Holland had cemented their ties directly with the Colombians during the latter half of the 1990s. That the FARC would deal with the Angels reflected the gang's substantial power on the continent of Europe.

The centre of this power rested with the Hells Angels Amsterdam chapter—the mother chapter of Europe. Steve Chocolaad knew them, and he liked the action with Diaz. Their partnership—and the shipments from Curaçao to Holland—took off in earnest in 2003. Of course, neither Diaz nor Chocolaad ever expected that one short year later, young Steve would be fish food in the Juliana Canal.

When Diaz learned of Chocolaad's fate from his Colombian contacts, it suddenly came home to him that what he had started a year earlier had veered out of control. At first he didn't know who was responsible, the Hells Angels or the Colombians. He just knew what both sides were capable of. Caught in the middle, he also knew he had to straighten things out. If he didn't, more bodies would end up in Holland's extensive canal system, and he was damned if his was going to be one of them.

Diaz's nightmare had begun back in November 2002. The Caribbean hurricane season had subsided, and the tourist season was just getting under way, when he was hit by storm winds of another sort. They came in the form of Dutch Hells Angel Paul de Vries, president of one of the most savage HA chapters in Europe, the Nomads from Limburg, Holland. He flew into Curaçao on KLM, first class as usual. Diaz had got a call from his Dutch brothers to meet an Angel at the airport and arrange accommodation. They didn't give him a name, but it hardly mattered. Diaz was dutifully at the gate when de Vries arrived and had no trouble picking the burly fifty-two-year-old biker out of the holiday crowd. His powerful arms and beefy hands were crawling with Hells Angels tattoos. His round meaty head was shaven clean, highlighting thick boxer ears and a sloping forehead. He wore big gold rings and a sinister smile that glittered with gold teeth and fillings like a discount jewellery shop. This was a man brimming with confidence, an outlaw biker who had come a long way from his roots as a trailer-park boy.

De Vries introduced himself. Diaz, who wasn't into body ornaments, just smiled, took his bag and led him out to his car. Diaz had never dealt with the Nomads but knew what was expected of him: keep quiet, do what he was told and treat de Vries as a visiting dignitary. He had no idea why de Vries was in Curaçao or how long he planned to stay. Nor did he really know who he was or that back home in Holland his fellow bikers referred to him as "The Butcher."

De Vries stayed four months. Almost the entire winter season. Diaz grew to like him, thinking he was a decent, trustworthy guy and after a few weeks considered him a friend. "We got close" was all Diaz would say later to police. But de Vries was not interested in friendship. He had come to Curaçao for two reasons: to hide from some Turkish and Belgian drug dealers he had ripped off, and to buy large quantities of cocaine. That's why he was sizing up Diaz. De Vries's Nomads chapter had been importing coke through a Canadian named Vic Trasmundi. Trasmundi, an Ontario biker who moved to Holland and joined the Nomads, was able to use his links in Canada to open a connection to the Colombians. But in 2002 he died of cancer, and his cocaine route died with him. De Vries wanted to establish a more direct line into Colombia.

"One time he asked me about the price of coke on the island," Diaz said.

Just US$3,000 a kilo, Diaz told him; depending on the amount. The more you bought, the cheaper it was.

De Vries did the math. Coke was selling for about eight times that amount—US$25,000 a kilo—in Europe. And cut to street purity, it could bring many times more.

Diaz later told the following story to a Dutch court about what transpired next.

De Vries was soon on the phone to his partner in Holland, Donny Klassen. He told him he had a major score.

Klassen was not a Hells Angel. He was a businessman who lived behind a security fence and video cameras in a large house in Maastricht. Although his name would later surface in court records in Belgium alleging he was partners with Paul de Vries in an October 2003 shipment of 195 kilos of ecstasy tablets to

Australia, his record was clean. Now, according to Diaz, Klassen was as keen as de Vries to open a fresh cocaine supply channel.

Diaz's Colombians flew in from Cartagena and met de Vries and Klassen at the Music Factory dance bar in Salina, a hangout for Colombian drug dealers. They decided their first shipment would be 300 kilos. The Colombians agreed to front the drugs. In exchange, de Vries and Klassen would arrange and finance the transportation to Holland. They would then split the drugs fifty-fifty, with de Vries and Klassen splitting their half and the Colombians selling theirs through their own European distribution network. De Vries and Klassen were staring at about US$3 million profit. Diaz would get a 5 percent cut—about US$150,000—from the Colombians for brokering the deal. The go-between, who would look after the shipping in exchange for 10 percent of de Vries and Klassen's profits, was none other than Steve Chocolaad.

Klassen arranged to have the drugs hidden inside a diesel electrical generator that he shipped over from Holland. The generator arrived in March, and Diaz and the Colombians immediately set to work removing the insides. They filled the empty shell with vacuum-packed cocaine and then welded the casing shut to make it "dog safe" so sniffer dogs couldn't smell it. Only 293 kilos could be jammed inside, leaving 7 kilos behind.

Diaz loaded the generator onto a container ship heading for Brazil. The exporter of record was a company owned by Diaz called, appropriately enough, All Smoke. As it left the harbour, the Colombians, Diaz, de Vries and Klassen sat in a bar watching their fortune in drugs head out to sea.

"There it goes," Klassen said, lifting his glass.

It was early March 2003, and the ship was supposed to dock in Natal, Brazil, where the local Hells Angels would look after it before it proceeded to Lisbon. From there the drugs would be trucked to Maastricht in southern Holland. The receiver was a bogus company in Belgium. In Holland, the parties would meet to break open the generator and divide up the drugs.

No sooner had the ship left the harbour than the Colombians grew nervous. They had fronted the cocaine from the FARC and had the most to lose. They expected the drugs to take no more than six weeks to get to Maastricht, so when they learned from Diaz at the end of March that the drugs had still not left Brazil, they were angry and suspicious. When another month passed with no sign of the drugs, they travelled to Holland to meet with Klassen. He told them that the shipment had arrived in Lisbon, and de Vries was there at that very moment looking after the transportation to Maastricht. So the Colombians waited another week. By mid-May the drugs had still not arrived. Suspecting a rip-off, the Colombians accused Klassen of lying. He tried to assuage their fears, suggesting they meet again the next day and he would have some answers.

Klassen did not show up. The Colombians complained to Diaz that they couldn't locate him. Then they read that Chocolaad's bloated torso had been pulled out of the Juliana canal.

It was as if Paul de Vries couldn't help himself. A deal wasn't any fun unless somebody was ripped off. The Colombians didn't realize it at the time, but the drugs actually had arrived in Holland in mid-May. De Vries and Klassen had trucked them to a farm outside Maastricht, selling them off almost as soon as they hit the ground. The Hells Angels had ripped off the Colombians.

Steve Chocolaad found out when he went to collect his 10 per-cent. That cost him his life. De Vries knew that Chocolaad would have to tell the Colombians about de Vries's theft, because if he didn't the Colombians would think that Steve himself was involved and his life wouldn't have been worth the price of a tulip bulb. De Vries had to keep the Colombians in the dark for as long as possible. In the end, he didn't want Chocolaad blabbing all over town and demanding his 10 percent. He couldn't be trusted, so he had to go. He was a security risk, a loose end.

Chocolaad went missing May 16, 2003. De Vries either lured or forced him to the home of his bodyguard, the Hells Angels Nomad Serge "Moon" Wagener, where they were joined by two other Hells Angels. There they strangled the unsuspecting Chocolaad, cut up his body in the bathtub and dumped it in the Juliana Canal along with a few bricks taken from Wagener's garden. When Serge's wife,

Ria, came home the next day from a visit to her parents, the place didn't seem right. The bathroom had been thoroughly cleaned and some of the furniture was missing. "Serge told me that he had killed someone, together with Paul," she said later. "They cut his body in pieces, put it in bags and threw it in the canal. When the newspapers mentioned this find, Serge told me that that was the boy they had killed." To Ria, it just seemed like Hells Angels business as usual.

Inside the Nomads' circle, people knew it wasn't the first time de Vries and his Nomads had slaughtered a drug dealer to cover up a rip-off. De Vries was proud of his killings. They said he laughed while he chopped. The happy butcher. His Filthy Few badge—a reputed symbol that a biker has killed for the club—was an eye-catcher. It was encrusted in diamonds. Not all the Nomads agreed with or liked Paul de Vries, although many admitted they were jealous of his success.

"Paul de Vries was busy murdering and doing rip deals, which is against Angel rules," Nomad Jan "Old Man" Laughs said. When Old Man confronted de Vries once about his rip deals, Moon Wagener threatened to kill him. "Moon took a knife and held it to my throat and asked Paul if he should kill me. Paul didn't want that. Paul killed eleven to fifteen people. Paul de Vries is the worst human being I have ever known, a filthy rat. [But] he meant something in the international bikers' world. He had many contacts all over the world. Paul de Vries wouldn't do the shooting himself. But Paul can cut. He was a butcher."

The Colombians didn't care about Chocolaad. They just wanted their money. And the man they put pressure on was Diaz. He had already learned the hard truth. He had heard from fellow Hells Angels that de Vries was driving around in a brand-new Mercedes. He knew then that the Angels had ripped off the Colombians' dope. By September, the Colombians had heard from their people in Europe that their coke had been sold on the street. They visited Diaz at his home in Curaçao and told him he had to return to Holland to get their money. They were furious, having been deceived, and now wanted 70 percent of the drugs.

They told Diaz not to come back unless he had at least $600,000 from the Angels to cover their costs to the FARC.

Diaz reluctantly flew back to Holland, hoping to settle the matter. But it wasn't going to be that easy. It was clear that neither Diaz nor the Colombians really knew Paul de Vries or Donny Klassen.

Diaz later told a Dutch court that he met met Klassen in Maastricht, and when he delivered the Colombians' demands, Klassen grew angry and defiant. He eyed Diaz and told him what he didn't want to hear: a suicidal message that no sane person would ever dream of relaying to the Colombians.

"You know what, Angelo? I took it," Klassen said. "Tell the Colombians I took it all and I am not giving it back. Whatever they do, I'm ready for war."

War was what Klassen and de Vries would get. But in the end it would come from a totally unexpected direction. More bodies would pile up as Holland's outlaw biker world imploded. By then biker wars would be all too familiar in Europe.

TEN

The Great Nordic War

―――

We are the country of Hans Christian Andersen.
We should not create crooks like that.
—Cmdr. Troels Ørting Jørgensen, National police,
Copenhagen, Denmark

Amsterdam's red light district is a lonely ghetto that's left largely to its own vices. It's located just beyond the city's oldest and most sacred church, the gothic Oude Kerk, and hugs two secluded dead-end canals. Sex and porno shops, window prostitutes, brothels, cannabis cafés, strip clubs and cheap hotels line the still waters in teetering buildings huddled shoulder-to-shoulder like shivering old men with tin cups. The district sits in stark contrast to the rest of the inner city with its broader streets, elegant townhouses and carefully planned waterways. You don't stumble across it. It's not on the way to anything. It's an end in itself.

It was here in 1983 that Joanne Wilson and her boyfriend, Stephen Hampton, came to work and play. They couldn't have known it, but they were moving into Hells Angels territory. Joanne was a flirtatious Irish girl with an eternal smile, bright brown eyes, a cute nose and a mass of dark curly hair. She came from one of the most violent and intolerant regions of Europe. Portadown in Northern Ireland is a small rural town whose history is soaked in sectarian conflict. When she was eighteen, she and her Ulster boyfriend hoped to leave all that behind by travelling the world—India, Asia—before settling in seemingly peaceful Amsterdam.

Joanne had trained as a dental nurse, but the only job she could land was as a chambermaid at a downtown hotel. It didn't bother her. She was young, and the money was enough to live on.

Stephen worked in a bar in the red-light district. Among his customers was Louis Hagamann, nicknamed Long Louis, who came in for a drink a couple of times a week. He was a tall, lean, muscular guy of thirty who wore his hair in a ponytail and tied a red bandana around his head. Most of all, what separated Long Louis from the rest of the red-light patrons was the fact that he was a full-patch member of the Amsterdam Hells Angels. Long Louis made his money dealing drugs and pimping in Holland's eager sex trade. He was also involved in armed robbery and extortion, but neither Stephen nor Joanne knew about that. Stephen said he found him "very friendly." Joanne also liked him. In fact, she liked him so much that she dated him in secret several times.

September 20, 1985, had been an all-nighter for Stephen. He had worked at the bar into the early morning and come home exhausted. Joanne was up early. She made him a breakfast and, before he drifted off to sleep, told him she'd be out most of the day but expected to be back for dinner. That was the last time he saw her alive.

Joanne later left their apartment and walked to Amsterdam's Central Station. Along the way she met up with a girlfriend. The two chatted briefly, and Joanne told her she was going to meet somebody. When they got to the station, the two girls parted, and Joanne vanished into the bustling crowds.

When she didn't arrive home that evening, Stephen thought that maybe she was staying with friends. When she didn't return the next day, he began asking around. He called friends—including the biker Hagamann. Nobody had seen her. Finally, he went to the police station. The police suspected it was a lovers' tiff and assumed she would show up sooner or later, so they did nothing other than file a missing persons report. After three days and still no word, a frantic Stephen launched his own investigation. With the help of Hagamann, he searched the streets and canals of Amsterdam.

Six weeks later, a sluice-gate operator in Amsterdam spotted a curious-looking plastic bag floating in his lock along the Amsterdam–Rijn canal. He grabbed a barge pole, hooked the end around the bag and hoisted it onto the concrete bank. Inside, he found human remains.

The problem for police was that the body had been dismembered, much like Steve Chocalaad's would be almost twenty years later. There were no arms, no legs, no head. There was a knife wound in the chest, but that didn't necessarily mean it was the cause of death. All they knew was that the torso was a woman's.

One week later, the gate operator found another plastic bag floating in his lock. He fished that out too and discovered a left leg. A pathologist concluded it belonged to the torso. Police began combing through missing persons records and found Joanne Wilson. A sandal in her apartment fitted the foot, and a hair found in her bathroom was similar to pubic hair on the torso. Still, they couldn't be certain; there was no DNA analysis at that time. They questioned Stephen and his biker friend, Hagamann, about their whereabouts the day she disappeared.

Louis Hagamann should have stayed at the top of the cops' list of suspects—not least because they were well aware he was a Hells Angel with a violent criminal record. Hagamann's apartment was only about three hundred yards from where the body was found. Joanne's girlfriend told police she had mentioned that she was meeting a man named Louis. Hagamann even admitted meeting her at the station for a drink, but after that, he claimed, he didn't know where she went. Police did not pursue him further, other than to mark him down as a suspect.

Police decided that they couldn't be sure the body was indeed hers, so they closed the file, which they callously labelled "Operation Annoyance." Because the identification was uncertain, they refused to release the body to her mother, Ann Donaghy, in Armagh. Instead, they had the body interred in a small corner of Amsterdam's largest cemetery reserved for unknown cadavers. And that's where the remains of Joanne Wilson lay buried for the next fifteen years.

Joanne had been Ann Donaghy's only child. Joanne's reassuring letters home had not assuaged a mother's fear for her daughter's safety. Now, her daughter's murder together with the remarkable indifference of the Dutch police would make Ann Donaghy's life what she later described as "a complete hell" for many years to come. Had the police been more astute or just a little more persistent, they likely would have discovered that Joanne Wilson was one of several victims of a lawless subculture of terror and intimidation proudly invented in America and now ready to sweep through Europe.

One of the leaders of this outlaw biker invasion was Willem van Boxtel, a muscular street-gang leader determined to become Europe's Sonny Barger.

Willem grew up in east-end Amsterdam, a lover of motorcycles, speed and gang violence. He gorged on American biker movies and tales of the Hells Angels. In 1973, at the age of seventeen, he started his own biker gang, calling it the Kreidler Ploeg East. The club quickly staked out its territory. On his eighteenth birthday, his gang beat up the manager of a late-night convenience store. When the manager complained to police, Willem and his boys came back and beat him up again. A few weeks later he raided a school, beating up two teachers, several schoolboys and some girls, throwing them to the ground and kicking them. His gang then tossed the husband of a teacher into a stairwell and bashed the owner of a nearby snackbar. Police arrested Willem and eleven other gang members. He got six weeks in prison and six weeks' probation, but that didn't stop him. He was determined to become the most feared outlaw biker in east-end Amsterdam.

Even though he didn't have an official charter, van Boxtel decided to call his gang the Hells Angels. Under that American banner, he was ready to take on all comers. When a British gang called the Mad Dogs came to Holland to party, his gang went to war, beating them badly in a sandlot fight before police broke it up. Alarmed Amsterdam youth commissioners decided that the way to tame Willem was to give his gang a place to hang out, so in

1974 they voted his gang 172,500 guilders (US$103,386 today) to build a clubhouse in east-end Amsterdam. The council then approved an annual grant of 21,300 guilders (US$12,772 today) to the biker gang to organize charity events and activities for young people and to promote motorcycle riding.

In 1977 Willem's Amsterdam club became a prospect chapter for the Hells Angels, with a clubhouse—called Angel Place—fully financed by Dutch taxpayers. It would prove a costly mistake. Far from being an oasis of goodwill, Angel Place would soon gain a reputation for murder, drug dealing, torture and gang rape.

It would take fourteen years before the council stopped paying the annual grant after they realized most of the Angels were well over thirty years old and had no interest in helping young people. Commissioners also discovered that Willem believed charity began at home and had used the money to expand his clubhouse while the youth department continued to pay the lease on the land.

Willem had command of his own fortress and the neighbourhood around it. He figured that what he needed now was a new name for himself—one that people wouldn't forget. He chose something straightforward and easy to remember: Big Willem. The name would stick. In fact, Big Willem would fast become a legend. He had caught the Hells Angels wave rolling in from California early: when he applied for a Hells Angels charter, there were just seven other HA clubs in Europe. England had five and Germany and Switzerland had one each. In other words, mainland Western Europe was a vast untamed territory ripe for the Hells Angels' picking.

Delegations of Hells Angels from the United States arrived to assess the Amsterdam club. German, English, Austrian and Australian Angels followed. The international attention was no accident. Amsterdam was becoming the drug centre of Europe, and the country's increasingly lenient laws meant it could serve as a safe haven for outlaws. The ports of Amsterdam and Rotterdam were already major drug transportation hubs. As the Angels planned an aggressive expansion throughout Europe, Amsterdam would play a pivotal role, quickly becoming the mother club. This was why the international Angels wanted to assure that the members who controlled it were up to scratch. Big Willem had to prove his mettle.

In May 1978 police raided Angel Place after the father of a nineteen-year-old girl claimed she had been gang-raped in the clubhouse. Some visiting Danish bikers had come to Amsterdam to party with the Hells Angels, who were hoping to expand into Denmark. They brought the girl to Angel Place for a drink, where they sexually assaulted her. The bikers were so drunk that she managed to escape when they passed out. She ran through the steel gates, up the small commercial road, under a railway bridge and into Amstel subway station, where she called her father. Police raided the clubhouse and arrested six bikers, who were convicted the following year. They never did serve their two-year sentences: the Dutch court allowed them to return to Denmark.

It was harder for Big Willem to calm his angry neighbours, who demanded that the city close down Angel Place. Willem defiantly declared, "We live by our own laws; one of them being that apart from our own girlfriends, girls are only permitted in Angel Place for sex." When opposition intensified, Big Willem took a more conciliatory tack out of the Toys for Tots gimmick book used by the North American Angels. He donated money and delivered free toys to children's hospitals. The chequebook diplomacy worked, and the incident was largely forgotten.

Big Willem's club finally gained full-patch status on October 28, 1978. At three o'clock in the morning, two members of Sonny Barger's Oakland club called with the good news. The German Hells Angels president from Hamburg was on hand to present them with their colours. Their wives and mistresses spent the night sewing the new Death Head patches onto their jackets. As Big Willem stood by proudly, his fellow Angels raised the Hells Angels banner above the clubhouse.

Big Willem's dream had come true. But his work was far from finished. He was determined to make his chapter the most powerful in Europe. For the time being, though, those plans could wait. For the next three days, the Amsterdam Hells Angels drank themselves into oblivion.

———

Nobody saw what was coming. Not the politicians. Not the police and certainly not people like Joanne Wilson, who found the outlaw bikers an intriguing, even exciting, subculture.

Big Willem wasted no time in expanding the Hells Angels throughout Holland. By 1980 they had opened a second chapter in Haarlem, about twelve miles east of Amsterdam. Then in 1986 the Nomads opened a clubhouse in Limburg, in southern Holland. Four years later the Angels added another club in the north. By the mid-1990s the HA had the four compass points of Holland covered. They owned the country and now could concentrate on the rest of Europe. Over the next twelve years, they would spread north through Denmark, Sweden, Norway, Finland and then into Eastern Europe and Russia. The expansion would spark one of the most vicious and daring internecine wars in the history of outlaw biker gangs.

Willem and his Hells Angels prospered in Amsterdam. They moved into the red-light district and established cafés and nightclubs with names like the Excalibur and the Other Place. Here they could build their forces and make alliances with existing crime figures while they fortified their drug business and began to build one of the most powerful underworld organizations in Europe.

They had little reason to fear arrest or conviction. Penalties were so lenient in the Netherlands that drug dealers rarely served much jail time. Holland became a country where, as one British journalist wrote, it seemed the legal system was drawn up "by a bunch of people out of their gourds on dope." In its more lunatic moments, the system allows criminals to deduct the expenses of their crimes. A Dutch court, for example, in 2002 ordered an armed robber to reimburse the 6,600 euros he stole from a bank—minus the 2,000 euros he had paid for his gun.

Dutch drug laws represent a tradition of tolerance and a will by the vast majority of its fifteen million people to decriminalize the use of soft drugs while at the same time perhaps stopping people from migrating to harder drugs such as cocaine and heroin. The Dutch regard drugs as a health issue. Licensed cannabis cafés—

there are about 860, including 290 in Amsterdam alone—can legally sell up to 5 grams of cannabis to patrons and can keep up to 500 grams (about a pound) on the premises. Dutch citizens can grow up to five marijuana plants for personal use, so it's not unusual to see marijuana plants popping out of the roofs of houseboats tethered to canal walls or among the lovingly tended flower gardens and windowboxes of Holland. Dutch authorities also tolerate the possession of up to 0.5 grams of cocaine or heroin.

What is illegal in Holland is trafficking in large quantities of any illicit drugs, including cannabis. Yet the Dutch have in the past largely closed their eyes even to that. Holland's politicians have made it clear that they would probably legalize all drugs, if not for opposition from the rest of Europe and the United States.

The Dutch ambiguity toward drugs has scored some successes as a social policy: a far lower proportion of the population in Holland uses cannabis than in the United States, with all its draconian drug laws. But it has been a disaster as a criminal policy, in effect allowing organized crime to thrive in Europe's open market.

For the outlaw bikers in Holland, the drug trade has been a gold mine: they have become the continent's gatekeepers. Cocaine flows in from Colombia, heroin from Turkey and Afghanistan, cannabis from Morocco. Laboratories in Holland pump out enough chemical drugs such as amphetamines and ecstasy to supply not only Europe but also parts of Asia, Australia and North America. Holland is the Colombia of synthetic drugs.

From his ever-expanding base in Holland, Big Willem launched his invasion of Scandinavia. Eager to bring the hundreds of ragtag Nordic biker gangs under the banner of the Big Red, he allied himself with a Danish biker as bold and ambitious as he was. His name was Bent Svang "Blondie" Nielsen, and he was eager to light up the land of Hans Christian Andersen.

Nielsen led a union of five local clubs operating under the surprisingly tame title Galloping Goose. In 1979 they were given prospect status under the Hells Angels. A year later the Geese acquired Angels' wings. Just two years after the Hells Angels had moved into Amsterdam, they had succeeded in creating their first Scandinavian club in Copenhagen, celebrating the new charter on New Year's Eve 1980.

Then the war began.

One club refused to join. They called themselves the Bullshit and they controlled a good chunk of the drug market in Copenhagen—especially the lucrative trade at an abandoned military base in central Copenhagen called Christiania. After squatters and hippies took it over in the 1970s, they declared it a self-governing state, and it remained as such until late 2005. They refused to pay taxes and utility bills. Tree-lined canals and brick walls brightly painted with graffiti art encircled and separated the community from the rest of Copenhagen. Christiania had its own sports clubs and social services. Thousands of visitors poured through its colourful gates each week to enjoy its cafés, restaurants, jazz clubs, theatres and art shows.

Christiania did a brisk business selling hash and pot out of numerous smoke shops. Police estimate they grossed anywhere from 500,000 to 1 million DK (US$78,600 to $157,200) worth of hashish and pot a day.

A lot of that money went into the hands of the Bullshit. They refused to ally themselves with the Angels, so the HA set out to destroy them. The Angels struck hard and fast, as if they were sending a message to all of Scandinavia.

Blondie Nielson seemed to have his spies everywhere. In 1983, after he'd received a telephone tip from a barman, he walked into a Copenhagen restaurant where he found four Bullshit. He instantly killed two with his knife, stabbing them and cutting their throats, and wounded a third.

Still the Bullshit refused to surrender. So the Angels struck at the head.

Hells Angel Jørn Jønke Nielsen drove a stolen van to the home of the Bullshit president, nicknamed the Mackerel, and shot him with a machine gun as he walked to his car. With the Mackerel's wife looking on, Nielsen calmly walked over to his prone body, rolled him onto his back and emptied his magazine into his chest.

Nielsen fled to Canada, where he hid out with the Vancouver Hells Angels. When he came out of hiding a year later and returned to Denmark he got a sixteen-year murder sentence. Prison turned him into a man of letters. He wrote an autobiography—*My Life*—and quickly became a popular author/murderer/biker guest on radio and TV. Nielsen bragged about his early days as a rebel biker: "Dirty, ragged clothes, and preferably with as many offensive symbols as possible. White Power T-shirts, swastikas and other Nazi badges could really get the bourgeois animals out of the armchair."

By 1988 thirteen people were dead, and the Bullshit no longer existed as a motorcycle club. Most of their members had been assassinated.

"They eliminated the Bullshit totally," Troels Ørting Jørgensen, commander of the Serious Organized Crime Agency (SOCA) in Copenhagen recalled. "They killed everybody. After that the HA were alone in the Danish criminal scene and in the Nordic as well."

For the next five years, the Angels enjoyed unrivalled supremacy in Europe. Sonny Barger's boys were firmly established in Holland, Copenhagen, France, the United Kingdom, Germany, Austria and Switzerland. Europe was their turf. But it wouldn't last. Their next adversary would prove far deadlier.

The Bandidos.

The Texas-based group rivalled the Hells Angels in numbers in the States and had moved into Australia in a big way; now they were eager for a European beachhead. Signs of an approaching war first appeared in France in August 1989, when the Bandidos patched over a club in Marseilles. Like the first Bandidos in Australia, the Marseilles gang was selling used Harley-Davidson motorcycles shipped duty-free from the brotherhood in the U.S. Harleys were rare in the Europe and commanded a premium price—at least double their American worth. The Hells Angels took immediate action to discourage the Bandidos' expansion. Four Angels from Geneva drove their bikes to Marseilles and shot the Bandidos vice-president dead and wounded two other club members. The murders sparked fears of a continent-wide battle for territory as both the Angels and the Bandidos planned massive recruitment campaigns, primarily among the hundreds of small biker gangs, many of them eager to wear American colours. Some included white supremacist groups such as Combat 18 (18 being the numerical initials of Adolf Hitler), soccer hoodlums and skinheads with a reputation for unbridled aggression. Some were culled from the ranks of Europe's prison populations. Others were just disaffected bourgeois youth. It was a recipe for extreme violence.

American executives from both clubs met in Paris in the late summer of 1993 to prevent all-out war and make a peaceful division of the continent. Both clubs wanted to avoid police and government countermeasures that could slow their expansion. In Germany, Hamburg officials had already outlawed the wearing of the Hells Angels patch, grounding the club and rendering it practically invisible. An Angel without his patch was clipped. The bikers wanted to forestall more of that kind of legislation, so they signed a non-aggression pact similar to the one they had in the United States. Basically, the Bandidos would inform the Angels where they would open a new club and give them the names of its members. If the Angels objected, some kind of compromise would be reached.

The Paris pact was the outlaw motorcycle gang version of Munich. As far as the European bikers were concerned, this was pure America hubris. While Europeans were impatient to embrace the American biker culture and adopt its most powerful symbols, they would do it on their own terms. As Churchill said in 1938, Europe had peace now; it would get war later.

It's not certain what exactly triggered the Great Nordic Biker War or even who fired the first shot. Both sides were primed for action. They were full of eager young disciples steeped in the lore of Sonny Barger and outlaw biker gospel. "Fuck the World." "Expect no mercy." "Real power can't be given—it must be taken." They were human tinderboxes dying to explode. Anything could set them off. So whatever the trigger, when the biker wars in Scandinavia began, they were bloody.

The Bandidos' expansion into Scandinavia began in Denmark in December 1993: they patched over a small gang called the Undertakers and set up chapters in Stenlose and Sandbjerg near Copenhagen. The Hells Angels sanctioned the takeover under the condition that the Bandidos confine themselves to just these two chapters in Scandinavia. "As far as we know the Bandidos promised not to expand further, but they did," Det. Insp. Christian Möller of the Danish police said.

The Bandidos leader was Jim Tinndahn, who was every inch as much an outlaw biker as Blondie Nielsen, the ferocious Danish leader of the HA. Determined to expand, he welcomed remaining supporters of the Bullshit plus several Hells Angels who had been tossed out in bad standing. "He filled his club . . . with this dirt," a Hells Angel said. "Tinndahn recruited all that garbage, and such a sick mixture produces more sick things."

The Angels, of course, had their own "sick things." Blondie's Copenhagen Hells Angels had already expanded into Sweden in 1990, awarding hangaround status to a club called the Dirty Draggles (Swedish for "scum") in Malmö, a port city on the southern tip of the country and just across the water from Copenhagen. The Draggles had won a violent struggle with two other clubs vying to become the first Hells Angels chapter in Sweden. It was typical of the way the Hells Angels selected new clubs. They sat back and watched as local clubs killed each other for the privilege of wearing the HA Death Head. The last club standing won. The Draggles became a full-patch HA club in 1993.

Tinndahn and his Bandidos had no intention of sticking to what they considered Hells Angels–imposed protocol. They too intended to expand. The Bandidos opened talks with the Morbids in Helsingborg, a port just north of Malmö. Once HA supporters, the Morbids were so angry with the Angels' recruitment of the Draggles that they opened talks with the Bandidos. That prompted the furious Malmö Angels to declare war on the Morbids. When Tinndahn patched them over as a Bandidos probationary club in late January 1994, the Hells Angels responded by sending a support club called the Rebels to spray the Morbids' clubhouse with bullets. The Angels launched a second attack a week later. The president of the Malmö chapter, Tomas Möller, a biker who, according to a Swedish police detective, used a giant Nazi flag as his bed cover and kept an elaborate museum of Nazi paraphernalia in his home, climbed onto the roof of a van with a high-calibre submachine gun and opened fire, riddling the clubhouse with bullets. Aside from one biker getting a finger shot off, nobody was hurt. The Angels then patched over the Rebels, making them their Helsingborg hangaround chapter. And the war began in earnest.

The first death occurred just after midnight on February 13, 1994. Fifteen Bandidos from Denmark held a party at the Roof Top Club in Helsingborg. The Hells Angels crashed the party. Thirteen shots were fired. When it was all over, one biker lay dead and three others were wounded, including HA hangaround Johnny Larsen. Nicknamed "Seven Bullets, No Problem," Larsen gained notoriety when he was shot seven times in a previous fight over either a woman or a motorcycle. Nobody ever really knew.

After that, the bikers brought in the heavy artillery. Literally. Throughout Sweden and Denmark, the military had built small-weapons' depots for their civilian militias. Most males undergo obligatory military training and therefore know how to use these weapons. They also know where the depots are located. But most of all they know that they are unguarded. On the night of February 20, 1994, the Bandidos raided a Swedish armoury, stealing sixteen shoulder-fired light anti-tank weapons. They also stole hundreds of hand grenades and crates of small arms, including pistols and military rifles, plus ammunition. The bikers would raid these depots many more times before the government finally took steps to secure them. "It was probably dozens of times that they broke in," one intelligence officer with the Swedish police said. "Only the defence department really knows." Bikers also broke into the homes of militia members and stole their army rifles. How many weapons in total were stolen from homes and military installations during the four-year war has not been made public. Swedish and Danish military authorities have kept these numbers a secret even from the police. But an analysis of official police reports from Denmark and Sweden show that between 1994 and 1997 there were at least 36 thefts, including at least 16 Bofors anti-tank rockets; 10 high-powered machine guns, about 300 handguns, 67 fully automatic military rifles, 205 rifles of various calibres, hundreds of hand grenades, land mines and 17 kilos of explosives, plus detonators. Police believe the Bandidos or their support clubs were responsible for most of the break-ins. For their part the Hells Angels obtained Russian- and Yugoslavian-made rocket launchers, as well as surplus machine guns from former East Bloc countries.

The bikers were well armed to fight the kind of protracted gang war that Scandinavians had never experienced.

Back in California, the Hells Angels worried about the Bandidos' expansion. They also wanted to avoid a drawn-out war and the legal repercussions it could entail. Sonny Barger's Oakland club summoned Swedish Hells Angels leader Tomas Möller of the Malmö chapter to California to remind him that the Paris pact was, after all, a non-aggression deal. At the same time, they emphasized that the agreement did give the Angels control of Sweden, and they were determined to hold the Bandidos to that. The Oakland chapter then met again with the Bandidos in Houston, where they reaffirmed that Sweden was indeed HA country. But the Bandidos central command in Texas could not seem to control the Morbids, who wanted to avenge the HA attacks. And European Bandidos leader Tinndahn reaffirmed his support of his newly chartered, violence-prone probationary club.

More futile diplomacy followed when a delegation of Bandidos from Houston visited Denmark and Sweden to meet with the Hells Angels clubs in Copenhagen and Malmö. Neither side would give in, and the talks ended in failure. That spring Helsingborg turned into Dodge City. "There were shootings almost every day," one police officer said.

The war found plenty of willing soldiers, even though at the time there was only one Hells Angels chapter in Sweden and one probationary Bandidos chapter in Denmark. But there were about fifteen homegrown biker gangs in both countries, most of them favouring the Hells Angels. That created several thousand bikers in Scandinavia itching to go into battle.

The war quickly revealed the differences in strategies of the two sides. While the Bandidos just blasted away in apparent indiscriminate attacks designed to terrorize the Angels into submission, the Hells Angels, if anything, showed themselves to be more strategically aware. They appeared to plot their attacks with the aim of decapitating the Bandidos. But neither side surrendered.

The first important attack on the Bandidos came on July 17, 1995: a carefully planned assassination of Swedish Bandidos president Michael "Joe" Ljunggren. As he drove his Harley along a largely deserted highway at more than seventy miles per hour, a sniper hiding in a roadside forest picked him off with five shots from a 9 mm automatic rifle. That same day saw two more assassinations of a couple of Bandidos outside their clubhouse in Helsinki.

The Bandidos responded over the next two weeks with two robust rocket attacks, one at the Hells Angels clubhouse in Helsinki and the second at the Helsingborg stronghold, where the rocket destroyed the roof, penetrated a wall and finally blew up a swimming pool. By sheer luck, nobody in either attack was injured.

As the war spread throughout Scandinavia, machine-gun battles broke out in Oslo and Copenhagen. Both sides lived in constant fear of attack from car bombs, drive-by shootings and rocket attacks. They heavily armed themselves, fortified their clubhouses and checked their automobiles for telltale signs of explosive devices. It wasn't unusual for a biker to find a hand grenade rigged to his ignition. Ample weaponry was within reach. Swedish police raided the apartment of the girlfriend of one Bandido and found machine guns, hand grenades, land mines and explosives.

Then, eight months after their first sniper attack, the Angels struck again at the Bandidos' leadership. This time the attacks occurred in broad daylight amid thousands of people.

March 10, 1996, began like any other day at the Kastrup

Airport in Copenhagen, with the busy cycle of arrivals and departures as cars and buses pulled up. Hundreds of travellers milled outside the glass-and-concrete terminal, expecting the safe and efficient processing of people. Except not on this day.

One of them was Jan Anderson. At 4:23 in the afternoon he was idly gazing out the window of a double-decker bus that was to take him to a ferry and then back to his native Sweden. "About eight or ten men emerged from a parking place," he later told a local newspaper. "Two of them walked over to a parked vehicle and began shooting directly through the windshield." The men jumped into a getaway car, which raced past his bus and disappeared down the highway. "I could see a guy dragging somebody away who was bleeding all over. The car was shot to pieces. Two of the tires were flat, but the driver had escaped."

Bandidos Danish leader Uffe Larsen was killed instantly. Three of his comrades were wounded. They had flown in from Helsinki, where they had attended a Bandidos party.

About 280 miles away at Fornebue Airport in Oslo an identical ambush was in process. Again the victim was a Bandido who had attended the Helsinki party. Four Hells Angels involved in the airport shootings got their Filthy Few patches.

"It was a very good professional job, like a military operation," said Commander Jorgensen of SOCA. "The Hells Angels are not like the Bandidos, who are kamikaze pilots. The Hells Angels always try to measure out the pros and cons, what is good, what is bad. The Bandidos have recruited the worst of the worst. The scum. But that made them extremely strong. So there was retaliation after retaliation."

After the airport ambushes, rockets rained down on the Angels.

On April 11, the Bandidos attacked the HA headquarters in Snoldelev, near Copenhagen, a prospect club in Jutland, and the HA club outside Helsingborg. A week later two anti-tank rockets were fired at two HA strongholds in Copenhagen, killing a woman and burning one of the clubhouses to the ground.

The Angels struck back a week later. On April 26 they somehow managed to cut through a perimeter fence at a prison in

Copenhagen, smash a window and lob a grenade into the cell of a sleeping Bandidos VP named Morten "Traeben" (wooden leg) Christiansen. The grenade rolled under his bunk and exploded. They then sprayed the room with machine-gun fire. Although badly injured, Christiansen miraculously survived, saved primarily by his wooden leg, which absorbed most of the grenade blast. The Hells Angels sent another imprisoned Bandido a shaver with a small bomb inside. In a third jailhouse attack, the Angels simply walked into a low-security prison and threw a hand grenade into a cell.

The violence continued throughout 1996. Another rocket was fired at the Angels' Helsingborg clubhouse in September. Four days later they tied the launcher to the second-storey window of an abandoned factory. They then rigged a string around the trigger, strung it to their getaway car and pulled the cord. It was exactly as diagrammed in the army manual for remote firing of the anti-tank weapon. The rocket cut through electric wires over railway tracks before hitting the HA fortress. Nobody was hurt, despite the fact that the Bandidos had also tossed two hand grenades and a smoke grenade into the building before making their getaway.

When the Bandidos struck again soon afterwards, the results were quite different.

Denmark is a flat country, so if you want a clear shot from a secure perch in a city crowded with apartments, you have to climb up onto on one of the steeply slanted tiled roofs. This was exactly what a prospect Bandido did one evening two weeks later, taking two anti-tank rocket launchers along with him.

Below, he had a clear view of the Hells Angels Copenhagen clubhouse compound, with its steel gate and chain-link fence. He could see guests arriving to help celebrate the Angels' anniversary party with a "Viking fest." About three hundred people showed up, plus about a hundred cops taking pictures and copying down licence numbers. One of them was Det. John Verlander. "I was talking to the people going in, and one of the Hells Angels told me to fuck off and lifted his beer to me as sort of a mock toast and closed the steel gate. He was lucky. If the steel door had been open, he would have caught the full force of the blast to come."

Seconds later the Bandidos prospect fired his first rocket. The projectile tore right through the clubhouse. Nobody saw it coming. All they saw was a huge explosion that rocked the compound. Verlander was the first one in.

"People were screaming and walking around, wounded. I called for two ambulances, but when I walked farther inside I told them to send everything they got," he said.

He started working on one victim, a twenty-nine–year-old woman named Janne Krohn who had been badly hit by fragments of stone from the wall, desperately trying to massage her heart, but she died in his arms. So did a man badly hit nearby, a Hells Angels prospect named Louis Niesen. Eighteen people were injured, many of them badly burned.

"If the rocket had hit about one foot to the right, it would have hit a steel plate and exploded with three-thousand-degree heat," Verlander said. "A lot of people would have been killed."

Police later found the abandoned launching tube on the roof of the apartment. Next to it was the second rocket. The prospect was too eager to escape to fire it.

The attack was a wake-up call for politicians and police, who, until then, had taken the stoic attitude that there was nothing they could do if two gangs wanted to kill each other. Now, however, another innocent woman lay dead, killed by a high-powered military rocket fired in the middle of Copenhagen. Within ten days the Danish parliament passed what became known as the "Rocker fortresses law," evicting bikers from their clubhouses. Police moved in quickly to execute the new law. In Copenhagen angry neighbours took sledgehammers to the Hells Angels Nomad clubhouse, levelling it to the ground. The irony was that many of the outlaw biker clubs had originally received state subsidies to set up their clubhouses, under the mistaken impression that the bikers wanted simply to pursue their passion for motorcycles. Some bikers sued for loss of property, while others went to welfare offices seeking state relocation subsidies. They were rarely successful. One mayor, however, decided to pay each biker an undisclosed sum to get them out of town. They took the money and ran.

In the end, the sudden flurry of evictions was too late. The bikers were so well entrenched and organized that they quickly re-established themselves in new and often improved accommodations, and the war continued unabated. Over the next ten months, well into 1997, police logged more than two hundred acts of violence, including three murders and twenty-two attempted murders. It seemed no one could stop the bloodletting.

Then Drammen happened.

Torkjel "The Rat" Alsaker had been carefully planning the attack for months. President of the Hells Angels chapter in Oslo, Norway, Alsaker, thirty-six, was eager to make his mark in the ongoing war with the Bandidos. On the evening of June 4, 1997, six members of a Hells Angels support gang packed a stolen minivan with explosives. Bikers wearing longhaired wigs drove the van to the front of the Bandidos' headquarters in Drammen, a small city just east of Oslo. The car bomb exploded at 11:45 P.M. collapsing the building, sending debris two hundred yards away and blowing out the windows of surrounding buildings. Three Bandidos were sleeping inside when the bomb exploded. The floor gave way beneath them, and the impact blew off their clothes. They walked out of the debris dazed and naked but uninjured.

The same wasn't true for Astrid Bekkevold. The fifty-one-year-old woman and her husband were driving home after an evening out. As they passed the minivan, the bomb exploded, and Bekkevold took the full impact. She died instantly. Her husband was badly injured but survived.

Fallout from the Drammen explosion shocked Scandinavia. Politicians from all four countries met to discuss banning the motorcycle clubs and pooling police resources for an intense clampdown. The sudden, universal condemnation spooked the biker gangs. According to a document later discovered in a raid on a Hells Angels clubhouse in England, the Angels began making plans to win public support and considered legal action if governments passed laws that they felt violated their freedom of association.

The bikers themselves, exhausted, bloodied and losing public support, seemed eager for an end to hostilities. Tensions had been at hair-trigger level for years. Bikers in Oslo had even shot a woman in the head when she drove by their clubhouse once too often. Most of all, though, "it was very expensive," Det. Insp. Christian Möller of the Danish police said. Wiretaps picked up bikers complaining about lack of money: the war was ruining their business. "We could see it in our investigations that they had no money and they had to use it all on this war," he said. "A lot of the bikers were older and had children and were not interested in having this war going on."

The incentive to find a solution was strong on all sides. American and European leaders of the Hells Angels and Bandidos met again in the United States, first in Colorado and then in Seattle in June 1997, to discuss yet another peace agreement. In the end, however, it had to be reached among the Nordic clubs. Police helped smooth the way by supplying security for peace conferences. "We picked up the people from the HA and the leaders of the Bandidos and brought them to the meetings," Möller said.

Finally, on September 25, 1997, on live television, Danish Hells Angel president Bent "Blondie" Nielsen, and Bandidos European president Jim Tinndahn shook hands. Dressed in their full-patch biker gear like two war-weary heads of state, they gave a press conference during which they declared an end to what police had dubbed the Great Nordic Biker War. The announcement headlined the news throughout Scandinavia. It seemed that the only thing missing was the declaration of a national holiday.

There were well over four hundred violent incidents during the three-year war, which killed eleven people and injured more than a hundred, many seriously. Given the ferocity of the war and the weapons used, it was miraculous that the mortality rate was not higher. Police say some people simply disappeared, their fates unknown. Authorities counted seventy-four murder attempts, but there were probably many attempts they knew nothing about.

The peace agreement held. The violence stopped. And the two clubs got down to the business of making money. What police didn't realize at the time was that this was more than a peace accord. This was a precursor to a Versailles Treaty, where the two gangs carved up Scandinavia and eventually all of Europe.

It began with the four Nordic countries. As police later discovered in raids on their Danish clubhouses, the bikers signed treaties designating exactly which areas they controlled, right down to individual bars, cafés, nightclubs and restaurants. "It was because they wanted to avoid a confrontation," Möller said. Police regard these documents as the strongest evidence of how far the enormous power of the two outlaw bikers clubs extends over Scandinavia's underworld economy.

The bikers quickly expanded into their allotted territories: By 2005 the Angels had added two more chapters in Denmark, going from six to eight, for a total of about 168 full-patch members. In Sweden they had eighty members in six chapters, in Norway five chapters and in Finland four.

Not to be outdone, the Bandidos formed thirteen clubs in Denmark with 171 members. They also have four in Sweden, plus two probationary, two clubs in Finland and five in Norway. Both clubs also beefed up their support gangs. In Denmark, for example, the HA formed twenty-five Red and White support chapters with 250 members and the Bandidos had about thirty support groups—called X-Team chapters—with 350 members.

For reasons that mystify the police, Denmark has the highest concentration of outlaw bikers in Europe and perhaps the world. "No one has ever done a sociological investigation as to why in this small, extremely peaceful country of Denmark we have so many chapters of outlaw motorcycle gangs," Commander Jorgensen said. "They are very much hardliners, they are fierce, they are violent. We are the country of Hans Christian Andersen. We should not create crooks like that."

From their Scandinavian base, the bikers were poised to conquer Europe—and with a peace treaty under their belts they were ready to take advantage of the newly emerging markets of the European Union. When the borders fell in 1992 between EU countries, it gave the bikers unrestricted access to one of the world's richest markets—376 million people with purchasing power of US$11 trillion. "Some of the greatest beneficiaries of a single market have been organized crime," said Europol, the police intelligence agency created to monitor organized crime in the EU. "Perhaps the most potent threat to the European Union, its economy and social fabric is organized crime groups that can now operate in a bigger, virtually unregulated, market. Sophisticated organized criminals are now operating closely together."

Indeed, since 1998 both clubs have doubled in size on the continent. Fifteen years after the Bandidos opened their first European chapter in Marseilles in 1989, they have expanded to seventy. The Hells Angels have moved into Spain, where the south is the central transit area for cannabis from Morocco and also a major money-laundering centre. Police investigations show that drug money has fuelled the enormous real estate boom along the Costa del Sol, helped somewhat by the transfer of some Scandinavian Angels to the Spanish clubs. In Italy the HA now have eight chapters, and the Bandidos have three. Europol officials are worried that police in both Spain and Italy are making the same errors that the Scandinavians made by ignoring the early-warning signs of the expansion of outlaw biker gangs in their countries. Already Italy has seen several high-profile biker murders in 2004 and 2005. "They are too preoccupied by their homegrown Mafias to care about what they think is just biker subculture," Mogens Lundh, a Europol intelligence officer from Denmark, said. "They are more or less developing this type of criminal society without really knowing it and understanding the danger."

That danger has been quite deliberately planned: documents found in 1998 by Danish police in a Hells Angels bunker in Roskilde reveal the Angels' intention to divide Europe into three power blocs. The first was Scandinavia, including the Baltics and Russia. The second was Great Britain and the third Western Europe, which would be in charge of expansion into Eastern Europe.

True to plan, both clubs have begun expanding aggressively into Eastern Europe and Russia. The Hells Angels opened a chapter in Prague in 2000 and a prospect chapter in Moscow in 2004, where they patched over part of the Night Wolves gang. The Bandidos moved into St. Petersburg that same year and established a prospect chapter in Turkey run by Muslims from Denmark.

The American-based clubs—the Hells Angels, the Bandidos and, to a lesser degree, the Outlaws—have in typical corporate fashion "rationalized" the outlaw biker gangs of Europe. During the past fifteen years, they have merged and amalgamated hundreds of largely white neighbourhood street punks, soccer thugs and racists into disciplined organizations that now rival traditional ethnically based organized crime groups such as the Italian Mafia and the Asian Triads. That has been the greatest success of the Hells Angels and Bandidos. They have empowered Europe's criminal underclass. They have given it structure and common purpose. They have turned the marauding punks of Europe into a finely tuned, intimidating machine without depriving them of their freewheeling independence. In so doing they have given them stature, power and wealth—or at least the expectation of wealth. It has been a typical American corporate invasion that has rewarded the Hells Angels and Bandidos with a truly global reach.

Indeed, many Hells Angels from North America are in awe of the stature their brethren have across the ocean. "There are European countries where we are literally looked on as gods," says Donny Peterson, a leader of the Ontario Angels in Canada. "In Scandinavia we're revered, feared."

It didn't take long for Europe's newly invigorated bikers to cast their eyes abroad—to Asia and Africa.

The Bandidos are expanding into Asia, where they have opened four chapters in Thailand led by Danish members. They have invested in bars and nightclubs. Commander Jorgensen thinks they are looking for a nice country to retire in. "It's all that they want. There's power, corruption, females, nice climate, no police to hamper them."

If Thailand is the retirement home for Bandidos, South Africa is where aging Angels want to settle. Danish leader Blondie Nielsen has bought a large estate in the northeast, close to the Elephant River game reserves. Malmö HA president Tomas Möller has an estate outside Cape Town on the cliffs overlooking the ocean. Möller lives in Cape Town half the year, where he collects 14,000 Kroners (US$1,707) a month in tax-free workman's compensation. He claims he has a bad back. "How did he hurt his back?" one Swedish detective scoffs. "He has a good doctor." Indeed, for a man who supposedly scrapes by on disability payments, Möller lives well. Swedish police records show he drives a Ferrari, a Hummer and two Harley-Davidsons. When not in South Africa, he has a number of apartments in Malmö, plus a small private museum for his collection of Nazi paraphernalia, including uniforms, flags and banners, weapons and even Nazi cars and motorcycles.

The police reaction to this renewed biker onslaught on Europe had been slow and uneven. Only in 1999 did one of Europol's priorities become outlaw motorcycle gangs. Headquartered in a large fortified former convent in The Hague, Europol set up a separate intelligence unit to monitor OMGs throughout the union. "Biker gangs are now entrenched in Europe," said chief analyst Mogens Lundh. "In the European Union there are outlaw motorcycle gangs present in every country except Cyprus, and the Hells Angels are present in almost all of them."

The brightest spot on the law enforcement map in Europe is Lundh's home country of Denmark, where police have applied tremendous pressure on the outlaw bikers since the peace treaty, designating them a "national security" issue. "We have had more or less a zero-tolerance policy," Lundh said.

As of the end of 2004 the 1,086 Hells Angels, Bandidos and supporters in Denmark had a total of 7,937 convictions, according to a survey by Danish police. In fact, only one biker in the two largest outlaw motorcycle gangs in Denmark did not have a criminal record.

"The whole philosophy here has been that after the biker war ended we would not allow ourselves to relax and let them share in their criminal activity," Jorgensen said.

Since the crackdown, many Danish bikers have sought safer harbours elsewhere. Norway was not much of a refuge. Police there have taken a similarly aggressive stance and convicted all six Hells Angels involved in the Drammen bombing that killed the fifty-one-year-old woman driving home. Torkjel "The Rat" Alsaker, the president of the Hells Angels chapter in Oslo, was sentenced in 2004 to life in prison.

Sweden proved to be more hospitable to the bikers. Almost none of the crimes have been solved there, primarily because police are too afraid to get involved: threats from the bikers are constant, and the government has done little to protect its police.

Swedish police got a taste of biker intimidation back in 1990 when they arrested every member of an Angels support gang called the Belkers, only to find themselves under siege. Bikers threw hand grenades into the homes of a detective and prosecutor. In the summer of 1999, when a patrolman approached a suspicious car in the harbour and opened the front door, he ignited a bomb that blinded him. A year later a bomb blew up a SWAT team member's car outside his house. Then in 2002 another bomb was placed just outside the door of a police officer's home, where he and his son were asleep; one of the clock hands on the timer snagged on a wire and stopped the explosion one minute before the scheduled ignition.

"Because of all the threats against police officers, I think policemen close their eyes," said one police intelligence officer who was reluctant to have his name published. "They don't want to see. They're afraid."

At least in Sweden the cops knew the power of the bikers. But in Holland, the police remained blithely unaware of the storm gathering around them.

For almost two decades, Dutch police had ignored the 1985 murder of the twenty-two-year-old Irishwoman, Joanne Wilson, whose body had been chopped up and the torso and left leg found in an Amsterdam canal. Despite the constant pleading from her mother no further action had been taken. Even after DNA analysis became a proven forensic aide in identifying victims and perpetrators, the Dutch police made no effort to use the science on the body parts they believed were Joanne Wilson's.

But one person didn't forget.

Peter de Vries is a journalist who specializes in digging up cold cases and solving them on TV. More than a million Dutch viewers watch each week as he unearths new witnesses and clues to the many unsolved mysteries that for one reason or another have stymied Dutch police. De Vries is particularly interested in murder where time is about to run out. Holland is one of only a few countries with a statute of limitations on murder. It's eighteen years; it's not good law, but as the clock ticks it can make great TV.

In 2001 de Vries decided to take one last look at a March 1984 murder in an Amsterdam apartment: someone had stabbed Corina Bolhaar and her two young children and then slit their throats while a third child, who was only one year old and too young to talk, looked on. The statute of limitations on the case would end in a year. De Vries didn't have much time. He learned from his police contacts that the main suspect was the Hells Angels' Long Louis Hagamann. He also learned that Hagamann had been a suspect in another long-forgotten murder: that of Joanne Wilson.

Now he had four murders to solve and one prime suspect. Because Dutch law had turned murder into a stopwatch game, de Vries found himself racing against time.

Since Joanne's death, Hagamann, known as the Hells Angels' assassin, had been a busy criminal. He had more than a hundred convictions for aggravated rape, drugs, armed robbery, assault, torture and tossing a hand grenade at a police officer. He had become one of the most feared men in Amsterdam's underworld. De Vries and his staff began questioning anybody who had anything to do with Hagamann and his case: old witnesses, pensioned police officers. At one point the Hells Angels Nomads attacked de Vries's crew with rocks, kicking in their car doors and forcing them to flee. Intimidation of journalists wasn't an entirely unusual occurrence in Holland. The Hells Angels had once walked into a studio and beaten up two TV journalists for daring to suggest on air that the HA were a criminal organization. But de Vries and his team were not easily frightened. Eventually they came across one of Hagamann's old girlfriends, with whom he had had a baby in the late 1990s. Renetta van der Meer's interview was the crucial break they hoped could blow both the Bolhaar and Wilson murders wide open.

She admitted that Louis Hagamann had bragged to her about killing a woman and "her brats." He also bragged about strangling a former girlfriend, cutting her to pieces and feeding some of her body parts to pigs and throwing the rest in the canal. "He laughed about how he walked around with one of her arms after cutting the body into pieces in a bath. It was horrible. He told me he would do the same with me if I ever crossed him." In fact, he once tried to strangle Renetta. He gripped her throat so hard that the veins in her eyes popped and she needed an operation to save her sight. She said that Hagamann had also shot her former boyfriend in the legs.

De Vries then discovered that after the Wilson murder, Hagamann had been forced to move out of his apartment because he didn't pay his rent. The next tenant made a chance discovery. He found Joanne Wilson's passport behind the wallpaper.

With only one week left before the statute of limitations expired, de Vries broadcasted his findings, and police were forced to reopen both the Wilson and the Bolhaar cases. (They had initially lost the Wilson file.) They still faced one major hurdle: they didn't know with 100 percent certainty that the body buried in the unmarked grave was Joanne Wilson's. Without a body, they had no case. Worse still, when they went to the cemetery, they found that the grave had been dug up and the remains dumped somewhere in a giant landfill. Joanne Wilson had vanished, again.

The police, while incompetent, were at least lucky. In their forensic laboratory they discovered a technician had preserved a vial of Joanne's blood. DNA tests proved the butchered cadaver pulled out of a canal eighteen years earlier was indeed Joanne's. Now police, if only in spirit, had a body. They also had plenty of reason to go after Hagamann.

Long Louis wasn't going anywhere: he was in prison serving time for rape. But the police had only a few days left to charge him with the murders. Two inmates came forward and signed statements that Hagamann had bragged about the killings of Wilson and Bolhaar. What body parts he didn't throw into the canal, he smashed with a sledgehammer and fed to pigs on a farm, one inmate said of the Wilson murder. "He told me that he slept in the same bed and snored away beside the corpse for a couple of nights."

In the end, however, the police were too late: they had no corroborating evidence about how or why Wilson had been murdered. Without proof of premeditation, the clock had run out on justice for Joanne Wilson. Ann Donaghy, her mother, was devastated: "Now he will not be punished for murdering my beautiful daughter. He will live the rest of his life as an innocent man as far as Joanne's death is concerned. The Amsterdam police have a lot to answer for."

But the police were more successful with the Bolhaar case. Hagamann, forty-seven, was convicted and given a life sentence, which means he could be out in fifteen years.

"He told me he'd kill me if he got a chance," de Vries said.

Too violent even for the Hells Angels, Hagamann was kicked out well before the trial, despite testimonials in court from Big Willem.

If the Dutch police thought they could go back to sleep, they were wrong. Another equally gruesome murder remained unsolved. Steve Chocolaad's Hells Angels killers still walked free. That would soon change, as even more bodies were about to come bubbling to the surface of yet another Dutch canal.

ELEVEN

Retribution

———

Paul was a man you couldn't say no to. He would walk over corpses.
—Dutch Hells Angels Marco "Moon" Hegger

While Scandinavia burned, Holland simmered. It was on a slow heat. Dutch police noted in a 1995 report that the Hells Angels Amsterdam clubhouse had become an "impenetrable criminal fortress guarded day and night by armed Angels." The Angels were prepared for any spillover from the biker wars to the north. In the end, however, the Netherlands remained an oasis of peace. The reason was simple. The country was completely controlled by the Hells Angels. It was a Big Red fortress that no other gang— not the Bandidos, not the Outlaws—dared attack. Such absolute power, however, has its own way of crumbling.

Big Willem van Boxtel and his Amsterdam franchise had carved out a monopoly in the Netherlands. For more than twenty-two years, the Angels had enjoyed unchallenged prosperity. With little or no interference from the police, they ruled the country's red-light districts, while quietly helping to expand the Hells Angels throughout Europe. Holland was their sanctuary. Requests from police outside the country for help to track down drug-trafficking networks traced to Holland frequently got the response from the Dutch police that it was "not our problem." Even when Interpol reported in 1989 that the Amsterdam Hells Angels controlled drug trafficking in Europe, the Dutch police did nothing.

Six years later, a Dutch parliamentary commission investigating lack of police cooperation in organized crime investigations defined the Dutch Angels as a "criminal network involved in the production of synthetic drugs and in the arms trade as well as stolen cars and motorcycles." Still, the report failed to raise the Dutch police from their deep sleep.

By 2000 Amsterdam was known as much for drugs and prostitution than for Rembrandt and van Gogh. The city had become home to criminal organizations from every continent—from Yugoslavia, Bosnia, Russia, Hungary, Italy, Spain, Colombia, Nigeria and Asia. Criminals all settled into the open city that had become the centre of Europe's drug and sex trade. Organized crime in Europe had exploded. In Amsterdam the Hells Angels comfortably serviced a profitable grey market at home while feeding the black market abroad.

There seemed enough profit for everybody. Organized crime laundered their money into legitimate business ventures, primarily real estate. But the biker peace didn't last. The attack did not come from outside. With little competition, the Angels turned inward and began to eat their own.

For some time, there had been too many rumours of drug rip-offs among the Hells Angels in Holland. Rip-offs were against the rules—one of the commandments the Angels imposed on every new charter. The worst offender was Nomads president Paul "The Butcher" de Vries. He had murdered Steven Chocolaad and dumped his body in the Juliana Canal in the spring of 2003, to silence him about de Vries's theft of 300 kilos of coke from the Colombians. De Vries had also cheated the Turks and Belgians. Now the whole club was feeling vulnerable.

"We are walking around as shooting targets," Hells Angels Nomad Marco Hegger later told police. "This is about millions of dollars, not just about the coke from the Colombians." Members of the Nomads were paranoid that the lunatic de Vries would get them all killed unless the Nomads acted decisively and quickly before the Colombians struck the first blow. That was why his fellow Nomad Peter Schumans travelled up from Limburg to Angel Place on Tuesday, February 10, 2004, to meet Big Willem. Angelo Diaz, the bikers' man in Curaçao who had negotiated the coke deal, would later testify that Schumans wanted Willem's permission to murder de Vries and settle with the Colombians.

The miracle was that Paul de Vries wasn't already dead. It was probably only because of his ferocious reputation—a reputation he had relied on for years as he murdered and butchered his way through life. He must have at least sensed the limits of his own mortality. A man like him would have had to worry about the loyalty of his own brothers, given his ripped drug deals.

Yet in February 2004 he was preoccupied by his daughter Sandra's upcoming marriage to one of his henchmen, Cor Pijnenburg. De Vries wanted every Nomad to contribute to the expense. The wedding dress alone cost US$4,237 (3,614 euros). Paul was a rich man who didn't share his wealth, and the other Nomads wondered why they should shell out for a stingy rich man's daughter. It just gave them one more reason to hate Paul de Vries.

While the bikers' internal feuds smouldered, the Dutch police were finally getting their act together. Faced with mounting gangland assassinations and pressure from foreign governments, they began in January 2003 a comprehensive investigation into the Hells Angels called Project Acronym. The goal was to prove that the Hells Angels were a vast criminal organization that should be outlawed. Canadian and American police supplied information on drug deals that had either originated in Holland or were headed there.

(Canada, in fact, was well represented in the Dutch Hells Angels with two Canadian members, including Vic Trasmundi, the Dutch Nomad who was a key link to the Colombian drug barons and had once been an Ontario biker.)

Then a year later, in January 2004, police in Limburg opened a second front: Project Fluor targeted the Nomads. Police were acting on evidence that the Nomads were the centre of a massive European drug-trafficking ring. As part of both investigations, police were bugging the phones of many of the Hells Angels, including the Butcher.

On February 11, 2004, at 3:37 P.M., they intercepted a call between de Vries and a Hells Angels buddy of his from Amsterdam named Theo. De Vries had spent the night with Theo partying on speed at a red-light nightclub and drinking at Angel Place. Theo mentioned what a great time they'd had, but then the conversation turned to more important business:

"We'll go to a sushi bar, and we'll talk about small things and then . . . That one out . . . get away. Everything out," Theo said.

"Yes, 100 percent," de Vries agreed.

"That's right."

"One thousand percent," de Vries emphasized.

Initially, police had no idea what de Vries and Theo were talking about. Only later did it become clear that the Butcher had gone to Amsterdam with his own plans about the future: he wanted to cleanse the Nomads of its disloyal members.

The Nomads were having their weekly meeting that night. De Vries had caught a bit of sleep at the home of his girlfriend, Deedee Sam, but not much. The speed had still not worn off. De Vries told Deedee he'd be at the meeting maybe half an hour, an hour at the most, and then come home. He threw on a white T-shirt and jeans, and the two drove over to the clubhouse, a former whorehouse just outside Oirsbeek, a village about fifteen miles from Maastricht. He hadn't even bothered to take his gun, which was unusual. "Paul didn't even wear underwear," Deedee later said. "He wanted to return home as quickly as possible."

Several of the Angels were milling around the front door when de Vries arrived. They all greeted one another with the usual back-slaps and hugs and then went inside. Only full-patch Angels are allowed at weekly church meetings, so Deedee had to wait with a prospect HA in a bar located in a barn behind the main clubhouse. Deedee was hungry, so de Vries phoned for a pizza before joining the rest of the Angels upstairs in their meeting room. The meeting started at about 8:30 P.M.

The Nomads clubhouse is a mundane, two-storey brick box

located on the main road leading into Oirsbeek. At that time of year the darkness weighs heavily, but there was enough light coming from the Nomads' headquarters for anyone who happened to be passing by at 9:15 P.M. to see Paul de Vries come flying out of the second-storey window and land with an ugly thud on the road. Local resident Hubert Rajh saw just that as he drove toward Oirsbeek. What looked like a man in a white T-shirt landed on the road about a hundred yards in front of his car. He slowed almost to a stop. After about ten seconds the man moved, and the frightened driver sped away, knowing well enough not to stick around.

How de Vries came to execute a swan dive out of the clubhouse is not clear. He could have been tossed out. Or he could have been trying to escape. Whatever the reason, several Hells Angels hauled him back into the clubhouse and up to the second floor.

The evidence indicates that de Vries, his bodyguard Cor Pijnenburg and his close friend Moon Wagener were then lined up against a wall and shot. De Vries must have been stunned. He had absolutely no forewarning. He thought the meeting would be short and he'd be out of there in half an hour, eating pizza with Deedee. Only that afternoon he was plotting to get rid of some of the fifteen angry Nomads who had turned against him.

It seems the Angels took their time. Three different guns were used. The killers shot each victim in the right arm, in the head and in the chest. A neighbour who was downloading music onto his computer heard the shots. He later said they seemed to come in bunches, but he couldn't pinpoint the exact direction. He heard shots followed by a pause, then more shots. Paul de Vries was shot seven times, Moon Wagener six times and Pijnenburg five times. The Nomads then carried the bodies down the stairs and loaded them into a rented van. A cold pizza sat on the hood of a nearby car, but nobody paid any attention to it. The delivery boy seems to have just dumped it there and left. He probably heard something he didn't want to hear and fled.

Deedee, meanwhile, was still in the barn when a Nomad came in and told her that Paul and the others had left. That surprised her because Paul had never just left her behind without telling her.

So she hung around for an hour or so and then went home—still hungry and worried. She swears she did not hear any shots.

The Nomads drove north six miles to Echt, where they dumped their former companions in a shallow aqueduct near the Juliana Canal. They made little attempt to hide the bloodied corpses. In fact, they wanted them found so that the Colombians would know the bikers had dealt with the men who had ripped them off. They hoped that would be enough to assuage their anger and placate the other gangs de Vries had cheated.

When they returned to their clubhouse, they tore the newly renovated meeting room apart and burned the red leather chairs and laminated furnishings in oil drums. Then they got to work rebuilding with fresh plaster and paint. When it was all done, they erected a huge sign next to the meeting room: "OMERTÀ"—the Sicilian Mafia's term that means keep your mouth shut or die.

The next day three Nomads returned to Amsterdam, where police said later in court that they informed Big Willem that the job was done. The Nomads and Big Willem said they were simply searching for their missing brothers, but police wiretaps picked up the Nomads talking about the assassination even before the bodies were found.

A canal worker discovered the bodies two days later, on Friday the 13th. That same day, Deedee went to Paul's house in Geleen to pick up her things. The house was small and insignificant. Only Deedee and a few others knew about it. And Paul wanted it to stay that way. It was a refuge. A place he could hide cash and a sanctuary where he and Deedee could go without fear of being disturbed. Paul had rented it a few months earlier. The door was still locked when Deeded arrived, but when she entered it was clear somebody had been there before her. The cash was gone along with other valuables.

Paul "The Butcher" de Vries and his two dead henchmen got the usual glittering send-off. Outlaw bikers came from across Europe and beyond. Their killers led the procession. Even Angelo Diaz and several of his Caribbean Brotherhood members flew over to take their place among the bereaved. They interred de

Vries under a Hells Angels headstone alongside other departed Filthy Few. Still, hardly any Nomads bothered to disguise the fact there was no love lost for de Vries. One later commented that he was one of the most hated men in the Nomads. At the wake Diaz heard whispers of what had happened, he later testified. "He kicked the bucket when I hit him in the face," one of the Nomads bragged about one of the victims he had shot.

Diaz quickly returned to the relative seclusion of Curaçao, wondering if he was next. He had good reason to worry.

With the Butcher dead, Peter Schumans took over as the new president of the Nomads and flew to Curaçao soon after the murders to talk to Diaz. It wasn't a social call. It was an official Hells Angels commission of inquiry: the Dutch bikers wanted to know what had happened to the 300 kilos of coke that de Vries had stolen from the Colombians.

Before he died de Vries had claimed that Diaz was in fact deeply involved and had benefited financially, Schumans told him.

Diaz was calm and direct: he had nothing to do with it.

Still, Diaz should come to Holland to convince the other Nomads, Schuman insisted.

Diaz knew he had no choice. If he refused, he would be killed and dumped in the ocean as shark food, probably by his own Caribbean Brothers. So he convinced himself that he could handle it. The president of the Caribbean Brothers, John Drop, was also instructed to go. The Nomads would hold him responsible if Diaz changed his mind and ran.

Diaz arrived on March 6 in Amsterdam and checked into a hotel. That same day Drop called him to say he was coming to pick him up. The Nomads wanted to talk immediately. Drop drove him to the home of Nomad Marco Hegger in Limburg. Peter Schumans wasn't around. Instead, he sent his brother Jack, a serious cokehead who had been kicked out of the club for drug abuse and debts. Now he was back, sporting a full patch and a Filthy Few badge, awarded to him just after the de Vries murder.

Diaz knew what that meant. A loose cannon was back in favour and had been unleashed on him.

Marco Hegger was no better. With his long, scraggly ponytail and beefy, pockmarked face, his tattoos and Filthy Few badge, Hegger was scary even in neutral.

While Hegger's wife and kids remained upstairs, Hegger and Jack Schumans went to work on Diaz. The tone was non-aggressive but not entirely friendly either.

Diaz later testified that Hegger told him, "We have scraped the shit off the pavement. We have done it so that if the Colombians come, we can say we did their work for them."

Schumans nodded in agreement.

Diaz said he understood, but he had nothing to do with the rip-off. He just brought the parties together and helped dog-proof the coke. That was it. The rip-off was de Vries's. But he sensed his story wasn't doing him any good. Hegger and Schumans weren't there to believe him. They were there to kill him. Diaz was scared, but he figured they wouldn't kill him in Hegger's house, not with the wife and kids upstairs.

And he was right. After a time they let him go. Told him that they had to check his story and instructed him not to leave town.

Diaz and Drop returned to Amsterdam, only to be ordered later that afternoon to again meet Schumans and Hegger, this time in the town of Sittart. When they arrived, the two Nomads told them to follow in their car.

Holland has few remote areas. Just flat, partitioned farmland surrounded by ditches with small clumps of woodland here and there. The odd fat windmill still stands in empty fields, offering a certain degree of privacy, but that doesn't account for much. Killers have to make the best of the country's few secluded nooks. Diaz and Drop followed the Nomads along a country road until they pulled over onto a small parking area alongside a railway track. Drop obediently pulled up behind them. Diaz noticed an old iron bridge down the narrow road surrounded by heavy woods. Perhaps he could just take off over that bridge. But Hegger and Schumans were out of their car pretty fast. Drop was the first to notice that Hegger wore a bulletproof vest under his jacket and that both Nomads were armed with machine pistols tucked in their belts.

Drop figured that maybe they wouldn't kill him. He hadn't done anything. This was about Diaz. Diaz figured they were definitely going to kill him. It was beginning to get dark and a bit frosty. The two Nomads motioned them toward the woods. Schumans and Hegger began chatting between themselves about having to talk to one other guy who was involved in picking up the coke in Maastricht and could verify Diaz's story. But Diaz knew that was just bullshit. There was no other guy. Just Donny Klassen and Steve Chocolaad. Chocolaad was dead. And Klassen was probably next on the hit list after Diaz. No, the Nomads just wanted to boost Diaz's hopes. They didn't want him running away before they shot him. Diaz was cold and terrified. It all seemed totally crazy. There he was obediently walking toward his death. But there was nothing he could do about it. Not now anyway.

Then suddenly, out of the mist, it happened.

"It" was a man walking his dog.

Schumans and Hegger saw him first. Diaz could see the look of concern and then resignation cross their faces. They quickly got back in their car. Hegger again said something about locating the third man to verify Diaz's story. And then they drove away, leaving Diaz and Drop alone by the railway tracks, their saviour having disappeared into the twilight.

The dog walker had just given them a second lease on life, and this time Diaz wasn't going to blow it. If there had ever been any doubt in his mind about the Nomads' intentions, they had just been dispelled. He pulled out his cellphone and punched in the number of a relative in Sittard. The relative had contacts, and before the night was out, Diaz and Drop each had a handgun. They were small calibre and unlikely to stop a rhino like Hegger, but they were all their money could buy. And anyway, the guns were a temporary solution. Diaz had other plans.

———

Angelo Diaz had decided to seek the protection of the state. He hoped the gun would safeguard his passage to the other side. After all, it's not something you just do. You don't just walk into a police station and make deals. At least not in Holland. You've got to be sure of whom you're talking to.

Back at his hotel he called a contact in Curaçao who had been a police informant. The guy gave him a number of a trusted police contact he once knew in Holland. Diaz made the call.

"John van den Heuvel speaking," said the voice on the other end of the line.

Without thinking, Diaz described his predicament and how he wanted the police to arrest him. He said he'd give them the whole story behind de Vries's murder and the Nomads.

The only trouble was, the guy on the other end of the line was not a cop. At least not any more.

John van den Heuvel had been a cop, but now he was a crime reporter. And Diaz had just given him his biggest scoop ever. He was savvy enough to let Diaz talk. Let him believe he was a police officer. He questioned Diaz long enough to unravel his story and then told him to sit tight and wait for his call back. The journalist then dialled his police contacts. In return for an exclusive story on the arrest of Diaz, he would put the cops in touch with Diaz. The police agreed. They had no choice.

In a prearranged takedown, police arrested both Diaz and Drop. They picked up Marco Hegger, and a SWAT team got Jack Schumans in his black Jaguar. Schumans resisted, but one cop hauled off and thumped him, breaking his nose. "I like arresting Hells Angels," the SWAT team member remarked. "They're too fat to run and too slow to react in a fight."

Drop was charged with illegal possession of a weapon and released after three months. Diaz, however, was in for the long haul.

Schumans refused to tell the police anything. Hegger, however, seemed only too glad to complain about de Vries. "Many more people would go the same way Paul did," he warned police. "This story isn't over yet." Hegger told the cops he and the Nomads had tried to persuade de Vries to stop his ripped deals, but to no avail: "Paul was a man you couldn't say no to. He would walk over corpses."

But Hegger was not going to tell the cops how the unpopular de Vries had died. Hegger soon realized he had talked too much. "If word gets out that I've told you all this, then I would rather shoot myself with a bullet through the head than wait for them to do it. Or have my wife and children worried. It's not only the Nomads I have to deal with. After that there's the HA Holland and then the whole world. That's so big!" He clammed up.

Diaz, on the other hand, wouldn't shut up. Until he spilled the beans, the police had no idea the Nomads were involved in the murder of their own president. Diaz made no less than twenty-seven statements to the police, implicating himself and the Hells Angels in numerous drug deals and revealing what he knew about the Nomads murders. For his snitching, he got thirty-six months for trafficking in the 293 kilos of ripped cocaine. In return the cops got the Nomads.

In June 2004, police rounded up the entire Nomad gang and charged them with the first-degree murder of Paul de Vries and his two henchmen in the Nomads' clubhouse. The prosecution demanded life sentences for all twelve accused. Police also busted Donny Klassen and charged him with drug trafficking and complicity in Chocolaad's murder.

It was Holland's first major case against the Hells Angels, and the Dutch were determined to do it right. A special courtroom was built in a small two-storey commercial building in suburban Amsterdam. While the exterior looked shabby and had none of the grandeur and formality expected of a courthouse, inside the security was impressive, with an array of X-ray machines, metal detectors and about thirty security guards.

Each of the dozen defendants sat behind Formica tables aligned in a semi-circle before a bench of five judges. The bikers lounged around in scruffy jeans and sweatshirts, flexing their muscles and scratching their tattoos. On the other side of a wall of bulletproof glass sat the relatives of the victims and the accused, plus a few reporters. No members of the general public were allowed. They had to watch the proceedings in a separate building in downtown Amsterdam equipped with closed-circuit television. The judges didn't want any of the usual intimidation from the Hells Angels showing up to pack the courtroom. It worked. The Angels stayed home.

Diaz, naturally, was the prosecution's star witness. For several days he recounted the story of the ripped deal, the murder of Chocolaad and the Nomads' boast that they had "scraped the shit off the sidewalk." He claimed the Nomads got permission from Big Willem to kill de Vries and then described how they tried to kill Diaz himself. Big Willem was subpoenaed to testify and denied Diaz's allegations that he had approved the murders.

Corroborating evidence included bloodstains at the crime scene from the three victims. Despite the efforts of the Nomads to rebuild their meeting room with fresh plaster and paint—spots of plaster were still wet when police raided the clubhouse—police found minute traces of blood on the stairway. There were also statements from the man who saw de Vries bounce off the pavement and the neighbour who heard gunshots. In all, the prosecution had about twenty-four hundred pages of evidence, wiretaps and witness statements.

Still, the evidence didn't amount to much. It all hung on Diaz, an admitted drug dealer. If the judges believed Diaz, the Nomads were toast. If they didn't, they walked. It was a tough call, and in the end, in typical Dutch tradition, they compromised.

The judges ruled that nobody could be found guilty of killing two of the bikers—Cor Pijnenburg and Serge "Moon" Wagener—because the prosecution had failed to prove who pulled the triggers. However, the murder of Paul "The Butcher" de Vries was a different story. The judges reasoned that after de Vries flew out the window and onto the road, none of the Angels stepped in to stop his murder. Therefore, they were all guilty. But since they couldn't prove that the murder was premeditated, the judges sentenced each of the twelve to only six years in jail.

In the end even his relatives didn't appear to shed tears for Paul de Vries. His daughter had to cancel her June wedding. After all, the groom, Cor Pijnenburg, was dead. Dutch law allows anybody who has suffered material loss from a crime to claim financial restitution and collect it from the perpetrators. She filed a claim for wedding costs. The court refused but agreed to award the families of the three dead Nomads 4,800 euros for the funeral costs. The twelve bikers were ordered to pay for the funerals of the men they murdered.

With the entire club dead or in jail, Paul de Vries's Dutch Nomads were disbanded. The Butcher was gone. That left one more powerful Angel in Holland—Big Willem.

In 2004 Big Willem turned fifty. For more than twenty-six years, he had been the undisputed leader of the most powerful Hells Angels chapter in Europe. That he lasted so long in such a deadly and unstable world testified to his charismatic leadership. That he had established one of Europe's most pwerful outlaw biker chapters reflected a vision and drive only a handful of biker leaders have ever displayed. Disciplining and corralling the energies of often ruthless, powerful men was no small accomplishment. Big Willem had been a master of force containment. His name was synonymous with the Hells Angels of Europe. Now, however, his power base was crumbing.

Allegations that he had approved of the killings of Paul de Vries and his henchmen did not sit well with some of his Amsterdam brothers. And it seemed that the entire underworld, which for decades had remained relatively stable, was in transition. Including the men at the top, the Hells Angels.

Big Willem himself seemed increasingly erratic and isolated. No longer was he seen at his nightclubs and hash bars in the city's red-light district—places like the Excalibur, with its ornamental castle battlements, along the narrow Achterburgwal, or the nearby Hanky Panky tattoo studio, run by his son Jerry.

Big Willem had gone into hiding. For the first time, he feared for his life. That anybody would dream of killing the most powerful of Europe's Hells Angels was astonishing. The protective wall of fear and intimidation he had built round himself normally would have seemed impenetrable. But these were not normal times.

The first signs that Willem was in trouble came as far back as the autumn of 2000, when two of his close associates were shot. One was a minor figure whose passing went unremarked, but the second victim was a major player with important contacts. Sam Klepper was an infamous and vicious Dutch bank robber, arms dealer and drug trafficker who had made more than enough enemies in his time, but nobody had ever dared to touch him because he had the backing of the Hells Angels.

Until now. It happened when Klepper was standing outside his apartment. The assassin drew a machine gun out of an umbrella and shot Klepper dead. His newly hired Serbian bodyguard then took off after the shooter. He chased him through a marketplace, firing as he went. The assassin turned and fired back. Shoppers dived for cover as the streets echoed with the rapid crack of automatic weapons fire, injuring an 80-year-old man. The killer escaped in a waiting car.

Amsterdam had never seen anything like it. Nor had its citizens ever experienced the huge mob funeral that followed. Klepper was a Hells Angels prospect. Though not a full member in life, he became one in death. The Hells Angels posthumously awarded the biker full-patch status and buried him in his colours after an elaborate funeral attended by everybody who was anybody in the underworld. Outlaw bikers came from all over Europe. To the dismay of Dutch citizens, the funeral procession of rumbling Harleys snarled its way through narrow downtown streets of elegant sixteenth-century townhouses and over the spiderweb of ancient canals. Led by Big Willem and escorted by a large police contingent, it stopped in front of Amsterdam's central police station, where the Angels lit fireworks. It then proceeded to the graveyard, where more fireworks were set off. It was as if the entire Dutch underworld had suddenly risen into the light of day. And there was Big Willem at the head of it all, waving an HA banner. The Hells Angels on parade. This was a message—loud and clear—about who really ran Amsterdam.

To this day, it remains unclear who murdered Klepper: there

was talk of an old drug deal gone bad. Still, the question was, Who would dare clip a Hells Angel? Normally that alone would spark immediate and violent reprisals. Klepper was one of Big Willem's allies. An attack on him was an attack on the Hells Angels and a challenge to Big Willem himself. Nobody could be allowed to get away with that. The franchise had to be protected at all costs.

But nothing happened.

Klepper's murder was the first crack in Big Willem's armour: not just because someone would dare kill a friend of his, but also because of his weak response.

Big Willem was oddly content not to take action. He seemed more interested in maintaining his comfortable jet-set lifestyle— commuting between his home in South Africa and his taxpayer-funded fortress in Amsterdam. He didn't want a gang war that would bring the police down on their heads. But down they came anyway. Early one morning a squad of Dutch Special Forces broke through the steel gates of Angel Place, followed by more than a hundred regular cops. They didn't find much. A Sokacs machine pistol made in Croatia, some handguns, twenty knives, a crossbow and some illegal fireworks. In Big Willem's bungalow at the rear of the compound they found a Beretta pistol and a Ruger revolver. They seized the guns and arrested Big Willem. When he produced gun licences for both weapons, the police had to give them back.

Still, the raid spooked him. So, like all chief executives worried about an unstable future, he called a meeting. Not just any meeting. All the top crime bosses were invited—and it was not optional. "He must come," Willem is heard telling a reluctant gangster on one police wiretap. The biker leader had to stop the killing before it got out of hand. He had to re-establish the careful balance that for decades had made his city a safe place to do business. His strategy worked, but only briefly. For the next seventeen months, there was peace. Then the streets opened up and the shootings began again.

From 2002 to 2004, assassins gunned down nine crime bosses in Amsterdam. The slaughter was confused and random. Life seemed to have descended to the blunt-edge reality of kill or be killed. Worried gangsters were seen making deals with police. Investigators were told of lengthy hit lists.

Big Willem got caught in the middle. Not only were most of his allies the targets of the shootings, but he himself got caught in a web of betrayal and backstabbing. It began in early 2002, when a second close associate of Big Willem's was the target of a shooting—and the twisted saga would eventually end with Big Willem's undoing.

John Mieremet was a handsome, professorial-looking gangster with wire-rimmed glasses and short dark curly hair. He had invested millions of euros in real estate holdings in Amsterdam. On February 26, 2002, he was shot in the stomach as he left his lawyer's office. A close ally of Klepper's—people called them Spic and Span—he had once escaped execution by rival gangsters by getting himself arrested with a carload of guns. He figured prison walls were safer than the streets. And he was right. He should have done the same this time. The shooter plugged him in broad daylight. Though the bullet tore through his insides, he miraculously survived and then retreated to his villa just across the Belgian border.

He didn't retreat into silence. Furious and vengeful, Mieremet started ratting to the media about Amsterdam's criminal class, naming names. He claimed two men were behind his assassination attempt: Willem Holleeder (known as "The Nose" for his most prominent facial feature) and Willem Endstra.

The name Holleeder surprised no one. He had already gained substantial notoriety when he was sentenced to eleven years in prison for the spectacular 1983 kidnapping of Dutch beer magnate Freddie Heineken. He was released from prison in 1990; since then, police had considered him one of Holland's top gang bosses, with strong ties to the Hells Angels.

Fingering Endstra, however, shocked the upper ranks of Dutch society. He was the scion of a wealthy Dutch railway and real estate family. A slick dresser, he liked expensive suits, big open collars and shiny black shoes. With his short-cropped salt-and-pepper hair, pudgy face and permanent tan, he had the aura of a highly polished middle-aged tycoon. To Mieremet he was little more than a "banker to the underworld," and his friend Holleeder was the "guardian of the bank vault." Mieremet claimed that Endstra had built a fortune laundering money for Amsterdam's drug lords and Holleeder's job was to make sure these investments were well protected.

Rumours of Endstra's involvement with the underworld had dogged him for years. In 1992 the Public Prosecutors office named him as a money launderer for a gang trafficking ecstasy, but he was never charged. He was rumoured to have paid off justice department officials to the tune of 1 million euros. Ten years later he was again named by the public prosecutor as a money launderer; again, he was never charged. Endstra always kept his mouth shut, eventually acquiring the nickname Willem the Silent. But Mieremet's disclosures forced him into the open and for the first time revealed a credible link between Holland's enormous illicit drug trade and the country's legitimate business interests.

The reason he was shot, Mieremet claimed, was that he had demanded repayment of a 22-million-euro investment. When Endstra refused to pay because the money was tied up in real estate, Mieremet went to his office and threatened Endstra with a gun. Endstra later called in his strong-arm man, Holleeder, to knock off Mieremet, Mieremet claimed. (Unfortunately for Mieremet, the first assassination attempt was not the last. In October 2005, he left his fortified villa in Belgium and travelled to Thailand where he had real estate investments. The trip proved fatal. A hit man tracked him down and on November 1 shot him dead on a busy street near the resort city of Pattaya. It was testament to the long reach of the Dutch underworld. There must have been no doubt in his mind that his life was still in danger because just two days earlier his lawyer had been gunned down in Amsterdam.)

By 2004 the tables had turned: Endstra found himself on a hit list. Gang leaders were growing concerned about their investments in Endstra's real estate empire. If Endstra had refused to pay John Mieremet his 22 million euros, how safe was their money? It was time to cash in. Endstra suddenly had a run on his real estate empire.

Endstra had for some time been a businessman under siege. His penthouse apartment overlooking the Seaport Marina (one of his many real estate investments) at the mouth of the North Sea Canal was encased in bulletproof glass. He rode in a chauffer-driven armoured BMW formerly used by the Dutch prime minister. He also had a team of bodyguards on twenty-four-hour duty. That was his defence.

His offence was Big Willem.

Endstra met secretly with Big Willem in early 2004 and offered to pay him 1 million euros, with 250,000 up front, if he could set up a hit on the man he thought wanted him dead: Willem Holleeder.

There was, however, one slight problem. Holleeder was a good friend of the club's secretary, Harrie Stoeltie, a tall, handsome, ambitious Hells Angel. Unlike many bikers, he's slim, fit and meticulously groomed. His job was "head of security" for Amsterdam's most expensive whorehouse, Yab Yum.

Increasingly anxious for his safety, Endstra went on TV on May 16, 2004, to claim he was being hunted and to deny any connection to organized crime. Willem the Silent was silent no more. But it didn't help him. The next day as he climbed into his armoured car in front of his head office in the fashionable Apollolaan district of Amsterdam, an assassin shot him dead in broad daylight.

Soon after the killing, an informant claimed to the police that Big Willem had planned to carry out the Endstra contract to assassinate Holleeder. The alleged plan was to blow up Holleeder when he paid his weekly visit to Angel Place. Police immediately arrested Big Willem and his two hired henchmen. According to police files, Big Willem confirmed that Endstra had approached him about "punishing" Holleeder but denied ever conspiring to kill him. After several days of interrogation, police were forced to free all three men for lack of evidence.

But it was enough evidence for the Angels. At an unusual press conference, they announced that Big Willem had admitted to them his role in the plot to kill Holleeder. The Angels immediately voted to kick Big Willem out of the club, ordered him to return his patches, sever all contacts with the Angels, sell his interest in his red light district nightclubs, which were Hells Angels hangouts, and burn off his tattoos. Big Willem's ruthlessness had brought the Angels power and wealth. Now it had destroyed him.

An obscure member, originally from Indonesia, replaced Willem as president, but nobody doubts that the real power behind the throne is Harrie Stoeltie. As for his friend Holleeder, outside of the Hells Angels, he is considered Holland's most powerful crime boss.

Theories abound about the downfall of Big Willem. Stoeltie said it was because his bomb plan endangered the lives of his fellow Angels. But now it appears there was something more sinister involved. Stoeltie had been part of an inner circle of Hells Angels— a gang within a gang—called "'t Setje," or "The Bunch." It included Nomads such as Paul de Vries as well as Hells Angels from Denmark and England. De Vries's murder, they say, turned Stoeltie against Big Willem, who is alleged to have sanctioned it. Then when Stoeltie learned about the plot to kill Holleeder, Stoeltie used it as an excuse to isolate and then to expel Big Willem.

For their part, the police, it is believed, intentionally leaked information about the Holleeder murder plot to the HA, hoping they'd turn on Big Willem and force him to come running into the arms of the police for protection—and become a star witness against his fellow Angels.

If so, it didn't work. Even under the threat of death, Big Willem has remained true to his outlaw biker creed. He vanished into silence, retreating to a secret location outside Amsterdam. Angels lawyer Vincent Kraal released a brief public statement:

"As far as the club is concerned, Big Willem no longer exists."

But he did exist. And he would resurface in late 2005, arrested with many of his former comrades on drug and gangsterism charges. And despite all the infighting, murders and arrests, his legacy remained: the Hells Angels still ruled supreme over the crime world in Amsterdam, and from there, across a new Europe that had become biker territory.

TWELVE

Tea with the British Bulldogs

———

The problem with the Hells Angels is here—but it's not in
the public eye. It's happening below the surface.
—DET. NICK CLARK, U.K. NATIONAL CRIMINAL
INTELLIGENCE SERVICE

The bikers' stared at the leather-studded knee-high boots and
then moved their eyes up slowly, along the fishnet tights, then the
leather miniskirt, finally settling on the low-cut Lycra top.

"We're all fighting over who will have her on the back of our
bike," Sinbad, a Hells Angels from Manchester, England, told the
local paper. "She looks fantastic in her leathers and many of our
wives and girlfriends are getting jealous."

What grabbed Sinbad's attention was Bev Callard, a star of
Coronation Street, one of England's, if not the world's, most pop-
ular soap operas. The soap queen was just one of several celebri-
ties eager to help out the bikers at a charity Christmas ride. From
Coronation Street to Westminster and Buckingham Palace, every-
one—from TV stars to cabinet ministers and even the late Queen
Mother—seems to have a soft spot for the Hells Angels in the
United Kingdom.

As the convoy of Hells Angels roared through the streets of
Salford, a bustling city next to Manchester, the good citizens cheered
and waved. It was just two weeks before Christmas in 2004, and more
than a thousand bikers—dozens of members of the Hells Angels,
along with a local group called the Mid-Life Crisis Motorcycle
Club—rode to the Children's Hospital to hand over presents donated

to their annual Toy Run. Toy Runs have long been favourite PR gim-
micks of the Angels in America and Canada, but the British Angels
have excelled in recruiting high-profile endorsements.

"I jumped at the chance to get involved," gushed Bev Callard.
The event went from soap opera to farce when the actress was
joined by the local Member of Parliament, Hazel Blears, who also
happened to be Home Office minister in Tony Blair's cabinet.
Blears's formal title is Minister of State for Crime Reduction,
Policing, Community Safety and Counter-Terrorism. Her official
Web site states that she has "overall responsibility for reducing
crime and the fear of crime."

Perhaps the minister thought the best way to reduce crime was
to socialize with the bikers. "Hazel was . . . really supportive and
even had a chat with the Hells Angels," said one organizer. "She is
a biker herself and has her own bike."

The Minister of State for Crime Reduction was in good company that day in Manchester. After all, the Hells Angels were front
and centre at the illustrious parade through the streets of London
to honour Queen Elizabeth's Golden Jubilee in 2002. Each biker
rode by on a motorbike built in a different year of her official role.
Leading the pack was a corpulent biker nicknamed "Snob," whose
real name was Alan Robert Fisher, the president of the London
chapter of the Hells Angels. The Queen Mother graciously waved
from her reviewing stand as the Angels rode by on their Harleys.

While the bikers were waging a bloody war in continental
Europe and shooting at one another in casinos in America, in
England they were literally getting the royal treatment. In no other
country in the world do the Hells Angels get as easy a ride as they
do in the U.K.—from politicians, the press, the public and even at
times the police. It is partly because England has a deep-rooted
motorbike culture: as the Manchester ride showed, many ordinary
people enjoy a weekend ride. The annual Bulldog Bash, a bike festival organized by the Hells Angels in Kent, draws tens of thousands of tourists every year. The Angels in the U.K. have done a
superb job of spinning a PR web while keeping the worldwide
criminal activities of their club well hidden.

"The problem with the Hells Angels is that their criminal activities are not in the public eye. It happens below the surface," says Det. Nick Clark, the most senior police officer in Britain to follow the outlaw motorcycle gangs. "You won't detect that. And it's not until you start looking for it that you find it."

Nick Clark started looking at the bikers in his country back in 1995. As a police officer in Lincolnshire, he had two passions: motorbikes and languages (he is fluent in French and German). By twenty-four he had signed up with the local police, but in 1995 he eagerly took a transfer to Interpol.

His first assignment was the drugs desk at the National Criminal Intelligence Service (NCIS) in London, where the Interpol liaison officers were stationed. Drugs, as Clark quickly discovered, meant bikers: "I started to see what was going on worldwide; it didn't take much to convince me that what you essentially had was international organized crime on a huge level."

Clark became the U.K.'s point person for Project Rockers, started by Interpol three years earlier. Police forces in Europe and North America had realized, belatedly, that the bikers were a growing menace, but they also realized they had little hard intelligence and even less coordination. The goal of Project Rockers was simple: to set up a network of police contacts in each country that would be in charge of biker intelligence in order to identify all known members by chapter, rank and group.

British police had not seriously looked at the British bikers before. "I was quite shocked to find that at the time outside of North America, the U.K. has the biggest population of Hells Angels anywhere in the world," Clark says. In the mid-nineties, there were thirteen chapters in the U.K.; today, there are sixteen charters spread across England and Wales, with over 250 members.

The London Chapter, which got its charter from California on July 30, 1969, is the oldest in Britain. Its well-spoken leader, Alan "Snob" Fisher, runs the fashionable Snobs Ultimate Customs in West London, where his finely tuned and crafted bikes can fetch more than £36,000. Fisher, who favours dark glasses and a black bandana, got picked to ride in the Queen's Jubilee because one of his customers was a BBC director. "Some people are afraid to be proud of being English. I'm not. I am very patriotic," he told one newspaper. "The Queen and Prince Charles are honourable and caring people."

Fisher himself came from fine stock, raised by a wealthy family in Kensington. He got his nickname Snob when as a youth his new-found working-class pals teased him about his background. Snob says he read an article about Sonny Barger when he was thirteen, and he was hooked. "Going out on a motorcycle allows me to be free, to express myself and to ride pretty much within the legal system," he once told the BBC.

"Pretty much" being the important qualifier, since many Angels have strayed over the line onto the other side of the law. Fisher himself had a minor record dating back more than twenty years: a 1980 charge for "affray" or assault and two convictions in 1983 for possession of amphetamines. That earned him only a small fine. Other officers listed in official corporate documents of his London chapter include Guy "Tricky Tramp" Lawrence, a director, who has a long list of convictions for everything from car theft to common assault and drugs; and two secretaries—Paul Floodgate, who served a four-year prison sentence for possession of 500 kilos of cannabis resin, and Andrew "Wilf" Bleu Brooks who was busted for theft and has four convictions for drug possession. The London roster is rounded out with members like David Clark, who was jailed on amphetamine and cocaine charges, and Martin "Rocky" Rock, who served eighteen months in prison for possession of cocaine, LSD and cannabis and seven years in prison for serious assault. "Snob" Fischer and his London pals were not connected to the murders or other acts of violence that some members of the Hells Angels would later commit in the U.K.

There is one Nomads chapter, as well as chapters for the South Coast and West Coast, plus clubs in Kent, Wessex, Lea Valley, Southampton, Tyne and Wear, Essex, Ashfield, Northampton,

Manchester, Wolverhampton, Windsor and Wales. By the end of 2005, the Hells Angels also announced they planned to set up a beachhead in Belfast.

If London is the oldest chapter, Kent is the loudest. It has the most bunker-like fortress, a sprawling farmhouse reminiscent of the red-and-white bunkers found in Canada. The most colourful biker in the U.K. was also from Kent: Ian Harris, the press officer for the gang in England. With his wraparound shades, neatly trimmed beard and shoulder-length dark hair, "Maz" as he was known, was a frequent guest on TV and radio shows. His eloquence came naturally. Harris had the distinction of being one of the few Angels in the world with a Ph.D. He completed his doctorate at Warwick University—with honours—by writing a dissertation on motorcycle gangs, titled "Myth and Reality: Motorcycle Subculture." Even police grudgingly admitted he was "'very very astute." Said Det. Nick Clark, "I had a lot of admiration for him as my nemesis."

Harris, like London leader Snob Fisher, also had the smarts for business. He owned the popular Kent Custom Bike Shop. Several of his fellow Kent bikers also ran successful businesses, belying the image of bikers as greasy losers. Brian "Boz" Raybould runs Boz Engineering; Paul McLean, nicknamed "Herman the German," owns a Home Services company (and also has a criminal record for theft and grievous bodily harm); Andrew Messer owns several Cottage Craft stores (along with convictions for assault, theft and burglary).

"The increased prosperity of the members" caught the attention of police, as a restricted report showed. The report noted that when the Hells Angels moved into England, the bikers went from being just bad boys to also being good businessmen: "Houses were purchased by chapters. . . . Individual members who were either unemployed or employed in low paid manual labour, were able to purchase houses for themselves; they acquired high value Harley-Davidson motorcycles which they retain as status symbols."

The police suspected that at least for some Angels their most profitable business was crime: stolen motorcycles and bike parts, extortion rackets and, above all, drugs. The various activities are often connected. Police say the bikers in north London practice extortion on clubs where they often also work as doormen. "They let their dealers in and other dealers get told to go away," says one senior officer from the London Metropolitan Police.

"They are up there with the Triads and the Mafia and the East Europeans," says Graham Weekes. "They are up there with the best organized crime people in the world." Weekes got a taste of the bikers early in life, when at sixteen he was beaten up by a group of bikers called the Scorpio in a Cornwall nightclub. "I was just a young lad chatting up the wrong women," he recalls. The bikers, wearing knuckle-dusters, tore a piece of cheek so deep that you could see his teeth; the scar is still there today. Weekes joined the Devon–Cornwall constabulary at twenty-six. Six years later, he took part in his first operation against the bikers, busting them for firearms and drugs.

Weekes got a better chance to take on the Hells Angels when he was assigned to the NCIS from 1992 to 1996. He assisted Britain's National Crime Squad in a massive, four-year investigation of a worldwide series of contract killings and drug operations centred on one member of the Hells Angels with British and world connections. "We had thousands of lines of inquiry," Weekes says, without being more specific because there are still offshoot investigations under way to this day. The drugs included amphetamines, ecstasy and cocaine; the countries included Holland, Sweden, New Zealand, Australia and the United States.

"I know they're dealing large amounts of drugs," Weekes says. "They're trafficking firearms. And we've never been able to hurt them."

When Nick Clark joined Weekes at NCIS, he took quickly discovered it was precisely their international ties that gave the Angels around the world the edge in the drug business. He got his first wind of the breadth of those ties early in 1995 when he ran surveillance of the Lea Valley chapter's tenth-anniversary celebrations. "Suddenly we found all these guests descending from different parts of the world," he says. "It was very professionally done—hire cars to and from the airport, good security. It really opened my eyes."

The U.K. provided the Angels with both a door to Europe and a bridge to North America. The London chapter, after all, was the first European base for the Hells Angels, and the U.K. Hells Angels were close to Europe but spoke the same language as the American boys.

The ties across the ocean were best illustrated by a bold biker venture to import more than 500 kilos all the way from Colombia directly to London, England, with the help of the Canadian Hells Angels. What the bikers unfortunately didn't know was that the money launderers and importers they were dealing with were undercover cops. Back in the early 1990s, the Royal Canadian Mounted Police (RCMP) had set up a storefront operation in the heart of downtown Montreal to collect evidence against members of the Italian Mafia and the biker gangs involved in a massive money-laundering racket. The Mounties were so successful in gaining the confidence of the criminals that they were asked to help broker the importation of 558 kilograms of cocaine.

The Mounties brought in an undercover agent posing as the owner of a London-based import-export business with ties to Amsterdam and the South American cartels. At a meeting in Montreal in the late summer of 1994, he got $907,000 as a first payment and was told the drugs were for the world Hells Angels, to be delivered to the U.K. The conspirators agreed to meet the following week in London.

Once the deal was cut, the Mounties leased a freighter, and on August 17, off Colombia's Caribbean coast, near the city of Baranquilla, they loaded it up with the white gold and headed out to sea. Unaware their plot had been infiltrated, the Hells Angels sent two Quebec members, Pierre Rodrigue and David Rouleau, to England to supervise the shipment. They waited at their luxurious suite at the London Hilton for news of the delivery and took in the sights. One Mountie sent over to help British police with the surveillance recalled the unlikely tourist couple: "They were like kids in front of Buckingham Palace, holding on to the gate."

They didn't hold on to their money. At a later business meeting with the undercover agent, the Angels agreed to fork over a lot more money to release what they thought was the cargo waiting in a British port. The next day, the British police swooped in and arrested the bikers—one at the hotel, the other in a car about to leave the Hilton with two international money launderers.

"When the rooms were searched, they found contact lists for all the U.K. chapters," says Nick Clark of the NCIS. "We suspected they were going to use that for a distribution network."

The two Canadian Angels were extradited and eventually each got fourteen years in prison.

Perhaps because they got burned so badly in a long drug haul from the Americas, but more likely because of England's close proximity to the continent, some of the U.K. bikers focused most of their international attention eastward. Several bikers moved back and forth with ease between the U.K. and the rest of Europe. Police reports indicated that one Kent chapter member was of Swedish origin and "travels extensively to Sweden and other Scandinavian countries." European bikers returned the favour. Dutch biker Marco Hegger—the Nomad who Diaz believed wanted to kill him and who had warned him that the bikers "have scraped the shit off the pavement"—was spotted by police in England in the fall of 1997. The British Isles were not Hegger's only travel destination. Police files say he had a record for possession of controlled drugs with intent to supply. His passport had recent details of trip to Colombia between March 10, 1997, and August 8, 1997, with various entries indicating authorized extensions of his stay in that drug mecca.

The Dutch connection was a profitable one for the British bikers, though not always a safe one. Steven Cunningham, or "Grumps," as he was known, was a major drug trafficker affiliated with the Nomads chapter based in Swindon, Wiltshire. He was an aggressive businessman: he lost his right hand when a bomb he planted under a rival dealer's car exploded prematurely. While he was in prison in the late 1990s, the South West office of NCIS received intelligence that he was smuggling drugs into the prison, but they could not come up with any proof. Shortly after his release, Cunningham headed to Amsterdam. "Intelligence indicated that the purpose of his visit was to buy drugs or explosives," says one officer. "But he just disappeared off the face of the earth." The one-handed biker made it as far as Ostend, Belgium, where he last used his mobile phone. Police know he had a falling-out with leaders of the Nomads club, but bikers don't readily come forward to police with their dirty secrets. Cunningham is still officially listed as missing.

His disappearance did not seem to deter some of the Angels from pursuing their ties with Amsterdam and other drug meccas. According to confidential police intelligence files, phone surveillance tracked "regular activity" between some UK bikers and South Africa, the Netherlands, Scandinavia and South America. One member flew from Heathrow to the Caribbean on the pretext of a two-week holiday, but according to the report, his trip "was for the purpose of carrying out a drug deal."

More recently, some Angels have also discovered the huge profits—and relative safety—of importing cheap marijuana from South Africa, where the Hells Angels have a strong presence. A kilo of dope bought for £20 in Africa can be sold for £3,000 in the U.K., and even if a person is caught smuggling grass into the country, the penalties are much lower than for harder drugs.

"Information was received from a source that the Johannesburg Hells Angels have been exporting cannabis to the U.K.," reported one memo in the late 1990s that was sent by police to the customs and excise authorities. A biker had been nabbed by the Swaziland police, who were "currently conducting the investigation of a syndicate to export huge quantities of compressed cannabis to the U.K." The Swaziland drugs were bought for the Johannesburg club, which in turn had "received the order from the U.K."

The botched deal was apparently the second transaction; the first had succeeded after the drugs were imported into England in custom-made wrought-iron furniture. So two bikers travelled to England to get their commission—"a considerable amount." Police tipped off Heathrow authorities, who stopped the two men waiting for their return flight on November 6, 1998. In one of their bags they found £25,000 cash.

Police intelligence files indicated that bikers in the U.K. and Africa had set up a trading company, a food business in Swaziland and a furniture enterprise in Johannesburg to facilitate their drug trade. In one case, police were able to seize 1.2 tonnes of compressed cannabis at London's Tilbury Docks in a container packed with furniture. But no one doubts that the vast majority of drug shipments from Africa—not to mention Amsterdam and Colombia—get in unnoticed and uninterrupted.

"It's a challenge," admits Nick Clark of NCIS. "At the end of the day, we're dealing with some very clever people. They're not bleeding idiots."

Almost from the moment they first set foot in England, the HA also displayed a passion for gruesome violence. In 1972, just three years after the Angels opened their first chapter in the country, a fourteen-year-old Girl Guide in Winchester was abducted, dragged to an HA party and raped. The judge who sentenced her attacker to nine years condemned the HA as "an utterly evil organization, evil and corrosive of young people."

Few people heeded his condemnation. And for more than three decades since, the British bikers have displayed an unrelenting willingness to use violence—often directed against their biker enemies, but many times against innocent civilians. While it never reached the fever pitch it did in the rest of Europe, the British bikers still managed to leave behind a long trail of blood.

In 1984 David Richards, a member of the Nomads chapter, was jailed for life after murdering a sixteen-year-old boy at his girlfriend's home in West Ealing, London. Richards left the victim with a bread knife in his chest and the words "Hells Angels" scrawled on the wall in a mixture of ketchup, lipstick and blood.

The following year, the Windsor chapter so terrorized their neighbours, a young family named the McSorleys, that they were forced to move out. The bikers threw drunken parties that featured axe-throwing competitions in the back yard. When the father, Pat McSorley, was away as a merchant seaman, the bikers exposed themselves to his wife and threatened his three children. "They had a meeting, and we could hear them deciding it would be easier to kill us. They were shouting, 'Kill them, kill them,'" said McSorley.

But the British Hells Angels—like their counterparts in North America—reserved their most vicious violence for rival bikers who dared to cross them. As one confidential police report puts it, "There was swift and severe punishment handed out to any person or group displaying the Death Head without authority." The police report cites an example of a man who showed up at the Reading police station with "a large, severe and untreated burn" on his right biceps. Though not an Angel, he had foolishly worn a Death Head tattoo. But not for long. The Hells Angels removed it by cutting out the offending patch of skin with a heated knife.

The man was not the first to learn the hard way that you don't wear the HA colours without official sanction. As far back as 1979, the Hells Angels were quick to impose their U.K. monopoly. Several overeager bikers in Windsor dared to call themselves a chapter of the Hells Angels without first getting the blessing from California. They also committed the sin of having a black member.

So the real Hells Angels surprised them as they slept on Easter Sunday. They shot the putative president of the upstart chapter three times—one bullet bouncing off his skull. A shotgun blast hit another Windsor member. Both men somehow survived. Ironically, five years later, the Windsor boys—minus their black buddy—followed the rules and were given official status within the club. A handful of bikers were eventually sentenced to several years in prison for the attack.

"If you believe yourselves to be above the law and able to do as you please, you are wrong," the judge berated the bikers.

He could have saved his breath. Three years later, the bikers showed they were quite willing to do as they pleased when a Hells Angels party in Cookham Dean, Berkshire, got out of hand.

The bikers had dragged a woman into their festivities and splayed her like an animal with four stakes at the ends of each of her limbs driven into the ground. They began ripping off her clothes; when one biker started taking pictures, violence erupted. Two bikers died of gunshots and stab wounds, and twelve more were injured in the violence. One man's arm was half severed by an axe; another was stabbed so intensely that his intestines were hanging out. After the incident, police found thirty-five knives, a pistol, a sawed-off shotgun, two axes, two hammers, two baseball bats and a machete.

It was petrol bombs in 1986, when there was another biker battle in Leamington. And then guns in 1992, when a prospect for the Wolverhampton chapter was charged with four counts of attempted murder—though he was later cleared—after a dozen shots were fired at a rival biker and two women in Birmingham.

The violence was escalating for a simple reason: the Hells Angels felt threatened. There had always been a coterie of U.K.-based motorcycle gangs, such as the Cycle Tramps, the 69s and Satan Slaves, but they were small and could never challenge the world-class HAs.

But by the late 1990s, the largest domestic gang, called the Outcasts, numbered about 200—just shy of the Angels' strength at 230. Concentrated mainly in London and East Anglia, the Outcasts had shown they could be just as brutal as the Angels. In 1987 nine of them were convicted after they crushed a rival gang by shooting one man, scalping another with a ceremonial sword and fracturing several skulls with axes and hammers.

Worse still, from the Angels' point of view, the Outcasts were loosely affiliated with the Outlaws, one of the Angels' long-standing North American rivals. The Outlaws had their own army of about 150 members in England, mainly in the Midlands. Together the Outlaws and the Outcasts would outnumber and outgun the HAs. The British Angels were beginning to feel the heat from their mentors across the ocean in California: quash your rivals—you're making us look bad.

The fever rose in June 1997, when the Outcasts made a bid to take over a small club called the Lost Tribe in Hertfordshire. No way, said the Angels, who put the screws to the Outcasts themselves: join us, turn in your patches, become prospects for the Hells Angels—or we'll crush you. Quite a few of the Outcasts caved in, including several senior members, but many did not heed the call. That November, two of them were arrested with loaded shotguns, probably en route to take on the Angels.

The rivalry would lead to a deadly battle early in the new year.

The Annual Rockers Reunion near the Battersea Arts Centre in south London has always been a nostalgic, if somewhat boisterous, festival for aging rock 'n' roll fans and Teddy boys, the rebels of the 1950s who sported pseudo-Edwardian clothes. By tradition, it was the Outcasts who policed the event; the Hells Angels always stayed away.

But not on January 31, 1998. This time, the Hells Angels were determined to send a message.

As night fell, about forty members of the Hells Angels from just about every chapter in the country surrounded the castle-like city hall with military precision. Several of them wore radio headsets: "Those Hells Angels were not there to enjoy the music but to act as spotters [to] identify Outcasts so they could be attacked," said the prosecutor at a subsequent trial.

Most of the Outcasts had already made it inside the building, but two of them had the misfortune to arrive late and alone. One of them was David Armstrong, known as "Flipper" because he had lost a leg. The Angels set upon him with baseball bats, machetes, iron bars, knives and axes, dragging him from his bike and hacking him to death.

"I got the bastard! I got him! I did him!" one gleeful Angel was heard shouting. Other witnesses reported that the Angels appeared unnaturally calm and "pleased with what they had achieved."

Another late-arriving Outcast, Malcolm St. Clair, rushed to his friend's side but was stabbed eight times. He managed to drag himself to the steps of the Lavender Hill police station, just a hundred yards away. "They were stabbing him to death in front of the police station," said Det. Sgt. Brian Charmer, who eventually led the murder investigation. "The Angels decided, We're going to teach you a lesson. It was an ambush, an absolute ambush."

Charmer, a veteran of the murder squad, was called out with his partner, Det. Geoff Hymans, to a chaotic scene on that chilly January night. Almost all the bikers—both Angels and Outcasts—had fled. Hundreds of potential witnesses were milling about, and weapons were scattered everywhere. Police tried desperately to preserve evidence along a blood trail fifty yards long.

"You try to stick your finger in their dike at the last minute and try to keep whatever is left of a dwindling crime scene," says Hymans.

"We knew we had a problem because of the audacity of it," adds Charmer. "It was obvious the Angels weren't concerned about witnesses. There was no attempt at disguise. It was in your face—stay out of this."

It also didn't take long for two homicide investigators to realize they had plunged into a world they knew nothing about. "I mean, you know the words 'Hells Angels,'" explains Hymans, "but when you actually stop and say, What does it mean? What's the structure?, you have to immediately start an intelligence operation."

Concludes Charmer more bluntly, "We tried to make some sense of it. Then we go, Help! What's this all about?"

Despite two decades of drug dealing and death by the bikers in England, police had paid scant attention to the Angels. Nick Clark, the only full-time biker analyst at the National Crime Intelligence Service, was about to be reassigned. He gave Charmer and Hymans the broad outlines of the Angels' history and structure, but the investigators needed more up-to-date information.

"They're not regarded as a particular problem here, so you

don't sink resources in, and you get what you pay for," complains Geoff Hymans. "Unless you actively put resources into keeping intelligence fresh, then intelligence is no good."

"It was a massive learning curve," says Charmer. "We started from scratch."

If the police intelligence files were thin, the pool of willing witnesses was proving even thinner. The bikers, both Angels and Outcasts, were obviously not talking. Hundreds of ordinary citizens had also witnessed the bloodshed, but most of them were too frightened to come forward. So Charmer and Hymans decided to use a basic investigative technique to solve a murder: get in the faces of the suspects, immerse yourself in their lives, find out enough dirt to make them want to talk to you. "We were really getting up their noses," says Charmer.

They spoke to hangarounds, prospects, girlfriends and wives— and to the biker bosses themselves. "We decided that we'd just call them unannounced, walk in their shops, knock on their doors," says Hymans. "They hated it." He recalls ringing up Guy "Tricky Tramp" Lawrence, a prominent member of the London chapter, at a T-shirt store he ran. "We would wander in there and have a cup of tea. 'Cause he's just a bloke, at the end of the day. You just have a chat."

Charmer visited Snob Fisher, the London biker leader, at his bike shop. "He'd engage you in an hour's conversation on the virtue of being an Angel. But they found our approach very odd because they're used to the police not bothering them. And they hated it, they just hated it."

They hated it even more when the detectives did everything they could to disrupt their activities: the constant phone calls and visits, the tipoffs to foreign police services when they travelled. Then in late March the police upped the ante by simultaneously raiding more than half a dozen clubhouses across the U.K.

Inside the Wolverhampton clubhouse on Penn Road, known locally as "The Fort," the lone prospect sitting guard got a rude awakening. Armed police used a JCB digger—a massive wrecking machine—to smash their way into the Hells Angels' property.

Unfortunately, the overeager operator took out most of the front wall and not just the door.

A shaken and dusty prospect stumbled out. "You could have knocked on the door," he said. "I'd have opened it."

Not likely. Inside, police found a machine gun and a hoard of ecstasy pills.

At other locations, the police picked up valuable intelligence, right down to the layout of their clubhouses. After the raids, Det. Sgt. Charmer phoned the president of a chapter in Sunderland, in northern England, one morning at six o'clock.

"Can I have an appointment with you in your office?" he asked politely.

"I haven't got an office," came the bleary reply.

"You have in your clubhouse," Charmer said.

"Bastard!" retorted the now suddenly awake biker leader.

Charmer's biggest intelligence haul, though, came from the raid on the mother chapter, the London clubhouse. "I found a computer with a disk in it. It contained the names and mobile phone numbers of every Angel in the world. There was the membership of every clubhouse."

The American authorities, in Charmer's words, went "ballistic" for the disk; the ATF flew over to get a copy. The Hells Angels were equally ballistic: "They knew we had it. It just chewed them up," Charmer says, laughing.

All their probing and pushing eventually helped police lay murder charges for the Battersea slayings against three bikers— Ron "Gut" Wait, the Essex vice-president, and two prospects, Raymond Woodward and Barry Hollingsworth. Both Woodward and Hollingsworth had been full-patch Outcasts until shortly before the attack; police suspected they had been instructed to take part as a test of loyalty.

"Our intelligence at the time indicated that the reason for the murders was the unauthorized expansion of the Outcasts, and that the Angels were told by California to sort it out or lose their charters," says Nick Clark, then with the NCIS.

Arresting the bikers was one thing; getting them to trial was another. For starters, notes Det. Geoff Hymans, "We had to be very careful about where we placed our prisoners because members of the opposition worked as prison staff." Indeed, the police found a full-patch member of the Outcasts working as a guard at one major prison. "Don't put me there, I'll get killed," Hollingsworth begged.

By the time the trials were set to start in November—almost a year after the killings—there were more problems. The prosecution suddenly dropped the case against Hollingsworth and Woodward. "The witnesses . . . have declined to come to court," said the prosecutor. "It would not be prudent in the circumstances for me to go into the reasons for it."

"My wife and I don't hold anything against them for not coming forward," the father of one of the victims, David Armstrong, told a London paper. "I would not have liked to be in the shoes of those witnesses."

But Ron Wait was not so lucky with the main witness against him. Wait, nicknamed "Gut" because of his 250-pound girth, was so fat that he had been driven to the event in a car, instead of showing up on his bike—which made his getaway clumsy and ultimately led to his downfall.

Ramak Fazel, a photographer with a keen eye and an even keener sense of civic duty, had followed the lumbering Angel to his car after the attack and promptly written down the licence number.

"He was absolutely appalled at what had happened," recalls Hymans. "He was the type of person to say, It's my moral duty; I don't want to do it but I have to."

When the trial started inside London's famed Old Bailey courthouse, the Angels paraded a bevy of character witnesses before the jury to try to save their Gut. Maz Harris, the press officer for the Hells Angels in England with the Ph.D. in motorcycle culture, testified that the Angels were, well, angels; their criminal history was a police conspiracy, he insisted. Other bikers were even looser with the truth. Wait had claimed he was not even at Battersea that night but at an Angel clubhouse in Reading. A hapless prospect was brought forward to cover this lie.

"You really want to go in there?" Charmer had asked the biker before he took the stand. "Because you are going to get ripped up for ass paper."

"I'm telling the truth—" he began, before Charmer cut him off.

"Don't! This is a stitched-up alibi."

The prosecutor shredded the prospect's tale. Nevertheless, after nearly four days of deliberations, the jury failed to agree on the murder charge: there was no solid evidence that Gut's axe had actually caused the Outcast's death, so the prosecution settled for nailing Wait for conspiracy to cause grievous bodily harm—and won.

"[Wait] was shocked," recalls Charmer. "Absolutely stunned."

Judge Geoffrey Grigson told the Angel vice-president, "You took an active part in . . . a conspiracy which led to the death of two men. In truth they were executed in a manner that was as ruthless as it was arrogant." He sentenced the Angel leader to fifteen years—an astonishingly high penalty for a charge of grievous bodily harm. In the end, the length of the prison term proved to be academic; Gut died of natural causes after a single year behind bars.

The other two bikers—who eventually got their full patches as a reward for their work—had walked out free men. "It hurt because we put a lot of work in it," says Det. Sgt. Brian Charmer. "But we had been warned they'd do it: get to your witnesses and you've got no case. They walked out [of the courtroom], not even looking over their shoulders."

"Don't mess with an Angel," he concludes.

Years later, the Battersea killings remain the signature event in the history of the British Hells Angels, epitomizing their supremacy in the biker world, their flouting of the justice system and their ability to recover from even the worst public relations disaster.

True, the ensuing months were a bit rough. In March 1998 they discovered a bomb at their Lea Valley clubhouse in Luton, Bedfordshire; then there was an arson attempt at Maz Harris's bike shop in Kent. The Angels retaliated by gunning down two

Outcasts as they were leaving an east London pub not far from their clubhouse. (A year later, an Outcast leader, frightened that he was on an Angels "death list," got three years in prison when police caught him transporting a .45 revolver, an Uzi sub-machine gun, an AK-47 rifle and a rocket launcher.)

Still, by the end of the summer of 1998, the Hells Angels were able to pull off their annual Bulldog Bash without a hitch. The bikers' bash had started back in the mid-1980s and has grown steadily in popularity and profit ever since. It was a brilliant concept: marry the outlaw image of the Hells Angels with the U.K. family tradition of weekend biking. Gang members from across Denmark, Holland, Sweden, France, Germany and North America attend, but most in the crowd are just ordinary folk. At one point, British home secretary Jack Straw urged mainstream bikers to distance themselves from the criminals, but to no avail.

After the violence of the Battersea murders, police feared the Hells Angels rivals might storm the event—so they helpfully provided security. "We worked very closely with the police," said Maz Harris. "The police were co-operative and friendly."

And when the police were not so friendly, the bikers always seemed swift enough to get out of trouble. After a Hells Angel from the Wessex chapter had dropped off a visiting biker from Canada at the local airport, he was stopped by traffic police who discovered a kilo of meth and an unloaded Magnum revolver in the glove compartment. The fast-thinking biker leaped out of the car—and promptly claimed he had stolen the car, thereby avoiding the more serious drug and gun charges.

Similarly, when a member of the Kent Hells Angels was found with 9 kilos of cannabis residue resin in a bag on the front seat of his car, he also had a ready explanation. "Officer, you've saved me a trip. I was on my way down to the police station. I think it's drugs," he said, claiming he had found the bag at a local bike show. Without any evidence to the contrary, police had to let him go.

The Angels had a network of sophisticated intelligence to keep them aware of police and other enemy activity. "They are very crafty the way they invite other people into their social world so they can use them—solicitors, accountants, telephone employees, Inland Revenue, police employees," says Graham Weekes. "They will try to court any type of civil servant that can help."

In the West Midlands clubhouse, police found lists of their radio frequencies; the bikers even had a map showing which police car and call sign covered which area. A supposedly top secret Interpol memo on fighting the bikers across Europe ended up being published in *Heavy Duty,* a magazine affiliated with the Angels. It was Maz Harris who wrote the article, he later admitted to police, under a pseudonym. He claimed he'd found the document on an airplane seat.

A more serious breach of security came when police found out that some of their own members were leaking information to the Angels. During one of the Battersea clubhouse raids, police made an unsettling discovery. "We found in one of their safes official police documents," says Detective Sergeant Charmer. The information included personal details on their enemies available only through the Police National Computer.

"There was going to be some sort of hit," Charmer says of one member of the Outcasts whose name was on the list. "There's only one reason they'd have his home address." Two police officers, including a member of the traffic squad, were eventually sacked.

Bad enough that the Angels seemed to have their fingers into the police. Even more unsettling was the discovery that the Hells Angels had disturbingly close ties to current and former military men.

In early 1998 British military intelligence began getting reports that the Kent chapter of the Hells Angels was particularly close to a motorcycle club called the Patriots. Military men as weekend bikers were nothing new. Since the 1980s, a biker group known as Soldier Blue, made up of serving army men, had evolved to include members of the other forces such as the navy and air force. By 1997 they had changed their name to the Patriots and aligned with similar groups in Europe and Australia. Their insignia featured a skull superimposed on symbols of the three branches of the military: the blood red and black swords from the

Army, the royal blue from the Royal Air Force eagle and the navy blue anchor from the Navy.

Like other regular bike clubs, the Patriots offered camaraderie: their UK Web site promised "serving and ex–serving members" of the armed forces "deep bonds and friendships . . . with like-minded bikers." But police feared that some of the Patriots could be used by the Hells Angels to obtain arms and ammunition in support of their war against the Outlaws, according to a detective at the Ministry of Defence (MOD) who cannot be named to protect his security. "We conducted intelligence to identify, prevent or disrupt that."

Reports were filtering out of Europe about the large-scale thefts from military barracks there to fuel the biker wars. One British military intelligence document warned, "The Patriots would be an ideal organisation for the provision of firearms to the Hells Angels and would be of invaluable assistance in the importation and distribution of drugs from the Continent."

Fears heightened when the MOD discovered that Belgian police had seized "an arsenal of firearms" from the local Hells Angels, stolen from military depots. "Club cards from the Patriots were discovered in seized documentation," according to one secret report.

Police got their first break when Richard Davey, a founding member of the Patriots and its sergeant-at-arms, died in a motor-bike crash in January 1998. An ex-Grenadier Guardsman, he was a serving as an officer at Whitemoor prison at the time. On his body, police found an address book detailing Patriot club members and worldwide associates, including "strong links" with the Kent Hells Angels and the Belgian bikers, plus the "contact names and telephone numbers of known cocaine suppliers from Belgium and Holland."

Surveillance at his funeral showed nineteen full-patch members from various motorcycle clubs, including the Hells Angels. Police determined that the local Patriots were "extremely well organised" under a president by the name of Martin Pocock. Pocock, who had a beer gut and extensive tattoos on both forearms, worked, according to military intelligence files, as a mechanic at the

Kent Custom Bike shop run by Hells Angels members. He had been employed by the Royal Engineers for fifteen or sixteen years, but most of his military records were password protected, "suggesting he was attached to a specialist unit." He left of his own accord, holding the rank of bombardier corporal.

By late June 1998 the MOD had amassed enough intelligence to produce a four-page memorandum. It said that the Patriots had been seen at numerous HA events, providing security and socializing with the Angels. At least seven Patriot members were "still currently serving" in the British military. The intelligence report issued a stark warning: "Hells Angels Kent had [armed forces] services personnel effectively under their control."

On November 12, 1998, police dropped by the residence of Martin Pocock, ostensibly to check on a minor vehicle offence. They were more than a little unnerved by what they saw. It wasn't so much the knife he had on him, or even the baseball bat to the left of the door. It was the shotgun hanging on the wall and "a military-NATO type shoulder rocket launcher." Just for good measure, the armaments were accompanied by a photo display of his military days and pictures of his biker gang.

Once inquiries confirmed that Pocock did not have a firearms licence for such an arsenal, police obtained a warrant and raided his home. A few months later, in May of 1999, Pocock pleaded guilty to possession of nine Russian rocket launchers, four anti-tank mines, one submachine gun, a sawed-off shotgun and a gas canister. He was sentenced to a year in prison.

The biggest danger, of course, was the political dynamite that might explode if word ever got out that some of Britain's military men—not to mention Her Majesty's weapons—might end up in the hands of outlaw motorcycle gangs. As one confidential police report put it, "The Home Office and Military Intelligence are concerned that the allegiance with the Hells Angels of the armed services would cause considerable embarrassment, especially with regard to insecurity of military equipment."

The Patriots were also concerned: they got rid of the people who were causing problems. They kicked out Pocock and a few of his henchmen. The club itself has never been accused of criminal activities.

In that sense, the MOD felt its intelligence operations had been successful, disrupting any possible thefts of armaments for the bikers at the height of the European wars. At the same time, the MOD continues to keep a close eye on the Patriots to this day. "They have recruited very heavily since then," says the MOD detective, including armed forces personnel "in very prominent positions." The Patriots now number between fifty and sixty and are still seen regularly at HA events and clubhouses.

"They are always there," says the MOD investigator. "They have full status within biker fraternity," he adds. "In that respect, they are always going to be in a position to obtain a service. They are leaving themselves wide open to getting firearms for the Hells Angels.

"They will obviously be monitored for the foreseeable future."

While the Hells Angels were stepping up their infiltration of police and military institutions, the British police were stepping back from theirs. As the furor over the Battersea murders faded from the headlines, so apparently did official police interest in the bikers, at least among the top brass.

Nick Clark, who had been keeping track of the bikers for Interpol and Britain's NCIS, was moved from the drugs desk to fraud in 1998. "I took the biker project with me because they had no one else to do it," he says. "A couple of years after that they wound it down completely. They finally pulled the plug."

NCIS management didn't say they weren't going to watch the bikers any more. What they said was that if there is a biker inquiry connected with drugs, it will go to the drugs desk; if you have a biker inquiry connected with frauds, it goes to the frauds desk. "To me, it was a complete fragmentation of intelligence," complains one former biker specialist. "There is no central contact. How could we—with a huge population of Hells Angels and Outlaws—have nobody? It was crazy, absolutely crazy."

Officially, a spokesperson for the NCIS says of the Hells Angels,

"We aren't shining the light on them." NCIS says the Angels are involved in what they call Level 2 and 3 (importation and trafficking) of amphetamine sulphates, but they have "very little" apparent involvement in the heroin and cocaine trade, although NCIS is "not ruling out" that business for the bikers because "they will try their hand at anything."

The police can't even stop the most famous biker in the world—much less illegal drugs— from coming to England. When Sonny Barger announced his plans to visit London for his book tour in August 2000, police tried to bar his entry on the grounds of his criminal record. "Immigration was put on alert," says one officer involved in the operation, "but he somehow got through."

"In this country the senior officers and government aren't bothered by the Hells Angels and the biker gangs. And it frustrates me no end," says Graham Weekes. For his work at NCIS, Weekes won a commendation at an international convention of biker investigators held annually in North America. Even when he left NCIS, Weekes continued to attend the North American meetings for the next decade—paying out of his own pocket. He was struck by how biker cops in Canada and the United States often devote their entire careers to taking on the motorcycle gangs. "The Americans and the Canadians regard it as a war: soldiers in a war against serious and violent crime. In this country, police don't regard it that way," he says. "Here, you just work on them a couple of years and then you go on to other things. Bikers don't. They stay loyal to each other for a lifetime or as long as they choose. And they develop an expertise, discipline and intelligence gathering. And they are far better at than we are because they stick to it."

Scattered across the U.K., there are still several local police experts on outlaw motorcycle gangs—an officer who knows the Outcasts well in Derby, another who is familiar with the Hells Angels in Kent. Weekes, with the blessing of his local police department, still serves as an informal point of contact in the U.K. for international investigators following the bikers because there is no one officially coordinating the intelligence nationally— much less internationally—and keeping it up to date. According to one senior police officer, "NCIS has been absolutely castigated because there has now been a resurgence of bikers in the Midlands involved in the meth trade and there is nobody in NCIS who has the intelligence on it—all the stuff there is five years old."

"If another Battersea happens, there'll be a big panic on. They'll have nobody to go to," he warns.

Indeed, after the Battersea investigations, Det. Sgt. Brian Charmer moved on to other homicides. He now works out of Surrey, south of London. And all the boxes of intelligence, photographs and documents he gathered from all those raids on the clubhouses back in 1998? The ATF from America got a copy of that valuable intelligence, but no central police agency in the U.K. has one.

"I still have a lot of it because I can't give it to anybody—there's nobody to take ownership of it. Nobody ever had ownership of the biker problem."

So the brown boxes full of intelligence sit on metal shelves, gathering dust in a police storage room in Surrey. Until the next Battersea.

Julia Rocket caused quite a flurry when she sat atop the £18,000 GDP Custom Chrome Chopper, though it was hard to say which smooth curves attracted the gaping stares of the men: hers or the bike's.

The twenty-three-year-old from Oxford was just one of many topless bike washers featured at the British Hells Angels' annual Bulldog Bash in August 2004.

After the Battersea killings, Bash organizer Maz Harris had promised that the bikers would expand the festival "to push the music and entertainment side of things to attract other people and families." The popular Hells Angels leader didn't live to see his success—he died in a motorcycle accident in June 2000. His funeral attracted Hells Angels from around the world; their eight hundred motorcycles stretched through town for two miles, and police ignored the many mourners who declined to wear helmets out of respect for their fallen comrade.

The ensuing Bulldog Bashes continued to grow as a major cultural mecca—and as an ideal way for the Hells Angels to keep their image squeaky clean. Every August, up to forty thousand people from across England now flock to land owned by the Hells Angels just south of Stratford-upon-Avon for the lavish biker party. "All that glisters is not gold," Straford's most famous son, William Shakespeare, once wrote. But the Bulldog Bash has certainly pulled in plenty of gold for the Angels: an estimated half million to one million British pounds every year from gate receipts and sales.

The bashes now feature a shopping village, an all-night dance tent, drag racing and, needless to say, a twenty-four-hour bar, plus live entertainment from the likes of Chuck Berry and a top American band aptly named the Fun-Lovin' Criminals.

When the London *Daily Telegraph* sent its correspondent to check out the Angels in 2004, he dutifully reported what "a fine bunch of friendly, entertaining chaps they turned out to be."

Back in his bike shop in West London, Alan "Snob" Fisher—who by default has become the country's most prominent Angel since the passing of Maz Harris—declines to be interviewed about the history of his club's criminality. "There is no such thing as justice," he says when reached by telephone. "I would love to have an intellectual debate with you," he continues, but insists all interviews have to be sanctioned by the club's unnamed press officer.

He tries to be charming even when hanging up: "I have my mother here. Even Hells Angels have mothers," says the biker who got a wave from the Queen Mum.

THIRTEEN

The Red-and-White Maple Leaf

———

I'm not saying we're all angels. We get unjustly accused of a lot of stuff.
Society needs whipping dogs.
—DONNY PETERSON, ONTARIO HELLS ANGELS

Bullies. That's all they are—bullies with stickers on their back.
—INSP. BOB PAULSON, RCMP, BRITISH COLUMBIA

The American Blackhawk helicopter takes off and soars through the skies, hunting for its prey. But the menacing military bird is not scouting over Iraq or Afghanistan; it's patrolling the U.S.–Canada border between British Columbia and Washington state. Since 2004, the Bellingham border station has added two helicopters and two boats to its arsenal for patrolling what was once described as the world's longest undefended border but is now recognized as a gateway for drugs.

U.S. customs officials have found "B.C. Bud," the popular and potent brand of Canadian marijuana, hidden in boats, cars, planes and backpacks, in frozen raspberries, crushed glass and hollowed-out logs. In 2004 authorities at this border crossing alone seized 20,500 pounds of the weed that Americans can't seem to get enough of, more than five times the amount seized in 1998.

At the other end of the country, three thousand miles east in the dense bush of central Quebec's upper Laurentian Mountains, another helicopter is on dope patrol. A Canadian Forces chopper lifts out of a clearing in the forest. Attached to its undercarriage is a thick steel-wired net stuffed with freshly cut marijuana plants. The noise from the chopper blades is deafening, and the wind force bends the surrounding spruce and pine trees as if they were fields

305

of wheat, momentarily dispersing the heavy, musty scent of the hundreds of marijuana plants. As the helicopter disappears over the treetops to dump its load at a base camp several miles away, dozens of police officers continue hacking down the remaining plants with machetes. The growers have carefully placed their plants in burlap bags filled with rich fertilized soil. The site was well chosen. The remote clearing offers plenty of sunlight, and the tidy rows of marijuana plants sit on a naturally irrigated bog. The growers would have shipped all their supplies into the bush on snowmobiles during the winter, returned in the spring to set up their plants and then waited until harvest. But this time the police got there first.

That anybody would travel so far into Canada's thick bush to grow marijuana is testimony to the huge amount of money the weed earns. Half of the B.C. Bud and "Quebec Gold" is exported to lucrative markets in the United States. American officials have seen pot seizures from Canada rise more than 700 percent since 2000. When it comes to marijuana, Canada has become the Colombia of the north. In his book *Ridin' High, Livin' Free,* Sonny Barger recounts the boast of one biker about "this amazing weed from one of my guys in Vancouver." Barger should know. The Hells Angels are behind much of the trade in marijuana and other drugs north of the border.

Indeed, in no other country of the world are the Hells Angels as dominant and unchallenged as they are in Canada.* With over five hundred full-patch members—a fifth of the world's total Hells Angels—Canada is the only country where the Red and White rule supreme. They have used that supremacy to profit not just from the lucrative export of cannabis but to dominate the cocaine market and expand into the exploding meth business.

Bikers around the world co-operate and compete with other crime groups, but only in Canada are they considered the top

---

*For a more complete look at the Canadian Hells Angels see our earlier book, *The Road to Hell: How the Biker Gangs Are Conquering Canada.*

dogs, the number-one organized crime threat to the country. It's a dominance for which Canada has paid a heavy price.

"People ask me what it's like, and I say it's like trying to drink water out of a fire hose. You try to make sure you don't put your whole mouth over it because it's probably going to come out the back of your head." These words would be funny, except that they come from Insp. Paul Nadeau, head of the RCMP's Coordinated Marijuana Enforcement Team in British Columbia. "There's nothing to compare with this," he says. "You can't keep up. We're just drowning in the numbers."

And the numbers are staggering. The RCMP's criminal intelligence division in B.C. estimates the province's marijuana trade at $7.5 billion annually. It's pure cash flow, says Nadeau, a flourishing industry that ranks just behind tourism and ahead of agriculture. Over the years, Canadian growers have carefully cultivated and cloned plants to nurture a much more potent product: genetic manipulation has made today's pot ten to fifteen times as powerful than what hippies smoked in the sixties. That potency has made Canadian weed a big seller south of the border. Depending on supply and demand, a pound sells in the U.S. at a wholesale rate of US$2,000 up to US$5,000—more than double or triple the price that Mexican marijuana can usually fetch.

It's become a well-integrated industry with enough profit to support a number of organized crime outfits: Vietnamese crime groups are the most prolific growers; the Hells Angels are active as the brokers, buying the weed and getting it to the streets, frequently using Indo-Canadian gangs to truck the product to market. "The Hells Angels have control from production to distribution, to brokering and smuggling," explains Nadeau. "They have their contacts in the U.S. already established, and they'll bring back the money and launder it themselves."

So it was hardly surprising when a U.S. grand jury in March 2004 indicted a dozen people for smuggling US$20 million worth of marijuana from Canada to southern Indiana as part of a ring "managed at the upper levels by the Hells Angels" in B.C.

Or that in May 2005, when the RCMP raided a Kelowna house owned by an East End full-patch member, they found a large grow op. Police seized more than a thousand plants; the cultivation room had a sticker on the door that read, "Support Your Local Hells Angels." The biker was not charged; he was renting out the house and claimed he knew nothing about the activities, although his truck, with a Hells Angels sticker on it, was parked outside when police conducted the raid.

A more imaginative Hells Angel from Nanaimo, along with a good business partner, came up with the idea for the "Big Red Shredder" a popular trimming tool sold on the Internet for about US$800. It is specially designed to cut marijuana buds in record time—sort of a K-Tel dicer for the drug set: no muss, no fuss.

"They made a pissload of money," says one biker source.

Marijuana has become the number-one money-maker for organized crime in B.C:

"Absolutely. No ifs, ands or buts," says the RCMP's Nadeau. "If you peel away the layers in every single major file in this province on organized crime groups, you'll find grow ops. Why not? Nothing happens to you. There's no risk." No risk because fewer than one in seven people convicted of growing pot in B.C. gets sentenced to any time in jail at all.

For the bikers, their marijuana profits are literally seed money—allowing them to finance their myriad other operations, from the emerging crystal meth trade to their trans-Canada cocaine pipeline. It helps when you have thirty-seven chapters coast to coast. It also helps when you have members and associates who work in the country's major marine ports.

More than three million containers pass through Canada's ports every year—and only an infinitesimal 3 percent of them are put through any kind of inspection. A blistering Senate report back in March 2002 exposed widespread organized crime activity in the ports of Montreal, Halifax and Vancouver. When this book's co-authors wrote their first book, *The Road to Hell,* about the extent of the Hells Angels' influence in Canada, it prompted the then federal transport minister Jean Lapierre to describe the ports as "sieves."

"It scared me," he said of the book. "I even bought a copy for my deputy minister. I think we have an enormous amount of work to do."

A secret RCMP report called "Project SALVE," later obtained by the media, warned that despite claims of improvement to security by port owners and some police leaders, organized criminals are "well entrenched" and "have rooted themselves firmly on the docks over decades," often operating in "crucial" positions. The RCMP said in random checks that tonnes of narcotics were found in everything from sofas to potato starch and cat food.

Customs officials have found that whole containers simply vanish off the docks of Halifax, Montreal and Vancouver. In Montreal in early 2005, Donald Matticks, a member of the West End Gang and a former container checker, was sentenced to eight years behind bars for importing more than 44 tonnes of hashish through the port. His father, Gerry Matticks, was already serving twelve years. A close associate of the Hells Angels, Gerry was the undisputed ports kingpin—controlling what illegal cargo came in and went out. Their ring had handled at least 44 tonnes of hashish and more than 200 kilograms of cocaine at the port since December 1999. Out west, a 2001 report by the Organized Crime Agency of B.C. identified at least five full-patch members of the Hells Angels who worked at the Vancouver and Delta ports, plus another two dozen associates. By 2005 police knew of three full-patch members or prospects still gainfully employed there. The numbers were not as important as the influence—it takes just a few people strategically placed when the shipments come in to make sure the right container gets sent to the right people.

So it was more than a little disappointing to see the union that represents longshoremen refusing to co-operate with Transport Canada's plans to impose the same kind of security checks on ports workers that are mandatory for all airport workers. "We're in a state of denial," warned Senator Colin Kenny, whose national security committee helped reveal the national port scandal. "The level of criminality in the ports is beyond belief. . . . We've called for a judicial inquiry; the government is ignoring that call. The Hells Angels are right outside your door."

It was back in 1977 that Sonny Barger's young organization first came knocking on Canada's doors, taking over a local gang outside Montreal and setting up the first Hells Angels chapter.

It didn't take long for the Hells Angels in Quebec to establish a reputation for murder and intimidation that far exceeded that of any other outlaw biker gang in the world. With its dozens of boutique gangs, Canada was fertile ground for a typical Hells Angels consolidation. Ruthless and determined, the Hells Angels, from the moment they established themselves in Montreal in 1977, began muscling their way to supremacy in a province whose biker gangs had been mere gofers and assault troops for more established and better organized crime syndicates. The Hells Angels, on the other hand, had no intention of being anybody's patsies. They were all business. Their product was drugs, and their goal was to make money.

By the beginning of 1985, biker warfare had already claimed 108 deaths from shootings, bombings and knifings. What was astonishing was that the vast majority of the killings could be traced to just one man: Yves "Apache" Trudeau, one of the original founders of the Hells Angels in Montreal. A desperate drug addict and psychopath, he alone killed forty-three people and had a hand in the murder of forty others. Trudeau's thin, square-jawed, gaunt face and blank, wide eyes became the image of the Hells Angels in Canada, establishing a tradition of death at bikers' hands that continued almost unabated for years.

From 1977 to 1985 Trudeau's gang ran wild. Many of the Montreal members became drug addicts. They killed with abandon. They didn't pay their drug debts and even stole $98,000 from the Nova Scotia chapter. Eventually, the other chapters turned against them. Members from Sherbrooke, Sorel and Nova Scotia, a group that had formed only a year earlier, invited Apache Trudeau and his Montreal members to a meeting on March 24, 1985. At a fortified clubhouse built in a wooded area just outside the small city of Sherbrooke, an hour and a half drive east of Montreal, the bikers massacred five members of the Montreal chapter, executing them with a bullet to the head. Other members were forced to watch as their comrades were gunned down. The survivors were stripped of their patches and thrown out of the club. The dead were wrapped in sleeping bags and dumped in the icy St. Lawrence River. In the following weeks, the Angels hunted down and murdered two more members. Three months later, police fished their bloated, shackled bodies out of the river's swirling waters.

Apache Trudeau was lucky. He had checked himself into a detox centre and had not responded to the invitation from his Sherbrooke brothers. Otherwise, he would have been among the dead. Convinced that his fellow Angels would eventually hunt him down, he ran to the police, confessed to his murders and got twelve years in prison for manslaughter in return for testifying against the Angels. A series of trials—one of which was temporarily halted after it was revealed that the Angels had bribed a juror—resulted in twenty-one of Quebec's fifty Hells Angels going to prison.

With the ranks of the remaining two Quebec chapters decimated, by 1990 police thought the Hells Angels were finished. But, as police would soon learn, once entrenched, the Hells Angels don't die off. The fact that death, jail and ejection from the club had reduced their ranks to a handful of brothers just meant that there were a lot of vacancies to fill. And there was no end of willing candidates. The Angels quickly regrouped into a stronger, more cohesive force. And an even more vicious killer than Apache Trudeau emerged as their leader: Maurice "Mom" Boucher.

Boucher got his nickname because he liked to cook breakfast for his fellow Angels. A man of few words but an ever-present smile, he was a natural-born leader. He grew up in the rough neighbourhoods of Montreal's east end, where he helped to start his own club called the SS. They were petty criminals who sold drugs and hijacked trucks. But Boucher always had his eye on the big leagues, and in 1987 he became a Hells Angel.

He was joined by one other biker, his English-speaking alter ego, who would prove to be a true visionary. Walter "Nurget" Stadnick was a little man of five feet four inches with a badly scarred face from a motorcycle accident. But he had big ideas. He was determined to bring the entire country under the banner of the Red and White. Linking up with Boucher was a stroke of good luck. Boucher would be the field general who led the Angels to war. Stadnick would be the diplomat who quietly worked behind the scenes, persuading recalcitrant clubs to join the Angels. Together Stadnick and Boucher formed a dynamic tandem with the goal of finally executing the Hells Angels' plan of dominating the drug trade in Canada.

First, however, they had to create a solid base in Quebec. They expanded to seven chapters, none more powerful than the elite group of Hells Angels Nomads based in Montreal. Boucher and Stadnick were the leaders. It was the Nomads and their eleven members who formed the core of the Hells Angels drug trafficking and launched the biker equivalent of total war against any gang or criminal organization that stood in their path. By the mid-1990s, bombs were going off in Montreal with a regularity that rivalled Northern Ireland. The police were caught totally off guard and at first didn't even seem to care. "I'll tell you honestly, the department didn't give two shits," André Bouchard, then the Montreal homicide commander, admitted. "They're killing each other. I give a hell if some guy pops somebody who just got out of jail? No. We didn't give a shit." That indifferent attitude quickly changed when the biker war claimed the life of an eleven-year-old boy.

August 9, 1995, a clear, warm summer day, found Daniel Desrochers playing idly outside with a friend. Suddenly, about fifty yards down the street a bomb blew up a Jeep, instantly killing the driver, who was a local drug dealer. Little Daniel probably didn't even feel the tiny piece of shrapnel that pierced his skull. He collapsed, and died later in hospital.

The public reaction was one of fury. Fury that the police had sat back like couch potatoes watching the action, allowing the

CANADA AND THE U.K.

Maurice "Mom" Boucher led the Quebec Nomads and was jailed in 2002 for ordering the murder of two prison guards. (John Mahoney, *Montreal Gazette*)

Ronald "Gut" Wait (top row, far right) poses with his "Hatchet Crew" as the Essex chapter of the Hells Angels is known in the United Kingdom. Wait, the chapter vice-president, was sentenced to fifteen years in prison after two rival bikers were butchered in 1998. He died of natural causes behind bars. (Photo News Service)

Bikies fire-bombed Don Hancock's Ora Banda Inn, his home, ore crusher and general store in the weeks after the Billy Grierson murder. The tiny desert town was almost wiped out. (Western Australia Police photo)

Neighbours dragged Lou Lewis's body out of the burning car and onto the road. He died soon afterwards. The bomb tore Don Hancock's body in two and blew the top half over the brick wall in front of his house and onto the patio beside his swimming pool. (WAP photo)

Lou Lewis (above) was driving his friend Don Hancock home from the racetrack when a bomb blew them both up. The target was Hancock. Lewis was just in the wrong place at the wrong time. (WAP photo)

The sartorially splendid retired police commander Don Hancock (left), known as the Silver Fox, was the chief suspect in the murder of bikie Billy Grierson in the Australian outback. He was killed by a car bomb. (WAP photo)

Speed addict and murderer Sid "Snot" Reid (left) agreed to testify against his friend Graeme "Slim" Slater. But the jury didn't believe him. (WAP photo)

IN THE OUTBACK

Inspector Stephen Brown (right) led a team of seventy detectives that took down bikie Sid "Snot" Reid for the murder of Don Hancock and his friend Lou Lewis. (William Marsden)

Detective Jack Lee had the almost impossible task of investigating his former boss for murdering a bikie. Then the case literally blew up on him. (William Marsden)

Western Australia Police believed that Graeme "Slim" Slater (left), among the most powerful Gypsy Jokers, was the mastermind behind the Hancock killing. But he had an ironclad alibi: his mother. (WAP photo)

Peter Hill (back row, right), whose father was a wealthy banker, was Australia's original speed manufacturer and distributor. With his friend Roger Biddlestone (second row, third from left) and a recipe from the Oakland, California, Hells Angels, Hill cooked up a multi-million-dollar drug business. Jealousy among his brothers in the Melbourne Hells Angels drove him into the arms of the police. (Police files)

Steve Chocolaad (right), twenty-nine, got more than he could handle when he started trafficking cocaine with Dutch Hells Angels Nomads leader Paul de Vries. In 2003 his butchered body ended up in a Dutch canal. (Dutch Police)

Fishing off Curaçao in the Dutch Antilles was Angelo Diaz's (above) passion, but he made most of his money as the Hells Angels connection with Colombian guerrillas and other drug traffickers. (Nieuwe Revu)

The tattooed and bejewelled leader of Holland's Nomads, Paul "The Butcher" de Vries, didn't murder people himself. He just cut them up afterwards. His butchering days ended when his Hells Angels brothers killed him because of a drug deal rip-off.

Dutch Hells Angels Nomads pose with their doomed leader, Paul de Vries (right), just before he left for Curaçao to organize a drug deal that would ultimately destroy him and his entire chapter. His close friend, the powerful Amsterdam Angel Harrie Stoeltie, is second from the left. De Vries's murder would have a grave impact on Stoeltie's Amsterdam club. (Ram van Meel)

ANGELS' POWER BASE

The legendary Hells Angels clubhouse in Amsterdam is on land owned by the city and originally was lent to the HA to promote youth activities and charity drives. Now it's considered the most powerful Hells Angels chapter in Europe. (William Marsden)

Big Willem van Boxtel almost single-handedly built the Amsterdam Hells Angels chapter into the most power-ful on the continent. Then a secret murder plot caused his demise. (RCMP photo)

In 1983 a city worker found parts of Joanne Wilson's butchered body in an Amsterdam canal. The outgoing twenty-four-year-old Northern Ireland woman had gone missing after meeting with a Hells Angels killer. Dutch police barely bothered to investigate and then misplaced her file. (Dutch Police)

GREAT NORDIC WAR

This bloodied victim is only one of many in the Great Nordic Biker War that raged from 1993 to 1997, when the Hells Angels and the Bandidos fought it out for control of Scandinavia's drug trade. Rocket launchers, hand grenades, machine guns and plastic explosives were the weapons of choice. (Danish National Police)

The Bandidos stole anti-tank rocket launchers from Swedish armouries to use against the Hells Angels. (Danish National Police)

Danish Hells Angels president Bent "Blondie" Nielsen (left), and Bandidos European president Jim Tinndahn met in September 1997 to make peace and end their five-year war, during which eleven people were murdered. There were another seventy-three attempted murders. (Police files)

Leaving an outlaw biker gang is not always painless. This biker was forced to burn off his tattooes. (Danish National Police)

Car bombs are a frequently used, highly lethal weapon in biker wars. (Danish National Police)

TERROR IN NORWAY

In what was one of the most spectacular assaults of the Nordic War, in 1997 the Norwegian Hells Angels blew up the Bandidos headquarters in Drammen just outside Oslo. The explosion totally levelled the headquarters and killed Astrid Bekkevold, 51, as she and her husband drove by. (Jarl Fr. Erichsen/Scanpix Norway)

bikers to turn their neighbourhoods into a war zone. Fury that a child had died as a result. Nervous politicians immediately promised to clean out the bikers. Millions of dollars were poured into a special joint police task force they called Wolverine. They promised the bikers' days were numbered. But things only went from bad to worse.

Jealousy and competition quickly destroyed any cohesion within Wolverine. Instead of fighting the bikers, the cops were fighting each other. Within a year, the Montreal police department had pulled its men out of the task force, and the government had launched a royal commission of inquiry into the provincial police force, the Sûreté du Québec (SQ). The commission concluded that the SQ was racked by corruption and incompetence. Within a few years, the vaunted police task force was dead.

Watching from the sidelines, the RCMP were quietly running their own anti-gang strategy. In 1994 an informant of theirs had infiltrated deep inside the Hells Angels, and they were running him as an intelligence source. Dany Kane was a disgruntled biker with a talent for spying. He had volunteered his services, and the RCMP jumped at the chance to penetrate the impenetrable. Kane's energy and courage were boundless. The RCMP gave him top-secret status and codenamed him C-2994. Their plan was to send him in as a sleeper who would become a full-patch Nomad and then take down the entire gang. For three years C-2994 performed flawlessly. He was the dream source, the super source. Then the handlers suddenly lost control of their man.

They hadn't figured on Kane's murderous, independent streak. The whole thing blew up in their faces when in February 1997 Kane killed a drug dealer in Halifax in a Hells Angels hit. Police later discovered that he had also directly taken part in the murder of at least two other biker assassinations. Kane's fellow assassin (and also his homosexual lover) was a psychotic named Aimé Simard. Several months later, police caught Simard after he had murdered three other people. He immediately informed on Kane, who was arrested and charged with murder. His life as a police informant was, at least temporarily, over. (For his part, Simard was found dead in his cell in the maximum security wing of the Saskatchewan Penitentiary in 2003, stabbed 106 times.)

With Kane in prison, the police lost their main source inside the bikers, and their task force was in shambles. Mom Boucher and his bikers had the field to themselves. Everything seemed to be going their way. They were unstoppable.

Boucher clearly relished his apparent invincibility. He was so confident that he turned his army of killers against the government, drawing up a hit list of judges, prosecutors, politicians, journalists, police officers and prison guards. The killings began in the spring and summer of 1997, when his henchmen murdered two prison guards and wounded a third. One guard was killed as she drove home after work, and a second was ambushed when he stopped his empty prison bus at a railway crossing.

One of the assassins was caught and after a six-hour interrogation finally confessed, agreeing to testify against Mom Boucher. The trial turned into a travesty as Hells Angels in full colours crowded the courtroom, intimidating the jurors. The jury found Boucher not guilty. He was back out on the street and fast becoming a folk hero. That evening he showed up at a boxing match, where the crowd gave him a standing ovation. Then the shootings began again in earnest.

Among the targets was Montreal's leading crime reporter. Michel Auger was shot seven times in the back as he leaned into the trunk of his car to fish out his computer. Miraculously he survived. Then a tavern owner who refused to allow the Hells Angels to sell drugs in his bar was beaten to death on his front lawn.

By the end of 2000 Boucher's biker war had claimed more than 160 lives, 12 of them of people like Daniel Desrochers who happened to be in the wrong place at the wrong time. The Hells Angels had achieved their goal of controlling the drug trade in Quebec. They formed a cartel with the Italian Mafia to fix cocaine prices at $50,000 a kilo, and they were bringing 250 kilos a week into Montreal alone. "Boucher now controls all of Montreal," one Hells Angel told Kane. "Montreal is his city."

What Mom didn't realize was that his old friend Dany Kane was once again burrowing deep inside his organization.

Kane had miraculously beaten his murder rap. Because of police bungling, the judge threw out the case and Kane was back on the street. The Hells Angels welcomed him as a hero. The cops, however, hadn't entirely given up on him. Although he was a killer, the former RCMP spy was still all they had. So this time the Montreal police—as part of a reinvigorated and newly united biker task force—rehired him as an informant and sent him back into the war zone.

Walter Stadnick, meanwhile, was successfully extending the Hells Angels' influence into Ontario and Manitoba. He made frequent trips to Winnipeg to nurture the new chapter there. In Ontario he pulled off a major coup: to break into Canada's largest and richest province the Hells Angels did what they had done only once before in the world, in Germany. Instead of obliging recruits from other clubs to go through the long screening process of prospecting, they instantly patched over close to two hundred bikers from a half-dozen gangs. Overnight, the Angels in Ontario went from zero to eleven chapters.

Back home in Quebec, the police were finally closing in on the Boucher/Stadnick empire. Kane was regularly tipping off police to gang meetings, which they photographed and bugged. They also located the Nomads' banking operations. The Angels had set up a crude system of safe houses in various apartments in east-end Montreal where couriers brought drug payments. Each night police secretly entered the unprotected apartments and copied computer disks that contained the Angels' weekly drug transactions. The accounting indicated that Boucher's Nomads were doing more than $100 million in cocaine, hashish and marijuana trafficking a year. The drugs were being transported not only throughout Canada but also into the U.S. and Europe.

Then disaster struck when one August Monday morning in 2000 Dany Kane was found dead. His reports to police had indicated for several months that he was depressed and disengaged. Later his wife admitted that he had spoken of suicide. That morning she found him behind the wheel of his leased Mercedes, a victim of carbon monoxide poisoning. A suicide note revealed a disturbed bisexual who was mentally and spiritually exhausted and had lost touch with who he was. "I have been squeezed dry and have nothing left to give," he wrote.

But even Dany Kane's suicide could not derail the mammoth police investigation. On March 28, 2001, the police launched the biggest biker raids in Canada's history: hundreds of police in Quebec and Ontario rounded up 138 bikers and associates, including all but one of Boucher's Nomads (the one biker who escaped is still at large). Stadnick, the Angels' little big man, was holidaying in Jamaica with his wife when police arrested him as he left his hotel.

Mom Boucher was rearrested for the guards' murders when the Court of Appeals ordered a new trial. It ruled that the original judge had erred in his instructions to the jury. This time he was convicted. At the age of fifty-two, he was sent to jail for twenty-five years without parole. He won't ride again until he's seventy-seven. Prison sources told a local tabloid that the fallen biker boss is "depressed, cantankerous, and aggressive" and, to make matters worse, he was placed in a cell that once housed one of the snitches who put him away.

For the rest of the outlaw bikers, the government built a $16.5 million bunker-like courthouse next to the prison, where three megatrials ended after almost a year in blanket convictions for crimes that included participation in a criminal organization, conspiracy, drug trafficking, money-laundering, assault and murder. Stadnick, fifty-one, faced twenty-three counts of murder, conspiracy to commit murder, drug trafficking and gangsterism. He was convicted of everything but the murder charges and sentenced to twenty years in jail plus a $100,000 fine.

Police were determined not to make the same mistake they had made in the early 1990s by thinking that the Angels were beaten. In February 2004 four hundred police officers arrested sixty-three people on drug-trafficking charges. These included twelve of the seventeen members of the Hells Angels Montreal South chapter.

That same month police arrested Jacques "Israel" Emond, who took over from Mom Boucher as the most powerful Hells Angels leader in Quebec. Emond, who had previously served time for trafficking cocaine and has a college degree in administration, was charged with operating a multi-million-dollar loansharking ring in Montreal. He pleaded guilty and was sentenced to twenty-two months in jail. While the Angels still have four chapters in Quebec with about a hundred members, the killings have stopped and the Hells Angels in the province have basically gone to ground, rarely parading their colours in public.

"Hundreds are behind bars," Crown prosecutor Randal Richmond says. "That doesn't mean we have got rid of all of the biker organizations. There's still a lot operating."

The crackdown in Quebec came too late. By 2001 the Hells had spread across the country. As in Quebec, it took time in the rest of the country for police and politicians to react. And as in Quebec, there would only be successes when police had overcome interagency rivalries and had formed specialized biker squads capable of finding, nurturing and running informants who could burrow into the secretive world of the bikers.

In Nova Scotia, for example, the Halifax regional police and the RCMP merged their biker and homicide teams seamlessly. They also realized it takes a thief to catch one. First they recruited Bill, a low-level drug dealer associated with the bikers who was unnerved when they murdered one of his friends. "I would either kill them or be killed," Bill says. Instead, he worked bravely undercover for the cops for eighteen months, recording multiple drug deals and helping the police nail three full-patch members on drug charges. Next, the cops struck a deal with Paul Derry, a long-time informant who had helped the bikers carry out a brutal murder of a ports worker in a drug dispute. "In the eye of the public, I come out of this looking like a hitman who got away with a murder. I appeased my guilt by ratting on everyone," Derry says. "But you gotta deal with it. It comes down to this: me going to jail for life or them." Derry got away with no jail time and a new life under witness protection, but his testimony helped put away one full-patch member for life and several associates on first-degree-murder charges.

The busts were a serious setback to Mike McCrea, the Halifax Angel leader and computer expert who had been selected by the Hells Angels to be the club's world secretary—an administrative role, not a decision-making one, but a high-status post just the same. McCrea flitted around the globe, attending world bike runs. But he couldn't keep his own house in order. His brother was one of those busted in the drug raids. The chapter was forced to forfeit its own clubhouse. With four members in jail, one kicked out and another departed for greener pastures out west, McCrea's charter fell well below the required six members and collapsed. The world secretary of the Angels turned in his Hells Angels patch ignominiously—another blow to the Angels' attempt to sanitize their global image.

In Western Canada, on the other hand, the Hells Angels' fortunes were riding high. In Alberta the Angels always had an imposing presence in the major centres, with three chapters and about three dozen members who took no guff from anybody. When the Angels turned their clubhouse in Calgary into a bunker without the proper zoning permission, the city moved in and demolished it. The bikers promptly tried to demolish their opponents: the then president of the HA chapter, Kenneth Szczerba, plotted to blow up the homes of a city alderman and a community leader. "The amount of explosives that the police found that were to be used to bomb my home was apparently enough to create a fifty-foot crater," says the neighbourhood woman who led the community resistance to the bikers. "Innocent children could have been victims. The Hells Angels exist within our society because we permit it. If citizens refused to allow their clubhouses and illegal activities and shone light on them, they could not function. Intimidation only works if people are willing to not resist."

Szczerba later got one year for the bomb plot and thirty months because police found cocaine when they arrested him.

The Angels' Alberta stronghold seemed briefly threatened at the start of 2004 when Asian gangs flexed their muscles and the Bandidos tried to muscle in; a murderous turf war looked as if it was about to start when one biker who had helped bring in the Bandidos was gunned down outside a strip club in Edmonton. Instead, the Canadian Angels pulled off another tour de force similar to their Ontario coup: by the fall they convinced the twenty-odd members of the Bandidos organization to patch over to the HA. It was an unheard-of event—something that could never have happened between the rival gangs in the U.S. or Europe. It was a testament to the unbeatable clout of the Angels in Canada. The Angels also sought strength in numbers: they set up various puppet clubs, including the Devil's Henchmen, Iron Steed and Red Demons. By the end of 2005, there were more than ninety members in those clubs and fifty seven full-patch Hells Angels in the province.

In neighbouring Manitoba, the Angel army was much smaller—only about fourteen Angels in a single chapter in Winnipeg—but that didn't stop them from wreaking havoc while managing to escape any serious retribution from the police or the courts.

In November 2003 four men with ties to the Hells Angels were released from jail when the Crown's key witness in a kidnapping and rape case had refused to co-operate. It was just the start of a legal meltdown. Two months later, a much-touted mega-trial against five Hells Angels associates became a mega-embarrassment. The men, most of them members of an HA support group called the Zig Zags, were charged with arson, gangsterism and conspiracy to commit murder in a wave of violence that hit Winnipeg—including the firebombing of a police officer's home. The Crown prosecutor sent a three-paragraph letter to the bikers' lawyers admitting that police officers "may have committed criminal acts" in their dealings with a key informant in the case, a dubious and unstable biker associate named Robert Coquette, who got $100,000 for his ultimately unreliable snitching.

By June 2004 the Crown had to drop the case, leading to a celebration on the streets outside the jail as the released bikers—in custody without bail for nearly two years—were greeted by supporters, happy girlfriends and stretch limos. "We won't raise the white flag to organized crime in this city," the police chief said lamely. "We won't throw up our hands and say we give up."

But it got even worse.

In September, charges were stayed against two more Hells Angels associates accused of firebombing a convenience store when allegations surfaced that the police might have forced the pair to make false confessions.

That same month, a major bust of a Manitoba-based smuggling network that shipped ephedrine—a main ingredient in meth—to secret labs in Western Canada and the United States should have been a police success story. It turned sour when a Winnipeg police officer was also arrested, accused of corruption and unauthorized use of a police computer, leading to speculation that he was communicating with at least one of the drug smugglers arrested.

As if the police needed another blow to their tattered image, there were even more damaging revelations about their failure to warn an innocent man he had been a long-standing target of a biker hit. Back in May 2002 Trevor "Boss" Savoie, who ran coke for the Hells Angels' Zig Zag club, was killed by one of his underlings. Daniel Tokarchuk had been snorting instead of selling, and accumulating a heavy debt to Savoie. Instead of paying it off, he killed Savoie. The bikers, though, were not ones to take kindly to someone who knocked off one of their own. Tokarchuk was in police custody, so Savoie's avengers did the next best thing. Exactly one year to the day after Savoie was killed, Daniel Tokarchuk's younger brother, Kevin, was executed with a shot in the head in the garage of his family's home—a murder that remains unsolved to this day.

It subsequently emerged that ten months prior to the revenge killing of Kevin, an informant in a taped interview warned that the Tokarchuk family might be in danger. The tip was never passed on directly to the family. When news of the ignored warning surfaced, the police chief suspended six investigators and two senior officers—including a deputy chief—for failing to act. All the officers were eventually cleared of any criminal wrongdoing; they insisted the tip was too unspecific. However, a lengthy hearing into the affair saw the police washing their dirty laundry in a very public way, spending more time fighting each other than the Hells Angels.

"Some very bad people got away with terrible, terrible crimes," one gang investigator complained at the inquiry.

Indeed, since the Hells Angels had set up their Winnipeg chapter back in 2000, close to half a dozen cases against them had collapsed, and more than a dozen of their members or associates had walked out of court. It was a combination of bad luck, bad informants and bad policing, with little co-operation between the local police and the RCMP. That seemed to change in early 2006 when—after a lengthy two-year undercover operation—a joint organized crime task force arrested more than a dozen people, including Winnipeg chapter president, Ernie Dew, and two other prominent Angels, on cocaine trafficking and other charges. Their trials are pending.

Still, for all their noise and bluster, the Manitoba Angels were limited to just over a dozen members in a single chapter. The key Canadian battlegrounds between police the bikers would be in Ontario, where the Angels had the big numbers, and in British Columbia, where they had the big bucks.

Like the businessmen they are, the Hells Angels in Ontario follow the rules of the market. In the competitive Toronto drug scene and throughout the heavily industrialized Golden Horseshoe of southern Ontario—where the bikers have to carve up the spoils with the traditional Mafia, Asian gangs and other competitors—they are obliged to keep the quality of cocaine on the streets as high as 85 or even 90 percent pure. But in the northern centres that the Hells Angels control—such as Sudbury, Thunder Bay or Timmins—they can get away with cutting the coke on the streets to a purity as low as 25 percent, thereby making higher profits.

"In the North the HA more or less control the market. It's Red-and-White coke or no coke," says Insp. Don Bell, head of Ontario's Biker Enforcement Unit (BEU). "In the North, they are the game."

Either way, North or South, the Hells Angels have dominated the game since they moved into the province in a big way in late 2000. They have grown to fifteen chapters, with about two hundred full-patch members and another forty prospects and hangarounds: Ontario alone has half the Angels in Canada and more HA than do many countries in Europe.

They are led—at least in their public relations campaign—by a handsome, smooth-talking entrepreneur named Donny Peterson, who runs the large Toronto Downtown chapter and a successful bike shop, and once addressed the business elite at the prestigious Empire Club. "I'm not a criminal—never have been, never will be. So why should I be treated differently from anyone else?" he says, and then adds, with no pun intended, "I'm not saying we're all angels. We get unjustly accused of a lot of stuff. Society needs whipping boys."

Peterson's Angels are showy and brash. In Toronto, their east-end clubhouse sports a flashy neon sign on a redecorated three-storey fortress. In Hamilton, the Hells Angels opened their newest clubhouse by installing eighteen red concrete pillars, a fence topped with barbed wire, four security cameras and a Death Head flag. In southern Ontario, the Angels also run several large support or puppet groups. One of these, the Foundation, has twenty-seven young punks eager to do the Angels' bidding, with branches in Richmond Hill and Toronto. A newer, more aggressive group called the Redline, with a patch showing a car's tachometer edging dangerously in the high-speed red zone, boasts as many as forty-three recruits and stretches from downtown Toronto to Barrie, Ottawa and Simcoe County.

The police have responded in kind. Learning quickly from Quebec's mistakes, Ontario set up the Biker Enforcement Unit, a single command structure under the Ontario Provincial Police that brings together OPP, RCMP and regional police forces. With over a hundred officers, it is North America's largest police force devoted exclusively to outlaw motorcycle gangs. But after significant mass arrests that came close to dismantling the smaller Outlaws and Bandidos gangs in 2003 in the province, the BEU has found the going against the Hells Angels a lot tougher.

The biggest blow—at least in terms of numbers—came in April 2003, when the BEU arrested fourteen Hells Angels and seventy other people in what it dubbed Project Shirlea, named after the street where the gang's clubhouse was located in Keswick, north of Toronto. Out of the Country Bebops, a seedy bar just south of Highway 401 in Scarborough, the bikers ran an extensive cocaine, marijuana and prescription drug network. The police were able to use a waitress-turned-informant to infiltrate the bikers' circle and ran extensive wiretaps and physical surveillance to document the trafficking operation of five different Hells Angels chapters—Toronto Downtown, East Toronto, North Toronto, Keswick and Simcoe. It was their new-found "Quebec connection" that provided most of the cocaine that the Hells Angels sold in the Scarborough area—a steady stream of coke that travelled by car along the 401 from Montreal.

The eavesdropping also revealed details of an attempted murder, when two bikers tried to knock off a suspected snitch in a drive-by shooting on a crowded street. "Tell him I'm coming to cave his fuckin' head in," one of the shooters threatened in a phone call. "Tell him he doesn't have a fuckin' hope in hell."

Project Shirlea took three years and cost $4 million, at one point involving more than two dozen officers from various forces, culminating in seventy-three search warrants and more than four hundred charges. But when it was all over, an overburdened Crown—at one point there were only two prosecutors to handle eighty-seven defence lawyers—had to drop the charges against more than half of the accused, and many of the bikers pleaded out to smaller sentences. The stiffest penalty of six years went to one of the ringleaders, Thomas Craig, the secretary of the Donny Peterson's own Downtown Toronto chapter—which seemed to deflate Peterson's public pronouncements that "as for drug shipments coming into Ontario, it's not been the Hells Angels involved."

The BEU was philosophical about the disappointing judicial outcome of their painstaking work. "Once the charges are laid, it's out of our hands," said Ontario's top biker cop, Don Bell. "If you're in this law-enforcement game for any period of time, you're going to get frustrated because you're not going to get the sentences you think people deserve."

Still, the police appeared to have redirected their energies into tighter, smaller and ultimately more prosecutable investigations. In August 2003, four months after the Shirlea arrests, the BEU co-operated with the RCMP and local police to take down a national drug network centred in Thunder Bay. Eight people, including two local full-patch members, were charged with using airlines, buses and private cars to ship cocaine and marijuana from British Columbia to central Canada. One of the ringleaders, Hells Angels Timothy Speak, got six years for possession and conspiring to traffic in cocaine and another six months for carrying it out in association with a criminal organization.

A rapid series of arrests continued throughout 2004 and 2005, culminating in a major cocaine bust in early 2006. In many of the cases, there was a direct connection to the Quebec Hells Angels, once more blowing the cover on Peterson's oft-repeated claim that his new Ontario Angels had nothing to do with their more violent French-speaking brothers from across the provincial border.

It began in April 2004, when Paul "Sasquatch" Porter, a Quebecker who now headed the Ontario Nomads chapter, turned himself in to police after the cops had raided his Ottawa clubhouse and arrested more than fifty people as part of a car theft ring. His trial is scheduled for January 2006.

Then in February, after a year-long investigation, the police broke up a cocaine distribution network led by the Windsor Hells Angels. The chapter had been sponsored back in early 2001 by a Quebec Angel, and according to police surveillance, three years later they were getting regular supplies of cocaine from Sherbrooke. Police arrested fifteen bikers, bookies and drug traffickers and seized $400,000 in cocaine and cash. (Former Detroit Red Wings enforcer Bob Probert appeared at the bail hearing for two of Quebec men charged in the bust. It was not the first time hockey stars had been linked to the Hells Angels. Over the years, pictures had surfaced of Montreal Canadiens goalie José Theodore at an HA party and of Pat Burns, a former cop and National Hockey League coach for the Canadiens, Maple Leafs and Boston Bruins, next to HA leader Walter Stadnick.) Nine men, including a leading full-patch member, pleaded guilty in the case.

The next month it was Sudbury's turn. Long the fiefdom of the Vachon brothers from Quebec, the Hells Angels chapter in that northern mining town got hit hard when police arrested a dozen people for cocaine trafficking. Police also issued a warrant for Michel Vallières, a full-patch member of the Sherbrooke chapter—and yet another regular Quebec drug supplier to an Ontario club. He eventually pleaded guilty and got a five-year prison term.

On June 2, 2005, an eleven-month investigation led by the BEU resulted in twenty-five arrests, including two Hells Angels, in the Peterborough area. Police seized cocaine, ecstasy, marijuana, steroids and $50,000 in cash. Among those charged was full-patch Hells Angels member Shawn Boshaw, a former Outlaw member who did what would have been unthinkable anywhere but in Canada and jumped ship to the Angels in late 2001. Also arrested was a Keswick member, Michael McIlmurray, who had already been nailed under Project Shirlea. Their trials are pending.

By late June 2005 the police had come full circle, striking again at the Ontario Nomads they had first targeted in the spring of 2004. This time, police barged into the Nomads' clubhouse to arrest another Quebecker, Brett "Lucky Luke" Simmons. Simmons earned the nickname—inspired by a popular Quebec cowboy cartoon character—when he managed to survive after a van he was driving full of dynamite for a murder job blew up. Police laid 102 charges of drug trafficking and operating as a criminal organization against more than a dozen Angels and associates, confiscating cocaine, crack, ecstasy and marijuana worth more than $1 million. Court proceedings were set to begin in early 2006.

"They now see that they are vulnerable, and law enforcement have come in, identified a cell and taken it down," BEU chief Don Bell said. The police had given the operation the appropriately hellish label Project Dante.

Clearly, the BEU's new strategy of picking off smaller drug rings instead of mega-busts—and the resulting mega-headaches—was working. "We've changed the way we do business," said Bell. "Our job is still to disrupt and dismantle. I think we can do as good a job at disrupting if we hit six to ten main figures than if we tackle fifty."

Donny Peterson's insistence that his boys were different from the gun-toting, bomb-throwing, drug-trafficking Angels in Quebec was definitely looking a little thin. Battered by arrests and bad press, the Angels tried a bit of publicity themselves, paying for a large billboard on the Don Valley Expressway for all of Toronto's commuters to see. Over a montage of the Death Head patch and roaring bikes, the Hells Angels proudly proclaimed, "Still Fighting for Democracy and Freedom."

Publicity of a different kind came in early 2006 when the BEU arrested five full-patch bikers and twenty-two others after an informant infiltrated the gang for two years. Four members of the Thunder Bay chapter faced cocaine charges, virtually crippling the northern Ontario chapter. Even more damaging to the biker image was the arrest on fraud and stolen property charges of André Watteel, for many years the president of the Kitchener chapter and a successful local businessman with popular support among local politicians. The trials of all the bikers are pending.

Nowhere in North America—and in few places around the world—are the bikers as rich and powerful as they are in British Columbia, where the marijuana trade is the most lucrative, the bikers' influence over the ports the strongest and the police crackdowns—until recently—the weakest.

It's not just the old-timers, like East End chapter president John Bryce, who owns his $600,000 home in Burnaby and three houses worth a total of more than $2 million, or his half-brother Lloyd "Louie" Robinson, who has no known occupation but lives in a

$1.1 million spread in West Vancouver. It's also the young guys, the up-and-coming movers and shakers.

People like Jamie Holland, a Nomad in his early thirties, who was convicted of carrying a concealed weapon. In a nondescript alley of small industrial storefronts along Vancouver's southeast end, a small wooden sign advertises his "Car Cleaning Company" with an offer for a complete wash and vacuuming for $22.95. Holland must be cleaning up a lot of profits from his businesses because, while still living in a $1 million condo at the downtown skyscraper known as the Wall Centre, he also bought a $1.2 million mansion in the Southlands that offers him a choice of seven bedrooms—all with ensuite bath—four fireplaces, a spiral staircase and maple floors. Plus, to help the busy Hells Angel relax, there's a home theatre, a billiards room and a sauna and steambath. The enterprising Nomad didn't get a chance to fully enjoy his new digs, though. In the late summer of 2005, Vancouver biker cops dropped by his home to warn him they had a credible tip that there was a contract out on him because of a drug rip-off he had allegedly engineered. The biker feigned indifference, but the next day he disappeared, lying low until the heat dies down.

Holland also runs several car leasing and rental firms, which perhaps explains his BMW, a Lamborghini, a Mercedes and of course two Harleys. With fellow Angel Gino Zumpano, he bought the Spinning Wheel nightclub in Vancouver's hip Gastown, now up for sale for $1.75 million. Zumpano himself runs an investment company that has about $5 million worth of shares in, of all things, the House of Brussels Chocolates, with a manufacturing and retail operations in Vancouver.

Not to be outdone, Damiano Dipopolo, also in his early thirties, runs Diggstown Clothing on East Hastings Street, a store so successful that he expanded it to include a tanning salon and a juice bar. Sgt. Larry Butler of the Vancouver Police biker gang unit calls the nearby neighbourhood in Burnaby "Dipopoloville" because Damiano and his family members own so many homes there. Damiano's estate, with a striking view of the water, features six gargoyles along the perimeter and another two sitting on the front porch. It is protected by a thick brick wall, topped with metal bars and grates and a camera nestled in the front arch. Dipopolo also owns two houses in Kelowna with Shane Bunting, a member of the Vancouver band Swollen Members, one of Canada's most popular rap groups, which did a video featuring HA bikers.

Other prosperous Angels have their fingers in the movie business, cellphone services, transportation and the mainstay of B.C. economy, forestry. Lyle Newton runs Alliford Bay Logging in Nanaimo; he quit the HA in 2005 only when publicity about his gang affiliation started costing him business. "He was an asset to them. He employed a lot of them," says one local police officer who follows the gang. James Williams, a member from Haney, and his brother Brian run Airth Industries, which is active in the lucrative cedar shakes and shingles trade.

Then, of course, there is that other economic mainstay, the sex trade. Not just the local strip joints—Randy Jones of the White Rock chapter, for example, runs T-Barz, which bills itself as an "Exotic Adventure Room"—but the entire industry. Insiders say that 20 percent of the lower mainland's strippers come from two biker-controlled companies: Deluxe, owned by former Haney chapter president Elie Bruneau, and That's Talent, run by Lloyd Robinson.

The "peelers," as the bikers like to call the women they employ, are not there just to bring in the cash and push the dope. "The girls are watching out all the time," says a biker associate. "Find out information about the targets to squeeze them," he says the girls are told, with instructions to watch for judges, cops or any prominent marks. The associate recalls a stockbroker from whom the bikers were able to extort a quarter of a million dollars.

Even criminal convictions do not appear to slow down the B.C. bikers' business boom. Full-patchers Ronaldo Lising and Francisco "Chico" Pires were sentenced to four and a half years in prison for cocaine trafficking. While awaiting their appeal all the way to the Supreme Court—which they eventually lost—Lising bought a new Lincoln Navigator and a $400,000 house in

Burnaby. Chico took over a Burnaby eatery and renamed it, appropriately, Big Shots Café.

The revelations about the surprising wealth of the B.C. Angels—originally disclosed in *The Road to Hell* and then in the local media—finally prompted the Canada Revenue Agency (CRA) to take a closer look at the bikers' finances. On the eighth floor of a grey building near Vancouver's waterfront, Wayne Fjoser is the team leader of the Special Enforcement squad. Fjoser hardly looks like a number cruncher: he favours casual jeans and a perpetual smile. His fellow investigator Garret Klassen looks every bit like the burly ports cop he once was. "I knew a lot of them on the waterfront," he says of the bikers.

"They flash the wealth, but nobody has ever really gone after them from our perspective," says Fjoser. "Now we decided to go out and do a proper job."

His team began by compiling lists of known members and their associates; by the spring of 2005 they had sent out demands for personal or corporate tax returns to more than sixty-five people who were in arrears just in the lower mainland; they then branched out to bikers in Prince George and hoped to target the Kelowna boys by the end of the year.

"They're in a real tizzy," says Klassen. "This is having an impact on the street. There's lots of scrambling."

Some bikers have been unfailingly polite when the taxmen show up, often accompanied by Vancouver biker cop Sgt. Larry Butler, who knows a lot about each of the Angels in his city. Jamie Holland drove up in his sparkling Lamborghini to his new Southlands estate and calmly talked about his real estate ventures. At his bike shop, East End president John Bryce was equally proper, if less co-operative when Klassen asked if he could meet with his guys to serve them all with notices.

"What do you mean?" asked Bryce. "The guys who work here?"

"No, the Hells Angels," Klassen said.

"Oh, so you're targeting the Hells Angels?" Bryce asked.

"We investigate citizens of Canada," said the tax man. "You are citizens of Canada?"

Other bikers were less inclined to even talk. When one full-patch member with numerous arrests for assaults, was stopped by the tax investigators, he snapped, "I'll rip your tongue out." Another biker who got the bad tax news at the airport when returning from a world bike run blurted out, "People like you get stepped on."

Several bikers did begin complying and filed their tax returns: one eagerly did it from jail and called two times to make sure everything was in order. Another unfortunate Angel sent in his paperwork, only to learn that the government had determined he owed $300,000—and the CRA wanted more information going back eight years.

The tax investigators are hitting a roadblock in their requests for detailed statements of the bikers' assets and liabilities—not something most Canadians have to file every year, but they can be required as part of an audit. The bikers and their lawyers have dug in their heels, arguing that the CRA is just on a fishing expedition, doing the dirty work for the police. The revenue men insist that the law bars them from sharing any tax information with the police or anyone else without legal warrants or court orders. Regardless of how the battle plays outs, Fjoser and his team feel they have already won by obliging so many bikers to declare their incomes. "We now have a base," says Fjoser. "We can track revenue, lifestyle. We now have a trail down the road, a reference point on each of these individuals."

Juan Roberto drives through the streets of Nanaimo, pointing out the business properties owned by the local Hells Angels—a car dealership here, an apartment block there, a logging company up the road. "You can just see these guys buying this town off piece by piece," he says. He works as a youth counsellor for the city and asks that his real name not be used for his own security because what really burns him up is the explosion of meth and other drugs in the schools that he blames on the HA: "What I find most difficult is watching these kids get hooked on drugs and watching their school fall apart," he says. "That's where I get my grudge—when I look at the human carnage."

"It's a problem in a town like this with such saturated organ-ized crime," agrees Dave Diemling, the RCMP officer who has been battling the bikers here for seven years. "They have contacts in every organization: we make an inquiry at a bank, they know about it."

A harbour town nestled on the east side of Vancouver Island, Nanaimo has seen better times but still gets by on shipping, tourism and fishing. The HA clubhouse is a fortified three-storey, red-and-white building well monitored by video surveillance. Just south of the city, the bikers own a sprawling eighteen-acre prop-erty worth close to half a million dollars called Angel Acres, where they have held public festivals and private parties over the years.

Drugs are nothing new among teenagers, but Juan saw a wave of cheap meth hit his schools about two years ago. Typically, meth is a white powder that easily dissolves in water, but a more popu-lar form these days is the clear chunks called "crystal meth." Five times more potent than speed from the 1970s, it is a powerful, addictive stimulant with side effects that include heart palpita-tions, severe anxiety, paranoia, violence and psychosis. "You can have a kid show up on Monday and he's not the kid who left on Friday," says Juan. "He's acting in irrational ways, mood swings, bipolar. Eventually we lose them because they're unable to main-tain themselves."

He estimates that 20 percent of the kids in his high schools have tried crystal meth. "Some can never recover from that. Even though they quit and manage to shake the habit, they can't do anything any more—reading, short-term memory retention, cog-nitive skills. It doesn't take a long exposure, either."

And it's not just meth. Chris Swan is a long-time drug importer who worked for the bikers for years. He brought in coke from South America for the bikers but ran afoul of them when they tried to rip him off. "Their agenda is to get the drugs to here and control the market. If you're a drug smuggler, they want you out of the market or working for them. That's their whole aim."

As elsewhere, they keep control of that market through vio-lence and intimidation. When a local bouncer had the nerve to kick one of the Angels out of his bar, they came back in force a few nights later, lured him out and beat him to a pulp. He told police he did not want to lay charges. The Nanaimo club earned a reputation for being vicious even with their own members. Long-standing club president Michael "Zeke" Mickle went out drinking one night in April 1993 and did not make it home. "What I heard was that Zeke fucked up a couple of deals and had to be whacked for that," says one biker source. To do their enforcing, the chapter recruited a hulking bully of a man, "Big Rick," who stood almost seven feet tall and weighed four hundred pounds. When they caught him stealing from the club till, they ganged up on the giant, held him down and were going to grind off his Hells Angels tattoos. They settled instead for simply burning them off.

For years the Nanaimo Angels—like their brothers across the province—had little to fear from the largely disorganized or uninterested police forces. That began to change in January 2001, when the Organized Crime Agency (OCA)—a new body set up specifically to take on the bikers and other sophisticated criminal gangs—began Project Halo. The operation targeted several members of the Nanaimo chapter "for cocaine trafficking, extortion, assault causing bodily harm [and] conspiring to keep a common bawdy house," according to search warrant documents. Slowly but surely, the investigation picked apart a drug-smuggling network that stretched from B.C. to Ontario. In April 2003 investigators found 10 kilograms of cocaine in a tractor trailer with Ontario licence plates near the Nanaimo ferry terminal. In court documents, police linked the shipment to Michael McIlmurray—the same Hells Angel from Ontario who was part of a drug ring exposed by Project Shirlea.

Finally, in March 2005, they arrested McIlmurray in Ontario, and in Nanaimo they picked up full-patch member Lee Scheppe on his way to his chapter's weekly meeting.

It was the first time police had dealt a blow to the Nanaimo bikers. Plagued by lack of money, lack of co-operation between police forces, and the absence of the huge number of officers needed for long-term surveillance and penetration, Project Halo fell far short of its original hopes.

"If we don't start treating it as a priority, it's not going to get better," says one police insider. "In order to take down organized crime, big changes have to be made."

Those big changes began to happen when the RCMP put Bob Paulson in charge as the major case manager for outlaw motorcycle gangs in the province in 2002. "I like the chase. I like working these guys," says the one-time military pilot instructor who worked his way up the RCMP ranks to become an inspector. "Bullies. That's all they are—bullies with stickers on their backs."

It was an open secret that for years there was bad blood between the RCMP and biker cops scattered among various police forces; "pissing contests between agencies" is how Paulson puts it, undiplomatically but accurately. It didn't help that the RCMP had most of the money and bodies but had shown little inclination to go after the bikers seriously. The Mounties had walked away from at least two high-level informants within the HA back in the 1990s; they blew a major bust when they pulled a plug on another informant who was bringing in kilos of coke by boat for the Angels. Police in B.C. had plenty of intelligence on bikers but took little action. "We had lots of people who knew about them but very few people prosecuting them," says Paulson.

He was determined to change all that. He brought his homicide mindset to the biker game. "Crooks is crooks," he says. "Target individuals, find the evidence." The RCMP's intelligence branch did a systematic threat assessment, asking police chiefs across the province to list their major organized crime threats—individuals and gangs. The Hells Angels came out on top.

Next, Paulson set about to build much-needed unity among the disparate police forces. He had little patience for petty rivalries and was known as an aggressive recruiter. He jokes that when commanders asked what kind of skill sets he was looking for for his team members, he answered, "A heartbeat. As long as they signed up to be a cop, I can point them in the right direction."

No one was happier with the RCMP's new approach than Andy Richards. A Vancouver cop who tried to bust the bikers' control of the downtown stripping scene in the 1990s, Richards made his name as a no-nonsense inspector for the OCA. He proved it could be done: with limited funds and people, his team had led the first successful undercover cocaine trafficking operation against the bikers that B.C. had seen in years, which led to the conviction of HA members Lising and Pires. In his office, a yellowed front-page newspaper clipping still shows the headline from 2001: "Hells Angels convicted for the first time."

Like many, Richards had not hidden his disappointment in the RCMP's lack of action against the bikers in the past, but today he has become an eager part of the RCMP's new biker-busting team. Richards and the rest of OCA's experts were folded into the Combined Forces Special Forces Enforcement Unit (CFSEU) of B.C.: they supply about ninety of the unit's people, the rest coming from the RCMP and municipal forces.

It was partly a cost-saving measure, partly a political move by the RCMP in B.C. to take back the initiative for organized crime investigations. And mainly a smart organizational move to get the best and brightest biker cops working on the same team. "Clearly in the past we weren't even in the same book. Now we're all at least on the same page, working very well together," says Richards.

Richards and Paulson got their first chance to bring their teams together in 2003, when alert officers in the RCMP's drug section in Prince George, a coastal town in northern B.C., recruited an informant with strong ties to the Hells Angels and their puppet club there, called the Renegades. As team commander, Paulson threw everything at this operation, code-named Project Essen. "We couldn't afford to fail at our first kick of the can," he says. He had upwards of forty-five investigators, plus support staff, working for twenty months. Larry Butler of the VPD sent over two of his men. Early on he brought in Richards's entire investigative team from the CFSEU. They ran wires, multiple surveillance teams and documented a long series of drug buys in Prince George, Langley, Cache Creek and other towns. For Richards, who, like many cops, had seen biker investigations tried on shoe-string budgets, it was a pleasant relief: "This was a national prior-ity investigation that was funded and resourced properly."

The operation cost $2 million; serious undercover penetra-tions of organized crime groups do not come cheap. In July 2003, the informant began purchasing drugs from the bikers, quickly graduating to kilogram buys of cocaine at $39,000 a pop. He was doing regular business with Cedric Smith, a veteran member of the East End, sending a pre-arranged code on his pager—"666"—to meet at a nearby Wendy's in Langley.

When the informant asked Smith if he could get a better deal, Smith introduced him to nobody less than Norm Krogstad, the president of the Vancouver chapter. They struck a discount price of $34,000. The informant made numerous other purchases over the next eighteen months. Then, on Monday, January 24, 2005, ten bikers were swept up in the biggest Hells Angels raids B.C. had seen to date. Six people connected to the Renegades support club were busted, along with senior full-patch members, including Krogstad and Smith, as well as David O'Hara, a member of the Mission chapter at the time of the offences.

By the end of the year, O'Hara pleaded guilty to marijuana, cocaine and firearms offences and got a thirty-four-month sen-tence. Norm Krogstad and Cedric Smith both pleaded guilty to eleven counts of trafficking cocaine and got four years each. Chapter president Krogstad was the highest-ranking member of the B.C. Hells Angels ever jailed. All the remaining bikers eventu-ally made plea bargains as well.

The arrests infuriated the Hells Angels in B.C., not used to such tough policing. "We don't have anything to do with criminal activity," insisted Rick Ciarniello, a garrulous, rotund biker from the Hells Angels chapter in Vancouver who has become the club's most public face. "We don't encourage it. We don't plan it." He neglected to mention that half of the ten bikers arrested under Project Essen had previous convictions or pending charges on everything from extortion to assault.

The Angels seemed to be losing their cool over the next few

months. In April, Damiano Dipopolo, the clothing store owner, was arrested for assault after he ran after an alleged shoplifter with a two-by-four, but the charges were stayed. That same month, Vincenzo Brienzo of the Maple Ridge chapter was charged with assaulting a Vancouver police officer. And the following month two Nomads were arrested on charges that they beat up a man outside the Au Bar nightclub. The case is still pending.

"The objective is not to get rid of the bikers—that's pie in the sky," says the RCMP's Bob Paulson. "The objective is to paint them as they are, marginalize them as the crooks that they are. We're on the offensive now. It's a good position to be in."

And it was just beginning. In a few months, Paulson and his team would unleash a new anti-gang offensive against the West Coast bikers that would send them reeling.

The B.C. Hells Angels were feeling bruised enough that they decided to take to the radio airwaves to try to defend their image. Rick Ciarniello, the bikers' media representative, debated one of this book's co-authors on a Vancouver radio's popular talk show in the early fall of 2004. The central issue was whether the HA would take responsibility for the criminality of its members.

"There's been a lot of misinformation recently; I felt it was time to set the record straight," Ciarniello began.

"Would you publicly condemn any notion of the smuggling of cocaine to young children or to people in Vancouver?" he was asked.

"I have no use for cocaine; it's an insidious drug. I don't think anybody should use it," he replied. It was pointed out to him that several HA members across the country had been convicted of drug smuggling, and a member of B.C.'s own Nomads was facing charges of trafficking 50 kilos of coke. "If he's found guilty, would you condemn him and say he's betrayed everything that the patch stands for?"

"No, I wouldn't condemn him for those reasons," Ciarniello answered. "I would condemn him for doing what is stupid."

"Have you ever condemned a member of the HA who was convicted on drug charges?"

"You know what? You're trying to back me into a corner here."

"You're doing a pretty good job yourself."

"You try to label the entire club with the acts of some people," the biker insisted.

"The HA, by your own admission, is a very elite group." Ciarniello was told. "You choose your members very carefully, and you're very proud of wearing that patch. You can't have it both ways. You can't say, 'We're an exclusive club,' and then when other members who wear this patch commit crimes you can't say, 'Oh, well, that has nothing to do with us.' Why would you not hold a news conference and demand that your organization, your HQ, your fellow club members, kick out the members who have been found guilty of violence and drug smuggling?"

"You assume too much," Ciarniello replied. "You assume that everybody in the HA is under some sort of hierarchy and that we all dance to the same tune. Nothing could be further from the truth."

The sad truth was that just weeks after that debate, two members of Ciarniello's own Vancouver chapter were arrested on cocaine trafficking charges as part of Project Essen. The even sadder truth was that it didn't take long for one of the co-accused to get a taste of biker justice at the end of a barrel of a gun.

Billy Moore, a good friend of Ciarniello's, was the thirty-five-year-old president of the Renegades—and one of ten Project Essen defendants, charged with three counts of cocaine trafficking. Like most of the bikers, he got bail; but that just gave Moore's killers a chance to give him a death sentence that the courts could never have imposed. On a Sunday night early in March 2005, he watched as his new forty-six-hundred-square-foot house went up in flames. He couldn't do much to stop it: his hands were tied to the steering wheel of his truck. His killers forced him to watch his dream home burn to the ground. Then they shot him dead.

"Bill was a nice man. I'm shocked," said a contrite Ciarniello to the newspapers.

Whether Moore was murdered because his former pals blamed

him for the arrests over a bad drug deal or for just generally screw-ing up really didn't matter. What did matter was that the graphic picture of the murdered man's house in flames on the front pages illustrated the fact that B.C. was now far from immune to the bloody settling of accounts that Quebec had seen in its biker war.

Even Chris Swan, the veteran drug smuggler who worked with the Angels in B.C. for years, shakes his head in disgust. "Burning some house down and forcing someone to watch and then killing him—that's what the Nazis did," he says. "Everything is about money for them. A lot of people die around these guys. They kill people regularly."

Five months after that interview, in September 2006, Chris Swan was gunned down outside of his Vancouver Island home. He died of multiple gunshot wounds in a slaying that had all the signs of a gangland-style hit. The murder remains unsolved.

PART V

AMERICAN RECKONING

FOURTEEN

The Last Temptation of Christie

———

He was the Al Capone of the city.
—KEN CORNEY, ASSISTANT POLICE CHIEF, VENTURA, CALIFORNIA

How do I respond? I take it as a compliment.
—GEORGE CHRISTIE JR., PRESIDENT, VENTURA HELLS ANGELS

Dressed in a fashionable black shirt and hip, baggy jeans, he struts around Main Street as if he owns the town. And in the eyes of many of his fans and enemies in Ventura, California, he does.

A small silver pendant dangles around his neck in the shape of the Angels' Death Head. A gladiator tattoo dominates his forearm. Today George Christie doesn't wear any other symbol that indicates he is the longest-serving chapter president in the Hells Angels history. He doesn't have to. Everybody knows George in this surfing and tourism centre sixty miles north of Los Angeles that hasn't quite shaken its 1960s hippie days.

Considered by many to be the number-two man in the Hells Angels and a potential successor and sometime rival to Sonny Barger, Christie has the kind of power in this town that says a lot about why the Hells Angels remain so popular in the United States—and remain so untouchable by law enforcement.

Street kids panhandling on the corner say hello to the affable biker. A housewife getting into her car waves and a former street gang member driving a big Chevy honks a salute.

"He's a sweetie," says Natalie, who runs a high-end dress store and wine bar down the street. "A lovely man," adds the woman who owns a baby-furnishings boutique as she takes out a photograph of

341

her two-year-old, and she and George, a new father himself at age fifty-eight, swap tales of raising toddlers.

Local police and prosecutors, who tried to prove that Christie runs a sophisticated criminal network that peddled drugs to schoolchildren, can only shake their heads in disbelief. "He's Mr. HA," says Mark Coronado of the Ventura Police Department (VPD). "People love him. They think he's a god down here."

George Christie perhaps never wanted to be a god, but he knew from a very early age he wanted to be an Angel.

When he was about six years old, he was awestruck by the power a lone biker exerted simply by roaring through his small town in the San Fernando Valley, turning heads and forcing everyone to stare. He bought his first bike as a young teenager, drifted to the rough streets of Los Angeles and was thrilled when Sonny Barger's still young biker gang asked him to join. "I wanted to make a statement of some sort," Christie says. "It really wasn't the thought of criminality; it was more an interest to rebel. It was a commitment."

Criminal or a rebel, Christie showed a commitment and a savvy that few biker leaders except Barger have matched. One of the few HA who not only finished high school but also attended college for a couple of years, he worked briefly as a high-voltage electrician for the defence department and married his high school sweetheart, Cheryl. Within a few years of signing up with the Red and White, in 1978 he became the founding president of the new chapter in Ventura, which had all the advantages of a small town while staying close to the Los Angeles scene. For the next three decades he devoted himself to steering the club through political storms, murder charges and drug raids. "It's like the marines. I wanna be one of the guys holding the flag up."

For many years, his Ventura boys were typical, tough old-time bikers. Guys like David Ortega, one of Christie's closest friends, who served time in state prison on meth charges. And Tim Heath, "one of the scarier ones," as the cops put it, convicted of trying to murder two Mongols with a bomb and of a violent assault on his wife. Christie himself had his first major skirmish with the law in

1986, when he found himself on the wrong end of secret tape recordings plotting a murder for hire. The target was Tom Chaney, a former associate of Christie's club who had turned snitch before being jailed on drug charges. The FBI sent an informant named Thomas Mulhern, a leader of another gang called the Mexican Mafia, to chat with Christie at his clubhouse about snuffing out Chaney.

"I'd do it myself if he was here," Christie said blithely about murdering Chaney, according to transcripts that Christie does not dispute. The FBI then faked Chaney's murder in prison, and in September 1986 Christie met with Mulhern at a Ventura motel, presumably to pay up. Mulhern later testified that Christie handed him $500 as a down payment.

"George just felt that something wasn't right. He's no dummy," says Mark Coronado, who was helping the FBI with surveillance. Christie stepped out on the hotel balcony and kept looking around. He walked in again and asked for the money back, but by then it was too late.

"The feds jumped out of the bushes. It should have been a slam-dunk case," says one cop who worked the case. Even Christie admits he was rattled: "At my first court appearance when they said, 'The United States of America vs. George Gus Christie,' it sends a little shiver down your spine. The most powerful country in the world and you're up against them."

It was all entrapment, Christie insists today. The money he handed over "had nothing to do with murder"—it was simply for an old debt. The talk about killing Chaney came up because the Mexican Mafia wanted him dead and offered Christie a chance to save a former club associate. "The only thing I was guilty of was the morality issue," Christie says, for not trying to stop the hit.

In court, Christie's able defence lawyer did a good job of turning the tables by putting the sleazy government informant—a long-time snitch and heroin addict—on trial. But in the final days, he came to Christie's jail cell to tell him there was only one witness who could guarantee a win at this trial: George Christie himself. Christie accepted the challenge and walked into the witness box, a rare and often foolish gambit for someone accused of murder. Ever charming and self-deprecating, Christie won over the jurors and they acquitted him. "George appeared to be very honest and very sincere, and very dedicated not only to his family but the Hells Angels," one juror said.

Two weeks later, five of the jurors attended a celebratory barbecue that Christie threw at the Hells Angels well-fortified red-and-white clubhouse in Ventura. "Some of them thought that I wanted this guy dead, and possibly at some point in time I would have had it done anyways," Christie says. "But that's not what the charges were."

At the time of his arrest, Christie had already proven himself a skilled media star. He was one of the local celebrities chosen to carry the Olympic Torch in 1984 through Ventura along the route to the LA Olympic Games. Now he parlayed his most recent judicial escapade into a bit of a public relations coup. He was a guest speaker at a criminal justice forum at a local high school. He later spoke at a college graduating class of journalists. No other HA leader besides Barger was as accessible as George Christie. Small in stature and unthreatening, he became a media darling, with his easy laugh and gravelly voice.

Christie's boys got special treatment at popular downtown hangouts, like the Ventura Theater and Nicholby's. That didn't stop them from beating the crap out of bouncers or boot-stomping patrons who annoyed them. Ken Corney ran the police gang unit at the time and would eventually be promoted to assistant chief. "We'd see the continual criminal influence in our city, the intimidation, the beatings and the drug dealing," he says. "We arrested little users all the time and small-time dealers who wouldn't give us any names but who readily admitted the methamphetamine and marijuana were from the HA."

Christie ran a tattoo parlour on Main Street known as the Ink House, a martial arts studio out of his home, a bail bond operation and a company called Erotic Images. He was an administrator with the legal firm of his daughter, a seasoned lawyer; her office handled much of the club's business and helped other local gang members and other criminals in trouble with the law. That gave him what he calls "legal intelligence" on who was being arrested, what the police were doing and who was likely to squeal and deal. "What better position for any businessmen [to be in] ?" Christie says proudly. "I knew what was going on around town. I knew who was doing what."

An internal police threat assessment on the HA in Ventura dated April 18, 1997, warned of "several new trends including the use of street gangs in the sale of methamphetamine, the extortion of businesses in the city of Ventura and money laundering through businesses owned and operated by members and associates." The report concluded: "Recent Intel indicates a power struggle will ensue when Sonny Barger dies and George Christie continues to be the main man on the west coast. It is believed that George Christie and the current president of [the] Oakland [HA chapter] will vie for the top position as national president."

Christie indeed flexed his muscles both within the club and for the public at large the next year when Ventura sponsored the 1998 World Run. It was the fiftieth anniversary of the birth of the Angels, and Christie was determined to put on a big show. "It was a coronation of his position in the club," says Ken Corney.

Mark Coronado, the police force's gang expert, was equally determined to make life as miserable as possible for the visiting Angels. The city was blanketed by cops, the downtown core plastered with special "No Motorcycle Parking" signs and police cameras clicked constantly. To counter police surveillance, the Angels ran a counter-intelligence operation. They had spotters serving as lookouts on street corners. They hired a local private eye who had been a policeman and tipped them off to what police frequencies to use (the cops foiled that by switching to an obscure frequency used by the local water department).

Still, close to a hundred bikers from more than twenty countries roared into the small town and dominated the streets. For their group picture, they took over the majestic steps of the historic old city hall like a conquering army. After the photo session, police spotted several world chapter presidents trudging to

Christie's Ink House for a business meeting. The entire event solidified Christie's position as a potential successor to Barger. "We were well on our way to becoming the HA hub for the world—or at least for the U.S.," said Corney. "He was the Al Capone of the city."

"How do I respond?" said Christie when told of Corney's label. "I take it as a compliment."

Christie's triumph as the crime boss of the city was secured when the local weekly, the *Ventura County Reporter,* put him on the front page and on the top of their list of the city's leading "Movers and Shakers." The Hells Angel chief beat out the district attorney, Mike Bradbury, the police chief and close to two dozen businesspeople and community leaders. "[A] colourful, well-spoken individual . . . ever articulate . . . Christie brings an undeniable sense of character to Ventura," crooned the paper.

There was only one person who could bring George Christie down. And that was the aging biker leader himself.

Rows of palm trees line the expansive front lawn at Ventura High School. The white stucco building stands out against the dusty brown hills overlooking the city. "Home of the Cougars," a sign proudly proclaims of the football team. The school was also home to an HA-sponsored gang of teenagers that ran drugs, carried out beatings and eventually even a murder. Nowhere in North America or the world had the Angels tried to bring in such young recruits—and the scandal of a biker gang accused of selling drugs to children would eventually tarnish even the seemingly untouchable image of George Christie.

Monty Pulido, the Ventura police officer assigned full time to keep an eye on the two thousand students at the local high school, first noticed something strange in the spring of 1998. "On one of the side streets near the school, I would see a couple of full-patch Hells Angels sitting on their bikes after school. They'd be talking to a couple of kids." Then school authorities caught a male student in a classroom selling Vicodin, an extremely addictive painkiller that can be used as a cheap high. The student told

Pulido that he and some of his friends had been to Christie's club-house, drinking, socializing and playing pool. They had done chores for the bikers—taking out trash and even helping them out with surveillance at the World Run.

The seeds of a youthful gang had been sown four years earlier in 1994, when George Christie broke HA rules and brought in his eighteen-year-old son, George Christie III, as a full-patch member, even though club regulations stipulate that members must be at least twenty-one. "Well, he must have had an ID that *said* he was twenty-one," Christie says with a fatherly smirk.

It was easy to dismiss the move as pure nepotism, but Christie had a more serious goal: he wanted to rejuvenate a club filled with "a bunch of old, potbellied men," as he put it. "My agenda is moving the Hells Angels forward into this next century."

Whether his son had the stuff to move anything forward in the current century or the next one was debatable. But it was undeniable that the teenage George helped bring a much younger crowd into the orbit of the Angels, starting with his friends in the Pierpont Rats. Named for the street in the south end of Ventura that runs along the ocean, the gang was made up of "rich little white kids" as one cop describes them, mainly into surfing and skateboarding. Todd Martin was one of the first Pierpont Rats recruited into the Angels; then came Bill Gaddie, Scott Sutton and William "Gunner" Wolf. The HA then recruited members from other street gangs, such as the Midtown and Avenue gangs—members like Matthew Garrett, Brian Applegate and Martin Kada, a former Eagle Scout and "straight-arrow kid."

"Suddenly our street gang members are hanging around with George. They'd never been on motorcycles!" says Det. John Castelanos, one of the Ventura cops who worked the streets for years. "I thought maybe George was going through a mid-life crisis because these guys brought the cute girls from the beach."

Indeed, Christie himself doesn't entirely dismiss that analysis. He admits he was going through a messy divorce at the time. "Did I have an attraction to young women? Consciously no [but] . . . you think, I'm reaching the end of the road here, and suddenly you got these young, good-looking women who think you're pretty good."

Castelanos watched in amazement as young people started showing up for celebrations at Christie's HA clubhouse, just a few blocks away from his home. "He was throwing parties for all these kids. It was ludicrous. Young girls were going in and out of there." Christie eventually met a smart, vivacious twenty-two-year-old named Nikki at a nightclub—he says he asked to see her driver's licence because he thought she was sixteen or seventeen—and they soon married, even though he was more than twice her age.

Aside from the young girls, there was another advantage to Christie's youth recruitment drive: he or his son knew a lot of the young men personally, trusted them and were certain they weren't snitches for the cops. At least not then. That gave him enough confidence to easily double his club's membership in just a few years.

But the membership boom came at a cost. By Christie's own admission, many of his older buddies didn't appreciate the young rebels—their hip-hop music, their skateboard dress, their punk attitude. Several of the veterans transferred to other chapters. Hells Angels from the other clubs also looked somewhat askance at the surfer boys turned bikers. Many of Christie's new Ventura recruits would show up at rides with their baseball caps cocked sideways, their skateboards attached with bungee cords to the rear of the bikes or sticking out their backpacks. "That's fucking bullshit. These guys are a fuckin' embarrassment!" one old-timer exclaimed to undercover cop Jay Dobyns from Arizona when they once met up with the Ventura crowd.

"The nucleus of the club George had formed was spinning out of control," says Ken Corney. "He had very different types of people in the club: different goals, different ways of looking at things. He had splintered his own club."

That was the least of George Christie's problems.

Young skateboarders were one thing. Young drug pushers were quite another. His own son George and several of the other young recruits to the Angels inspired a loose group of teenage punks who became known as the Outfit in the spring of 1998. Christie insists his Angels had nothing official to do with the Outfit. "We were not directing this. Those guys created their own group." In fact, the ties between the Outfit and Christie's Angels were intricate. Several of the Outfit boys were good friends with many of the former Pierpont Rats and Midtown boys that had become Hells Angels, including Christie's own son George; police even found a photo of the young Christie on a ski trip with his Outfit buddies. The mothers of some Outfit members were girlfriends of the bikers.

The Outfit was noticeable at the Ventura high school and youth hangouts because they would wear the Hells Angels' distinctive red and white colours, often with the Angels' emblematic flames up and down their sleeves and black boots with red and white laces, red and white T-shirts and shorts. They carried the same kind of small plasticized cards that the bikers always had, with club members' nicknames and phone numbers. "It was like they came out of nowhere," says Eric Jensen, now an FBI agent in Ventura but at the time a gang officer for the local police, tasked with dismantling the Outfit. "I have never seen anything like it, as far as how the youth in this community look up to the Hells Angels as role models. It was very alarming."

At one point as strong as thirty members, the Outfit was an informal band with little leadership and less structure. In some of their bedrooms, police later found video libraries of old gangster movies and cutouts of Mafia boss John Gotti plastered on the wall. "It goes back to the whole romantic image of the outlaw," says Eric Jensen. "In Ventura, the Hells Angels are a very visible presence. These young kids were trying to be part of something— like most young kids—and they saw an opportunity to associate with the tough guys."

It didn't take long for the cops to catch the Outfit kids doing grunt work for the Angels. During the World Run, they helped out on surveillance. On March 17, 1998, police stopped three Outfit members coming back from a clubhouse party and arrested one on dope charges. That same night on a highway near the clubhouse, the sheriff's department stopped two Outfit members dumping a truckload of trash for the Angels.

Frustrated with their run-ins with the cops, the Angel wannabees tried to learn lessons from their elders. In a letter that later fell into police hands, one Outfit member wrote to another, "Do you ever see George Christie in jail? That's because he runs his shit right. What I'm seeing and hearing is that our shit is known. We are targets for the police."

But George Christie and his youthful admirers were soon to discover that the old man was about to get into his own deep shit—and it would be his son's ties to the Outfit and the high school drug scene that would be a large part of his undoing.

It began, appropriately enough for the self-styled Al Capone of Ventura, with a tax raid.

The authorities decided it was time to try to go after George Christie. Ventura County DA Michael Bradbury—who could not have been pleased that the Hells Angels leader had beaten him out in the local paper's top list of "movers and shakers"—gave his chief deputy DA, Jeff Bennett, unmistakable marching orders: Get Christie.

"Nobody's ever done a goddamn thing. I want people prosecuted, whatever it takes," Bennett recalls his boss telling him. "That's how this started. I had no fucking idea what I was getting into." Bennett was a straight-shooting, square-jawed prosecutor who looked every inch the ex-cop, ex-football star he was. He put together a team of investigators and attorneys, including an aggressive partner named Mark Pachowitz, to begin probing Christie's empire. They began with his Ink House business on Main Street and eventually uncovered enough evidence of what they felt were minor tax and employee deduction violations to get a series of warrants. On May 18, 1998, police burst through the doors not just at Christie's tattoo parlour but also at his home and the house of his estranged wife, Cheryl, who also happened to be the club's accountant.

What police found stunned them, "You have to got down here right away!" the cops told Bennett.

It wasn't the half gram of cocaine that police found in a night-stand next to Christie's bed that excited them—the coke, found with a women's magazine, probably belonged to a girlfriend. It was the bottles and bottles of Vicodin, the addictive narcotic painkiller. Seventy-five in all: at his home, Christie had just a few dozen pills; but his Ink House stored 1,393 pills and at Cheryl's hillside condo there were forty-three sealed bottles of Vicodin with 500 pills each, and twenty-eight bottles with 100 pills each.

Alarm bells went off because at about the same time, Outfit members at Ventura High School were getting picked up peddling Vicodin and other addictive prescription drugs on campus. While a person with severe pain and proper prescription might take one pill every four hours, kids—and bikers—were popping as many as fifteen to twenty-five a day, often mixing it with alcohol to get a cheap, if dangerous, high. "Where do you sell this Vicodin stuff? There aren't desperate housewives walking on the streets," deputy chief Ken Corney said. "You sell it in the school. It makes you feel good. It's very addictive. They're pushing it on campus. Typical drug dealing stuff: give 'em some candy and then wait until they gotta have it."

If the Vicodin was getting into the schools via some of the Hells Angels and their youthful followers, as the cops suspected, how was that much illegal Vicodin getting to Ventura in the first place? Investigators tracked the lot numbers of some of the seized bottles back to the manufacturer. That led them to Joshua Adams, a twenty-three-year-old purchasing clerk at a clinic on a Los Angeles air force base who had figured out a way to steal more than 700,000 pills. He in turn got them to a Hells Angels associate in Ventura named Rogelio Botello.

With hidden GPS tracking devices, secret cameras and wire-taps, police began watching the network. The sheriff's department ran informants who started making drug buys and recording conversations. The dirt they collected was damning. In October 1998 Botello told one informant that the Angels were the only street source for Vicodin and the going price was $700 a bottle. A full-patch Hells Angel named Kenny Collins told the same informant over lunch at Lalo's on Ventura Avenue—this according to detailed indictments later filed in court—that the Angels set the price and controlled the Vicodin and methamphetamine market in Ventura. Collins told the informant he was going to get more Vicodin back at the clubhouse, where indeed there seemed to be quite a brisk drug trade going on. Another Angel and former Pierpont Rat, Gunner Wolf, sold five tablets of ecstasy to an informant there. Undercover recordings picked up George Christie himself laughing and joking with several other bikers about one member's Vicodin addiction and his drug busts.

Even more disturbing were the repeated instances of the young Outfit boys pushing drugs, according to those same indictments. The indictments alleged that the Hells Angels and their associates furnished several members of the Outfit with Vicodin and diazepam (commonly known as Valium) between June 1997 and January 1999 "to sell and distribute to minors." One teenager was alleged to have sold Vicodin at least ten times and diazepam at least five times to a seventeen-year-old girl during the school year.

When two other Outfit boys met up at the De Anza Middle School, the talk quickly turned to the ready supply of diazepam.

"Where did you get all those from?" asked one seventeen-year-old. "From the HA?"

His eighteen-year-old partner nodded. "Yeah."

On September 11, 1998, one Outfit member called his buddy for more drug supplies. "I need to re-up," he said.

The two teenage traffickers then met at the De Anza Middle School to exchange a clear plastic bag with fifty diazepam pills. One rode his bike, the other his skateboard; their youthful antics would have been laughable if what they were peddling hadn't been so dangerous. A few days later, the skateboarder received yet another bag of pills "for the purpose of selling . . . on and around the Ventura High School campus during school hours," the court documents allege.

The skateboarder, who according to the court filings distributed at least 150 pills, was one of several Outfit members who partied at Christie's clubhouse; the indictment even alleged that "Hells Angels members allowed [him] . . . along with other Outfit members to celebrate a birthday" at the clubhouse.

"I find that is a vague and broad statement," Christie says when asked directly about the allegation. "Did we get a cake for him? I don't know who this kid is. I couldn't pick him out of a crowd." In fact, the indictment states that on at least one other occasion, that teenager asked explicitly to be allowed into the clubhouse; a biker "asked George Christie for permission and permission was granted."

Christie does not deny that high schoolers were allowed into the closely guarded clubhouse. "Make sure these kids are not drinking alcohol," he insists he warned his boys. "I would be specific with them: 'Don't give these kids drugs.' You know, you see five or six Hells Angels walking out of a bathroom . . . I'll leave it to your imagination what went on in there."

Photographs of the parties inside the clubhouse show girls in tight pants and T-shirts and other teenagers packed inside; one young blonde is holding a drink in her hand. A sign posted on the wall says it all:

> What you do here, what you see here, what you hear
> here, let it stay here when you leave here.
> —Hells Angels Ventura

Christie knew that the allegations that his Angels were funnelling drugs to schoolchildren were explosive. "I don't care about respectability, but I command respect," he says. "How can you respect a man who sells drugs to kids?" Christie insists he would never have allowed his members to push Vicodin into the schools through the Outfit. He concedes that he does know Rogelio Botello, the HA associate who was the main pipeline for getting the pills to Ventura, but "not very well at all. There is no phone call between me and him."

The small amount of Vicodin pills found in his house, he admits, was illegal but for his own use and that he "got [them] on the street to save money." He doesn't try to make the same excuse for the twenty-five thousand pills found at his estranged wife's house: "I'm not a foolish man, and I would not make a statement that those are for personal use." He simply says he had nothing to do with her.

The pills police found at Christie's own place of business were more problematic. "They never found my prints. My prints are on nothing," he says. True, but when police entered the Ink House with a warrant, it was Christie who had the keys to open the door to the small office where the bottles—and a gun—were found. "I do have a key," Christie says. "I wasn't involved, but it came back to bite me."

"He wasn't involved?" asks a skeptical prosecutor, Mark Pachowitz. "Even though everybody's selling them and everybody's doing them. You're all laughing and joking about it. What's your reason for them being in your business? How do you not know everything, considering everybody tells you everything?"

It was a question the prosecutors were dying to ask George Christie in court. "They assured us, based on everything they had, that Christie was looking at ten to fourteen years," one cop says.

Getting the case from the investigation stage to a trial would prove to be a tortuous and ultimately disastrous process, plagued by jealousies, infighting and incompetence. The rivalries between various agencies had begun long before the raids on Christie's business and home. In the mid-1990s, the ATF had put together a large task force to investigate Christie's Angels, including local police, the sheriff's department, the DA's office and even the IRS and the Secret Service, who were looking into counterfeiting and credit card scams. "We subpoenaed tens of thousands of financial records on the top players," says one investigator. "We had a roomful of papers and an IRS forensic accountant."

But when the DA's office abruptly pulled out of the team and upstaged the feds by raiding Christie's business on its own in May

1998, looking for financial shenanigans, the task force collapsed. Several cops working the biker files felt that the DA wanted all the glory for himself and had unwisely shut out the federal agencies, losing much needed resources and experience. Then, when the raids unexpectedly turned up the stash of Vicodin, the DA's office was forced to turn to the sheriff's narcotics team for their drug expertise. The rival investigating squads seemed to spend as much time spying on each other as on the bikers.

"We weren't really co-operating with the DA's office because they were too snaky," admits one of the sheriff's deputies. The narcotics team would be on stakeouts, only to discover the DA's own investigators lurking not far away. They discovered that the DA's investigators would go out on surveillance and listen to the sheriff's department's radio frequencies. It got to a point where the sheriff's deputies were snapping surveillance pictures of the DA investigators to prove their point.

"They didn't trust us, and we didn't trust them," says one of the cops involved.

But these weren't the Keystone Kops snapping pictures of each other: their antics had serious consequences. Senior deputy assistant DA Jeff Bennett says his team had prepared an elaborate reverse sting, making fake bottles of Vicodin and setting things in motion so that chief pill pusher Rogelio Botello would, they hoped, make a delivery directly to George Christie. "We were ready to rock," Bennett says, but the sheriff's department jumped the gun. "They spilled the beans to the law enforcement agencies and arrested Botello before he had a chance to do it."

It only got worse when the police began to develop top-level informants inside George Christie's circle. When full-patch member Gary Wilson was sitting in jail on a drug bust, an alert sheriff's deputy spotted him as a weak link. Wilson broke, agreeing to snitch for the cops. For several months, he made numerous drug buys from other members and wore a wire to the clubhouse. "Christie isn't stupid," notes one of the cops who ran Wilson. He made sure the bikers often used an eraser board during their meetings rather than say anything compromising.

The police reeled in an even bigger catch when they flipped Wilson's friend and mentor Dave Gerradin—who was also the chapter vice-president and Christie's second-in-command. Gerradin was looking at a long jail spell under California's stiff three-strikes law when he failed to register as a sexual offender. He approached the Ventura Police Department, but the VPD quickly farmed him out to the DA's office, where the investigators assigned to him had little experience in running Angel informants. "We screwed up. We should have kept him," says the VPD's biker gang expert, Mark Coronado.

Gerradin, a heavy drug user, had a big ego and even bigger biceps. He enjoyed intimidating and bullying everybody he came into contact with and would have been a difficult informer for even the toughest agent running him. Still, Coronado thought the police should have tried to wire him up and get secret recordings: after all, he was close to the top man, George Christie. Instead, the DA's office used him only for intelligence and debriefing and shipped him out of state.

"He could have gone in and talked to George about anything in the world. They never did it. There was so much potential to take down the Ventura Chapter, but they let it get away from them," says Coronado, whose offer to help the DA's office was rebuffed. "I could have sworn that we were all on the same side working the same crooks!"

Even after managing to alienate investigators in the ATF, the sheriff's department and the VPD, the DA's office perhaps could have salvaged something—if they'd had their own act together. But the prosecutors themselves were beset by infighting and indecision. At one crucial point, DA Mike Bradbury pulled senior deputy assistant Mark Pachowitz off the case, leaving the chief prosecutor, Jeff Bennett, crippled. "Half the case was in Mark's head, the other half was in mine. I tried to tell the boss it was like sawing off my leg."

On his office bulletin board, Pachowicz had posted a prophetic quotation he had found from New York Mafia boss John Gotti: "You know why the feds will never get us?" Gotti asks one of his underlings. "'Cuz they got no fucking cohesion. They got no fucking unity."

While trying to co-ordinate as best they could, the sheriff's department and the DA pursued their parallel investigations. For a year after the May 1998 raids on Christie's business and home, the sheriff's narcotics team—with a number of informants—bought drugs twenty-five times from Hells Angels members, sometimes posing as high school students on their way out of school. In April 1999, the sheriff announced that no fewer than nine full-patch Angels had been arrested on drug charges—everything from Vicodin to Valium, cocaine and meth.

The DA's case against George Christie would take much longer to build. It was not until July 2000 that prosecutor Bennett went before a grand jury—and it took eight months and 186 witnesses before he won an indictment. Armed with what they thought was a sure-fire indictment, police on February 23, 2001, arrested twenty-four suspects, including nine full-patch Hells Angels, on 132 criminal counts of theft, fraud, tax evasion, firearms possession, drug sales to minors and the use of a street gang in a criminal conspiracy. They picked up George Christie and his son, plus his estranged wife and his daughter; all told, the Christie family faced 57 counts. Most of the other suspects made bail, but Christie and his son were slapped with an almost insurmountable $1 million bond. For almost a year, the Hells Angels leader had to cool his heels behind bars. When Christie finally walked out on January 9, 2002—after a judge agreed he could use $2 million in property put up by supporters to post bail—he was frail and withered. "He'd aged tremendously," says Bob Griggs, a close friend. "He was a changed man. It was night and day."

It hadn't been much easier on Christie's nemesis, prosecutor Jeff Bennett. Overworked, understaffed, his investigation riddled by infighting, Bennett was beginning to face grumbling in the press about how long—and how costly—the four-year-old case was becoming. It didn't help when police made foolish PR gaffes, like crashing a wedding reception to serve a subpoena to a woman who had just married a Hells Angel member connected to the drug bust. More seriously, Bennett and his team also faced intimidation by the Angels. One Sunday he heard the roar of motorcycles outside his house and walked out to see a pack of bikers at the foot of his driveway.

"I didn't know you lived here," one of them said innocently.

"I'm not afraid of those guys, but I've got a family—that changed a lot of things," Bennett says.

But he got the worst news when a court ruling in an unrelated case in effect shattered the very foundations of his case. A Santa Barbara judge and later the Court of Appeal dismissed the indictment of a suspected murderer simply on the basis that women were underrepresented on the Ventura County grand jury—the same body that had indicted the Hells Angels. The ruling threw into doubt the validity of the indictment that Bennett had painstakingly won against Christie. The prosecutors faced a dismal choice: take a chance, go ahead with a trial and risk having a guilty verdict overturned on appeal, or start all over again with a new, equally costly and time-consuming grand jury process. "Everybody was tired of fighting," admits Bennett.

In the end, just four days later, the DA and Christie reached a plea arrangement. Both parties claimed the other side caved in. Christie said the prosecutors were eager to deal not because of the court ruling but because they knew they had a shaky case. The DA said Christie pleaded because he knew he was guilty.

"Hey, they want their pound of flesh," Christie said in recalling his lawyer's advice. "Maybe this is the time to give it to them. You never know in a trial."

On Tuesday, March 19, 2002, George Christie admitted guilt to a single count of conspiracy to possess Vicodin for sale and pleaded no contest to filing a false tax return; his son pleaded no contest to two counts of possession of drugs for sale; his ex-wife pleaded guilty to one count of accessory to grand theft after the fact. Charges against his daughter were dismissed. In the end, the three had 143 charges against them reduced to five felony counts.

When it came time for sentencing one month later, the prosecution—more as a last gasp than anything else—asked for seven years of prison for Christie. The judge instead gave him only 390 days, which really meant no extra jail at all because of the time he had already served, plus three years' probation. Christie was naturally delighted: "I am a lucky criminal. Yes, I am lucky," he said, and then he added almost as an afterthought, "But I also wasn't guilty."

Street cops like Mark Coronado who had been going after Christie's bikers for years were livid. "He ended up pleading out to a lightweight crap," he says. "As far as I'm concerned, it was a complete failure." Others, like deputy chief Ken Corney, were more upbeat about the case: "It had really crippled the club. If their vice-president could turn informant, no one knew who to trust in the club any more."

In the end, it seemed that everyone lost in the longest and costliest criminal case in Ventura's history. The police and prosecutors looked overzealous in the eyes of many citizens, spending millions over several years with little to show for it. But it was also undeniable that George Christie's public image took a serious tumble as well —at least temporarily.

The biggest losers, sadly, were the teenage drug users, the young addicts who became hooked on the Vicodin that flooded the schools. Says prosecutor Jeff Bennett: "It ruined a lot of lives."

The boys who joined the Outfit as Hells Angels wannabees also lost out, picking up juvenile records—or worse. They got busted for assaults, stabbings, drug possession—and then some of the young punks graduated to murder. On a hot summer evening in July 1998, a couple of Outfit members got into a fight in an alley with two strangers after a concert at the county fairgrounds. After what police described as a "stabbing frenzy" that left one man dead and another wounded, one teenage Outfit member eventually got twenty-nine years for murder and the other eighteen-year-old Outfit member got four years for involuntary manslaughter.

Eric Jensen and his team started hitting the Outfit hard, arresting more than half of them and eventually dismantling the group.

"A lot of them were just misguided youth," Jensen says, "They obviously were going down the wrong path in a hurry."

Plenty of the bikers and their associates also paid for the Vicodin frenzy. At least sixteen members of the conspiracy pleaded guilty. Joshua Adams, the air force clerk who started it all, got a four-year prison term; Rogelio Botello, who funnelled the pills to the Hells Angels, received six years. Five bikers who had been full-patch members pleaded guilty to various drug offences. Especially damaging to Christie's Angels was the fact that several of them admitted the "crime was committed . . . in association with a criminal street gang." Christie's personal reputation as a national leader in the Hells Angels took a further blow because so many of his own members turned snitch. "Before it all ended, no fewer than eight full patches volunteered to become informants," says one of the sheriff's investigators. Christie's bold recruitment drive among Ventura's youth was also in tatters. Many of the Pierpont Rats who had become Angels were busted for drugs and quit the club. "At first they liked the power, the glory. Then they started realizing that George was just using them," says gang cop John Castelanos.

Worse still, Christie's own son, George Christie III, threw in the patch. Bad enough that he walked out of jail and promptly announced he was leaving the club. Nobody likes a quitter. But he left Harleys for haute cuisine, becoming a chef, of all things. Not a profession that ranks high on the scorecard of macho bikers. Much as he tries, Christie can't hide the hurt in his eyes when he talks about his son's departure from his beloved Angels.

"I tried to talk him out of it," he says. "Maybe someday he'll come back. The door is open."

But Ventura cop Mark Coronado says pushing his son into the club at eighteen and up the ranks to vice-president was one of the worst mistakes Christie made in his storied biker career. "And he knows it. His son ended up biting him in the butt."

The Olympic torch George Christie carried through Ventura during the happier days of 1984 hangs on the wall in one corner of his spacious living room; in the other his weather-beaten Hells Angels vest with the proud patch "Ventura President" hangs below a stained-glass Death Head. On another wall there are several Filthy Few patches and banners; Christie scoffs at the notion that those are awarded only to those Hells Angels who have killed in the name of the club: "That's what law enforcement says. I say that it's [for] the people that are the core of the partying aspect of the club."

He proudly shows a visitor a painting of himself by the artist Michael Baylog. He rattles off the names of movie stars like Mickey Rourke whom he counts as friends and shows a photo of Hollywood Kung Fu actor David Carradine at his new baby son's recent birthday party. Next to a large screen TV—and two smaller security camera monitors—a bookshelf holds a catalogue of a Monet retrospective and *The Yale Shakespeare* alongside the DVD volumes of the last four seasons of *The Sopranos,* the complete *Godfather* collection and rows and rows of every conceivable Mafia movie.

The Al Capone of Ventura lives well. In addition to this family home not far from the clubhouse, he has an estate on a hillside in Oak View outside Ventura. When police raided his homes and business back in 1998, they found a total of $224,000 in cash. When it is suggested to the biker leader that that's a lot of money for the ordinary person to leave lying around, he shrugs: "Well, yes and no. I didn't bank at the time. I bank now."

Six years after the raids and three years after his guilty plea, the cloud of suspicion still rankles. "I don't want my legacy to be that I sold drugs to kids, that the Ventura HA sold drugs to kids or that the Hells Angels at large sold drugs to kids or had anything to do with that," he insists. "Because we didn't."

It was all a plot by police and ambitious prosecutors, he says, to get back at him for bringing the World Run to Ventura in 1998 and showing off his political clout. If, in fact, the Hells Angels were selling drugs to high school students, he argues, why did the police do nothing about it for years: "Why did the police let it go on?" he asks.

But the year in jail and the battering in the press have made the Ventura patriarch, now nearing sixty, more reflective. He's still trying to fight his age: his short grey hair is teased and gelled on top for that punkier look, and a gold earring adorns his left ear. He favours long, loose dark boxing shorts, comfortable sneakers and a black Ventura Hells Angels T-shirt. But looking back, George Christie now admits publicly for the first time that recruiting teenagers from the Outfit to help during the World Run or letting high school students into the clubhouse was a mistake: "It was bad judgment," he says. "I never thought in a million years, that the police would take this allegation of selling drugs to kids, latch on to it and just beat it into the ground."

No minors are allowed into Hells Angels parties any more, he insists: "I am very specific about who goes in the clubhouse."

Still, Christie has lost none of his touch, none of his charm and none of his apparent ability to charm the authorities. He wooed his probation officer, a burly, muscle-bound weightlifting champion named Steve Hall, who became an outspoken fan of the Hells Angels leader: "He's a nice guy once you get to know him and you realize he's not the devil incarnate." Hall recommended an early end to Christie's three-year probation, though his superiors quashed that idea.

Christie's continued clout reaches much higher into the police establishment. When the city's long-serving police chief, Mike Tracy, retired in late 2004, the assistant chief and his successor asked the Hells Angel leader to participate in the send-off video. Christie also signed one of the few remaining "No Motorcycle Parking" signs the police had put up during the World Run with a "Best of Luck" wish to the chief. The joking between the top men in blue and the top man in leather was indicative of what Christie says is still the unwritten understanding in the city: "George Christie has his power and we have ours."

And Christie clearly revels in his power as the city's unchallenged gang leader: "I am who I am, and I make no apologies for anything I've ever done," he says. "We are a society unto ourselves. We govern ourselves. We discipline ourselves."

He shifts uncomfortably when it is pointed out to him that as the powerhouse behind the Hells Angels in Ventura, he can't have it both ways: either he was at the pinnacle of the drug conspiracy to which so many of his members pleaded guilty, or he was an incompetent leader who didn't know what his own troops were doing.

"Certainly nobody wants to be considered a bad leader," he says after a long pause. "So the question you're asking me encompasses a lot of issues of morality, friendship. You can't control what everybody's doing all the time and sometimes it's better not to know. You know we're not Boy Scouts, nor do we pretend to be Boy Scouts."

He points to the expensive jade chess set that sits on a table in his living room. He did not feel he faced a checkmate during his recent battle with the police, he says, but it was close.

"They are learning from their mistakes and I'm learning from my mistakes."

And, he is asked, who is winning now?

"I think we're having a rematch."

FIFTEEN

Slaughter of the Innocents

———

Their whole organization was on trial because that's why a five-year-old
and her family were murdered. It happened because of the
Hells Angels. It's their job to get into trouble. It's their
job to deal drugs. It's their job to kill people.
—MENDOCINO DEPUTY COUNTY SHERIFF PHIL PINTANE

She lay clutching her little Matchbox car in her right hand, huddling behind the dresser, where she had fled in terror. Her blue
eyes glaring wide open, her long blond hair falling loosely below
her neck. A neck that had been sliced open by a Hells Angel.

Five-year-old Dallas Grondalski was not the only victim in her
home on California's northern coast on that Sunday in October
1986: the corpses of her stepbrother, her mother and her father lay
still warm in the other rooms and hallways. Dallas's only sin was
having a father who had tried to leave the Hells Angels to start a
new life. Two bikers ended up massacring the family and having
the house set on fire to cover their tracks.

In the biker heartland of California, where the Hells Angels
were born, leaders like George Christie and Sonny Barger seemed to
enjoy an easy ride from an adoring media and public as they
crafted for themselves a daring but essentially harmless image. One
determined cop, however, uncovered a darker side to the Angels—
but it would take him almost twenty years to bring the killers of
Dallas and her family to justice. "It's the case that will never go
away," says Phil Pintane. "You can't help thinking of Dallas."

As the deputy sheriff of Mendocino County in 2005, Pintane
patrols the sprawling territory that reaches from the coastal com-

SLAUGHTER OF THE INNOCENTS 365

munities along the Pacific Ocean to the rolling hills of California's northern wine country. Alcohol isn't the only intoxicant that made Mendocino famous: it is equally renowned for its potent marijuana crop. Growing and selling dope is a bigger cash industry than the county's failing lumber business. Whether he is looking for dope growers or murderers, Pintane always makes sure his grey uniform is neatly buttoned and pressed. A bulky walkie-talkie and a gun dangle on his belt. His neatly trimmed moustache is darker than the short cropped hair beginning to grey along the temples.

His hair was black two decades ago, when he first heard of the killings that would change his life. Back in October 1986, Pintane had just been promoted from detective to sergeant. He was working the graveyard shift when news came in about a fire that had burned down a house in the coastal town of Fort Bragg with four bodies inside. The flames couldn't hide the bullet holes in the corpses: they had all been executed. Billy Grondalski, a former member of the Vallejo chapter of the Hells Angels, had paid the ultimate price for crossing the bikers— and he had doomed his family as well.

The slaughter of the Grondalski family was set in motion weeks earlier in a series of cold-blooded business meetings conducted at the Oakland clubhouse. At the time Sonny Barger was still in charge of the mother chapter; his move to Arizona was still several years away. He ran a tight ship: breaking the rules meant beatings, expulsion—or worse. In April 1986 Sonny's chapter expelled a veteran biker named Terry Dalton who had been with the gang for fifteen years after he was caught stealing money from the club till. On May 14, the bikers decided to distribute a photo of Dalton because he was "fucking up" by continuing to have contact with several members of the Hells Angels—particularly from the Vallejo chapter north of Oakland.

Two months later Barger and the Oakland chapter invited the Vallejo boys down to their clubhouse for a chat. And promptly proceeded to beat the crap out of them. Anthony Tait, the infiltrator being run by the FBI at the time, witnessed and recorded the entire evening. "Several people gathered around [Vallejo president Derrick] Kualapai and took turns beating him," Tait reported.

"That's enough!" Sonny Barger said after two minutes of pummelling. He then interrogated the hapless Vallejo biker about the whereabouts of the disgraced Terry Dalton: "Now if you know where the motherfucker's at, we want to know!"

By August 21 Sonny and his boys had cleaned house in Vallejo. Gerry "Butch" Lester was installed as the new president. At a meeting of top officers of the West Coast chapters recorded by Tait, Lester announced that several members of his chapter had been booted out. But Billy Grondalski and a few others remained in "good standing."

It didn't last. On September 27, Lester told Barger and others gathered for their regular officers' meeting in Oakland that Billy's status had suddenly changed. "Billy has, uh, since become the, uh . . . in bad standing," he said. "Tattoos need to be covered, and notify Vallejo if anybody sees him. We wanna talk to him, and that's it basically."

The passing reference to tattoos was significant: in the pantheon of biker mystique, one of the most sacred rules is that nobody but members—and especially not disgraced ex-members—can wear a Hells Angels symbol on their clothes or skin. Lester talked about simply wanting to "talk" to Billy, but in the end the bikers would get their pound of flesh from Billy Grondalski in the most gruesome way.

Grondalski had been a member of the Vallejo chapter since 1982, soon after the charter was formed. A labourer from the rough working-class town of Martinez just across the bridge from Vallejo, he was a lifelong "wrencher" who loved tinkering with bikes. He married Patty, a girl he had known since high school, a petite but tough-minded strawberry blonde. Billy, like many in Martinez, worked at the local refinery, while Patty brought in extra money as a receptionist in a beauty salon. When a back injury forced Billy out of work, they made ends meet by selling hot dogs outside the plant. He met the Hells Angels, who had already recruited several members from the refinery and local shipyards. "They made Billy a part of their family—that's how they pulled him in," says Phil Pintane. "Christmastime they went over, showered them with gifts, paid their overdue rent."

Patty had a teenage son, Jeremy, from a previous marriage. By the time Billy was signing up with the Angels, he had a one-year-old daughter with Patty, named Dallas: a blue-eyed spunky kid. "She was just a smart little girl for her age," recalls her aunt, Debbie Kast. "I think that's what got her killed. Because she knew her killer."

The Angels became the Grondalskis' new family. One of them, Charles Diaz, hung around enough with Dallas to be called "Uncle Chuck." A creased photo shows Diaz, with a dark full beard and long hair, clutching Dallas in his big arms, cheek to cheek, as the little girl gazes out with an impish grin, seemingly without a care in the world.

"It made us sick," says Debbie, who never liked or trusted the Angels. Her brother-in-law Billy suddenly seemed moody or stressed all the time, on drugs or drinking. Whisky. Meth. Her once perky sister was acting strange. Secretive. Making phone calls from the back bedroom at Debbie's house.

The two sisters had always been close, bonded by family tragedy. One of their brothers had died in a bike accident; another brother and a sister had taken their own lives. "We made a little pact together," Debbie explains. "She meant everything in the world to me. I was supposed to protect her, and she was going to protect me. When we told each other that, we hugged each other."

So Debbie, only five foot four, wasn't going to take any guff or grief from any burly, towering bikers who tried to stop her from seeing her sister.

"I've got to see my sister," she told Butch Lester, the Vallejo club president, when she heard Patty was staying at his house.

"If you know what's good for you, you'll get out of here," the biker warned, threatening to sic his pit bull on her. "You're being watched."

Debbie just laughed at him and kept coming back, leaving notes on the porch. "I would not stay away."

It paid off. By 1985 Patty had grown disillusioned with the Angels and estranged from her husband. "I'm sick of all it," she told Debbie. "He's changed; he's not the same person." She filed for divorce and took the kids.

Billy was torn between his real family and his adopted family of the bikers, but by the next year he was having his own problems with the Angels. With his fellow Vallejo bikers, he trudged down to Sonny Barger's Oakland clubhouse that fateful summer of 1986, only to witness the brutal beatings and expulsions of those members who had dared to maintain contacts with the disgraced Terry Dalton. Billy escaped punishment and kept his patch, but within three months his status had gone from "good" to "bad standing." Later in his investigation, Pintane determined that despite his denials, Billy almost certainly had kept up ties with Dalton. Pintane also heard stories that Billy may have encroached on the drug territory of other Angels. Whatever the reason, by the fall of 1986 Billy Grondalski was on the outs with his former Angel pals.

He chose to tell his family the day they were gathered in a Martinez hospital room where Patty's father was recovering from a stroke. "I'm out of the club," he announced. "We're going to start our family all over again."

He showed them his tattoo which read "in 84, out 86" signifying his years of duty. Debbie gave him a hug.

"I'm so glad," she said.

"Deb, I'm going to start a new life," he promised.

There were smiles and tears. But Debbie Kast could not shake a cold dread deep inside her. "I knew it wasn't over."

Her sister, Patty, was just as uneasy: "It's not over," she murmured. "It's not."

Billy knew he was a hunted man. When Vallejo president Butch Lester had told Sonny Barger and the other officers gathered in Oakland that they "wanna talk to him," everyone knew they didn't mean a friendly chat over a beer. The Grondalskis moved to Martinez but lay low. "He couldn't have people see him or know that he was in town," Debbie remembers; she even had to go down-town to buy him some new clothes. She took care of the children, Dallas and Jeremy, as Patty and Billy hunted for a safe place to live.

They shacked up in a house trailer for a while, travelling up and down the coast of Mendocino. Finally, they found a two-bedroom wooden house in Fort Bragg, about four hours from Martinez and Vallejo. It was just two hundred yards from the harbour, a plus for Billy, who loved to fish. He dreamed of opening a tow truck business, baptizing it Dollar Bill Towing. They began moving their furniture from Martinez—but only at night, always fearful they were being watched. Indeed, one evening friends helping them out thought they were being followed. Another time they spotted a biker in a phone booth. Pintane later confirmed that one of the oldest Angels in the area, named Father John, had been poking around Martinez looking for Billy.

Uneasy but hopeful, the Grondalskis settled into their new home on Wednesday, October 1, 1986. That very same day they enrolled little Dallas in the local school's kindergarten. On Saturday, Billy and Patty decided to head back down to Martinez to visit her sister. Ever cautious, Billy called ahead to make sure Debbie cleaned out the garage so he could keep his truck out of sight there.

"Billy seemed nervous; they all seemed nervous," Debbie says. That afternoon she took a walk with her niece to the local deli, never suspecting it would be the last time she would see Dallas alive. The little girl, oblivious to the turmoil and fear swirling around her, couldn't stop chattering. She rambled on about her new neighbour, her new friends, a pony near her new home.

"You talk too much," Debbie kidded her.

"I know, Debbie, I know," Dallas said, laughing.

That evening Debbie and her mother, Louise, set out to play bingo. "You're welcome to stay," she told the Grondalski family.

"We may go to a show," Patty and Billy said, "but if we do we'll use somebody else's car. If we don't stay, we might go back for some fishing Sunday."

They must have opted to stay, because a babysitter showed up.

She later reported the supper meal was on the table when the phone rang around six-thirty. Billy answered and hung up after only a few seconds.

"Come on, we're out of here!" he shouted.

Billy, Patty, Jeremy and Dallas scrambled into their truck and left. It was the last time anybody in the family saw them.

Whether that Saturday-night phone call was a tip from a friend that the Angels were on to him or a direct threat from the bikers themselves, it was clear the Hells Angels now knew where Billy Grondalski was hiding out. While he was rushing his family back to Fort Bragg, hundreds of bikers were gathering that weekend in nearby Sonoma County for a weekend of partying and runs at a local campground. It was not an official Hells Angels event, but the HA were out there in force.

(One of the big shots on hand was Otis "Buck" Garrett, a one-time president of the Vallejo chapter who was now a prominent Nomad. He was the central player in another grisly family massacre that had eerie overtones for what was to befall the Grondalskis that weekend. Garrett had ordered a hit on a twenty-four-year-old named Margo Compton who'd had the nerve to quit her job at a sleazy nude bar and testify against him in a pimping trial. Garrett tracked her down to a small town in Oregon and sent two biker wannabees to silence her. The men first forced her to watch as they executed her six-year-old twin girls as they lay face-down in their bed, clutching their favourite teddy bears. The Angel assassins put a .22-caliber bullet hole behind the left ear of each girl. Then they did away with the mother with three shots to the head. For good measure, they also murdered the nineteen-year-old son of her boyfriend, who had the misfortune to be in the house at the same time. Garrett would eventually be convicted of four counts of murder.)

Among the bikers attending the weekend party from the local Sonoma chapter were "Little Mike" Tankersley and Charlie Haas. Tankersley had a lengthy record of assaults and drugs. Haas was just back from Germany, where he had served eight years for killing a man and stabbing another man seventeen times. On Sunday morning, two Angels from Vallejo—club president Butch Lester and his friend Chuck Diaz—approached Tankersley to borrow his Blazer truck. They had located Billy Grondalski in Fort Bragg, they reported, and were going up to see him.

"Leave me something I can drive," Mike Tankersley said as he tossed them his keys. Butch left him his new bike. On their way out, Butch also told Charlie Haas they were heading out to Fort Bragg to see Billy. No one thought anything of it. When another biker, Dick Roach, spotted Tankersley doing wheelies, he noted "Little Mike" was fooling around on a new set of wheels.

"Hey, is that your bike? It looks like Chuck's bike," he asked.

"Oh, Butch and Chuck borrowed my Blazer to go see Billy in Fort Bragg, and if they don't bring it back I got myself a new bike," Tankersley explained.

"Little Mike" went on partying until around 3 P.M., when Lester and Diaz returned. Lester was ashen-faced.

"What's goin' on?" Tankersley asked.

"It went bad. It all went bad," Butch replied.

"What do you mean?"

"They're all dead," the Angel answered.

Even a veteran biker like Tankersley, no stranger to assaults and violence, was stunned. "What do you mean, they're all dead?"

At 10:23 on Sunday morning, Billy Grondalski had walked into the Payless store in Fort Bragg to buy some planting bulbs and fishing equipment. He drove home and parked in the back yard. The visiting Angels must have arrived soon after that, because the gear was found in the truck; Billy hadn't even had time to bring it in. The events of the next few minutes can be pieced together from later testimony and evidence gathered during the investigation and trials.

Butch Lester and Chuck Diaz confronted Billy. Or tried to. At six foot three and 240 pounds, Billy was not one to take anything from anybody. So it wasn't long before Butch Lester pulled out the .45 pistol he had just been given as a birthday present. He wasn't used to it; he usually carried a 9 mm. "I took it out and pointed it, and the fuckin' thing went off," he later said.

Billy took a bullet right through the teeth and tongue and then out through the back of his head. He dropped dead to the floor. It was a tragic accident. But what happened next was a calculated biker bloodbath.

Lester and Diaz made an instant decision that they were not going to go to prison for accidentally killing a disgraced Angel. They would simply have to dispose of the rest of the family. Patty, knowing what was coming next, screamed in horror. She raised her arm to protect herself, but the bullet penetrated her forehead. She collapsed in the hallway.

Seventeen-year-old Jeremy started running to the back room, perhaps hearing his mother's screams, to protect little Dallas. He was the only one not shot at close range; the fatal bullet pierced his left eye.

That left a terrified five-year-old, huddling in the spare bedroom in the back where furniture had been stored. Two dressers had been left there, pulled away from the wall. Dallas cringed behind one of them, clutching her tiny Matchbox car for dear life. Her "Uncle Chuck"—Hells Angel Charles Diaz—took out a knife and began slicing. The blood splattered on the wall indicated repeated knife movements up and down. Diaz made at least four or five cuts—to her ear, her cheek, her neck and a large slice that severed her spinal cord. There was no blood on her ponytail, so it is likely that Diaz held up the girl by her hair. "What I envision is her hanging by the ponytail and swinging as he's doing this," says Susan Massini, the DA who would later prosecute Diaz for the slaying.

It was brutal but, at least for the bikers, not very efficient. Butch Lester came in and muttered, "Oh, this is taking too long!" He promptly put a bullet in the girl's chin that went through her collarbone and out the centre of her back, lodging in the wall behind her.

"They let her fall," says Massini. "She lay in the corner, obviously not fighting: she had nothing in her fingernails. Her eyes are wide open. She's just begging. You can see right into her."

———

A couple of hours after the slayings, back at the hiker run, Mike Tankersley could not believe what he was hearing from Butch Lester.

"We had to kill the rest of the family."

"Even Dallas?"

"Even Dallas."

"Why? Why?"

"I had to. I had to."

As horrified as he was by the news, Mike Tankersley was a true-blue Angel. And the code of the club was that you protected your brothers. Lester gave him the murder weapon and an extra clip. Later that night, Tankersley—joined by Butch's wife, Sammie Lester—melted the gun down with a blowtorch. The two of them were also supposed to drive up to Fort Bragg to burn down the house and destroy any evidence. They didn't get far.

"Fuck it. I ain't going to do this," Tankersley said.

"I don't want to do this either," Sammie agreed, and they turned back.

Meanwhile, other bikers were scrambling to help cover up the murders. "Everyone in the club knew about them," said Tankersley.

Butch Lester dropped by the motor home of Dick Roach and his wife, Mary Anne—a woman so tough that it was said of her, "she'd be a Hells Angels if she had a dick." Butch asked for coffee.

"There's coffee in the coffee pot," Dick Roach said.

"No, Butch wants a new pot of coffee," Mary Anne said.

"Well, Butch can make it himself."

Mary Anne made a fresh pot and then watched as Butch proceeded to take the coffee after it had cooled a bit to wash his hands and arms—an old trick to remove gunshot residue.

Mary Anne wasn't through her work for the boys. She washed the blood off their vests. Early the next morning, she woke up a biker associate who ran a port-a-potty business and went by the unfortunate moniker of "Shithouse Carl." She had some evidence that Butch had asked her to get rid of, she said, holding out a brown paper bag.

Shithouse Carl glanced inside to see what looked like a piece of meat, greenish in colour, with lines on it. Either as a trophy or as proof of a job done, the Hells Angels had carved Billy's Hells Angels tattoo from his left arm. Carl and Mary Anne burned it in a barrel.

At 2 A.M., Charlie Haas—the biker just back from serving time for a murder in Germany—got a call from Butch. There was some club business that needed taking care of that morning, the Vallejo president told him. About eleven on Monday, Haas met up with Butch Lester, who told him about the murders and asked him to travel up to Fort Bragg to torch the crime scene. Butch felt he could rely on Haas, who had already killed for the club. Haas borrowed a truck from another Sonoma chapter member, Robert Huffman, and made the journey to the death house on the coast.

Haas found it spooky when he entered the silent, darkened home with the shades all drawn. He only made it as far as the main room, where he saw Billy sprawled on his back. Reminded him of Jesus on the cross, he later told police. But a biker's work is never done. Haas calmly poured gasoline over Billy, the curtains, the sofa and much of the house. Then he set a simple delayed ignition device—a book of matches stuck to a lit cigarette with its filter removed, next to a rag soaked in gasoline.

It happened to be a training night for the volunteer fire department, but that made little difference. By the time the firemen made it to the Grondalski residence, the searing flames had consumed much of the building. It didn't take long, though, for the firemen to realize they had stumbled on more than a deadly blaze: Billy was a pile of cinders. They spotted Patty's corpse, then Jeremy's crumpled body on the floor. As the fire chief made his way slowly through the house, next to Jeremy he could see a pool of blood around his head.

When he got to the back bedroom, which had been spared most of the fire damage, he saw Dallas, with her eyes open. He reached over to feel for a pulse—and his fingers went right through her neck.

———

"When I heard they were dead, I knew who murdered them, right off the bat."

Debbie Kast first got the news from Jeremy's teacher, who called to say there had been a fire but no bodies had yet been identified.

"I knew right then and there it was them, and I knew it was the Hells Angels—not the fire—that killed them," she said. "I walked down to my girlfriend's and said, 'They killed them. They finally did it.'"

At the funeral home a few days later, a bouquet of thirteen red and white bleeding hearts showed up with a message from the Hells Angels: "We are really your family." Enraged, Debbie tossed them out the side door. The family had little hope, though, that the killers would ever be brought to justice. "They're never going to find them," Debbie's father told her. "I'm never going to live to see it." He was right; he died three years later, in 1989, and by then the case was already dormant.

From the start, it had been marred by bad luck, bad witnesses and the biker wall of silence. Because the fire had been set on the Monday, everyone assumed the murders had been committed shortly before on the same day. A neighbour told police she was pretty sure she had seen a woman in the house in the window, washing the dishes on Sunday night, before the fire. A coroner quickly put the time of death to Monday.

Once the police discovered Billy's history with the Angels and heard Debbie Kast's stories about the frightened family, they quickly suspected the Hells Angels were behind the murders, but proving it was not going to be easy. Most bikers refused to talk. Others lied. Charlie Haas had a burn scar on his hand, but he claimed it was from a tool grinder. Potential leads were not pursued because the cops were convinced that the murders took place on the Monday. Diaz, when questioned, admitted they knew he was in Fort Bragg and had headed out to see him on the Sunday but returned because of a flat tire. The case was dying a slow death.

Phil Pintane could not let it drop. He had not been on the original investigation but could not get the murders out of his mind.

A couple of years later, in 1988, he went back to conduct several new interviews and failed to turn up any leads. Pintane had to wait five more years before his first big break. In late 1993 he got news that Charlie Haas, the man who had set the Grondalski home ablaze, had been arrested and convicted on a drug charge in Arizona. Looking at thirty years of prison time for the manufacture and distribution of methamphetamines, Haas told his sister to get in touch with the Mendocino authorities to tell them he had some information on "a murder." He knew that even after a conviction, co-operating with the police could get him some reduction in time behind bars.

Pintane had no certainty that it was the Fort Bragg massacre Haas wanted to talk about, but he got on a plane. He waited in a small office in the prison, tucked away underneath a stairway: nothing but a small desk and three chairs.

In walked a giant of a man, his feet in chains. "Who the fuck are you guys?" Haas bellowed.

"Hey, you called us," Pintane shot back.

"I don't co-operate with cops," the biker said. It went back and forth like that for about an hour with Haas giving up little until he asked, "Do we have a deal?"

"You haven't told me stuff I don't know," Pintane said.

Then Haas opened up with everything that had happened on the Sunday. He stopped when he saw the stunned look on Pintane's face.

"You do know these murders happened on a Sunday, don't you?" the biker asked. "You didn't know, did you? How could you not know? With a pathologist and all that, you couldn't tell?"

Pintane just looked at him.

"Oh. I know." Haas paused when it finally sank in. "Because of the fire."

Pintane's mind was racing: *How could that be? He sets the fire on Monday, but the murders actually took place on Sunday? Is this guy a liar?*

"Okay, I'll take what you have and see what we can do," he said, and the meeting was over.

Pintane went back and talked to the new district attorney.

Susan Massini was a tall woman with flaming red hair. She cut her teeth as a public defender, and in that role her first encounter with a no-nonsense cop like Pintane did not augur well. Back in 1983, he was interrogating a suspect in a stabbing murder when Massini burst in: "That's my client, and you can't talk to him any more!" she said.

"Who is that bitch, and who let her in here?" Pintane sputtered.

They soon learned a grudging respect for each other, which only intensified once Massini crossed over to the prosecution side. "She was too good to be a defence attorney," Pintane jokes.

Massini agreed that Haas would not be charged if he had nothing to do with the murders; they would also put in a good word for him to help get his sentence reduced. So six months later, in June 1994, Pintane went back down to Arizona to take a tape-recorded, sworn statement. Eight years after the murders, he finally had one of the conspirators willing to break the biker code of silence.

Debbie Kast had just returned home from a shopping trip when she got the news that somebody named Phil had called about the murders. After so many years, she had come close to giving up on the police. "What? Oh my God!" she exclaimed. She called back; Pintane told her he was on the case now and that somebody had finally spilled the beans.

"Within minutes, you just knew he was the guy for the case," she says, remembering the start of what would become a warm and close relationship with the officer who seemed as devoted to her family's memory as she was. "He can make you feel so good. He's just so mellow, so caring and so smart. He would know just what to say."

Giving the family hope was one thing; busting the case was another. Charlie Haas's testimony had left Pintane with a major dilemma: "We had no evidence at that time that the murder had occurred on Sunday other than his statement," Pintane explains. So he began combing through the old files, tracking down old and new witnesses. "There were so many reports, people and locations that it was mind-boggling." By the time he would finish almost a

decade later, Pintane had spoken to close to three hundred witnesses in almost every state, because so many of the people who
knew the Grondalskis or the local Hells Angels had scattered
across the country.

Pintane began to assemble a truer picture of what really happened that weekend. He knew that Lester and Diaz had told
enough people and were seen by enough people leaving on Sunday
for Fort Bragg; what he needed was proof that the murders had
indeed occurred on that day and not Monday as originally
believed. Pintane came up with at least three pieces of evidence.

First, Dallas did not show up for school on Monday.

Second, he found a receipt that proved Billy had bought his
fishing gear on Sunday morning, yet the gear and his other purchases remained untouched in the truck in his backyard.

Third, he traced two phone calls made from the house to
Father John, the Nomad leader in Martinez; he surmised that the
panicked killers were trying to reach him for advice.

Later on, Pintane was able to remove one last nagging obstacle
to nailing down the day of the murders. He returned to Fort Bragg
to re-interview the neighbour who had claimed she had seen a
woman washing dishes at the Grondalski home on the Sunday
evening. All it took was some persistent questioning. The woman
admitted she had misinformed the police: she had inadvertently
confused the events of that weekend with an earlier sighting. The
only place to see the Grondalski kitchen window from her home
was on tiptoes standing next to her washer-dryer, and she had not
done the laundry that weekend. In fact, she now recalled that
when she and her husband got back from a camping trip on
Sunday, the house had been entirely dark.

It was all enough to get arrest warrants issued for Diaz and
Lester by May 1995. Both men had become huge liabilities to the
club: killing a five-year-old and her family was not the kind of
publicity the Hells Angels wanted. The HA would protect its
members, but it would protect the club above all: the Angels had
been known to wipe out their own brothers to either keep them
quiet or permanently out of the picture. Butch Lester quit back in

1987, lying low in Tahoe, then Arizona, and finally settling in Arkansas. Diaz, though, was still a full-patch member when the police came knockin on his door.

Pintane made sure both men were arrested simultaneously. A SWAT team moved in to arrest Diaz at his home. "You're under arrest for murder," Pintane told him. Diaz didn't utter a word. Pintane then got on a plane and flew to Arkansas to bring back the former club president, Butch Lester.

"Aren't you going to advise me of my rights?" Lester asked.

"I haven't asked you anything about the murders yet," Pintane answered.

"Well, I'm not telling you anything," Lester said. "I want my attorney."

Gratified that he had now had the two bikers behind bars, Pintane was seasoned enough to realize that the most difficult battles in his war to get justice for the Grondalski family lay ahead—the trials. Now it really starts, he thought to himself. Now the hard part starts.

Even a skeptical cop had no idea how hard and long that battle would be.

The Hells Angels certainly realized how damaging the court battles could be to his organization. "They didn't like the situation at all," Pintane remembers. "They were trying to distance themselves."

Early on in the legal proceedings, Fritz Clapp, who had a long history of acting for the club, showed up. Clapp wanted to argue that the Hells Angels name should be kept out of the trial. The judge promptly shot him down, telling him that he could file whatever papers he wanted, but he had no standing in the courtroom. Pintane, shocked at the club's brazenness given that, at least in his mind, the blood of the Grondalski murders was all over the Hells Angels, went up to the lawyer afterwards.

"I can't believe you did that," the cop said.

"Why?" said the Angels lawyer. "It's a good upstanding organization."

As the trial got under way, the police still had not located Mike Tankersley, leaving Charlie Haas as the main bulwark for the prosecution. A convicted murderer and the admitted arsonist who burned the Grondalski bodies was not the most sympathetic witness. "He got chopped up pretty good by the defence attorneys," Pintane admits.

The result was the first of several setbacks: at the end of the preliminary hearings in late 1995, the judge committed Butch Lester to trial but ruled there was not enough evidence to proceed against Diaz.

"We had to put it back together," said a frustrated Susan Massini. Pintane redoubled his efforts to locate Mike Tankersley, the key witness who had lent his truck to the killers and had heard directly from both of them about the day's bloody events. It had been a trying decade for "Little Mike" since the murders. Booted out of the club, he had ignored the Angels' warnings to leave the state. He tried to stay hidden but kept getting into beatings and even shootouts with the bikers. At one point he had to escape from a speeding car, convinced that the Angels who had seized him were going to kill him.

Through his girlfriend's phone records, the police finally tracked Tankersley to a small community in Arkansas. The county sheriff and two of his deputies drove by his house in an unmarked van with blackened windows. On the second pass, Tankersley got suspicious and made a dash for his car. The cops did a quick U-turn. A panicked Tankersley rammed their car as the sheriff pulled out his gun and emptied his magazine. His deputies leaped out and put two more shots into the driver's side.

They opened the door of the fleeing car, and Tankersley, wounded but miraculously still alive, burst out with a desperate plea: "Don't kill me, don't kill me!"

Later he explained to Pintane, "I didn't know if it was the cops or the Hells Angels. I knew both of them wanted me, and I was just trying to get the hell out of there."

"When did you realize it was the cops?" Pintane asked.

"When they opened the truck door."

"Why?"

"Because If It Was the HA they'd have shot me. The cops wouldn't do that."

As Tankersley sat there, all bandaged up in his hospital bed, he initially refused to talk to Pintane much about the Grondalski killings. Until the cop told him that Butch Lester's lawyers were trying to pin the murders on him and Haas.

"You're going to end up going to jail for the murders," Pintane said. "They're accusing you of doing it."

That opened up the floodgates. "It wasn't right that it happened," Tankersley told Pintane. He spilled his guts about everything he knew of the murders; he was fearful that the Angels would kill him and his family once word got out he had squealed.

Indeed, it didn't take long for the bikers to find out. When Phil Pintane returned to Vallejo to arrest Chuck Diaz yet again, this time he was more talkative: "Been waiting for you guys," Diaz said.

"Why's that?" Pintane asked

"Well, I knew you got little Mike," Diaz replied. "That rat. He's a rat."

The rat's testimony was enough to put the case back together. District attorney Susan Massini dismissed the charges against George Lester and had him rearrested so that once again her office could try Lester and Diaz together. "We wanted them both sitting there for the jury to see," she says. After a short preliminary hearing in July, both men this time were committed to trial—but the judge ruled that Diaz should only be charged with the murder of Dallas and ordered individual trials for each defendant. "So everything we did was for naught," Massini says.

They elected to start Lester's trial first, figuring the case against him was the strongest. Massini herself didn't try the case; her office farmed it out to an independent prosecutor. Unfortunately, the case came off as confused and complex, while Lester benefited from a strong legal team: one of his attorneys had been campaign chairman for Susan Massini when she'd run for the office of DA; the second man was Norman Vroman, an up-and-coming lawyer with an eye on public office. After five months the jury was hopelessly deadlocked, splitting eight to four in favour of an acquittal. The trial collapsed with a hung jury in April 1997.

Debbie Kast was devastated but determined not to give up on getting the Angels. "You're not going to get away with it. We're going to get you," she remembers thinking.

Equally adamant that the case not be dropped, Phil Pintane stormed into Massini's office. "We need to have another trial," he said, pushing her to take over the case and prosecute it herself. "Susan, you have to do this."

"Sorry, this is over. This is over," said Massini. "Get this case out of here. I don't want to deal with this any more." But it didn't take long for the persistent Pintane to win her over. "I realized that that was not fair. It wasn't fair to the family, it wasn't fair to Dallas," she concluded.

Massini accepted the challenge. She knew little about the details of the case, but she knew the courts would not countenance a long delay for a new trial. A former teacher, she realized she had to pare down the complex investigation to a simple story. She made short notes on each of the 217 witnesses on her list. "I created an image in my mind of what had happened, and by doing that I created the story to tell the jury in a manner that made sense to them."

She was ready to go in six weeks.

Massini decided that she had to make a jury of ordinary citizens understand that the Hells Angels would kill over something as seemingly insignificant as a patch that a disgraced member refused to remove. "When you think of it, to an average person that's just the dumbest thing they ever heard," she says. "For the Hells Angels, it was a real thing. Someone wearing a tattoo they're not supposed to is a real problem. You can get killed over it."

To illustrate her point—literally—she brought in a big, burly truck driver who had been kicked out of the Angels. His back was one huge scar where he had been forced to burn off his HA tattoo. Even after he'd been out of the club for years, the bikers tracked him down to Idaho to check out his compliance and forced him to get more skin removed.

"It was an amazing demonstration of how far they will go," Massini says.

It was working. The defence team was outgunned and out-manoeuvred. But Massini made one mistake. She accepted one young woman on the jury who seemed to come with impeccable credentials: she gave all the right answers and her father was a retired judge. The next day she came back wearing a Harley T-shirt.

"I just shuddered when she walked in with that T-shirt on," Massini recalls. Halfway through the trial, she got word the juror had asked for the day's proceedings to end early so she could catch a weekend motorcycle run. "Oh my God, we're in trouble," Massini recalls thinking.

As the jury began its deliberations, the woman refused to budge. She deadlocked the jury in an eleven-to-one vote for conviction in June. Once again, the trial against Butch Lester ended in a hung jury. Undeterred, Susan Massini went after him a third time a few months later. And finally won. In October 1997—eleven years exactly after the slaughter of the Grondalksi family—the former president of the Vallejo chapter was found guilty of their murders and was sent to prison on four concurrent life sentences.

Debbie Kast was in the courtroom for the verdict, along with her aging mother, Dallas's grandmother, Louise. Lester turned to the elderly woman and just laughed.

"You're going to hell, you bastard," Debbie Kast said. "You will go to hell. You're going away."

One down, one to go.

Chuck Diaz had been waiting for almost three years for his trial to start. "I knew we were only halfway there," Pintane says

"We wanted him just as bad," adds Kast.

But it wouldn't come easily.

After countless delays caused by a change in lawyers and legal manoeuvres, the Diaz trial was finally scheduled to get under way in January 1999. But a funny thing happened on the way to trial: in elections for the district attorney's office a couple of months earlier, Susan Massini went down to a narrow defeat—a margin of just 927 votes out of more than 26,000 cast—to none other than Norman Vroman, who had been the defence lawyer for Diaz's co-accused, Butch Lester, at his first trial. Vroman also had served a nine-month federal prison term for failure to pay income taxes and had twice filed for bankruptcy. But he campaigned in part on the decriminalization of marijuana, which no doubt proved popular in Mendocino's vast rural areas where dope was the biggest cash crop. (Ironically, Lt. Phil Pintane at the same time had made a bid to succeed his retiring sheriff, but he too was narrowly defeated by a candidate who called for the decriminalization of the weed.)

It left Susan Massini in a gut-wrenching dilemma for the final weeks of her term, before Vroman took over officially in the new year. Vroman, throughout the original preliminary hearings and trial, not only proclaimed the innocence of his client but also insisted the case should never have even come to trial in the first place. While he had defended only Lester and not Diaz, it was impossible to imagine a scenario where Lester was innocent but Diaz was guilty.

Massini felt uneasy leaving a former defense lawyer like Vroman who had worked for one accused Hells Angels to take over the prosecution against another Angel accused in the same murder. So she made one of the most difficult decisions of her career—and, she knew, her last. She walked into the courtroom in January 1999 and announced that she was dismissing the case against Diaz.

"It was a horrible day," she recalls. "It was my last day in office in a job that I loved. Diaz was there looking at me. It was horrible."

Diaz was exultant. It looked as if he had beaten the rap one more time. He must have been a little disappointed when the club asked him to leave shortly after the case was dismissed; he was damaged goods, after all, legally not guilty but a walking public relations embarrassment nonetheless. Still, he was a free man.

Or so he—and his long-time Hells Angels buddies—thought.

Phil Pintane had a surprise waiting for the bikers. In California the state prosecutor is allowed to pick up a local case if there is a perceived conflict of interest or if the case is complex and costly. Pintane asked the state's department of justice to review the legal possibility of filing the charges once again. Mike O'Reilley, the deputy attorney general, determined that while most cases can only be filed twice, a unique California law allows for a third chance in murder cases, providing there has been negligence by the court or the prosecutor.

It was a daunting task. By this time, there were twenty-five thousand pages of police reports, hundreds of binders and thirty thousand pages of transcripts. "I had mixed feelings," O'Reilley admits. "After reviewing the evidence, I knew it was a very thin case." Some of the witnesses had died, and those still alive were scattered across the country. There was virtually no physical evidence—no murder weapon, no fingerprints. "We had to rely primarily on the testimony of other gang members, and it was questionable whether a jury would believe them," O'Reilley says. "But I felt I had a moral and ethical obligation to go forward. I was certain that Diaz was guilty—and this was an innocent defenceless little girl who was murdered in such a horrific fashion."

He got a grand jury indictment not only against Diaz for murder but against three other gang associates for conspiring to cover it up. Mary Anne Roach was charged with threatening witnesses and getting rid of evidence (including the lump of tattooed flesh); Robert Huffman for lending a van used in the arson and Sammie Lester, Butch's wife, for melting down the gun. Sammie had the dubious distinction of having being married at different times to both of the Hells Angels' most infamous child murderers—Buck Garrett, who ordered the hit on Margo Compton and her twin girls in Oregon, and Butch Lester, who killed Dallas and her family. When Pintane arrested her, she was tight-lipped: "Hell, I had to protect one husband when I was married to him. I might as well protect this one too."

By early 2000 O'Reilley had cleared all the legal hurdles and was ready for trial. But nothing ever turned out to be simple when it came to prosecuting the Hells Angels, and it would take four more years of interminable legal wrangling. The case went through three judges and three defence lawyers: the first judge left the case early; the next one assigned had to step aside because he was a good friend of the defence attorney; the first judge then returned, only to be challenged on bias. He fought for the right to stay, all the way to the Californian Supreme Court—and won— only to then withdraw on his own. Meanwhile, Diaz's public defender kept pushing for continuances, and when after two years he could get no more delays he promptly quit; a second defence attorney was eventually disqualified when police discovered he had once acted on behalf of one of the prosecution witnesses. A third public defender had to be named.

Through it all Pintane never lost touch with Debbie Kast and her family, visiting them every couple of months. Her mother, Louise, was getting weaker and weaker as time went on. The prosecution was worried enough that they decided to film her testimony, a not so subtle hint that they felt she might pass away before a trial ever began.

"Phil, you've got to get this to trial," Dallas's grandmother begged the deputy sheriff.

"Well, I'm trying," he said.

"I'll stay around as long as it takes," she declared. "I'll crawl on my hands and knees to Ukiah if I have to, but I will be there."

She didn't make it, at least in body. She died three months before Diaz's trial, never knowing if the man who sliced her granddaughter's neck would be punished. But Pintane was convinced that she was there in spirit: "I'm not a real religious person," he says, "but I'm sure she was there watching somewhere."

If so, she saw quite a spectacle. On the first day of the trial, March 4, 2004, the defence asked for a mistrial because during the lunch break family members had sat on courthouse stairs with T-shirts that read, "Justice for Dallas." The judge declined.

"I hope you will hear in my voice the voices of Billy, Patty, Jeremy and Dallas," prosecutor Mike O'Reilley told the jurors. "Frankly, there is no one else to speak for them, and they deserve to be heard."

Diaz's lawyer was quick to try to defuse the scope of the crime. "The Hells Angels are not on trial here," he said. "Mr. Diaz is on trial here."

Throughout the trial O'Reilley rebuffed that position: "There's this rotten, idiotic stupid ethic of the Hells Angels that permeates everything about this case."

To prove his point, O'Reilley brought in Anthony Tait, the FBI's super spy who had recorded the officers' meetings in Oakland where Sonny Barger and other leaders passed judgment on wayward members like Billy Grondalski who went from good brothers to enemies in "bad standing." Tim McKinley, Tait's handler and by this time retired from the FBI, enthralled the jurors with his detailed exposé of the Angels' strict protocol and brutal discipline. "It was the HA culture that really was the driving force behind these murders," O'Reilley explains. "The Vallejo chapter was in danger of having their charter pulled because they were not able to take care of HA business. They had to show the rest of the club that they could discipline their members."

In fact, what shocked the jurors even more than the murders—after all, even ordinary people knew about revenge killings—was the gruesome testimony of the rotting flesh of Billy Grondalski's Hells Angel tattoo that the killers had taken with them. "Cutting off part of his arm and bringing it back was even more horrendous to many jurors," says O'Reilley.

During most of trial, Chuck Diaz kept his eyes focused on the table in front of him, constantly taking notes on a laptop and then later on a notepad. The defence produced the photo of Diaz hugging a smiling Dallas, arguing that "Uncle Chuck" loved the girl and would never have harmed her. The prosecution turned that argument on its head: precisely because Dallas knew him, Diaz had to silence her and prove to the Angels he was not weak.

Toward the end of the trial, prosecutor O'Reilley projected a large photograph of Dallas's body as it was discovered at the murder scene. Debbie Kast, in the courtroom that day, covered her face in her hands and sobbed uncontrollably.

"You could hear her crying in the background," Pintane remembers. It was a moment of reckoning for him too. For years, he had seen those photos, used them so often in interviews—though never with the family—that he had become almost nonchalant about them. That day in court, the full impact of the crime struck him. "I realized that Dallas was a real person; she had people who loved her. If she was alive she'd be a grown woman."

Phil Pintane's wife, Yvonne, happened to be in the court as well that day. She and her children had not seen a lot of him over the years as he spent countless days on the road, tracking down evidence and witnesses. He missed graduations and birthday parties. "All those years that I missed with Phil, it was made up for right then and there," she told Debbie. "The whole thing is worth it now."

Still, a trial could go either way. And so far in the countless preliminaries and jury trials that had marked this case over nearly two decades, the Hells Angels had come out on top more often than not. Prosecutor O'Reilley was optimistic but not absolutely confident. He took a stroll the first night the jury began its deliberations and bumped into the court bailiff who takes care of the jurors, an elderly man he knew well.

"Hey, Frank, how's it going? What do you think?" the tired prosecutor asked.

"Don't worry," the bailiff assured him. "I think in about a week there's going to be a guilty verdict." On Wednesday, May 5, 2004, Charles Diaz stood up to hear the jury's decision. There would be no hung jury this time. No dismissal. No mistrial.

Guilty.

Diaz blanched, clenched his fists and muttered something inaudible. It had taken eighteen years and cost more than $4 million, but now both of the killers of Dallas Grondalski, her parents and her brother had at long last been brought to justice. Diaz was eventually sentenced to twenty-nine years to life, his chance at parole virtually nil. His co-conspirators got sentences varying from twenty to thirty-two months.

"It was one of the most incredible feelings of my entire life," says Mike O'Reilley. "I cried. My eyes watered up in court."

Debbie Kast, the only surviving member of her family to finally see justice done, was overjoyed. "I'm so happy. I believe in the system again," she said that day.

Susan Massini, though no longer a prosecutor, worked across the street from the courthouse and had dropped in regularly to watch the proceedings. "That was the happiest day of my life. It was a sense of completion. This was the man who had inflicted the greatest injury on Dallas."

Perhaps the most satisfied person in the courtroom that day was Phil Pintane, the policeman who had spent close to two decades of his life waiting for this moment. He took comfort from the fact that not only had Dallas been avenged, but a criminal gang had been exposed. "Their whole organization was on trial because that's why a five-year-old and her family were murdered. This never would have happened if they didn't have these stupid club rules that make them so frickin' macho. It happened because of the Hells Angels. It's their job to get into trouble. It's their job to deal drugs. It's their job to kill people."

Still, Pintane—now retired—would be the first to admit he had only put two killers behind bars: the club that spawned them was as strong as ever. Prosecutor O'Reilley also had no illusions. "Did I feel that we had caused any damage to the HA? No. They are a very large organization—if anything, they are more powerful now than when the murders occurred."

At last count, the Vallejo chapter boasted eighteen active members, more than they had when the Angels killed Dallas and her family.

Debbie Kast did not leave the Martinez area. At forty, she gave birth to a girl, Carlie, who at five years old looked strikingly like Dallas, the cousin she never got to see.

Not a day goes by that Debbie doesn't think of her sister, Patty. When she finally realized her dream and opened up her own nail salon, Debbie knew exactly what she would call it: True Colors Nail Salon—a direct dig at the Hells Angels.

"I knew her true colours, and they weren't red and white."

One day a couple of young women came in wearing tight-fitting Sonny Barger T-shirts with the slogan "Support Your Local Hells Angels." Debbie politely but sternly asked them to leave or go home and change their clothing. "Like they think it's so cool. They don't know what they are," she says. "Because they don't understand. They need to understand that they will use you, they'll rape you, they'll murder you. They'll do anything to you. And it's not a fun thing."

At the school that Dallas had attended, they planted a tree in memory of the little girl who didn't get a chance to grow up. She'd be in her twenties today, if not for the Hells Angels. The tree now stands tall and splendorous, its branches reaching up to the sky.

SIXTEEN

The Racketeering Rap

———

You did what it takes. . . . Welcome, you're Hells Angels now.
—TEDDY TOTH, PRESIDENT OF THE HELLS ANGELS
SKULL VALLEY CLUB

We were overjoyed. They're telling us we're members.
There's no way we can end this now.
—ATF AGENT JAY DOBYNS

Sonny Barger must have looked at the run-ins with the law that some of his fellow Angels were enduring in his former stomping grounds of California—the convictions for the Grondalski family slaughter and the legal headaches of his sometime rival George Christie —with a mixture of pity and relief. In his new base in Arizona, the Angels felt immune, never suspecting how close the cops were to closing in.

Indeed, the Arizona Angels had grown so trusting of Jay Dobyns and the rest of the ATF undercover team of Black Biscuit that they let them housesit their homes when they were away (even giving them the keys to their gun cases) and invited them to their weddings. They displayed pictures of the Solo Angeles on their walls and in their photo albums. By the late spring of 2003, Jay and his crew had become family.

For more than a year, under case agent Joe Slatalla's direction, the Solo Angeles had bought drugs from the Hells Angels, trafficked in illegal weapons with them, partied at their clubhouses and ridden alongside them on their bike runs. They had also catalogued a lot of evidence they believe documented a network of crime. The undercover agents had filed hundreds of pages of reports on gun and drug deals, extortions and assaults—and even murderous shootouts: on more than one occasion, Arizona Hells Angels bragged about their roles in the Laughlin casino brawl.

The Solo Angeles gambit had worked so well that the ATF suddenly found itself closer to the Hells Angels than they had ever planned on being. Dobyns and his crew were putting on such a show that the Angels were begging them to join, and the ATF agents were resisting.

It was a delicate dance that was going to have to end soon.

"No thanks, we're not interested in coming in with you guys; we have a good thing going right now," Dobyns kept telling the Hells Angels.

But the Angels were getting pissed off. "You're either going to be a Hells Angel or you're going to get the fuck out of this state!"

On April 13 members from the Skull Valley chapter, Robert Reinstra and George Walters, met with the undercover agents at a bar to give them their Skull Valley tabs to be placed on biker vests as a public sign that they were official prospects. Reinstra scoffed at other biker clubs like the Sons of Silence in Colorado that had allowed themselves to be so easily infiltrated by cops. Their recruitment rules were "too easy" compared with the lengthy period the Hells Angels impose, he boasted. "Cops don't have the patience to get through our prospecting time," he said, although he was quick to reassure Dobyns and his gang that they would become Hells Angels members "fast."

The Arizona Angels were definitely rushing things. By May 31 the undercover agents were each given an official Hells Angels bottom prospect rocker. "Now that you're members, you just need the vote," chapter president Teddy Toth said, referring to the unanimous vote of charter members needed to obtain full membership. Bob Johnston, the leader of the nearby Mesa chapter who had wanted Bird and his gang so badly for himself, told them they appeared to "be on the fast track" to becoming full members. "Skull Valley is low on members," he said. "You guys will make it quick."

Indeed, Skull Valley was hurting. They had once had nine members, but now one was a fugitive, one had been booted out, one had left and two had transferred to other chapters in the state—leaving only four, well below the HA's required minimum of six full-patch bikers for a club. But they were a tough bunch. Dobyns saw more than a little of himself in these Angels: "They were much like me—quiet intimidators."

If the Hells Angels were desperate for the undercover cops to prospect quickly and become full members, the ATF seemed equally desperate to slam on the brakes.

Cops joining the Angels had never been part of the original operational plan for Black Biscuit: cozying up to the HA, yes; becoming members, no. Dobyns, of course, was thrilled with the chance to infiltrate the Hells Angels on a deeper level. But Joe Slatalla, the agent who had created the Solo Angeles ruse and was its mastermind, was not convinced.

Aside from strategic differences, it came down to the underlying tensions that almost always exist between the undercover agent who lives for the thrill of the chase and the manager who feels that caution saves lives and gets results. ATF management feared they were about to lose control of their own agents. Once they joined the Hells Angels, the Angels would call the shots. When the Angels snapped their fingers, the agents would have to jump. It was too much like flying blind, and Slatalla was far too rigorous an organizer to want to take that trip. But Jay Dobyns, who had been shot and run over on the job and got juiced by the excitement of it all, was dead keen on making the move. And that's where the problems began.

Slatalla pushed Dobyns: "What is prospecting or becoming a Hells Angel going to bring to this investigation that staying a Solo Angele is not bringing?"

Dobyns couldn't argue with that. Trouble was, they were stung by their own success. With or without the Hells Angels patch, his crew had already compiled so much evidence, so many secret recordings, drug buys and illegal gun purchases, that they could easily walk away and call it a day.

More important than the long list of offences were the connections. By being on the inside, close to the bikers, the agents were able to see how the club operated: who made the decisions, how crime was organized. It became clear to Slatalla that his undercover operatives were painting an intricate portrait of a "criminal enterprise" as defined by RICO, the American racketeering law originally used for the Mafia. Slatalla had already drafted various reports to convince first the U.S. attorney's office in Phoenix and ultimately the Organized Crime and Racketeering Section of the Department of Justice in Washington that Black Biscuit was amassing enough evidence to arrest many Hells Angels under the much-feared RICO gang charges. Slatalla got on well with the attorneys, but he never imagined a dispute between him and prosecutors would eventually jeopardize the entire case.

Meanwhile Dobyns just wanted to keep driving forward and see how far they could go. The prospect of burrowing into the inner sanctum of the Hells Angels—right in Sonny Barger's backyard—was just too enticing.

By late spring the choice was clear: either Jay Dobyns and his team were going to become HA members or Black Biscuit was over. The ultimatum the Angels had given Bird and his gang— join us or get out of Arizona—had in effect become an ultimatum to Joe Slatalla.

So the ATF came up with a compromise of sorts. Slatalla agreed to let his agents become prospects, but he also set a hard date for the entire Black Biscuit operation to be shut down: July 8. It would take several weeks to tie up the loose ends, in any event. But once the ATF took the decision to terminate the project, it was as irreversible as a speeding locomotive.

Dobyns would not be above throwing himself on the tracks in one last desperate gambit to keep his infiltration going.

For most of May and June, Dobyns and his team were way too busy as prospects to worry about how it was all going to end.

Being a prospect—in effect, a glorified gofer—could be gruelling at the best of times; for undercover cops it was especially draining and demeaning. "It's a completely degrading and humiliating process to have people that you don't respect—criminals—snapping their fingers and pushing you around," Dobyns says. "They run your ass into the ground, and they don't give a shit. And your partners are seeing you have to put up with this."

"Hey, Prospect—you have a nice truck. Bring it down to the clubhouse," was a typical command the Solo Angeles once got.

"What's going on?" they asked.

"Just bring the fuckin' truck down here—don't ask what's going on," came the stern rebuke. It turned out the bikers were doing renovations and they obliged the Solo Angeles to lug heavy cinder blocks. Bird, Timmy and Pops also did all the other chores foisted on hangarounds. They were reduced to pinning up HA banners at parties, selling T-shirts at runs and manning HA booths at public events. Prospects were expected to show up long before a major biker event began to start setting everything up and to stay late afterwards cleaning up. "Then when it's over and they get to sleep it off, you have to go log your evidence and write your reports," Dobyns says. "It's a killer lifestyle: trying to prospect and then trying to prospect as a cop is damn near impossible."

Because of Bird's reputation as a debt collector and gunrunner and Timmy's expertise as a martial arts expert, the Solo Angeles were also recruited to do security—and not just in Arizona. Dobyns stood guard outside Sonny Barger's Cave Creek clubhouse for a state officers' meeting alongside Mike Coffelt, a club prospect who had befriended the Solo Angeles and helped them through the harsh days of kowtowing to the full-patch members. The Solo Angeles provided security at several Hells Angels funerals and acted as personal bodyguards to a couple of full-patch members. In California they manned the front door of the San Bernardino clubhouse, and in San Diego they held a nervous watch during the height of the Mongols–HA war.

"They have a bunch of violent guys on both sides," says Dobyns. "We were on the edge, waiting for a bomb to go off or a shootout to take place between these two clubs. Not a comfortable place to be as a cop pretending to be a Hells Angel."

It got even scarier on June 12, when the Arizona Angels directly recruited the cops as frontline soldiers for what they thought was a looming battle against one of their rivals, the Texas-based Bandidos.

"Hey, get all your guns, get all your knives, get all your weapons, come to the clubhouse," came the call from the Angels that the undercover cops had always been dreading. "This was the event that we feared, the one that made us think, How do we overcome this?" says Dobyns. Violence is a way of life—and death—in the biker world. How could the Solo Angeles maintain their cover if asked to commit violent acts and yet not break the law as cops?

When the ATF operatives arrived at the Skull Valley clubhouse on Yuma Drive in Chino Valley, they found the bikers itching for a fight. The word on the street was that the Bandidos planned to crash a large coalition meeting of biker gangs sympathetic to the Angels scheduled for that night at the Eagle Lodge in Las Vegas.

"If they show up at this meeting, we're taking their asses out," the Angels vowed. "Fuck Laughlin, we don't give a shit what happened there. We'll fuckin' kill some more fuckin' bikers. They want to fuck with us, they want to fuck with our meeting, we're taking them down ourselves." The details of what police say happened next were laid out in a court-filed ATF affidavit that forms the basis of a pending trial against certain members. The police version of events still has to be proven in court.

Bobby Reinstra came out of the bedroom area of the clubhouse, putting a Bersa .380-calibre pistol in his pocket. George "Joby" Walters, planning to bring a sawed-off shotgun, told the prospects they should anticipate going to jail or having to leave the country following the confrontation.

Shortly after 2 P.M., Dobyns and his men dutifully loaded a cache of guns into the back of Dobyns's Jeep and started driving to Nevada with Walters. Dobyns's mind was racing: how were the cops going to get out of this one? He managed to make a quick call to his ATF cover team, pretending he was talking to JJ. "We've got some problems; we're loaded up and heading to Vegas."

The task force scrambled into action. When they stopped for gas, Dobyns found a moment to make a furtive call to Joe Slatalla. "We've got to protect this meeting," he said. "Put cops in there, whatever you got to do. Make sure the Bandidos don't get close to this thing because we're going to have a war."

And the undercover cops were going to be caught right in the middle. "You know what," the Angels told Dobyns and his crew. "If the Bandidos come in heavy, they've seen us, they know what we look like. But they don't know who you dudes are. Take all your HA stuff off, no support gear. You guys are going to be undercover HA." Undercover cops playing undercover Hells Angels. It would have been funny if the stakes had not been so deadly.

"You'll be staged at the gate," the Solo Angeles were told. "If these dudes show up, you smoke them off the bikes before they even get their kickstands down. We're not even going to let them stop."

Luckily, it never came to that. Slatalla had managed to saturate the area with cops. If the Bandidos had shown up—and wisely, for whatever reason, they decided not to—they would not have made it close to the Eagle Lodge. And once again, the ATF had turned a near disaster into a bonus. The Solo Angeles' apparent willingness to kill and even die for the cause only served to heighten their status in the Angels' eyes as all-out warriors: "Those guys were ready to go to war," the bikers spread the word. "Those guys are going to be members soon."

The Angels wanted them in fast; the ATF wanted them out just as fast. And the agents themselves were quickly running out of gas. Still, Dobyns, whose energy seemed as boundless as his determination, wanted one more play, what he called "the icing on the cake."

And what a play it would be: to convince the Hells Angels that the Bird and his gang had carried out the cold-blooded murder of a member of the hated Mongols.

The ruse had no major legal or evidence-gathering value against individual gang members, although Dobyns would get a gun from an HA member. The stated goal was broader: to air out the criminal intent of the Hells Angels and show them as the warring, organized crime syndicate they were, men who celebrate and reward assassinations.

Dobyns and his crew also had an unofficial, unstated objective: if they could make this scheme fly, perhaps it would be even harder for the bosses to pull down the operation.

The Hells Angels had made no secret of their policy toward the Mongols. "If I meet a fuckin' Mongol, how am I supposed to handle that?" Dobyns would ask regularly.

"You see a Mongol, your responsibility is to kill him," he was told in no uncertain terms. "You gotta kill him and you gotta get away."

Dobyns filed away those instructions; now he figured he could use them. He told the Hells Angels there was a troublesome Mongol down in Mexico: "One, he's bad-mouthing the Angels, and I don't stand for that. Two, he's in Mexico—in my territory, where I got juice. Now I want to go down and take his ass out."

The Solo Angeles told the bikers they were first sending Pops down as a scout; once he found the target, Bird and Timmy would join him for the kill. The story had the added advantage of easing Pops out of the picture as Black Biscuit was supposed to be winding down. As the only non–police officer in the Solo Angeles undercover team, the informant was burning out even faster than the cops. "He was not prepared physically and mentally for the amount of stress and the pace we were running," Dobyns says. The ruse would be a good way to cover his exit.

Dobyns approached Joby Walters for a throwaway gun: "I need to smoke this dude and leave something down there," Dobyns said, and the Skull Valley member quickly came up with a pistol.

The other chapter members gathered to say farewell to their Solo Angeles comrades, hugging them and giving words of encouragement. "Come home safe and don't get hurt."

"It's like I'm being sent off to war," Dobyns says.

In reality, he and Timmy got a few days of well-earned vacation in Tucson while the Hells Angels thought they were Mongol-hunting in Mexico. Still, as prospects they were supposed to check in with their full-patch sponsors every day. They made the requisite calls, but one day they phoned at 3 A.M., knowing they were going to get voice mail only.

"Hey, it's Bird. We had a problem down here. Pops is gone. The Mongols . . ." he left the sentence unfinished. "I'll talk to you when I can talk to you."

That had the desired effect of unsettling the bikers, letting their imaginations run wild. They started contacting JJ.

"Hey, what's happening? Have you heard from them?" they asked.

"Man, I don't know. You're scaring me," came her rehearsed reply.

A few more days slipped by with still no word from Mexico. At one point, the bikers called JJ when she was at a restaurant. No, she hadn't heard from Bird and the boys, she reported, but she was sure they were okay. Probably they were just waiting until it was safe to cross the border back into the U.S.

In fact, Jenna MaGuire could hardly keep a straight face. Sitting opposite her were Dobyns and Billy Long, making faces and trying to make her laugh. "We were all extremely giddy at that point," MaGuire says.

Finally, two days later, Bird reached the Angels and told them the story. "Okay, here's what's happening: Pops tried to take the Mongol on his own. He was trying to impress you guys—he wanted to be an HA so bad; he wanted to do this on his own. The dude smoked Pops. We got Pops's body. We went and found the guy, took his ass out and we buried him. We're trying to get back to the States. Be patient."

In reality, the agents were staging their perfect Mongol murder in a dry riverbed west of Phoenix. It was a sweltering 115 degrees. Long had recruited a colleague from the Phoenix homicide squad to assure authenticity. Another cop played the victim, dressed in a Mongol cut supplied by the ATF team in Los Angeles. They bound his hands and feet with duct tape and dumped him in a hole. They created wounds by spreading cow blood, some of it liquid, some so coagulated that it looked like bloody cottage cheese. They laid small pieces of cow lung on the skull, where the hair was matted with blood, making it appear as if there were deadly protrusions of brain matter. It was a little too realistic: in the blistering sun, the blood and guts smelled like rotten flesh. Then they took graphic digital pictures as souvenirs—and proof.

Once back at the Solo Angeles trailer in Prescott—fully wired with hidden cameras and tape recorders—they called the Hells Angels to say they had returned safely. Joby Walters rushed over, along with club president Teddy Toth, Bobby Reinstra—the victim of the "Mr. Big" scam in Vegas—and Rudy Jaime. Bird began by telling the story of how, enraged at the slaying of Pops, they had tracked down the Mongol. "I hit him in the head with my ball bat. We dragged him out to the desert. He was still alive, and Jimmy popped him in the head with the gun that Joby gave us."

"That was the best $200 I ever spent," Joby Walters said.

"We knew we had to bring some evidence, so we brought pictures," Bird continued, adding that they had cut off the Mongol's patch and FedExed it to JJ to avoid carrying the evidence of murder across the border.

Joby walked over to the couch and started opening the FedEx package, his back to the others.

"Wow!" is all that escaped his mouth.

"What is it?" Bobby Reinstra asked

"It's a Mongol cut," Joby replied with awe and held it up for all to see.

In the ritualized biker world, no one hugs a biker or touches his patch without permission. But the Hells Angels were so moved by the death of Pops—one of them actually shed tears—and the courage of the Solo Angeles that they embraced the undercover agents as comrades in war.

"We can take Pops's cut and hang it in the clubhouse," one of them said. "We can put JHAP—'Jesus hates a pussy'—under it, since that was your guy's motto."

"You did what it takes," club president Toth said. "Welcome, you're Hells Angels now."

Dobyns could hardly believe what the Hells Angels were saying. They expected the fake murder would advance them along the path to full membership. But they didn't expect the ruse would put them over the top.

"They're telling us we're members," Jay says. "There's no way we can end this now."

Jay "Bird" Dobyns, along with Billy "Timmy" Long, were on the doorstep of entering the Hells Angels' inner sanctum. A fortress that no police officers had ever penetrated. They were, in effect, already members.

Their Skull Valley mentors advised them that their prospecting days were over and all the other members would be told they were to be treated like full Angels. Joby even offered Timmy an extra Hells Angels patch that he had. Bobby Reinstra told Bird that the undercover leader could wear his cut while he went without until the official word came in. Both cops declined, insisting they wanted it done the right way.

"I came to the Hells Angels in the front door," Dobyns said. "I won't sneak in the back to get my cut. I'll walk in the front door for that too."

The Skull Valley bikers decided they would tell the story of the Solo Angeles' bold killing of the Mongol at the international biker run in early August in Laconia, New Hampshire, where the world council of the Hells Angels was expected to meet. They would get the formal blessing to patch over the Solo Angeles. Joby Walters had personally briefed Sonny Barger and reported to Dobyns that Barger was proud of them: it was as good as gold, he vowed.

"I had Hells Angels officers from other clubs telling me that when you get in I'd like you to come and work with us," Dobyns says. "So the other charters were still hunting us." There would have been no limits to where the undercover agents could have gone.

Dobyns was more convinced than ever that Black Biscuit had to keep going. But his managers were angry.

"You guys did this just to try to force our hand, just to keep the case alive," came back the dismissal.

"How can we not keep going?" Dobyns insisted. "We're in the position right now where we can really hurt these guys. How can you say we're done?"

"You know, I don't care if frickin' Sonny Barger is delivering to you a semi-tractor load of M-16s, this case is coming down on July 8," Dobyns remembers his managers saying.

There were many more "screaming, finger-pointing" arguments between the ATF agents. From management's point of view, it came down to numbers. With perhaps as many as two, three or four dozen defendants, the judicial juggling was already a monstrosity—how could they handle it if it was twice as big in six months? Black Biscuit had more than accomplished its original goals. Money was running out, and the costs of mounting a full-bore Hells Angels penetration would be prohibitive.

"So, yeah, at that point everybody was getting sick of everybody else," Jay says. "The cover team guys were sick of the undercovers, the undercovers were sick of the case agent, the case agent was sick of everybody and my family was sick of me."

Dobyns had been in his biker role as part of Black Biscuit for more than a year. Prior to that he had already spent a year undercover in Bullhead City. Going undercover now as a full-patch Hells Angel would add on at least another year or two. A four-to-five-year undercover stint was way too long for anybody's sanity.

Still, Dobyns felt that stopping then would have been like stopping a marathon at the twenty-mile mark: sure, you could console yourself with the fact that you had done something few people could accomplish, but why not go all the way once you've suffered so much to get that far? "You know it's going to be painful, it's going to suck, I'm going to hurt, I'm going to pay for it afterwards. But I'm going to run the six more miles that I need to finish it."

Jenna MaGuire, who admits to being "pretty frustrated" with the shutdown of the operation, also didn't buy the exhaustion argument: "We were the ones doing it, so we didn't understand this fatigue excuse." Still, she was more philosophical about pulling the plug: "In the end I told Jay everything happens for a reason: something bad could have happened if we continued."

MaGuire and Dobyns, though, were both good soldiers. "Up to the end, I was saying, 'We're making a mistake; this is fuckin' bullshit. We should not be knocking this down right now.'

I never gave up the fight until the very end," Dobyns says. But once it was clear, by late June of 2003, that nothing he could say or do would change the ATF's mind, Jay Dobyns did his job and obeyed his orders.

As the hot summer days rolled in across the Arizona desert, Sonny Barger was blissfully unaware that the Hells Angels were about to be hit not just by Black Biscuit but by three major police sweeps in the next six months. For the time being, the biker icon was too busy enjoying his ever-increasing international stardom. His second book, *Ridin' High, Livin' Free,* was coming out in paperback, with more "hell-raising motorcycle stories."

But the heat was about to come down on the Angels in a triple blow of arrests like his gang had not seen since the 1980s.

The first blow came on June 10 at 8:30 P.M. at the Hells Angels' stark, boldly red-and-white clubhouse in San Diego, or "Dago," as the bikers often called it. Not far from a Church of Christ, the temple to biker garishness stands on a busy corner of El Cajon Boulevard. A large American flag flutters on one side of the building; red gates flank the fortified front entrance. In the back, painted white flames lick the bottom portions of two large red gates. The austere white-brick walls surrounding the clubhouse have a small sign in the corner:

> Warning:
> The Surgeon General has determined that marking
> these walls will be dangerous to your health.
> HAMC DAGO

Needless to say, the white walls are spotless. But the walls or the warning sign didn't stop more than 150 officers from the DEA, the San Diego County sheriff's office, the San Diego police and the ATF from storming the clubhouse that June evening and arresting president Guy "Big Daddy" Castiglione along with sixteen other Hells Angels and associates. It was the successful conclusion of Operation Five Star, a case based primarily on wiretaps.

The bikers were charged with violations of the RICO Act and the Violent Crimes in Aid of Racketeering (VICAR) Act. Castiglione—often described as "one of the most feared members of the HA"—and other Hells Angels officers were singled out for conspiring since 1995 to murder members of their hated rivals, the Mongols. They also stood accused of extorting drug traffickers, robbing and assaulting people and running large-scale pot, cocaine and meth trafficking operations. Along with related arrests, the takedown put twenty of the twenty-eight known Hells Angels in San Diego County behind bars.

The next blow came just twenty-seven days later, in the early-morning hours of Tuesday, July 8. After all the months of risky undercover work, drug buys and gun deals, Black Biscuit was heading toward its climactic takedown. On that July day, hundreds of police officers swept across the state. In Phoenix, Tucson, Flagstaff, Prescott, Kingman and Bullhead City—all the towns where Dobyns and his Solo Angeles had hung out with the Angels—the cops knocked on doors and took away stunned, disbelieving bikers. The police also carted away 560 illegal weapons—everything from pipe bombs to sawed-off shotguns and machine guns—along with $50,000 in cash and drugs.

The raids were carried out without a shot being fired—with one exception. Mike Coffelt was pulling all-night guard duty at the Cave Creek clubhouse, a usually boring task foisted on prospects. He was about to get a nasty wake-up call. Shortly before 5 A.M. an armoured vehicle rumbled through the white gates. A blinding grenade burst through the windows. Coffelt rushed to the door and caught four bullets from a policewoman's rifle, but none of them proved fatal. While there were plenty of bikers Dobyns had come to despise and secretly would not have minded if they did something foolish enough to merit a harsh police response during the raids, Coffelt was one of the rare bikers he liked. "I did not want to see him get hurt. The moral of the story: don't answer the door with a gun in your hand when the SWAT team knocks."

Except that Coffelt's gun stayed in his hand, unfired. Police nevertheless charged him with assault, but a judge eventually ruled his gun-toting behaviour was "reasonable" considering that the assault team had waited just seconds after yelling "Police! Police!" to smash into the clubhouse.

In all, police nabbed more than thirty suspects that morning: the Hells Angels in Arizona had never seen anything like it. There were several arrests from Dobyns's early days undercover in Bullhead City, when he was running murder-for-hire ruses. At least four wives or girlfriends were jailed on various drug charges, including Dolly Denbesten, who had invited Dobyns and MaGuire to her wedding. There were two prospects from the Nomads club and a couple of associates from Tucson. Four full-patch members from the Nomads and Mesa faced gun and drugs charges.

The most serious offences were eventually rolled into a wide-ranging organized crime indictment against sixteen Hells Angels, including three chapter presidents. Slatalla's infiltrators had done serious damage to several charters. They arrested four from Skull Valley, the club for which Dobyns and his crew had been prospecting, three from Mesa and Tucson and a couple of patches from both the Nomads and Phoenix chapters. Escaping unscathed was Barger's Cave Creek chapter and other chapters, such as Flagstaff, with which Dobyns and his team had had too little contact.

Bob Johnston, the president of the Mesa chapter who more than anyone had vouched for Dobyns and his Solo Angeles gang, was charged with threatening undercover informant Rudy Kramer and for conspiracy to distribute methamphetamines and marijuana.

George "Joby" Walters, another early booster of the Solo Angeles, was accused of conspiracy to murder a Mongol and for giving Dobyns a gun when the Solo Angeles staged their fake murder. Walters also faced another conspiracy-to-murder charge for recruiting Dobyns and the undercover team to prepare for the shootout against the Bandidos in Vegas. Joining him in that charge were Skull Valley club president Teddy Toth and Bobby Reinstra, who, according to the ATF, was eager for Dobyns to cut him in on some of his mob action with "Mr. Big."

In Tucson chapter president Craig Kelly—among the first to meet and deal with Dobyns and Carlos Canino—faced an assault charge and three gun charges; Douglas Dam, another early contact for the Solo Angeles, faced gang and racketeering conspiracy charges. Robert McKay, the tattoo shop owner who was so eager to join Dobyns's Mafia enforcement and debt-collecting ruses, was hit with three assault charges. In one case, according to police, a former biker had a falling-out with the HA over a drug debt and was summoned to Mac's tattoo parlour, where he was badly beaten; they allege McKay would not stop beating the victim with his fists and a flashlight until the officers drew their weapons on him.

Drug charges were also thrown at Cal Schaefer, as well as Donald "Smitty" Smith (who had tried to recruit Jenna MaGuire for wet T-shirt contests), Dennis Denbesten (who had invited the undercover cops to his wedding) and Rudy Jaime.

All the charges still had to be proved in court. And the ATF would soon find that laying charges against the bikers was one thing; keeping a complicated conspiracy case from falling apart before it got to trial was quite another.

"The Hells Angels arrested by ATF today don't contribute to Toys for Tots," she said. "These are the guys who contribute to firearms and drug trafficking."

The bikers could only cringe. And they had no idea that in less than six months the ATF would hit them even harder one more time.

Sonny Barger was not among those arrested in the July raids. He was doubtless relieved that the Black Biscuit infiltration had been stopped before the ATF agents could get close enough to many of the senior leaders of the club across the country.

Still, the statistics alone were staggering: forty-two search warrants; more than five hundred undercover operations involving over a thousand suspect contacts; sixteen hundred pieces of evidence; and hundreds of guns seized. Dobyns alone had had personal contact with more than three hundred HA members from the U.S. and Europe.

All the usually loquacious Barger could summon were a few bitter words against the tactics used by law enforcement to ensnare his fellow Angels: "It's too bad they get away with what they're doing."

Privately, Barger was bitter that his members had let themselves be hoodwinked by the cops. According to what some biker sources later told police, Barger told bikers itching for revenge, "They got us fair and square. Leave them alone. We need to re-evaluate how we prospect members."

Indeed, the comments the ATF collected from the Arizona Angels they arrested ranged from incredulity to admiration for a wily enemy.

"You're fucking kidding me—that chick JJ was a fucking cop too?" said one astonished biker.

"It took some really big balls to come in on the Hells Angels," said another. "People have died for less."

In the immediate aftermath of the July arrests, more bikers fell, largely because of their own arrogance and bullying. Furious at the sweep, the bikers orchestrated a series of threatening phone calls and threats against the ATF, especially case manager Joe Slatalla, whose name was on the affidavit. The cops responded with a three-for-one policy: for every one of our agents you threaten, we will arrest three of your thugs. Among those nabbed was Robert "Chico" Mora, the fearful Phoenix patch member who came so close to unmasking undercover cops. Chico was eventually convicted of being a felon in possession of body armour.

For their safety, the undercover officers had been whisked away just prior to the arrests. Billy Long and his family were removed from Phoenix; Jay Dobyns and his wife and two children got a vacation on a beach for a month far away from their Tucson home. Jenna MaGuire was already back home in San Diego. She was going to take some vacation time, but her superiors stepped in to fly her home to visit her parents back east and gave her several weeks of administrative leave.

Joe Slatalla, who had dreamed up the scheme at the start and steered it to its conclusion, realized its success could never be repeated: "We sent guys out there wearing patches of a legit club and when they see that patch, their defences go down. It won't happen again."

Slatalla's team had done what police had failed to do in fifty-five years: infiltrate deep inside the HA circle. "The most dangerous and difficult outlaw motorcycle gang penetration ever, bar none," says Jay Dobyns. "It will be surpassed. But for now, it's the mark that others are striving for." Still, he still couldn't shake the nagging feeling that he could have done more. He thought the ATF had shortchanged itself. The Angels agreed.

"Thanks for quitting the investigation when you did," said one arrested Angel. "Can you imagine how bad you guys would have nailed us if you'd kept going?"

John Ciccone, the ATF case agent who had run Billy Queen as a full-patch member deep inside the Mongols, understood the reasons why ATF managers shut down Black Biscuit, but he could also see the big advantage of having a cop as a member inside and not just as a prospect on the outside. "The thing that you missed out on was being able to record all the meetings and the one-on-one conversations between patch and patch. You missed all that."

"That was a once-in-a-lifetime opportunity. You're not going to get that shot again."

After living the biker life for so long, the ATF agents faced the daunting challenge of re-entry into their normal lives. Billy Long, the Phoenix policeman, had the easiest time of it: never far from his family, he had managed to see them regularly. For Jenna MaGuire, the transition was more difficult, because she had been so isolated during the entire operation.

"I didn't have anybody," she says. "My family didn't know what I was doing."

Not wanting to worry her parents—and initially expecting her Arizona assignment to last only a couple of months—she had told them only that she was on "surveillance detail" out of town. When she flew home over the summer and told them the truth of her "biker chick" days with the world's most notorious motor-cycle gang they were understandably unnerved, though her mother could not help exhibiting a little "way to go, girl" parental pride.

For Jay Dobyns, who had plunged the deepest into the dark world of biker crime, the climb back to normalcy was the hardest. He talked to his old buddy Chris Bayless from Chicago, who reminded Dobyns of one his own bleakest moments. Pulling an all-nighter, Bayless had just had a gun put to his head by a biker he charitably describes as "a total asshole" at one of the clubhouses. "Going home next morning, I was just friggin' whipped," he says. But as soon as he opened the door, his wife complained about his long absences and told him they were out of bread.

"I just wanted to tell her I just had a gun put to my head. But other people don't really care about those kinds of problems. So I went and got the bread."

Dobyns took his friend's advice and tried his best to become a father and husband again. He mowed the lawn, played with the kids, talked with his wife, Gwen. "But I was still so wound up," Dobyns admits, the abrupt end to Black Biscuit still eating away at him. "I still couldn't get it out of my head. I just couldn't stop thinking about it. I was a mess at that point."

He and his daughter, Dale, fessed up and told Gwen about Dale's close encounter with Hells Angel Robert McKay—not the kind of news a mother wants to hear.

"Excuse me?" she said in shock. "I wanted to pound him out," she recalls with a nervous laugh.

"I did some serious, serious damage to my family, and I don't feel one bit good about that," Dobyns says. "They're still trying to recover from what happened. I lost their confidence. My son—I can't get him off me. When I get into a car to go the airport, he thinks Dad's going to go away for two more years.

"It eats families alive."

Once his family returned to Tucson from their security-imposed vacation, Dobyns knew they were still not safe from the bikers. "They know where I live," he says. A simple Google search would turn up details of his football career and biography. In Arizona, ATF agents are not classified as police officers, so they cannot hide their personal information from the public record. Anyone could access Dobyns's name and housing data from county tax records.

"So I was resting on the fact that these guys are going to hurt themselves worse by coming after a cop than they would by leaving me alone."

Still, there were worrisome signs not all bikers were so cool-headed. On a secure section of their Web site, the Hells Angels had posted prominent pictures of "The Arizona Rats"—Dobyns as "Bird," Timmy, JJ and Pops. The email messages posted gave a tenor of the hatred: "Hope all is well. Snitches are a dying breed. Get it?"

As angry as the bikers were toward Dobyns and his infiltrators, there were a lot more disruptions to come. The ATF had held off many of its arrests in the July 2003 sweep until John Ciccone's work with full-patch biker Mike Kramer had run its course. By August of that summer, Mike Kramer had formally completed his undercover snitching for the ATF. On November 10, 2003, he pleaded guilty to the murder of Cynthia Garcia. The ATF's star Confidential Informant 784000–376 got the sweetheart deal of a lifetime: five years of probation. No time in jail.

It was the ultimate, distasteful trade-off police felt they occasionally had to make in the dirty underworld of bikers. Sometimes the gamble works, sometimes it blows up in the faces of the cops and prosecutors. No one doubted Kramer had been involved in a heinous crime; the question was: could he deliver? On the morning of December 3, 2003, the ATF launched the widest series of coordinated attacks against the gang in law enforcement history. Across five states—Alaska, Nevada, California, Washington and Arizona—the ATF led raids against Hells Angels clubhouses and homes. By the time the sweep was over, fifty-five Hells Angels and their associates were behind bars—at least until they made bail. The vast majority of them were caught up directly in the Laughlin fallout: forty-two defendants were charged with nine counts of violence and racketeering.

Among those charged were three of the Arizona Angels who, according to the ATF affidavits, had boasted of their role in the Laughlin shootout directly to the undercover ATF agents in Black Biscuit: Donald "Smitty" Smith, the Nomad who was the first to befriend the undercover cops and had said the Mongols "ran from the casino like little girls" at Laughlin; George "Joby" Walters, who the police say had told them he was considering fleeing to Mexico to escape prosecution; and Cal Schaefer, who had allegedly told the undercover cops he "was sure he would receive some prison time."

Included in the massive sweep around Laughlin were two other arrests on the other important front of Mike Kramer's work for the ATF: nailing the men accused of Cynthia Garcia's murder. In the long list of indictments, those were the only two names that mattered for Chuck Schoville, the Tempe gang cop for whom the Garcia murder had become a personal passion. Paul Eischeid and Kevin Augustiniak faced one count for kidnapping Garcia and another for her murder; both acts were charged as racketeering crimes committed for the purpose of "maintaining or increasing" their stature within the Hells Angels. Chuck Schoville had been waiting for this moment for two years.

When the City of Mesa Police Department's Tactical Team stormed the clubhouse of the Mesa chapter of the Hells Angels at 7 A.M. as part of the nationwide raids on December 3, it was hard for Schoville not to think of the horror Garcia had suffered there on that October night two years earlier.

Simultaneously, police knocked on the door of Paul Eischeid's home on North Saint Elias in Mesa. The stockbroker biker was calm and professional, although inside his house police seized the kind of arsenal most commercial workers don't have: a Ruger .22-calibre semi-automatic pistol, a Mossberg 12-gauge pump-action shotgun, a Glock pistol, a Bushmaster semi-automatic rifle, sixteen hundred rounds of ammunition, a bulletproof vest, numerous knives and the Hells Angels trademark ballpeen hammer.

Chuck Schoville gave the Garcia family the good news that their mother's suspected killers had been arrested. "We were thrilled," said Olivia, one of Cynthia's daughters. "I was so glad. Finally some justice."

For Schoville, who had waited nervously for so long for the ATF to move in on the killers, there was a sense of fulfilment. "Of the whole case, that was the most rewarding to me. Being able to go to the family and say, 'You know what? It's done.'"

Or so he thought.

When Paul Eischeid appeared at his bail hearing shortly after his arrest, his lawyer argued that his client had "no significant criminal history" except for a dismissed misdemeanour charge back in October 2000. As a stockbroker for the Security Trust Company, he was pulling down $3,000 a month and had mortgages on two homes totalling $300,000. "The government has a burden to show Paul Eischeid is a flight risk," the lawyer concluded.

The problem was that the government's hands were tied. The ATF and the prosecutors were not yet willing to divulge all the secrets Mike Kramer had collected against Eischeid: it was too early in the judicial game, too risky for Kramer and the cases against the other Angels. So the judge granted Eischeid bail, and Cynthia Garcia's accused murderer was once again a free man.

A few months later, in the early summer, Schoville was driving down the freeway when he caught sight of a massive Harley in his rear-view mirror. He knew instantly it was Eischeid. Emblazoned on the front was the number "666"—the sign for the devil and a favourite symbol for the Hells Angel.

"There's something not right about this," he muttered, finding it hard to believe a Hells Angels accused of a brutal murder was riding around, carefree.

Sure enough, on July 28, 2004, Eischeid threw a party at the swank home he had bought not more than five miles from the desert road where Cynthia Garcia had been murdered. It was a going-away party. The next day, he broke the ankle bracelet he was forced to wear as a condition of his release and fled. When Olivia Garcia saw on the news later that night that one of her mother's accused killers had fled, she was aghast. "It's just been so frustrating for all of us."

In the days that followed, the ATF issued its usual bulletin for an "armed and dangerous" man on the run. Eischeid got his fifteen minutes of criminal fame when he was featured on the tabloid TV show *America's Most Wanted*. He had an easy way to evade the law: the Hells Angels had a worldwide network of chapters. All eager to lend a hand to a brother in need.

The summer should have been one of relative calm and rest for Jay Dobyns. Over the past year, he had been busy on new undercover assignments. So far, he had successfully beaten off ATF pressure to move with his family out of state. The agency often relocated operatives after an operation that gained them too much notoriety.

The tranquility would not last.

Late at night on August 30, Dobyns was heading to the Club Congress, a downtown Tucson establishment known to have its share of rough characters, with his friend and fellow ATF agent Darrin Kozlowski. Koz, who had infiltrated the Vagos in California and the Warlocks in the Northeast, had already lent Dobyns a hand in Laughlin back in 2000. The two agents were working on a guns-and-drugs case and were headed to the bar to see if they could catch some more action.

Once inside the bar, scoping out the crowd, Koz suddenly gave Dobyns a flip of the arm.

"Out the corner of my eye, I see a full patch, so I nudge Jay," Koz recalls. It was Robert "Mac" McKay, the tattoo artist who had done some work on Dobyns's arms, bumped into his daughter and fallen victim to one of his fake debt collection ruses. The details of what happened next are based on police accounts and a prosecution motion filed before a judge. McKay has yet to tell his version of events in court.

"What do you want to do, Jay?" Koz asked his partner.

"I'm not leaving," Dobyns said. "I'm not going to let this guy bug me."

Dobyns turned his head again to see McKay standing right next to him.

"Mac, we meet again," the ATF agent said.

McKay was clearly steaming for a fight: "So you're a U of A football star. We've been checking on you."

"Mac, I bet you there are all kinds of things you're finding out about me that you didn't know before," Dobyns said.

"What name are you going by these days?" McKay asked.

"I have thousands of names I use."

McKay pointed to the cigarette in Dobyns's hand. "Your smoking makes you look nervous."

"Nervous?" Dobyns shot back. "Mac, you know what? I wasn't nervous when I was under on you guys. Why would I be nervous now?"

"You're going to spend the rest of your life nervous. You're going to spend the rest of your life on the run from us," the biker warned. "You're a marked man."

McKay then turned to the scruffy-looking Kozlowski, whom he assumed was another legitimate biker being scammed by Dobyns. He asked Koz if he knew what Dobyns did for a living. Koz shrugged and said no.

"You should check him out before you spend any more time with him," McKay warned.

McKay then slipped away. Dobyns could see him moving to different corners in the bar, eyeballing him all the time and talking on his cellphone.

"Maybe he's rallying up the boys," Koz said.

"Koz, you're going to have to trust me on this one," Jay said. "If he puts out an emergency call, there's no way these guys can get their shit together and come here and do anything about it."

"No one knows what I look like, Jay," Koz insisted. "Let me just poke my head outside."

As soon as Koz left, though, an even angrier McKay stormed up to Dobyns and pointed to his dark sunglasses. "Take off those fuckin' glasses and look me in the eye like a man!"

"You think I'm fucking afraid of you?" Dobyns retorted, pulling his shades up. "I didn't have a problem looking you in the eye when I was a part of the club, and I surely don't have a problem with it now."

"You're a punk snitch!"

"If that's the case, then the Hells Angels made a punk snitch a member of their club," Dobyns retorted. "What's worse for you is that you tried to get me to be a part of your chapter. You recruited me to Tucson. I was a Hells Angel, and you helped me get in."

"That's bullshit," the biker insisted.

"Is it, Mac?" Dobyns replied. "Remember, everything you ever said to me was recorded. You wanted me to be a Hells Angel, you wanted to sponsor me in Tucson, you did my ink [tattoos]. I got over on you and you're embarrassed about it."

It was too much for the two-hundred-pound biker. McKay stepped directly nose-to-nose with Dobyns and yelled, "I think you're a fucking piece of shit! You're a fuckin' asshole!"

"Well, you know what, dude? You're entitled to your opinion, man. But I ain't going anywhere, I ain't running."

By this time, Koz had returned and had inched his way behind the fuming biker. "If this guy is going to get stupid, I'm going to crack it right over his head," he remembers thinking.

It looked as if Koz might indeed have to act. McKay jacked up the pitch: "You scared?"

"Of you? Are you kidding me?" Dobyns snickered. "You guys are used to scaring people and making them run. That ain't happening here."

"You need to watch yourself," the Hells Angel responded. "This is dangerous shit."

"You need to step off right now," Dobyns said, the professional cop in him winning over his gut desire to pound the crap out of a gang member. "This is not personal to me, but you're making it personal. Step off right now or this is going to turn out real bad for you."

It was the turning point when the confrontation could have gone either way. McKay walked away, but not before he turned over his shoulder to bellow one final threat: "You're going to get hurt!"

McKay left the bar at 1:15 A.M.; the two ATF agents left ten minutes later.

The next day, Dobyns called Joe Slatalla. "If we put this out, I'm going to get moved," Dobyns said, dreading the upheaval for his family. "I'm not going to be able to survive this one."

"Hey, look," Slats pointed out, "when he tells you that they know where you live, that you're going to get hurt, that they know you were a football star, they've done their research into you and they probably do have the intention of hurting you. It was a threat and it has to be reported."

The incident was duly filed. The next day, police arrested Robert McKay in his tattoo shop. He originally denied he had made any threats, insisting it was his word against Dobyns's—until Slatalla told him, to his horror, that there was a second witness: the "biker" standing next to Dobyns was a cop as well. McKay had been fooled one last time.

His five minutes of rage cost him dearly. Out on bail under the original Black Biscuit gang charges, McKay now found himself charged with a violent racketeering offence: he was accused of issuing the threats not as a personal warning but under the name of the Hells Angels.

But for Jay Dobyns and his family there were more immediate consequences.

The ATF gave Dobyns no choice: he and his family had to move. For the children, it meant leaving their schools and their lifelong friends. For Gwen, it meant abandoning the high-end clients she had developed for her interior design work that was becoming the talk of the town. For Jay Dobyns, it meant leaving the ranch house he had so lovingly built by himself, brick by brick. It was a striking hacienda on an isolated road outside Tucson, with a curved stone driveway that led to fountains and cactuses. Behind it, the desert seemed to stretch for miles.

Now he would have to abandon it.

"My family loves it here," Dobyns says. "Again, my family is going to take the hit for what I do for a living. My family is going to pay the price for it."

And their own private hell was not over yet.

PART VI

"HELLS ANGELS FOREVER"

SEVENTEEN

The Long Road to Justice

——

Let's not kid ourselves. If we're going to make out the Hells Angels to be a criminal organization, we better have our powder dry.
—RCMP INSP. BOB PAULSON

At the offices of the Arizona district attorney on the twelfth floor of a downtown Phoenix skyscraper, they want you to know they mean business. On the wall greeting visitors are fourteen pictures of "victims who died as a direct result of violent crime" at the hands of various assailants who have since been brought to justice. One is a sixty-five-year-old grandmother; three others are just nine years old.

Cynthia Garcia's picture is not up there. And probably never will be. Federal prosecutors had wanted to convict members of the Hells Angels of Arizona for her murder as part of a broad racketeering case, but it was not to be.

Pity Sonny Barger. The ailing Hells Angel patriarch could not have picked a worse location to set up his new home base when he moved to Arizona in the late 1990s. Bad enough that he picked the city and state where Joe Slatalla and the ATF had decided to launch one of its major undercover operations against the bikers. Worse still, Barger had inadvertently chosen the only state in the country where one of the top prosecutors was a biker expert and longtime Angel foe.

Pat Schneider is the assistant U.S. district attorney (AUSA) in Phoenix. He had tangled with the Dirty Dozen, the Angels'

421

predecessors in Arizona. He had sent several Arizona Angels away to prison for a major drug importation scheme from South Africa. It was Schneider who handled some of the initial negotiations with the ATF's super snitch Mike Kramer.

Schneider also happens to be one of the few non–police officers who is a member of a little-known but effective group called the International Outlaw Motorcycle Gang Investigators Association (IOMGIA). In fact, he had been IOMGIA's president for the past four years. IOMGIA is a loose network of biker cops from across the United States, Canada and as far away as Europe and Australia. Hundreds of officers meet once a year, discreetly and with little publicity, to exchange intelligence, contacts and experience. More important, throughout the year IOMGIA gives cops the ability to pick up the phone and speak to a frontline investigator with expertise on any biker gang anywhere.

"Biker gangs like the Hells Angels are nothing more than multinational corporations—and they're certainly interested in pursuing business opportunities around the world," Schneider explains. "They're globally aware. And we have got to be globally aware too."

That coordination and intelligence-sharing is vital because, as any cop will tell you, knowing who did a crime is one thing; proving it in court is a whole other matter. When it comes to the Hells Angels, closing the gap between knowledge and legal proof is that much harder. The Hells Angels have always been well fortified behind a wall of silence.

"Anybody can go out and arrest people and indict someone, but my hat's off to you if you can put someone in jail," says Ted Baltas, the recently retired ATF veteran who had worked with the FBI and the informant Tony Tait back in the 1980s to send Sonny Barger to a federal prison for several years. "When you get involved in a more elaborate, professional organization like the Hells Angels, it's much harder. They have the money and the wherewithal, and they understand how we work."

In the United States—as well as Canada, Australia and Europe—police and prosecutors were realizing they were going to have to come up with innovative ways to put the bikers behind bars. And success might always be partial at best.

By late 2005 four major operations in the American Southwest were winding their way through the U.S. courts: the drug-and-murder conspiracy case against the San Diego chapter, the Laughlin casino shootings, the Black Biscuit busts in Arizona and the Cynthia Garcia murder investigation.

The San Diego case—Operation Five Star, as it was code-named—was in many ways the easiest because it was largely a straight-up wiretap investigation. And it didn't take long for most of the arrested members and associates of the powerful Dago chapter to fold. By August 2005, all but two of the eleven bikers nabbed back in June 2003 had pleaded guilty to an array of charges involving conspiracy to commit murder, drug trafficking and extortion. What was remarkable was that several had also pleaded guilty to gang enhancement charges—a surprising reversal of the strict policy of the Hells Angels forbidding their jailed comrades to ever plead to any racketeering or organized crime charges. In other words, take the fall but never blame the club.

Then on September 22, Guy Castiglione caved in. The president of the San Diego chapter of the Hells Angels pleaded guilty to racketeering charges, admitting that he had conspired to distribute methamphetamine and kill members of the Mongols. Castiglione, sentenced to six years, tried to weasel out of the fact he was in effect confessing to being part of criminal gang by telling the judge, "I was its president, but I joined [the conspiracy] as an individual." And the wily chapter president was able to negotiate careful wording in his plea agreement so that the name "Hells Angels" did not appear. But the damage to the cherished image of a biker gang that was not a criminal enterprise had been done.

"It was significant because the Hells Angels hate to admit they are a criminal organization," says the ATF's John Ciccone. Ciccone was hoping the San Diego pleas might set a precedent and open the floodgates to similar admissions in his massive Laughlin case. But it did not happen. By the end of 2005, the Hells Angels were hanging tough. So the federal authorities struck back, adding two more accused bikers to the casino conspiracy—bringing the total to forty-four full-patch defendants from California, Arizona, Nevada, Washington and Alaska. The government also laid additional charges for attempted murder and using firearms to commit violence. Each defendant was charged with 19 counts under the Violent Crimes in Aid of Racketeering Act. That was the clincher: the accusation that the bikers carried out the shootings, stabbings and beatings "in aid of racketeering" as part of a "highly organized criminal enterprise"—the dreaded organized crime charges that the Angels feared so much.

If everyone was convicted of all charges, the bikers would go away for 136 years. But that was unlikely. In size and complexity, the federal Laughlin trials—set to start in early 2006—would be extremely challenging. The Nevada Supreme Court had already suspended the separate state prosecution against seven Hells Angels, agreeing with defence motions that there were "major flaws" in the indictments against them. While the ATF's federal prosecution was a distinct legal procedure, the setback at the state level did not bode well.

At the state level, the Angels had invoked the self-defence argument—they were just protecting themselves against the Mongols. For the federal trials, the bikers were also likely to turn the tables and put the cops and their informants—with Mike Kramer front and centre—on the hot seat. In pre-trial motions, defence lawyers charged that at Laughlin the police and their undercover agents were "present and aware that this attack was brewing and imminent and did nothing to defuse it." In fact, some HA leaders such as George Christie were going further, suggesting that the shootings had been sparked by police provocateurs. It was a ludicrous charge, but Ciccone and his star infiltrator, Mike Kramer, were going to have their hands full—especially since the prosecution of the forty-four bikers was to be broken up into at least six separate trials, one after the other.

Meanwhile, in Arizona, there were mounting legal headaches in the trials of the sixteen Hells Angels and their associates who had been snared in the ATF's Black Biscuit undercover operation. A trial date kept getting pushed back, as the lawyers fought over what police files should be disclosed and whether all sixteen accused should be tried together. In the early fall of 2005, the judge assigned to the case issued a stinging rebuke to the prosecutors for dragging their heels on disclosure, blasting them for being "inaccurate, inconsistent and sometimes legally incorrect." A chastened government team admitted they had sought to bury the defense with piles of less relevant documents. They promised to be more forthright and speedy in releasing details of their case to the defense, but insisted they needed to protect government witnesses against the Hells Angels: "The targets are all members of an international crime organization with a well-known record of using violence and an equally well-known capability for gathering intelligence," the government brief said.

Finally, a firm court date was set for the end of April 2006—almost three years after the arrests. For their defence team, the bikers chose an array of lawyers ranging from the gruff to the gifted. Joe Abodeely is a portly former prosecutor turned criminal defence lawyer who has little patience for polite small talk. His client is Craig Kelly, the president of the Tucson chapter, who was one of the first to be targetted by Jay Dobyns's undercover attempts at weapons-buying. On Abodeely's cluttered bookshelves stands a white aerosol can with the label "Bullshit repellent." His office is filled with photos of his days as a Marine commander in Vietnam, and he spits out his arguments with the rat-a-tat-tat of a machine gun.

"Do I believe that there are badass bikers in the world? Of course there are," he bellows. "Do I know whether or not Craig Kelly is one of them? I don't know. Do I believe he's done shit in his life? Probably. Can I prove it? No. Do I give a fuck? No. Can they prove it? Probably not."

"Probably" wasn't good enough for Bob Johnston, the president of the Mesa chapter who was instrumental in accepting the Solo Angeles spies into the fold, only to find himself facing two counts of racketeering. So he turned to the experience of Brian

Russo, the self-assured lawyer who had ably defended Sonny Barger back in 2003 on the shaky gun possession charges by hammering away at the FBI's fumbling and by exposing his wife Beth Noel as an unreliable witness. Johnston no doubt hopes Russo can do the same legal handiwork for him. "My client didn't sell drugs, didn't sell guns. He's not accused of anything except being the president of the Hells Angel chapter of Mesa," Russo says, not untruthfully. There were no specific drug or weapons crimes levelled at Johnston—only that he was part of a criminal enterprise. "I don't like it when innocent people are charged simply because they wear a patch on their back. It's guilt by association."

Perhaps the defence lawyer with the biggest battle on her hands is Patricia Gitre, whose client, Kevin Augustiniak, faces the most serious charges of the Arizona defendants: the murder of Cynthia Garcia. Gitre, respected for her steely doggedness, knows her best defence was an offence against the snitch who had fingered her client—Michael Kramer.

"There is no question that Michael Kramer is a murderer," Gitre argued in one pre-trail motion. "His drug and alcohol use, violent conduct and ATF paid-informant status bears on his motive, credibility and reliability as the sole witness against Mr. Augustiniak."

In a brief telephone interview, Gitre is even more forceful against Kramer. "They gave him a licence to lie, cheat and steal. He did meth on a daily basis. He used a knife, he carried a gun. And all because he could," she says. "The guy got away with murder. That's what I find offensive." Gitre's tactic to focus her fire on Kramer made sense: Kramer's credibility as a star prosecution witness would be crucial not just against Augustiniak but against many of the defendants in the Laughlin case as well. Jurors often distrust informants, and it was far from clear that Kramer could get a jury to look beyond his unsavoury past and believe his snitching.

So there was more than passing interest from all sides when Kramer got to perform in a trial run, so to speak, at his first court appearance—the prosecution of former Hells Angels from the

San Fernando Valley chapter in California in the summer of 2004. Under the direction of ATF agent John Ciccone, Kramer had bought meth from Daniel Fabricant—a one-time partner and protégé of Ventura Hells Angel leader George Christie. Prosecutors and defence attorneys showed up from Arizona and Nevada to see if Kramer could pull it off.

At his debut performance in the witness box, Kramer came in for quite a beating. Fabricant's lawyer, Ellen Barry, pummelled Kramer with revelations that he had used some of the meth he was buying instead of handing all of it over to his ATF handler. She also charged that Kramer was often drunk and that he took part in vicious beatings. "It just happened. [I] didn't intentionally go against it," Kramer said about respecting his contract with the ATF, which ruled out any law-breaking. "[I] did [my] best to live by it except for beating the guy with a bat."

In the end, Barry couldn't break Kramer's credibility. "He's a lot slyer and way more devious than you'd expect going in," she admits. Kramer convinced the jurors that he was no angel—but he was no liar either. They found Fabricant guilty on all counts. (A repeat offender, he eventually was sentenced to life in prison with no chance of parole.) The bikers and their lawyers got the message—Kramer could do them serious damage. One of his potential targets apparently heard that message loud and clear: it was on the day after the verdict against Fabricant that Paul Eischeid, one of the accused murderers of Cynthia Garcia, chose to skip bail and went into hiding.

Then suddenly on February 17, 2006, the case imploded. Half of the bikers charged were given deals on lesser offences and none of them would face the most serious charge of racketeering, being part of a criminal enterprise. Where they could have faced life on the gang rap, none of the bikers would serve more than five years. Bob Johnston, who could have gone to jail for twenty years under the RICO charges, pleaded guilty to a minor charge of not telling authorities he knew about a meth transaction. "It's a victory," his lawyer, Brian Russo, said. "He was the alleged godfather of this great RICO conspiracy!" Teddy Toth, the president of the Skull

Valley chapter, copped to a plea of obstructing justice. Robert McKay was cleared of racketeering and assault charges, but pleaded guilty to a misdemeanor of intimidation for his barroom run-in with Jay Dobyns. Cal Schaefer had five counts dismissed but pleaded to a simple firearm possession, though he still faces charges in the Laughlin casino shooting. Dennis Denbesten and others also got reduced charges.

The one biker who did not escape was Kevin Augustiniak. His murder charges were simply transferred to the state level, where an experienced gang prosecutor would try him for the slaying of Cynthia Garcia—and announced he would seek the death penalty if he won a conviction.

Bob Johnston, who had spent so much time with the fake ATF bikers, complained bitterly to the *Arizona Republic* about the "abuse of power" by the police, but he also paid Dobyns and his team a compliment of sorts: "Those guys are damned good actors, I'll tell you that." And Johnston—the Mesa chapter president for several years—did something surprising: he quit the Hells Angels.

Still, the collapse of the federal racketeering case was embarrassing. The government tried to pass off the result as a "good thing" because eight of the defendants pleaded guilty but no one was fooled. The authorities gave no explanation, but insiders said in addition to the judge's harsh rulings against them on discovery issues, there was also turmoil between the ATF managers and the prosecutors over how the case should proceed. Specifically, they fought over thousands of pages of investigative reports that the ATF refused to turn over to the defence. "Slatalla and US attorney's office couldn't see eye to eye on anything," said one ATF source. "The bosses let it spin it out of control."

It was not the first or the last time a complicated biker investigation would be crippled by internal infighting. But this was not the way the ATF agents had wanted their work to end. Still, Jay Dobyns and his team had managed to inflict a lot of damage and disruption on the Arizona Hells Angels. Before Black Biscuit had begun, Sonny Barger had helped lead the Arizona Hells Angels to a tripling of their forces from forty-two members in 1997 to more than 120 by December 2001. But by 2006—three years after Dobyns and his team had infiltrated the bikers—the once impervious Angels had been cut in half, down to sixty-two. And even that number included a dozen behind bars, on the run or on parole without the right to associate with fellow club members.

The ATF perhaps had not won, but the Hells Angels were also the losers in the Arizona battle.

The legal battlefield is equally complicated north of the border. In Canada, police and prosecutors are hoping the country's anti-gang laws will give them more clout against the Hells Angels, which dominate the organized crime scene in a way not seen in most other countries. There were early indications that it was working.

Many of the Quebec Hells Angels had been sentenced to much longer jail terms, thanks to the original anti-gang law under which those convicted of gangsterism could face an additional fourteen years in prison—and even life if they are gang leaders. A revised, toughened version of the law widened the number of offences, but it still imposed a heavy burden on the Crown to prove a crime had been committed for the benefit or with the help of a criminal organization. The first test of the law came in January 2002, when two full-patch Hells Angels from the Woodbridge chapter in Ontario, Steven "Tiger" Lindsay and Raymond Bonner, were accused of trying to extort $75,000 from a businessman in a dispute over TV satellite equipment. The bikers, decked out in Hells Angel leather, first showed up at the man's house demanding their "fucking money" right away and frightened him so much that he stopped sleeping at home. A week later at a restaurant meeting, one of the bikers warned the victim, "If you toy with me, man, your days are numbered."

What the bikers didn't know was that the businessman had gone to the cops—and he was wearing a wire during the meeting. Authorities slapped extortion charges against the two Angels, but then in a bold move the Crown also decided to lay charges under the anti-gang law. In effect, it meant putting the Hells Angels as an organization on trial. Crown attorney Graeme Cameron, a sixteen-year veteran of the prosecutorial wars and deputy director of the criminal branch of the Crown law office, faced a triple challenge. He had to prove the two Hells Angels committed the alleged extortion. Then he had to convince the court that they committed the crime with or for the Hells Angels. To top it off, he had to prove that the biker club itself qualified as a criminal gang.

It was a gamble—a precedent-setting gang charge resting on the foundation of a minor extortion. At times that foundation looked exceedingly shaky, as the defence punched holes in the story of the only witness to the underlying crime, the victim of the extortion. On the substantive gang issue, the defence lawyers argued that branding an entire group as a criminal organization was an affront to civil liberties: "We would not have the nerve" to brand the Chinese or Italian communities as criminal because of the actions of few, they said. They conceded that the Quebec bikers had a bloody criminal history but insisted the Ontario chapters were peace-loving clubs devoted to charity events. Cameron countered with a lineup of biker cops and experts to show that the HA were a "homogeneous, unified organization in Canada" engaged in the lucrative business of drugs, loansharking and extortion.

After a six-month trial—most of it devoted to a debate on the history and actions of the HA—Ontario Superior Court judge Michelle Fuerst issued her historic decision on June 30, 2002. She not only found Lindsay and Bonner guilty of extortion but also ruled that their gang was indeed a criminal organization. "It simply defies common sense that a group so deeply involved with crimes in Quebec would have any interest in establishing benign counterparts in a neighbouring province," she wrote. Fuerst's ruling was significant because, in effect, she found that the Hells Angels constitutes a criminal organization not in Ontario alone but in Canada. Lindsay was eventually sentenced to four years on the extortion charge and an additional two years for gang affiliation; Bonner got two years for the main offence and an extra year for carrying it out as a Hells Angel. Both are appealing.

Prosecutor Graeme Cameron didn't have time to celebrate. He was surrounded by security guards and whisked out of court. A week earlier, a dummy pipe bomb—filled with sand instead of explosives—had been found beneath his car in the underground parking lot of the attorney general's downtown Toronto office. Somebody apparently was trying to send him a message.

The Barrie court ruling sent the Hells Angels reeling. "They're licking wounds and they're trying to regroup," says "Ears," a one-time drug dealer with the gang who stays close to the bikers throughout Eastern Canada. "All the PR that they did is going down the tubes." The Hells Angels desperately tried to crank up their faltering publicity machine. The Web site of the Toronto chapter featured a picture of a tombstone with the words "Freedom died June 30, 2005." But the bikers, as usual, were being disingenuous. The ruling did not infringe on their freedom of association or anyone else's; it did not ban the HA or make it illegal to join the club. All it did was leave members of the Hells Angels open to longer prison terms—if and only if it could be proven that they committed specific crimes as part of the criminal organization. Fuerst's ruling made case law and might set a precedent, but each judge or jury would have to make up their own minds on a case-by-case basis. Each trial would have to start from scratch, proving each time that the HA acted as a criminal enterprise.

Out West, the RCMP's top biker cop in British Columbia, Bob Paulson, had an even bolder idea. Up to now, anti-gang charges had basically been tacked on—sometimes almost as an after-thought—following a successful criminal investigation. Paulson wanted to turn things around: start with the goal of proving or disproving the idea that the Hells Angels are a criminal organization, select a target chapter or chapters and gather the evidence to see where it leads. Paulson didn't want just experts testifying about why the HA were a criminal organization, as had happened in other gang trials. He wanted the evidence to speak for itself.

He knew the police and prosecutorial track record in B.C. had not been great. An investigation by *The Vancouver Sun* had revealed that more than thirty criminal prosecutions against the B.C. Hells Angels in the past decade had failed—a stunning 60 percent of the cases. It was a sorry contrast to Quebec, where prosecutors from a specially trained and staffed Organized Crime Bureau had sent more than half of the Angels to prison. Quebec has close to fifty Crown attorneys dedicated to organized crime. B.C.—until recently—had only one. In 2005 a dedicated provincial team was finally established.

On the federal side—where most of the serious drug busts end up—rank-and-file biker cops seldom hid their frustration at the lack of prosecutions under the anti-gang law. "I do appreciate where they are coming from," responds Martha Devlin, the deputy director of the Federal Prosecution Service in B.C. "But we also know the challenges of what the courts place on us: what is a reasonable conviction? What do we have? What don't we have? The fact that they are Hells Angels and they wear their patches doesn't make it a criminal organization."

Paulson agreed: "It's an eight-letter word and it starts with *E*," he says. "E-V-I-D-E-N-C-E. Let's not kid ourselves. If we're going to make out the Hells Angels to be a criminal organization, we better have our powder dry."

Paulson selected Vancouver's East End chapter as his target. It had at least two members who were on the RCMP's national priority list of top organized crime figures. "The East End chapter is the most senior, the most powerful," he says. "If we were successful in taking them out, that's where we would have the most impact on their operations."

The police nurtured a close friend of the chapter and turned him into an official police agent—an informant contracted like Mike Kramer in Arizona—to go in and spy on the Hells Angels under close police supervision. He was paid handsomely—$1 million, according to police sources. Project E-Pandora, as it was called, had a core investigative team of thirty-five people and a support network of as many as another thirty. As before, the RCMP pulled in resources from the Vancouver Police Department's anti-gang unit and Andy Richards's biker experts at the Combined Special Forces Unit. For twenty-three months they patiently gathered secret audio recordings, video surveillance and documentation of drug buys, assaults and extortion. But the main purpose was to gather evidence that the East End chapter was operating as a criminal enterprise. "We relied heavily on the structure and the nature of the organization to point out that it facilitates the commission of criminal offences," says Paulson.

On Friday, July 15, 2005, more than sixty officers armed with search warrants and battering rams smashed through all six of the reinforced steel doors at the East End chapter's clubhouse in a quiet residential neighbourhood of Vancouver. By the time the weekend was over, police had arrested nineteen people—including eight full-patch members—on drug trafficking, weapons and extortion charges. Over the course of the investigation, police seized an estimated $7 million worth of illegal goods, including 20 kilograms of cocaine, 20 kilograms of methamphetamine, 70 kilograms of marijuana, five handguns, eleven sticks of dynamite and two meth laboratories. Half of the coke—and several of the suspects—came from Kelowna, where the East End club had been expanding aggressively in the hope of setting up an independent chapter in the booming tourist town.

It was not only the largest crackdown against the once untouchable B.C. Angels in that province's history, it was also the biggest sweep against the Angels in Canada since Operation Springtime 2001 that hit the Quebec bikers. More important, this wasn't your typical drugs and weapons bust: seventeen of the B.C. bikers were also charged with committing their crimes as part of a criminal organization—the East End chapter. Three of them were charged with being a leader "who knowingly instructs" someone else to commit a gang offence, leaving them liable to imprisonment for life.

One of those was Ronaldo Lising, a full-patch member of the Nomads chapter in B.C. and one of only a few B.C. Angels to be convicted of a serious offence: at the time, he was out on the street, awaiting a Supreme Court appeal on his 2001 sentence for cocaine trafficking. (He lost.) Another was John Punko, who became a full-patch member of the Hells Angels after he was found guilty of threatening the Crown prosecutor who had convicted Lising.

Jonathan Sal Bryce, the twenty-four-year-old hangaround son of East End chapter president John Bryce, was charged with four counts of trafficking cocaine and one count of assault and extortion, plus two counts of committing offences "in association of a criminal organization"—his dad's club.

Bryce *père* was perhaps the most senior and powerful HA member in the province. He found out about his son's arrest as he stood near his clubhouse, watching the police raid. A police officer handed him the search warrant. He flipped through the pages, then stopped when he caught sight of his son's name. He turned white and walked away in silence.

Later, when he regained his composure in front of the media, he trotted out the oft-repeated line that if any Angel committed a crime it was a freelance fling: "Whatever they do, it's on their own— it's not to do with the organization itself," he said. Aside from the dubious coincidence of so many members and associates of his club getting snared in the same criminal enterprise, Bryce was not being entirely forthcoming. According to police sources, surveillance teams with E-Pandora spotted the older Bryce at one point in control of ten twenty-five-kilo barrels of methylamine—a main ingredient in speed as well as in the designer drug ecstasy. They also observed him getting the shipment to his son, who ultimately gave it to another man. Bryce Sr. was, according to police, making calls from phone booths and transacting the deal in a parking lot of a Home Depot—not the usual method of business for someone who runs a legitimate motorcycle shop. But it is not an offence to handle methylamine, since it can in theory be used for other, perfectly legal, things. (Bryce's son eventually pleaded guilty to trafficking cocaine, extortion and possession of the proceeds of crime.)

The arrests caused some serious damage to Bryce personally and to his beloved club. Predictably, B.C. Hells Angels spokesman Rick Ciarniello took to the radio phone-in airwaves again, proclaiming, "We are a bunch of nice guys and we like to ride motorcycles." But this time he was laughed at and berated by many listeners. The Hells Angels PR in B.C., as in Ontario, was finally wearing a little thin. All they could do was wait until November 2006, when they faced the grim prospect of watching more than a dozen of their members stand trial on gangsterism charges.

The bikers got a glimmer of hope in the dying days of 2005 when B.C. Supreme Court Justice Heather Holmes struck down an important provision of Canada's anti-gang law, ruling it was too broad and vague and therefore unconstitutional. Bob Paulson—whose tough work against the bikers had earned him a promotion to RCMP headquarters in Ottawa as director-general of major and organized crime intelligence—was stunned. "This is a real setback," he said.

Holmes did not trash the entire anti-gang law: she singled out one clause in the law which makes it a crime to be member of a criminal organization who instructs someone to commit an offence. Only a handful of the bikers were charged under this so-called "leadership" clause – but it did come with a possible life-time sentence. The federal justice department vowed it would appeal the ruling, but for the time being a key weapon in the fight against organized crime was hobbled.

Meanwhile, all across Canada, governments were trying to come up with less draconian, more innovative ways to curtail the bikers. The province of Manitoba, for example, as part of its Civil Remedies Against Organized Crime Act, bars the Hells Angels from wearing their colours, the winged Death Head or support gear anywhere liquor is sold. Several Hells Angels charged under the law, including bikers from Ontario ticketed while passing through town on their way to a national biker event in British Columbia, have vowed they will appeal on constitutional grounds all the way to the Supreme Court. Still, a store on one of Winnpeg's main streets run by the bikers that sold T-shirts and other HA gear has been forced to close, presumably because of lack of business. And in August 2005, the city of Kelowna—where the Angels expanded aggressively—asked the B.C. government to bring in similar legislation.

Manitoba and Ontario also have civil forfeiture laws on the books that allow police to seize the assets of any member of a criminal organization, whether convicted or not. The "reverse onus" of these laws obliges the suspect to prove the assets are not the proceeds of crime.

Municipalities are also getting into the act. When the Hells Angels opened up a new chapter in Hamilton and refurbished a clubhouse used by a former support club with steel doors, pillars and security cameras, the city began preparing a bunker-busting bylaw that bans "excessive" fortifications. Ontario municipalities such as Burlington and London already have such measures, as do many locales in Quebec that had to deal with fortress-like HA encampments built in the 1990s. Manitoba has a province-wide anti-bunker law.

In Quebec, the government moved to seize the Angels' homes, vehicles, real estate holdings and bank accounts, but their attempts were only partially successful. Nomad Normand Robitaille is serving a twenty-year jail sentence, lost $500,000 in cash and investments, including ownership of a strip club. But he was all smiles when the judge announced the seizure. His lawyer wife got to keep the family home, and the government couldn't touch several other real estate holdings held through front companies. Police have never found Robitaille's profits from the deals. The Angels were also gifted stock investors. Robitaille and fellow Nomad Gilles "Trooper" Mathieu, who is also serving a twenty-year sentence and who was making $2.7 million annually from drugs, invested money in a Montreal technology firm called GSI Technologies. In 2000 the company obtained a listing on the NASDAQ. The stock went from 25 cents to $3.81. Both Angels cashed in before the company collapsed following a Quebec security commission investigation. By that time Robitaille and Mathieu were in jail.

What's more, when it came to the Nomads' vast drug profits, the government was too late. The Angels' millions of narco dollars had already disappeared offshore and have never been found. Some of the Nomads could be out of prison by 2012. Their riches will be waiting for them. Well, some of their riches will be. A couple in the town of Trois-Rivières found $100,000 in cash hidden in the ceiling of the newly acquired home they were renovating. The home had belonged to the leader of the local chapter of the Hells Angels, Marc-André Hinse, who is still on the run from the police.

In Australia, too, they were trying to follow the money. Les Hoddy was among the most notorious bikies in Western Australia when police seized more than $500,000 of his assets, including vehicles and real estate. Founder of the powerful Gypsy Jokers in the glistening seaside city of Perth, he was one of the first bikers to feel the sting of the state's new asset seizure laws. And he didn't like it one bit.

"I know where you fuckers live!" the bearded Hoddy yelled at authorities as they towed away his cars and slapped liens on his home and businesses. "I'm going to dedicate the rest of my life to get even with you fuckers."

That was on July 3, 2001. And for the next four years he battled in court to get the law overturned and his assets returned. A major setback came in 2004, when he was charged with drug trafficking. Unfortunately for Hoddy, he won't be around to see the results of his court case. In January 2005, at the age of fifty-six, he dropped dead of a heart attack. Dying was a big mistake. According to the Criminal Property Confiscation Law, Hoddy had "absconded" and thereby forfeited any rights to the property. His children will get nothing.

Since the seizure of Hoddy's assets, police in Western Australia have confiscated more than $45 million from bikers and other drug dealers. Theirs are among the toughest asset seizure laws in the world. The state makes no apologies for its draconian reversal of the burden of proof that basically forces a defendant to prove he or she isn't a trafficker. Nor do police apologize for specifically targeting the bikies. "Doesn't matter if you inherited it or worked for it," Fred Gere, superintendent of the Western Australia Police Service, says. "You deal in drugs and you are going to lose everything."

Fact is, in most Western countries it is becoming increasingly difficult for criminals to hide their profits. The days when gangsters could flaunt their wealth without any legitimate source of income are gone, which almost takes the point out of high-profit crimes such as drug smuggling. Since the murder of retired police officer Don Hancock—in what bikies saw as revenge for the slaying of one of their own—Western Australia and several other Aussie states have reacted with new laws specifically aimed at disrupting and dismantling bikie gangs, which they claim have become the most powerful organized crime syndicates in the country. They have strengthened asset seizure laws and closed loopholes. In Victoria, traffickers can no longer hide behind rented cars or properties, which can be seized. The new laws allow police to seize goods of equivalent value or like for like. In other words, nothing is out of reach. In a show of blind justice, police have also seized the property of corrupt officers.

In June 2004 police targeted the forty-two-year-old leader of the Hells Angels in Melbourne, Stephen Rogers. They seized $3 million in assets, including six properties, bank accounts, trucks, cars, motorcycles and other items such as a model car set valued at $46,000. All these seizures followed the discovery of a mere 230 grams of amphetamines.

Some states have specifically targeted bikie businesses such as security companies. South Australian police claim about 80 percent of licensed nightclubs in Adelaide use security companies linked to bikies to guard the premises and supply doormen. Police claim the security agents oversee drug trafficking in the bars. So in 2005 the state imposed regulations that deny permits to security companies or nightclubs owned by or linked to bikies. Indeed, bikie gang warfare over control of the city's nightclubs has gripped Adelaide with various degrees of intensity since 2004. In one very public incident, shots were fired during a brawl between gang members in front of six hundred invited guests at a black-tie Dance Music Awards dinner at the Adelaide football stadium. It turned the dignified event into a barroom brawl. Several Hells Angels sitting at a table purchased by the Heaven nightclub began battling members of the Rebels, who were at a table paid for by the rival Rise nightclub. The evening festivities ended with panicked diners racing for exits when the bikies started hurling tables and chairs at each other and firing guns.

Authorities almost greet these territorial battles with a sigh of relief. In Australia and Europe, their worst fear is that the bikers will put aside their territorial differences and unite under one banner, much as they have done in Canada. "Imagine if tomorrow the Hells Angels amalgamated with the Bandidos [and] amalgamated with the Outlaws—what force you would have with those gangs together," Gere says. "I can tell you now in a very straight-forward manner that law enforcement would be up shit creek."

In fact, it's already happening. In Australia, by 2004, bikie gangs in three states had formed cross-border alliances. In May 350 police in three states raided speed labs run by a joint venture involving the Rebels, the Nomads, the Gypsy Jokers, the Finks, and the Hells Angels. Police claimed drugs seized were worth about $23 million. The bust showed that the business of drugs is changing. So many different gangs are involved that monopolies are hard to protect, making alliances a necessity. The Hells Angels remain the most powerful bikie gang in the country, even though they have fewer members than other gangs such as the Rebels or the Gyspy Jokers. Their assets remain considerable and include retirement homes, nightclubs and vacation resorts. According to the Australian Crime Commission's 2004 report on crime, bikie gangs are now the biggest underworld threat in the country.

Flush with cash, Aussie bikie gangs are expanding. Some have even gone abroad. On September 3, 2004, the Perth-based Coffin Cheaters established a chapter in Norway, patching over the Forbidden Few and becoming the first non-American club to go international. Norway is controlled by the Hells Angels and the Bandidos. Gere speculates that the Coffin Cheaters must have struck a deal for the right to establish in Norway. The Coffin Cheaters were supported in the patchover by an HA associate club in Norway called the Wizards. The new chapter will give them access to the vast ecstasy laboratories in Scandinavia. Already, Gere says, police have seen a spike in that market. But that's not the only expansion. The Australian Crime Commission reported that "out-law motorcycle gangs are establishing connections in Southeast Asia and are believed to be increasingly sourcing amphetamine-type stimulant precursors from Thailand and Vietnam."

The number of clandestine drug labs uncovered in Australia has risen steadily over the past few years at a rate of 19 percent a year. Two hundred and forty labs were detected in 2001. More powerful speed-based drugs are also on the market. A pure form of speed called "P," similar to crack cocaine and crystal meth, has become the drug of choice in New Zealand, police say. "These potent forms are increasingly being linked to psychotic and violent behaviour," the commission says.

In Europe, too, police have shown a renewed interest in aggressively pursuing the biker gangs. The Danish government, in particular, gave police new powers of search and seizure. To avoid intimidation by the bikers, witnesses can testify anonymously and even in disguise. Police also have the power to seize the assets of crime, putting the onus on the bikers to prove they bought the goods with legitimate funds—a tough task, since the vast majority of bikers have no jobs.

Danish police have also created a massive database on every known outlaw biker in the country, with thousands of names and an enormous amount of detail: not just addresses, phone numbers, assets, automobiles and the names of wives, mistresses and associates but also daily movements, frequent flyer numbers, credit card records, tax and criminal records, photos and voice samples. "We have the most comprehensive computer system in the world here," Jorgensen said.

As a result, the police succeeded in completely closing down the support clubs because so many members are in jail and those still out can no longer endure the constant pressure from the law. It's too risky. Danish police have solved every major crime committed in Denmark during the biker war—including the 1996 airport ambush and the Copenhagen rocket attack.

Using the combined efforts of the police, customs and tax departments, Danish authorities have also tracked down the bikers' assets, seizing millions of dollars in cash and property and emptying bank accounts. In 2004 they seized the Bandidos' European defence fund, which collects fifty euros a member each month, and charged European president Jim Tinndahn with more than $2 million in tax fraud.

Then, a year later, it was the turn of the Hells Angels in the Netherlands. On October 17, 2005, at two o'clock in the morning, the police invaded the sanctuary of Big Willem Boxtel, who had been lying low since his fallout with his fellow Angels, and arrested him. At the same time, more than a thousand officers fanned out across the country, raiding the Angels' six clubhouses as well as sixty-four of their homes and seizing an assortment of arms—guns, grenades, a grenade launcher, a flame thrower and a machine gun. The Hells Angels apparently knew the raid was coming. Three months later, police arrested one of their own national police investigators for allegedly tipping off the bikers. Still, by the time the autumn sun had risen over Holland, a total of forty-five Angels, including Harrie Stoeltie—who had replaced Big Willem as the most powerful Angel in Holland—and ten other members of the Amsterdam chapter were behind bars.

The mass arrests were a result of the investigation that had started more than two years earlier, with the murders of drug dealer Steve Chocolaad, Paul "The Butcher" de Vries and his two henchmen, and gathered momentum with information supplied by Angelo Diaz and another informant whose identity the police have refused to reveal. This informant was slated to testify in disguise in court that all major European criminal activities by the Hells Angels were overseen by the Amsterdam Angels, a claim Scandinavian police had been making for years. Police asserted in court documents that the Angels were being investigated for using violence and intimidation to drive out competition in the tattoo and hash-café business. Within two months police had released all forty-five Angels but not before charging eighteen of them, including Big Willem and Stoeltie, with assault, extortion, gun and drug trafficking, money laundering and participation in a criminal organization. Then during the night of January 29, 2006, police arrested Stoeltie's pal Willem Holleeder charging him with extortion of the murdered real estate developer Willem Endstra and uttering threats.

Meanwhile, the appeals case involving the twelve Nomads convicted for the 2004 murder of Paul de Vries was unraveling. The prosecution had appealed their six-year sentences (they wanted life sentences) while the bikers appealed their convictions. The case was taking so long that by the summer of 2006, a key prosecution witness had disappeared. The prosecutors had to admit they had no idea where he was and the case hung in the balance. As of this writing, police were still looking for him.

Still, the legacy of Big Willem remains strong.

With more than two hundred members in Holland, the Dutch Angels are still a potent force. Amsterdam's Angel Place seemed untouched by the storms that raged around it, a monument to the bikers' enduring presence in Europe.

Indeed, despite the constant pressure there are no signs that the global power of the Hells Angels has been reduced. Biker cops around the world have no illusions. The Hells Angels and other outlaw motorcycle gangs are not going to disappear. At best, the police can hope to destabilize or even cripple them, marginalize them, keep them constantly off balance.

"These guys are looking left and right now because they don't know who to talk to, who to trust," says John Ciccone of the ATF, who helped put dozens of bikers either on trial or behind bars, thanks to a constant stream of snitches and undercover cops. "That's all you can really do—you're not going to save the world, but you always keep one step ahead of them so they never know what's going to happen next."

The Hells Angels had shown before that they were more than able to roll with the punches. They had the ingenuity to build a worldwide organization that was as disciplined as it was flexible. Every member, every chapter, every national club has to follow the strict rules and protocol set down for those honoured few who carry the Death Head patch. Club officers meet regionally, nationally and internationally to set major policies, approve new clubs, and discipline—more often than not with violence—any troublemakers. At the same time the cellular structure gives each member and club freedom and autonomy. So the arrests in Arizona don't disrupt the expansion of the Hells Angels in the northeastern United States; the takedown of several chapters in Quebec doesn't stop the drug trade from flourishing in Western Canada; the fall of Big Willem in Amsterdam doesn't weaken the rest of the European Angels.

In fact, on a worldwide scale, the biker gangs worry much more about their criminal rivals than about the cops. While still dominant worldwide, only in a few countries like Canada are the Hells Angels unchallenged. In the American Southwest, the Mongols continue to nip at the HA heels and the Bandidos are seeking to expand. In the Northeast the Pagans are trying to encroach on HA turf. In Australia the bikies remain the number-one criminal organization. In Europe the biker truce is holding, but all eyes are on the lucrative new markets of the former Soviet republics and Eastern Europe.

"In the past ten years, they've been expanding like mad," says Pat Schneider, the Arizona prosecutor and past president of the International Outlaw Motorcycle Gang Investigators Association. Schenider takes solace from the fact that the explosion of biker gangs around the world also leaves them vulnerable. "As long as they're in this mad competition for who is going to rule the world, they're going to take risks. When you are so eager to expand so fast, you open yourself to possibility of infiltration."

And there will always be another bold cop like Jay Dobyns, or a desperate snitch like Mike Kramer, ready to step in and beat the bikers at their own dirty game.

But standing up to the bikers comes at a cost—as both cops like Jay Dobyns and innocent victims like Cynthia Garcia have learned. After uprooting his family from their Tucson home to a safer location, Dobyns hoped the worst of the threats from the Hells Angels was over. He was wrong.

By the fall of 2005, Dobyns got word he and his family would have to relocate yet again. The ATF learned that there were indications that the Hells Angels had put out a hit on Dobyns, and offered the contract to the Aryan Brotherhood. Dobyns had done undercover work against the white supremacist Aryans in the past—now his exploits against them and the bikers were coming back to haunt him and his family.

Meanwhile, in a noisy living room of a cramped house in a Hispanic neighbourhood of Mesa, Arizona, another family was trying to cope with the fallout of the Hells Angels' wrath. Two of the grandchildren of Cynthia Garcia scamper around, oblivious to the sorrow of the adults around them. Two of Garcia's oldest daughters, Bianca and Olivia, open a small wooden box that has a faded wedding picture of their mother on its lid. A jumble of family photos falls out, along with the remnants of Cynthia Garcia's last night alive—an empty cigarette box, a little black wallet with a few pennies inside and a broken makeup kit with blue eyeliner.

Four years after their mother's murder, the Garcia family is fed up with the waiting and the legal games. "It's just been a nightmare for us," Olivia says, admitting that she still shudders whenever she hears the roar of motorcycles in her neighbourhood, which is not far from the Mesa clubhouse. "I'm in fear. Every time I see bikers, it just haunts me. It gives me the creeps. It just brings back images of my mother's murder."

Bianca, for her part, vows that if and when Kevin Augustiniak or Paul Eischeid ever stands trial, she will be there, watching the bikers. "I want to see who they are," she says. "I want them to see who she was. She had family. She had people who cared for her."

EPILOGUE:

Return to Hollister

___

If you treat me good, I'll treat you better.
If you treat me bad, I'll fuck with you.
—Ralph "Sonny" Barger

Mile upon mile of rolling thunder is heading toward Hollister, California. Leather-clad bikers ride two abreast, jackets billowing, faces strained bone tight against the dry, hot wind pressing at deadly speeds. The endless motorized cavalcades climb more than three thousand feet over the Coastal Range past the still, blue waters of the San Luis Reservoir, before descending into the southern end of the Santa Clara Valley and the rural town of Hollister. It's the July 4th weekend run in 2005, and tens of thousands of bikers are making their annual pilgrimage to the birthplace of the outlaw motorcycle gang culture—the Hollister Independence Rally.

For 362 days of the year, Hollister, with a population of only 36,500, jealously guards its rural roots. The region, which is about two hours south of San Francisco, is lush with endless fields of irrigated fruit and vegetables. Cattle graze on the brown grasslands that cover the surrounding hills. Mountains rise in the distance. The air is often cooled by the foggy breezes that drift inland from Monterey Bay. But on this three-day weekend, the sleepy town is hot and dry and echoes with the harsh complaint of growling Harley-Davidsons and custom motorcycles pouring over the distant mountains and into the city. The cowtown becomes oil and grease, black leather and T-shirts, steel, chrome and tattoos as more than 150,000 often warring bikers mingle on Hollister's neutral territory. Rival gangs such as the Hells Angels, Mongols, Outlaws and Vagos share the streets and sidewalks with other more obscure patched clubs as well as the thousands of recreational bikers that flock to Hollister just to be part of an American outlaw legend.

That legend was born here back in 1947, when about two thousand bikers tore up and down the main streets of Hollister in a rally that included motorcycle races, loud music and drinking. Life magazine featured a large picture of a man on a motorcycle surrounded by empty beer bottles. It didn't matter that the photo was staged. It was enough to engrave into the American psyche the rough, freewheeling image of the outlaw biker taking over small-town America, inspiring Hollywood classics like *The Wild One* with Marlon Brando and Lee Marvin.

Back then, police drove the marauding bikers out of town with shotguns and wooden batons. Now the bikers are welcomed with open arms by a city thrilled to exploit America's fascination with the bikers. What a difference a few decades and the shrewd stewardship of Sonny Barger can make. The bikers have gone from rebels to rock stars. The Hollister Independence Rally now features top-flight rock bands, beauty pageants, tattoo contests and bike shows. "It's so funny. We won," Barger once boasted to local reporters. "Here we were, being run out of town at gunpoint . . . and now the citizens are paying us to come back to their town and do events there, and have the sheriff's office and police protect us."

It's been a long ride for Sonny Barger.

As a fourteen-year-old back in 1953, he saw *The Wild One* and decided then and there he'd be a biker just like Lee Marvin's rebellious character, Chino. Within five years he was leading the Oakland chapter of the Hells Angels. And for the next nearly five decades, he would witness the Hells Angels' worldwide expansion, not to mention the countless drug busts, murder raps and vicious biker wars with rivals from Europe to Australia to Laughlin, Nevada.

And each year the ride to Hollister gets a little longer for the aging biker. Sonny is sixty-nine years old. He is blind in his right eye, deaf in his left ear and short of breath from an inoperable clogged artery in his heart. Since he had his vocal cords removed because of throat cancer, he continues to speak through a valve inserted in his throat. Anybody else would be dead. But not Sonny. Sonny Barger is still a powerful force as he takes his annual 675-mile run to Hollister all the way from his tiny ranch outside Phoenix, Arizona, on his black Road King because "riding motor-cycles is what I do." His religion, philosophy and politics—his entire life—is wrapped up in a two-wheeled steel machine.

Sooner or later—and probably sooner rather than later—Barger's body is going to ride the last mile and the world's most famous Hells Angel will die. Or get knocked off by a rival. Many in his own gang will pretend to mourn, but silently they'll be glad: they feel the Old Man has grown soft, too commercial, too selfish. Rivals like George Christie are eager to fight to become the new leader of the pack.

But for now, Sonny Barger, like his bike, is still the Road King. A week earlier in Reno, Sonny married his fourth wife, Zorana. She's a platinum blonde in her forties. Standing behind Sonny and his Hells Angels, she looks middle class and somewhat out of place. No leather. No weather-beaten face. No loud tattoos. Just soft and fem-inine and motherly. Maybe Barger hopes he'll be luckier with wife number four than he was with the first three. His last wife, Beth Noel, who accused him of assault and later said she got paid by the FBI, is somewhere "living on the street," according to Sonny's lawyer and court adviser, Fritz Clapp. His second wife was a model and drug addict. His first wife died trying to self-abort her baby.

Sonny and his new bride are staying where he always stays when he makes the Hollister run—at the Cinderella Motel, a small U-shaped inn on the main drag into the city. Motels jack up their rates to more than $200 a night during the rally, but Barger says, "I work a deal."

Sonny has been working deals of sorts all his life. Indeed, he has become the consummate deal maker and businessman. So much so that his Web site—sonnybarger.com—is all about Sonny and his products and very little about the Angels. He pushes sweatshirts for men and tight-fitting tube tops for women with his photo and the slogan "An American Legend." Like a Paul Newman wannabee, he markets Sonny Barger Cajun Salsa with "just enough spice to make it hot enough, but not too hot." He peddles his books and Sonny Barger beer.

Now he's back at Hollister to work another deal. He's promoting his new book, *Freedom: Credos from the Road*. It's a small jet-black hardback decorated with the profile of a silver motorcycle. Sonny's name is in Hells Angels red. The man who more than any other created the universally recognized image of the Hells Angels has transformed himself into a writer and a kitchen-table philosopher of life on the road. It's the biker's version of a self-help book with chapter titles such as "Screw Fightin' Fair" and "Nothin' States Your Position More Clearly than a Punch in the Face." There's even a swipe at George Bush's America called "Don't Trade Freedom for the New Security"—an uncharacteristic attack from the usually flag-waving, patriotic bikers who staunchly supported the Vietnam War. On the other hand Barger makes sure he is still all-American and apple pie and Father Knows Best, cautioning people not to take drugs or drink too much ("Streamline yourself and clean up"); be punctual ("Early is on time, on time is late"); and be your own man ("Don't be so damned run-of-the-mill and buttoned down"). It's his fourth book and he says he wrote it so he could express his thoughts "on what it takes to be free in America."

For a man who spent thirteen years of his life in prison, freedom has become a state of mind. "If you treat me good, I'll treat you better. If you treat me worse, I'll fuck with you," Sonny says. "That's always seemed to get me by in life. If you do what you think is right, ninety-nine times out of a hundred it's the right thing to do."

Sonny sits patiently for hours signing books. He's warm and friendly, pudgy and chipmunk-cheeked—far from the steely-eyed Hells Angel he used to be. He's smooth and easy-going, joking with fans and posing for pictures. Members of the Soldiers for

Jesus biker club, with large red crosses on the backs of their leather jackets, crowd round his table. A young woman introduces herself as Chastity, and as Sonny signs her book he wears his warmest smile. "That's a nice name," he says.

Barger is holding court at the Hells Angels booth on Sixth Street just off Hollister's main drag of San Benito Street. Among the numerous patched bikers, nobody can mistake the Angels. Their red and white colours are always the boldest. Under a huge red-and-white canopy with the words "Hells Angels" emblazoned around the fringe, Sonny Barger sits behind a table, a king surrounded by his adoring subjects.

And as befits a king, he has some imposing protection. Since the assassination of Dan "Hoover" Seybert, the president of Sonny's Cave Creek chapter and Sonny's surrogate son, back in the spring of 2003, Barger is taking no chances. His bodyguard is Louie Valdez, the sergeant-at-arms from Cave Creek. Where Sonny goes, Louie goes. He's small, wiry and muscular. Were it not for his horn-rimmed glasses, he could pass as some kind of weird video game warrior. His narrow thin face is weathered, taut and deeply tanned. His hair is shaved into a thick black Mohawk. He has tattooed horns onto his forehead and dark Hells Angels wings onto the sides of his head. Tattooed flames crawl round his neck from behind his white Angels sweatshirt and leather vest. He's a living, breathing warning and he looks like the devil himself. Everything about him is watchful, alert, on edge and ready for battle. The Mongols are in town, and he's guarding the Angels legend. You never know what's going to happen—especially since the shootout at Laughlin.

Earlier in the day Sonny was signing books at Corbin's motorcycle supply shop just outside Hollister. Corbin's is famous because of its customized motorcycle seats, and Sonny ordered a new one for his Road King. Sonny's lawyer, Fritz Clapp, was in the diner next door finishing off a plate of sausages, eggs and hash browns while he dictated the rules of engagement for a brief interview for this book. Fritz is Sonny's chief of staff, his final gatekeeper. Nobody gets to Sonny without going through Fritz Clapp.

Fritz is a longtime biker who became a lawyer for the Angels when they met in a California court disputing a state helmet law. On September 2, 1989—a date forever branded on his memory—Fritz got into a terrible motorcycle accident where five of his biker friends were killed. With burns all over his body, he took a year to recover. The incident served as a sort of epiphany. He gave up his law practice and took to the road full time. With a tiny white goatee and a thin Mohawk haircut dyed orange, Clapp looks disturbingly like Colonel Sanders gone punk. But don't let that fool you. He's tough, direct and all business, in charge of promoting Sonny through his company Sonny Barger Productions. Clapp explains that his goal was to make Sonny independently wealthy while assuring that the Hells Angels are "treated with respect." He's accomplished both, he announces, making his master a hero to the worldwide biker community.

"When we were in Europe he was greeted like the pope," Clapp says. "Limos at the airports, anything we wanted. It was a great time."

Clapp clearly doesn't want any interview with Sonny messing things up. For starters, Fritz says that Sonny doesn't comment on the Hells Angels. Nor will he comment on the biker wars in Canada or Europe, which he claims are an "embarrassment" to the club. "It's a bunch of biker clubs that want to be Hells Angels by showing how tough they are," Clapp says. An astonishing sleight of hand since the murderous wars in Quebec and all through Europe were conducted by full-fledged, official HA chapters approved by the Oakland mother chapter.

Most important, Clapp warns, do not refer to the Hells Angels as a "gang." "You use it once and Sonny will correct you. But he won't correct you again." Sonny prefers the word "club."

Despite Clapp's admonitions, the word "gang" inevitably crops up in the interview. But Sonny smoothly dismisses the line of questioning.

"We don't use the G-word," he says quietly.

"I don't know anything about [the biker wars]. I have never been involved in one, and therefore I cannot talk about it," says

Barger, apparently forgetting his prison sentence for his role in a conspiracy to murder rival bikers. "I don't talk about other clubs. What's their business is their business. I'm not one of them. I don't know anything about them."

Sonny lives in a dream world of his own creation. In Sonny's world, Hells Angels are simply motorcycle enthusiasts. They are rebels and brawlers who never back down from a fight. It's the police who are the outlaws. They and the prosecutors plot against them to get bigger crime fighting budgets and advance their careers. That's what he insists precipitated the bloody shootout at Laughlin.

"Really, that's what it was, a barroom fight. Cops made that happen. They infiltrated the other club. They tried to infiltrate against us. They got into the other club. They agitated them. They agitated us. They were there when it happened. They claimed they knew it was going to happen."

Sonny interrupts the uncomfortable topic to sell another auto-graphed book and have his picture taken. Then he turns back and tries to steer the conversation away from the Hells Angels. "We sort of got to get away from the club because I'm not the spokesman for the club anymore. I mean, I've got to answer a few questions because I'm a member, but I don't want to get into the club."

Polishing his self-image does not include discussing murder.

But it was Sonny's vision that turned the Hells Angels into a tightly disciplined gang where the Hells Angels is always greater than its members. Members don't even own their own patches. They belong to the Hells Angels Inc. It was Sonny who legally incorporated the Hells Angels and then drew up a code of conduct that would ultimately link the members worldwide to a single strict orthodoxy. But he brushes aside questions about the mounting evidence that his society of "motorcycle enthusiasts" attracts often psychopathic characters bent on murder and may-hem, for which they show no remorse. The victims are many: Cynthia Garcia in Arizona; Margo Compton and her six-year-old twin girls in Oregon; Joanna Wilson, and Corina Bolhaar and her two children in Amsterdam; the slaughter of the entire Grondalski family in California; eleven-year-old Daniel Desrochers in Quebec—not to mention the many unnamed victims of the brutal biker wars in the United States, Canada and Europe.

Sonny Barger can try to sell as much beer and salsa as he wants, but he can't run away from his legacy. Indeed, in their own promotional video, called *Hollister: 50 Years, Bikes and Brotherhood*, two Hells Angels are unabashedly proud of the gang's outlaw image. "We got a set of laws I live by and that's all I care about. . . . I don't buy into all that social bullshit. How you ought to act. How you ought to be. I'm where I want to be and I'm proud of it. People follow Billy the Kid and some of the famous outlaws—and that's what we've become."

But Sonny Barger, the rebel who once revelled in his image as a rabble-rouser, has become the ultimate American legend: a merchandiser hawking his own brand name. "I'm not an outlaw," he says defiantly. "I'm a Hells Angel."

It's his parting statement. With that, he and his bodyguard, Louie, climb on their bikes, pose for a photograph, gun their engines and leave. Only they don't just leave, they rocket through the crowded parking lot like twin missiles.

Raw speed and power, and to hell with anybody who gets in their way.

AFTERWORD
TO THE PAPERBACK EDITION

Jay Dobyns wanted his day in court badly. The ATF undercover agent had long wanted to testify against the Hells Angels he and his team had worked so hard to infiltrate. "That is where I will get my satisfaction. To be able to walk in that courtroom and look at those guys and say: 'Despite all your propaganda and all your bullshit, now everyone is going to hear the true story. And I'm going to tell it.'"

He never got that chance. In the year since the original edition of this book was published in the spring of 2006, the legal skirmishes between the outlaw bikers and law enforcement escalated—and it was a see-saw battle with victories and setbacks for both sides.

After the collapse of the Black Biscuit prosecution in Arizona, attention shifted to Las Vegas where a series of racketeering trials against forty-two Hells Angels members got underway in the fall of 2006 for the shootings at the Laughlin casino in 2002. Dobyns, along with John Ciccone's long-serving snitch, Mike Kramer, was set to testify. But after just three weeks, the first trial against eleven of the Angels fell apart.

Again, as in Arizona, controversies over disclosure bedeviled the prosecution. But the biggest problem was that from the start, the judge made it clear he did not want to see the Hells Angels put on trial as an organization—a serious handicap considering that even though the charges were against individuals, it was precisely a gang racketeering case the federal prosecutors were trying to prove. They brought in two former senior members of the Hells Angels from Minnesota and Arizona to explain the inner workings of the Hells Angels, but the judge twice interrupted the testimony to say that it was as unfair to blame all Hells Angels for the crimes of a few members as it was to blame all Roman Catholic priests for the sexual abuse carried out by a few members of the clergy. But the analogy fails on two counts. Surely the point is that any disciplined, hierarchal group with strict rules—be it a church or the Angels—has to take responsibility for the repeated illegal actions of its members. More importantly, no one would argue the Catholic church's main goal is to abuse children; but the historical record shows the Hells Angels—proud to call themselves outlaws—exist to expand their criminal empire.

Sensing they were never going to get their best evidence in front of a jury, the prosecution folded and opted instead for plea deals with what they called "the six most active and culpable participants" in the casino fighting. Five of the six men were looking at less than two and a half years in prison—a lot better than the possible life terms they might have served if convicted on the racketeering and attempted murder charges. Cal Schaefer—seen on security video firing his handgun at a Mongol—pleaded guilty to a deadly weapon charge and faced up to five years; his sentence would run concurrent with his guilty plea in the Black Biscuit case in Arizona. The judge dismissed all charges against the thirty-one remaining Hells Angels members whose trials were to follow.

In effect, six Angels had fallen on their swords to protect the organization as a whole. In a bizarre legal contortion, the Angels pleaded guilty to a single count of racketeering but not as a gang: the racketeering "enterprise" officially consists of those six, but only as individuals.

"Once again the prosecutors underestimated the Hells Angels," said retired FBI investigator Tim McKinley, who had led a probe against putative biker leader Sonny Barger in the 1980s. He sent Barger to federal prison on murder conspiracy charges—one of the few major successes against the gang in the United States.

The Hells Angels continued to be underestimated in England, where they expanded their activities under the radar of a complacent police and public.

In Australia, where bikie crime had been more violent and in-your-face, there were signs of a more serious legal offensive. In the late fall of 2006, three Hells Angels were ordered to stand trial for refusing to answer questions at secret Australian Crime Commission (ACC) hearings. The ACC was investigating the gang's activity in South Australia, including drugs, money laundering, bribery of public officials and firearms offences. The ACC has the power to use so-called coercive hearings in major investigations into organized crime, which oblige the suspect to answer questions or risk a penalty of up to five years in jail.

But despite some draconian measures to seize assets and outlaw their fortresses, bikie gangs in Australian continue to expand, merge and consolidate. This was amply demonstrated in 2006 when tensions rose in Sydney between the Bandidos and the Hells Angels, leading to several shootings. Both clubs had been organizing associate crews to strengthen their presence in the city. The Bandidos, however, were temporarily distracted by an internal struggle in April when Bandido Russell Oldham murdered downtown Sydney president Rodney Monk before killing himself. Part of the reason Australia continues to have problems controlling its bikies is that it lacks a powerful national police force. Its six states are largely autonomous when it comes to criminal justice and there is insufficient communication between forces. Bikie gangs, on the other hand, are masterful organizers for whom borders do not exist.

Even within state jurisdictions, police are criticized for not working together. In Western Australia where the Gypsy Jokers continue to rule, the state's crime commissioner Kevin Hammond complained in 2006 that police don't bother to work with the commission and use its so-called exceptional powers of subpoena to fight organized crime.

In Queensland, police made the bizarre request for the right to work with private security companies to gather intelligence. This was put on hold when one member of the state legislature pointed out that bikie gangs had penetrated many security companies. "Clearly issues like that would have to be resolved satisfactorily before we believe you could go too far down this path," Liberal member Rob Lucas said.

One of the most dramatic moves of 2006 took place in Europe where one of the countries hardest hit by the biker gang wars—Holland—began to consider an outright ban on the Hells Angels. Dutch prosecutors, apparently frustrated in their attempts to bring individual members of the gang to justice, in November 2006 asked the civil courts to outlaw the gang and confiscate its clubhouses. Calling the Angels a "well-oiled criminal organization with branches worldwide," the prosecutors said in a court statement that "It's become sufficiently clear that the activities of the motorcycle club are in conflict with public order . . . In our firm opinion, this is not a case of a few incidents, but a chain of criminal activities. This criminal behavior is . . . part of the culture of the Hells Angels."

The prosecutors are asking the court to close down all seven Dutch chapters as well as their affiliated clubs. The move to ban them outright has won the support of all political parties in the Netherlands.

At the same time, Dutch prosecutors were continuing their criminal prosecutions of the Hells Angels chapters in The Hague, Rotterdam, Haarlem, Maastricht, Leeuwarden and Zwolle for fraud, forgery and embezzlement. Twenty-two Hells Angels are scheduled to go on trial in the summer of 2007 on charges of extortion, theft, blackmail, possession of drugs and weapons, and murder.

The Hells Angels have vowed to fight the ban, claiming it is illegal. It could take years for the case to wind its way through the courts. "Because a number of members have committed crimes, the entire club is being branded as criminal," Hells Angels lawyer Benedicte Ficq said.

A similar battle was underway in Canada, where Rick Ciarniello, the frequent spokesperson for the British Columbia Angels, launched a constitutional challenge to the country's gang laws in front of the B.C. Supreme Court. Like his Dutch counterparts, he argued all Angels were being unfairly branded as criminals and wanted sections of the legislation struck down because they were vague and overly broad. As examples of public snubs he claimed to have suffered, he listed patrons in a restaurant not wanting to sit next to him when he wore his Hells Angels colours, employees treating him rudely at a local supermarket and many people simply avoiding him altogether.

In November 2006, a judge dismissed Ciarniello's complaints, but the biker had good reason to wish the legislation would go away. As a result of the E-Pandora raids that saw nineteen of his fellow full-patch members and associates arrested on cocaine, extortion and weapons charges, three trials were scheduled to start in 2007 that took direct aim at the powerful East End chapter of the Hells Angels as a criminal enterprise as defined by the law. In pre-trial motions, the defence tried to turn the tables and put the RCMP's chief snitch on trial, arguing before the B.C. Supreme Court that the charges should be thrown out because the police agent committed crimes of assault and drug trafficking.

Indeed, the judge heard evidence that Michel Plante, the former strip club bouncer who infiltrated the bikers under RCMP supervision for two years, was permitted to participate in the trafficking of more than 20 kilograms of methamphetamine, plus small amounts of cocaine and steroids. By law, police can allow agents to traffic drugs by getting an exemption under the Controlled Drugs and Substances Act, Chief Supt. Bob Paulson told the court. Since revitalizing the police assault on the bikers in B.C. with several successful undercover probes, Paulson had been promoted to become the RCMP's Director General of the Organized Crime Intelligence branch in Ottawa.

"The Hells Angels uses all sorts of methods to combat law enforcement," Paulson said. "Without this strategy we could never infiltrate them." He had made as strong a case as possible for the necessity of law enforcement to get down and dirty with the bikers if they were ever going to take them down. By late 2006, Paulson and the bikers were waiting to see how the judge would rule.

That is the central issue facing all the countries grappling with the invasion of outlaw motorcycle gangs: How far is a society willing to go to curb organized crime and how far can police go without crossing the line into that same dark netherworld where their biker targets flourished?

After their birth as freewheeling rebels in the late 1940s, the Hells Angels spent much of the next five decades expanding into lucrative criminal activities—but they were left largely unchallenged by law enforcement. Only in the mid-nineties did some countries begin to set up dedicated police agencies or investigative units to take on the bikers. There were some notable successes in the decade that followed and, by 2006, in some places—notably Canada, Denmark and Holland—the Hells Angels were on the defensive.

But the police have also discovered that when they push the outlaw bikers, the bikers push back. Hard. No one ever said taking on organized crime is easy. And the Hells Angels, like their inspirational patriarch Sonny Barger, will keep riding hard, as far and fast and furious as they can.

Acknowledgments

———

After the success of our first joint investigation, *The Road to Hell: How the Biker Gangs Are Conquering Canada*, our curiosity was piqued: how did the biker gangs manage to conquer so much of the organized crime territory around the world? This book is the result.

It could not have been done without the tips and insight from biker informants, including Bill, Paul, Ears, and others who, for obvious reasons, cannot be fully identified. Among the law enforcement experts who spared us their time are J. P. Wilson of the Phoenix Police Department, Tom Mangan of the ATF, Billy Guinn of the San Diego Sheriff Department and John Schlim; in Canada, Jean-Pierre Lévesque and Bruce Macdonald of the RCMP. In Australia, retired police detective Bob Armstrong; and in Europe, several Swedish and Spanish police officers who preferred not to be named for security reasons.

And, of course, "Bubba."

Several journalists around the world are working hard to investigate the bikers. We received special help from Dennis Wagner in Arizona and Tony Thompson in the U.K. Sam Bagnall, who produced a comprehensive documentary on the Hells Angels for the BBC, was also especially helpful with his contacts and analysis. We'd like to thank Paul Vugts, Rob Cox and Henk Schutten in Holland, whose insights and help in unearthing important details and translating key documents are greatly appreciated. In the United States, the court reporting of Ken Ritter of *AP* and Adrienne Packer was invaluable. In Canada, we were aided by the published work of Neal Hall, Lori Culbert, Judith Lavoie, Timothy Appleby, Michael Den Tandt, Bill Dumphy, Gary Dimmock, Pat Brooks, Richard Dooley, Bruce Owen and Mike McIntyre.

Student researchers who lent an invaluable hand include Elaine Mills and Joost van de Loo in the U.K. and the hard-working Montreal team of Elisia Bargelletti, Karen Biskin, Christopher Hazon, Stavroula Papdopoulus and Yannis Themelis. Our devoted crew at Knopf Canada/Random House of Canada Limited, as usual, made a difficult task much easier. This book would never have seen the light of day without editor Diane Martin, rights director Jennifer Shepherd, publicist Stephanie Gowan, copy editor Alison Reid and managing editor Deirdre Molina. Nick Davies of Hodder & Stoughton in the U.K., Philip Turner of Carroll & Graf Publishers in the United States, and the translators at Éditions de l'Homme in Quebec and Uitgeverij Luitingh-Sijthoff in the Netherlands all helped make this book an international reality.

As always, our wives, Janet and Lisa, deserve medals for putting up, yet again, with another two years of the biker wars.

William Marsden
wjmarsden@hotmail.com

Julian Sher
julian@sher.com

Montreal
February 2007

Index of Proper Names

——

WILLIAM MARSDEN and JULIAN SHER are Montreal journalists and co-authors of *The Road to Hell: How the Biker Gangs Are Conquering Canada*. WILLIAM MARSDEN is a senior investigative reporter for *The Gazette* in Montreal. He has won numerous national and international awards for journalism including two National Newspaper Awards and an IRE award in the United States with the Washington-based Center for Public Integrity's International Consortium of Investigative Journalists. JULIAN SHER is the author of several books, including the national bestseller *"Until You Are Dead": Steven Truscott's Long Ride into History* and the forthcoming *One Child at a Time: The Global Fight to Rescue Children from Online Predators*. An award-winning documentary producer for many years at the CBC, he has also worked on investigative projects for *The Globe and Mail*, the *Toronto Star* and *The New York Times*.